Appropriate Dispute Resolution

WILLIAM J. BARRY

Wolters Kluwer

Published by Wolters Kluwer in New York.

Wolters Kluwer Legal & Regulatory U.S. serves customers worldwide with CCH, Aspen Publishers, and Kluwer Law International products. (www.WKLegaledu.com)

To contact Customer Service, e-mail customer.service@wolterskluwer.com, call 1-800-234-1660, fax 1-800-901-9075, or mail correspondence to:

    Wolters Kluwer
    Attn: Order Department
    PO Box 990
    Frederick, MD 21705

Printed in the United States of America.

1 2 3 4 5 6 7 8 9 0

ISBN 978-1-4548-4125-8

Library of Congress Cataloging-in-Publication Data

Names: Barry, William J. (Lawyer)
Title: Appropriate dispute resolution / William J. Barry.
Description: New York : Wolters Kluwer, 2017. | Includes index.
Identifiers: LCCN 2017021810 | ISBN 9781454841258
Subjects: LCSH: Dispute resolution (Law)—United States. | Legal
    assistants—United States—Handbooks, manuals, etc.
Classification: LCC KF9084 .B375 2017 | DDC 347.73/9—dc23
LC record available at https://lccn.loc.gov/2017021810

Appropriate
Dispute Resolution

About Wolters Kluwer Legal & Regulatory U.S.

Wolters Kluwer Legal & Regulatory U.S. delivers expert content and solutions in the areas of law, corporate compliance, health compliance, reimbursement, and legal education. Its practical solutions help customers successfully navigate the demands of a changing environment to drive their daily activities, enhance decision quality and inspire confident outcomes.

Serving customers worldwide, its legal and regulatory portfolio includes products under the Aspen Publishers, CCH Incorporated, Kluwer Law International, ftwilliam.com and MediRegs names. They are regarded as exceptional and trusted resources for general legal and practice-specific knowledge, compliance and risk management, dynamic workflow solutions, and expert commentary.

This book is dedicated to Dr. John Zacharis, who planted the seed for it
many years ago when I was a graduate student at Emerson College
in Boston, Massachusetts. I still remember his comment after reading my first
graduate school paper: "Your paper demonstrates excellent abilities to
synthesize, organize and present information clearly and succinctly.
You should write a book." Little did Dr. Zacharis know that his comment
would remain with me for years and provide the confidence to undertake
writing this textbook. To him I will be forever grateful.

Dr. Zacharis earned his BS and MS degrees from Emerson College; after
earning his PhD at Indiana University, he returned to Emerson to teach in the
Speech Department. He also served as president of the college from 1989 to 1992,
when he passed away much too early. He is remembered for his devotion
to teaching, concern and support for students, congenial manner, and warm
personality. I am fortunate to have known Dr. Zacharis.

SUMMARY OF CONTENTS

Contents   xi
Acknowledgments   xxi
Introduction   1

CHAPTER ONE
Understanding Conflict   5

CHAPTER TWO
Litigation   29

CHAPTER THREE
Negotiation   47

CHAPTER FOUR
Mediation   79

CHAPTER FIVE
Arbitration: An Overview   107

CHAPTER SIX
Settling Disputes with Arbitration   131

CHAPTER SEVEN
Online Dispute Resolution: The Beginnings   161

CHAPTER EIGHT
Online Dispute Resolution: Settling Disputes   181

CHAPTER NINE
Restorative Methods   201

CHAPTER TEN
Court-Annexed Alternatives   221

CHAPTER ELEVEN
The Paralegal and ADR   245

APPENDIX A
Uniform Mediation Act   279

APPENDIX B
Sample Mediation Agreement   285

APPENDIX C
Proposed Arbitration Fairness Act of 2013 287

APPENDIX D
Answers to Practice Test Questions 289

Glossary 291
Index 295

CONTENTS

Acknowledgments   xxi

Introduction   1

What Is Alternative Dispute Resolution?   1
Legal Disputes and Conflicts   2
Summary of the Book   2

CHAPTER ONE
Understanding Conflict   5

Introduction   5
Definitions of Conflict   7
Understanding Human Needs   7
Sources of Conflicts   9
Factors Affecting Conflict   9
How People Approach and Avoid Conflict   10
Conflict Avoidance   12
Power and Conflict   12
Power and People   13
    Power Over   13
    Power With   13
    Powerlessness   15
    Empowerment   15
Sources of Power   16
Power and Context   16
The Application of Power in Conflict   17
    Coercive Power   17
    Reward or Exchange Power   17
    Ecological Power   17
    Normative Power   18
    Referent Power   18
    Expert Power   18

Power and Alienation   18
Culture and Conflict   19
Constructive Conflict   23
Conclusion   23
Key Terms and Concepts   23
Practice Test Questions   24
Review Questions   25
Application Questions   25
Practice Exercises   26

CHAPTER TWO
Litigation   29

Introduction   29
  Who Will Participate in the Process?   30
  What Are the Basic Stages of the Process from Beginning
    to Final Resolution?   30
  Where Will the Proceedings Occur?   32
  Which Claims and Issues Will Be Considered?   32
  What Information Will Be Considered, and How and When
    Will It Be Exchanged?   32
  Who Determines the Outcome?   33
  What Types of Outcomes Are Possible?   33
Advantages   33
  Ensures a Resolution   33
  Predictable Process   34
  Enforcement   34
  Precedent   34
  Discovery   35
  Due Process   35
  Openness of Process   36
  Appeals   36
  Interim Relief   37
  Parties Do Not Have to Deal with Each Other   37
  Provides Justice   38
Disadvantages   38
  Expensive and Costly   38
  Slow   40
  No Privacy   40
  Not Flexible   40
  Does Not Preserve Relationships   40
  Need for an Attorney   41
  Can't Choose the Decision Maker   41

Conclusion   41
Key Terms and Concepts   42
Practice Test Questions   42
Review Questions   43
Application Questions   43
Practice Exercises   44

CHAPTER THREE
Negotiation   47

Introduction   48
Negotiation Defined   48
Types of Legal Negotiations   49
    Transactions   50
    Civil Disputes   50
    Labor-Management Negotiations   50
    Criminal Cases   51
    Domestic Relations (Including Divorce and Child Custody)   52
    International Negotiations   52
The Lawyer and Client Relationship   52
Two Methods of Negotiation   53
    Distributive Negotiation   53
    Problem Solving   53
Negotiator Styles   53
    Competitive Negotiators   54
    Cooperative Negotiators   56
The Negotiation Process   57
    Preparation Stage: Setting Objectives and Limits   57
    Preliminary Stage   60
    Information/Positioning Stage   60
    Distributive/Competitive or Integrative/Collaborative Stage   61
    Reaching Agreement or Collapse Stage   62
Laws Affecting Negotiation and Settlement   63
    Promotion of Settlement   63
    Constraints Imposed by Contract and Tort Law   64
    Regulations for Specific Types of Negotiations   67
Ethical Constraints Affecting Negotiations   68
Conclusion   70
Key Terms and Concepts   70
Practice Test Questions   70
Review Questions   72
Application Questions   72
Practice Exercises   76

CHAPTER FOUR
Mediation 79

Introduction 79
What Is Mediation? 80
A Brief History of Mediation 81
  The Pound Conference 81
  The Uniform Mediation Act 82
The Advantages and Disadvantages of Mediation 83
  Advantages 83
  Disadvantages 87
The Mediation Process 88
  Stages of Mediation 88
The Role of the Mediator 90
  Educating the Parties 90
  Organizing the Sessions 91
  Developing and Maintaining Communication 91
  Managing Emotions 91
  Maintaining Interest 91
  Generating Solutions and Reaching Agreement 91
Caucuses 92
Mediation Forms 92
  Evaluative Mediation 92
  Facilitative Mediation 93
  Transformative Mediation 94
Mediator Qualifications 95
Mediator Skills 95
Ethical Issues in Mediation 98
  Standards of Conduct for Mediators 98
Med-Arb (Mediation-Arbitration) 99
Conclusion 100
Key Terms and Concepts 100
Practice Test Questions 100
Review Questions 101
Application Questions 101
Practice Exercises 104

CHAPTER FIVE
Arbitration: An Overview 107

Introduction 107
A Brief History of Arbitration 108
  Biblical Times 108
  Greeks and Romans 109

Middle Ages	109
The United States	110
Arbitration vs. Litigation	112
Advantages of Arbitration over Litigation	114
Speed and Cost	114
Privacy	115
No Precedent	115
Finality	115
Informal Atmosphere	116
Flexibility	117
The Parties Choose the Decision Maker	117
Preservation of Relationship	117
Disadvantages of Arbitration over Litigation	118
No Due Process	119
No Appeal/Finality	119
No Discovery	120
Absence of Record and Reasoned Opinions	120
Too Much Like Litigation	121
May Not Be Fast or Inexpensive	121
Arbitrator Bias	121
Conclusion	123
Key Terms and Concepts	124
Practice Test Questions	124
Review Questions	125
Application Questions	125
Practice Exercises	127

CHAPTER SIX

Settling Disputes with Arbitration

131

Introduction	131
The Federal Arbitration Act	132
Revised Uniform Arbitration Act	134
Agreements to Arbitrate and Arbitrability	135
Consent and Fairness: Adhesive Arbitration Agreements	136
Supporters of Adhesive Arbitration Agreements	143
Common Types of Arbitration	143
Labor and Employment Arbitration	144
Consumer Arbitration	146
Securities Arbitration (Investor/Broker Disputes)	146
Commercial Arbitration	148
International Commercial Arbitration	149
The Arbitration Process	149
Filing a Demand for Arbitration	150

Selection of Arbitrators   150
Preliminary Meeting   150
Prehearing Conference   150
Exchange of Information and Discovery   150
The Hearing   151
The Award   151
Judicial Enforcement of Awards   152
Manifest Disregard of the Law   153
Arbitrary and Capricious   153
Irrationality   153
Violates Public Policy   153
Conclusion   154
Key Terms and Concepts   154
Practice Test Questions   155
Review Questions   156
Application Questions   156
Practice Exercises   159

CHAPTER SEVEN

Online Dispute Resolution: The Beginnings   161

Introduction   161
What Is ODR, and How Does It Work?   163
The Evolution of ODR   164
First Period: Pre-1995   165
Second Period: 1995-1998   168
Third Period: 1999-2000   171
Conclusion   175
Key Terms and Concepts   176
Practice Test Questions   176
Review Questions   177
Application Questions   178
Practice Exercises   178

CHAPTER EIGHT

Online Dispute Resolution: Settling Disputes   181

Introduction   181
eNegotiation   183
Assisted eNegotiation   183
Automated "Blind-Bid" eNegotiation   183
eMediation   184

eArbitration   185
   American Arbitration Association   186
   Virtual Courthouse   187
Advantages of ODR   188
   Convenient   188
   Saves Money and Time   188
   Speed   188
   No Physical Presence   189
   Avoids Jurisdictional Issues   189
   Data Storage and Retrieval   190
Disadvantages of ODR   190
   No Face-to-Face Contact   190
   Confidentiality   192
   Deception   192
   Lack of Trust and Confidence   193
   Enforcement of Agreement   194
   Access to and Proficiency in Technology   194
What's Next? Holography and Artificial Intelligence   194
Conclusion   195
Key Terms and Concepts   196
Practice Test Questions   196
Review Questions   197
Application Questions   197
Practice Exercises   198

CHAPTER NINE

Restorative Methods   201

Introduction   201
What Is Restorative Justice?   204
The Advantages and Disadvantages of Restorative Justice   205
   Advantages   205
   Disadvantages   207
Restorative Methods   209
   Victim-Offender Dialogue (VOD)   210
   Conferencing   211
   Circles   214
Conclusion   216
Key Terms and Concepts   216
Practice Test Questions   216
Review Questions   217
Application Questions   218
Practice Exercises   218

CHAPTER TEN
Court-Annexed Alternatives 221

Introduction: Brief History of ADR in the Courts 221
The Court-Annexed Alternatives 222
Mediation 223
Settlement Conference 225
Early Neutral Evaluation 228
Nonbinding Arbitration 231
  Referral 233
  Prehearing 233
  Hearing and Award 233
  Demand for Trial De Novo 234
Summary Jury Trial 235
Mini-Trial 237
Conclusion 238
Key Terms and Concepts 238
Practice Test Questions 238
Review Questions 239
Application Questions 239
Practice Exercises 242

CHAPTER ELEVEN
The Paralegal and ADR 245

Introduction 245
Paralegal Mistakes Become Attorney Mistakes 246
Paralegal Tasks 247
  Motions 249
  Explain the Designated ADR Process to Client 251
  Write Legal Memoranda of the Facts 253
  Research the Neutral 253
  Prepare Subpoenas 263
  Prepare Memoranda Summarizing Each Witness's Expected
    Testimony 263
  Preparation of Exhibit List 266
  Attend the Proceeding and Take Notes 269
  Prepare Agreements and Other Documents 269
Conclusion 274
Key Terms and Concepts 275
Practice Test Questions 275
Application Exercise 276
Practice Exercises 277

APPENDIX A
Uniform Mediation Act   279

APPENDIX B
Sample Mediation Agreement   285

APPENDIX C
Proposed Arbitration Fairness Act of 2013   287

APPENDIX D
Answers to Practice Test Questions   289

Glossary   291
Index   295

ACKNOWLEDGMENTS

I want to first and foremost thank my wife Mary and my two children, Deanna and Kayla. I thank them for enduring my many absences while I worked in the law library researching and writing this book. Deanna and Kayla have also been my teachers. I have learned many things from parenting them and the joy they have brought into my life has sustained me in many ways. Thank you Julie Welch, retired law librarian at the University of Maine School of Law, for your encouragement, support, and research help. Thank you also to Maureen Quinlan, University of Maine School of Law librarian, for your assistance with my research. Thanks to my friends for their encouragement, support, and help: Paul and Nancy Krasnow, David Freeman, Amanda Nelson, Angie Cannon, Jennifer Ackerman, Tracy Gorham, Robyn Dahms, Julie Webber, Stephen Dasatti, Amanda Nelson, Laura Berry, Jessica Hollencamp, Juliana O'Brien, Jon and Eileen Munroe, Paul Cereste (K1CGZ), Martin Orloski (N1WST), Brian Selee (N1OXG), Mark Bonderud (N1NYX), Gene Giddings (AA1XD), Dr. Michael Garnett, and Donna Barthe. I also want to thank my former students who were always in my mind while writing to make sure the information was understandable, interesting, and useful. Thank you to Betsy Kenny for your valuable suggestions, help guiding me through the publishing process, and patience. Thanks also to Lisa Wehrle for your outstanding editing skills and suggestions and to Dana Wilson for managing the production of my book. And thank you to David Herzig and Wolters Kluwer for providing me with the opportunity to write this textbook and allowing me the time within which to do it.

And a great big thank you to Faye Luppi, Esq., and the Honorable Roland Beaudoin, retired judge, Maine District Court. I am so grateful for the countless hours you both spent reading my manuscript drafts and making corrections and suggestions.

I also want to thank the following copyright holders who kindly granted their permission to reprint the following materials:

American Arbitration Association, Agreement to Arbitrate and Arbitrability (Submission Agreement) from *Drafting Dispute Resolution Clauses: A Practical Guide*.

Brazil, Wayne D. *Early Neutral Evaluation or Mediation? When Might ENE Deliver More Value?*, 14 Disp. Resol. Mag. 10, 11 (2007).

Cicognani, Anna. Excerpt from *A Linguistic Characterisation of Design in Text-Based Virtual Worlds.* © Anna Cicognani, September 1998.

Craver, Charles. *The Impact of Negotiator Styles on Bargaining Interactions,* 35 Am. J. Trial Advoc. 1, 2 (2011).

Danois, Diane L. The Cost of Litigation Versus Mediation in Family Law. Blog post from the Huffington Post, December 27, 2012.

Ellis, Katherine. Photo of Two Sisters and an Orange.

Family Circus © 2004 Bil Keane, Inc. Dist. By King Features Synd. (Cartoon)

Handelsman, J.B. "You have a pretty good case, Mr. Pitkin. How much justice can you afford?" J.B. Handelsman/The New Yorker Collection/The Cartoon Bank.

International Institute for Restorative Practices. *Conference Facilitators Script.*

The International Institute for Conflict Prevention and Resolution, Inc. *Comparison of Arbitration and Litigation* from the publication *Suitability of Arbitration and Litigation.*

Kelly, Russ. The Kitchener Experiment, used with permission.

Mencimer, Stephanie. *Eat Burger, Waive Right to Sue* (January 31, 2008). Copyright © 2008 Mother Jones and the Foundation for National Progress.

Noll, Douglas, excerpt from *Peacemaking: Practicing at the Intersection of Law and Human Conflict.* Copyright © 2003 by Cascadia Publishing House.

Robinson, Mark Lee. Excerpt from *Just Conflict: Transformation through Resolution.*

Shields, Allison C. Effectively Dealing with Difficult Client Situations. Legal Ease Consulting, Inc.

Steiner, Peter. "On the Internet, nobody Know You are a Dog." Peter Steiner/The New Yorker Collection/The Cartoon Bank.

Uniform Law Commission. Excerpts from the Uniform Mediation Act (© 2003 National Conference of Commissioners on Uniform State Laws) and the Revised Uniform Arbitration Act (© 2000 National Conference of Commissioners on Uniform State Laws).

Victim-Offender Reconciliation Program Information & Resource Center. "Is Restorative Justice Appropriate for Your Client?" Used with permission.

Virtual Courthouse. Excerpts from website at http://virtualcourthouse.com.

Welch, Craig. *Environmentalists, Loggers Push New Wilderness Deal in Northeast* published in The Seattle Times, July 27, 2010. © The Seattle Times Co.

Zehr, Howard. *Commentary: Restorative Justice: Beyond Victim-Offender Mediation,* 22 Conflict Resol. Quarterly 305, 307 (Fall-Winter 2004). © 2004 Wiley Periodicals Inc. and the Association for Conflict Resolution.

Appropriate
Dispute Resolution

Introduction

Litigation may not always be the best way to resolve a dispute. See whether you agree after reading the following account of a lawsuit between a co-op housing owner and the governing board.[1]

New York City requires window bars for apartments in which children under the age of 10 live.[2] One co-op housing board assessed the cost of this equipment only to residents who needed it; those without children under 10 were not charged. When co-op owners Alec and Suzi Diacou were billed for $909, the charge for installing the window bars, they refused to pay.

The Diacous refusal set in motion a long and expensive legal process that included numerous court filings and appeals. The result: a New York appellate court ultimately found for the co-op board, ruling that the Diacous owed $909 for the window bars. But that was not all they owed. Because the co-op ownership contract they had signed required them to pay legal fees if they lost in a dispute with the co-op board, the pair was responsible for the co-op lawyers' fees: $73,547.

The Diacous then brought another suit, this time seeking to prevent paying the co-op's legal fees. Eventually, the parties settled the dispute. They agreed that the co-op board would pay $43,547 of the legal fees and the Diacous would pay the remaining $30,000. Of course, the pair also owed their own attorneys' fees, which totaled $30,000.

At the conclusion of this long legal battle, Alec was quoted as saying, "I'm a man converted. Anything you can possibly do to avoid a lawsuit, do it."[3]

One would be hard pressed to argue that litigation was the best way to resolve this dispute. The only winners were the attorneys. There are better, less costly, and faster ways that could have been used to satisfy the parties. This is not to say that litigation doesn't have its place in dispute resolution but, there are alternatives, and that's what this book is about, choosing the appropriate dispute resolution.

WHAT IS ALTERNATIVE DISPUTE RESOLUTION?

The genesis of dispute resolution theory and practice in modern history is generally recognized to have begun in 1976 at the Pound Conference, where lawyers, judges, law professors, and court administrators came together to study problems in the legal establishment. Two important concepts originated at this symposium: (1) the creation of Neighborhood Justice Centers, which laid the foundation for community dispute resolution centers throughout the United States; and (2) the "multidoor courthouse" approach to resolving disputes, proposed by Harvard Professor Frank E.A. Sander who suggested that courthouses could offer multiple dispute resolution "doors" or programs to help alleviate the increased demands on U.S. courts. Sander envisioned that some cases would bypass litigation and instead use alternative dispute resolution processes (e.g., mediation, conciliation, or arbitration).

This idea of resolving disputes in ways other than litigation caught the attention of businesses. Around 1980, corporate attorneys were concerned about the growing costs of litigation and formed the Center for Public Resources. The organization's objective was to reduce the legal expenses associated with business-to-business and consumer disputes.

Since the Pound Conference, **alternative dispute resolution** (ADR) has become an integral part of the U.S. court system. Many courts now require parties to participate in an ADR process before granting them a formal trial. Parties also may opt to use private dispute resolution in lieu of seeking resolution through a court. ADR traditionally refers to **negotiation**, **mediation**, and **arbitration**. Today there are added methods: **summary jury trial**, **early neutral evaluation**, **mini-trial**, **mediation-arbitration (med-arb)**, **online dispute resolution**, and **restorative justice**.

LEGAL DISPUTES AND CONFLICTS

To appreciate the different re/solution processes, we first have to understand the nature and dynamics of disputes or **conflicts** (these two terms are interchangeable). People have individual needs that sometimes go unmet or are incompatible with those of others. Most people do not like conflict because it is emotionally draining, takes time away from what they would rather be doing, requires them to deal with people they do not like or agree with, and forces them to use limited resources. However, conflict is sometimes very useful. It has helped our society evolve, as the women's suffrage and civil rights movements show. Conflict excites our interest and curiosity and, arguably, is essential for advancement and progress.

SUMMARY OF THE BOOK

Chapter 1 introduces how conflict arises, how people approach or avoid it, and what variables affect it. The next chapter looks at the traditional judicial method of solving disputes, litigation. Chapter 3 explains negotiation, which forms the foundation of all ADR methods. Parties use negotiation to choose the ADR

process for their dispute. This chapter discusses the types and methods of negotiation, the process, legal and ethical concerns, and the relationship between
lawyer and client during a negotiation.

Mediation is explored in Chapter 4, including the advantages and disadvantages of mediation, the process, the different forms (evaluative, facilitative, and
transformative), the mediator's role, qualifications and skills, and ethical
concerns.

Chapters 5 and 6 cover arbitration. Chapter 5 discusses the history of arbitration, the advantages and disadvantages of using arbitration, and the similarities
and differences between arbitration and litigation. Chapter 6 looks at the Federal
Arbitration Act and the Revised Uniform Arbitration Act, arbitration agreements, common types of arbitration, the process, and judicial enforcement of
arbitration awards.

Chapters 7 and 8 address using technology in dispute resolution. This relatively new field is exciting and holds much promise for the future resolution of
disputes, especially by "digital natives."[4] Chapter 7 describes what online dispute
resolution (ODR) is, how it works, and how it developed. Chapter 8 discusses the
electronic forms of negotiation, mediation, and arbitration; the advantages and
disadvantages of ODR; telepresence; holography; and artificial intelligence.

The restorative approach to dispute resolution is the subject of Chapter 9. Often
associated with criminal acts, restorative justice principles and methods apply
equally well in other contexts, such as workplaces and schools. This chapter
explores the meaning, philosophy, and principles of restorative justice, its advantages and disadvantages, and the three most common restorative methods.

Chapter 10 concerns the adoption of ADR by the U.S. courts, including how
this came about, the role judges play in the use of ADR, and the various methods
used.

In Chapter 11, you will learn about the various tasks frequently assigned to
paralegals. These include preparing motions, subpoenas, settlement agreements,
exhibit lists, memoranda, and client letters. Additionally, because paralegals
often attend many proceedings, this chapter discusses shorthand note taking.

As you begin your study of conflict resolution, remember: "Conflict has many
positive functions. It prevents stagnation, it stimulates interest and curiosity, it is
the medium through which problems can be aired and solutions arrived at, it is the
root of personal and social change."[5]

Endnotes

1. The account here is based on Wade Lambert, *Ever Hear the One About the Lawyers and the Window Bars?*, Wall St. J., Mar. 23, 1994, at A1.
2. N.Y.C. Health Code § 131.15.
3. Lambert, *supra* note 1.
4. The term "digital natives" was coined by Mark Prensky in his book *Digital Game-Based Learning* (MCB University Press 2001). You will learn more about this in Chapter 7.
5. Morton Deutsch, *The Resolution of Conflict: Constructive and Destructive Processes* 8-9 (Yale University Press 1973).

CHAPTER ONE

Understanding Conflict

Chapter Outline

Introduction

Definitions of Conflict

Understanding Human Needs

Sources of Conflicts

Factors Affecting Conflict

How People Approach and Avoid
  Conflict

Conflict Avoidance

Power and Conflict

Power and People

  Power Over

  Power With

  Powerlessness

  Empowerment

Sources of Power

Power and Context

The Application of Power in Conflict

  Coercive Power

  Reward or Exchange Power

  Ecological Power

  Normative Power

  Referent Power

  Expert Power

Power and Alienation

Culture and Conflict

Constructive Conflict

Conclusion

Key Terms and Concepts

Practice Test Questions

Review Questions

Application Questions

Practice Exercises

> Nature desires eagerly opposites and out of them it completes its
> harmony, not out of similars.
>
> —HERACLITUS

INTRODUCTION

What do you think or feel when you see the word "conflict"? Whatever reaction you experience, it is about to increase dramatically as you prepare for a career as a legal professional. After all, conflicts form the basis for most legal actions.

Not only do individuals view conflict through their own set of lenses, societies and cultures do too. James Schellenberg presents "three myths" to explain how Western society has viewed conflict.[1] The first is found in the Bible. Prior to Adam and Eve eating fruit from the tree of knowledge, God supervised human behavior. Once the fruit had been eaten, conflict arose, and although humans looked to God for guidance, they were left to their own devices for structuring society and controlling those who broke the rules.

The second myth portrays human society as one in perpetual discord and chaos. In the absence of any moral compass of right and wrong, physical strength was the dominant means of resolving conflict. However, the power of a single individual could always be overcome by people joining forces to destroy him. Still others could band together to oust the first group and on and on. These repeated clashes kept society in a constant state of turmoil. Eventually, humans recognized that if they ceded power to some superior authority, conflict would cease because this superior authority could create principles for governing behavior and methods for enforcing compliance. Thus, according to this myth, a system of government developed that could provide the safety needed for the advancement of human civilization.

The third myth, according to Schellenberg, posits that human society was somewhere between ideal ecstasy and limitless fighting. There was an awareness of right and wrong and the existence of basic human rights; missing, however, was a method to resolve disagreements that arose about these rights. Thus, people came together to develop a system of government. As Schellenberg points out, this depiction is found in the American system of government as evidenced by these words in the Declaration of Independence:

> We hold these truths to be self-evident, that all men are created equal, that they are endowed by their Creator with certain unalienable Rights, that among these are Life, Liberty and the pursuit of Happiness. — That to secure these rights, Governments are instituted among Men, *deriving their just powers from the consent of the governed.*

This third view of conflict, that disagreements can be settled through the democratic process using the art of persuasion, is the one most prevalent in our society today. In essence, we try to use our intelligence, rather than power, to resolve disagreements. Schellenburg points out that there are two major traditions in Western society for using intelligence to solve problems. The first is the "rationalistic" view, which "sees human intelligence as useful primarily to seek out general principles to apply to concrete problems."[2] The second is the "pragmatic" view, which "sees human intelligence as useful primarily in wisely assessing the detailed realities and managing them as effectively as possible."[3]

Our culture has conditioned us to see conflict as harmful, as something to be avoided. The end result is the emergence of a winner-and-loser mentality that rather than resolve the dispute may serve to energize and perpetuate it. Unfortunately, this competitive approach shields us from seeing conflict as an opportunity for good. Mary Parker Follett, acknowledged as the mother of the contemporary field of negotiation and dispute resolution,[4] writes:

> As conflict [difference] is here in the world, as we cannot avoid it, we should, I think, use it. Instead of condemning it, we should set it to work for us.

Why not? What does the mechanical engineer do with friction? Of course, his chief job is to eliminate friction, but it is true that he also capitalizes friction. The transmission of power by belts depends on friction between the belt and the pulley. The friction between the driving wheel of the locomotive and the track is necessary to haul the train. All polishing is done by friction. The music of the violin we get by friction. We left the savage state when we discovered fire by friction. We talk of the friction of mind on mind as a good thing. So in business too, we have to know when to try to eliminate friction and when to try to capitalize it, when to see what work we can make it do. This is what I wish to consider here, whether we can set conflict to work and make it *do* something for us.[5]

Social theorist and psychologist Morton Deutsch also suggests that "[c]onflict has many positive functions. It prevents stagnation, it stimulates interest and curiosity, it is the medium through which problems can be aired and solutions arrived at, it is the root of personal and social change."[6] Much of our advancement as a society is the result of conflict. The creation of the United States and the civil rights and women's movements are examples of change brought on by conflict. Rather than looking at human conflict as basically either good or bad, it can be viewed as vital and necessary for growth and development.

Now that we have discussed various views of conflict, we'll look at different definitions and types of conflicts.

DEFINITIONS OF CONFLICT

Let's begin by looking at three definitions of **conflict**:

"Social conflict [is defined] as the opposition between individuals and groups on the basis of competing interests, different identities, and/or differing attitudes."[7]

"Conflict [is] a feeling, a disagreement, a real or perceived incompatibility of interests, inconsistent worldviews, or a set of behaviors."[8]

Conflict is a "disagreement or incompatibility."[9]

Essentially, conflict can be described as a competition between people or groups who have incompatible interests (values, goals, and needs). But where do these incompatible interests or needs come from? How do they develop? The following discussion will help to answer these questions.

UNDERSTANDING HUMAN NEEDS

Human needs are at the core of all conflicts. Conflict arises when people's needs are unmet or incompatible with others'. Abraham Maslow, a psychologist who worked in the first half of the twentieth century, posited that all people seek to satisfy certain needs, which he structured hierarchically (see Exhibit 1-1,

Exhibit 1-1. MASLOW'S HIERARCHY OF NEEDS

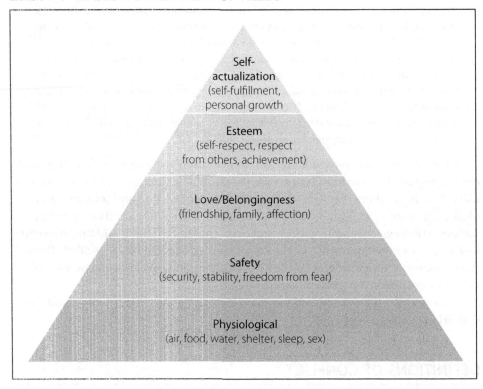

Maslow's Hierarchy of Needs). According to Maslow's theory of human development, each need must be fulfilled or almost fulfilled before moving to the next level.[10] The most basic needs, those found at the base of Maslow's pyramid, are physiological (air, water, food, shelter). Next are safety and security needs. Once these basic needs are met, people seek love and belongingness. Next is the need for self-esteem and esteem by others. Maslow believed that once individuals meet all of the needs just discussed, they strive for "self-actualization," or the ability to be all that they are capable of becoming. An impediment to satisfying any of these needs creates conflict. For example, wars have been fought over land on which to grow food or graze animals. Labor strikes can be attributed to the need for safe working conditions and fair wages. People go to college seeking, among other things, self-esteem culminating in the awarding of a college degree.

Christopher W. Moore offers another view, describing what he calls "interest needs." Moore suggests that people have three types of interests: *substantive interests* (concerns about tangible objects); *procedural interests* (concerns about the way people discuss their differences and the method for implementing an agreement); and *psychological interests* (concerns about the way people are treated).[11] Conflict arises when a person perceives any one of these interests as being unmet or challenged.

We now know that human needs can produce conflict. The next section presents examples of tangible and intangible objects that can be the focus of the conflict.

SOURCES OF CONFLICTS

Conflicts arise from any number of different sources, too many to discuss fully here. This section recognizes some of the most basic sources of conflicts.

Resources. These conflicts involve a dispute over the rights to or control over something valuable. Tangible objects such as money, food, water, land, natural resources, and property are included in this category. So too are intangibles such as prestige, respect, recognition, time, and power. Conflicts over resources can be difficult to resolve unless a satisfactory substitute is found.

Values and beliefs. People use these to guide their own actions and to evaluate others'. Applying these standards, people judge others' behaviors, opinions, and ideas as either moral or immoral, good or bad, right or wrong. Values develop over a long period of time and are influenced by such forces as families, peers, education, religion, and ethnicity. Because values are closely connected with personal identity and rarely change, disputes involving clashes of values may be difficult or impossible to resolve.

"Preferences and nuisances."[12] These conflicts arise when one person's habits or behaviors disrupt another person's preferences. The issue is not whether a person has a right to her preferences, but whether she can exercise her right when it disturbs another. A neighbor who lets her dog bark incessantly or plays loud music are typical examples of nuisances. These conflicts can usually be resolved by changes in the environment. Closing the windows or soundproofing the room may alleviate the sounds of the barking dog or loud music.

Communication. Many factors affect people's ability to communicate effectively: emotional and physiological states, cultural differences, language differences, educational backgrounds, gender, and class, as well as the complexity of the matter being discussed. Whatever its cause, miscommunication increases the odds that a conflict will remain unresolved or even escalate. Because communication is key to discussing and resolving conflicts, it is a necessary skill to develop.

Conflict can be generated by scarce resources, differing values and beliefs, individual preferences, and ineffective communication. However, other variables also affect a disagreement. These are discussed next.

FACTORS AFFECTING CONFLICT

No matter who the parties are, understanding what effect the following variables have on a disagreement is useful when analyzing a particular conflict.

1. The attributes of the conflicting parties (their values, goals, and objectives; their resources for pursuing the conflict or reaching a settlement; and their beliefs, strategies, and tactics)

2. The relationship of the parties with each other prior to the dispute (their views, attitudes, and beliefs about each other and what they expect from the other)
3. The characteristics of the issue(s) giving rise to the conflict (its range, meaning, implication, and firmness)
4. The attitudes of the parties toward conflict resolution (cooperative or competitive)
5. The possible impact on other interested nonparties (how the outcome may affect their relationship to others)
6. The strategies and tactics the parties are likely to use (their use of threats or coercion, their openness to information sharing, their credibility)
7. The outcome and how it will affect the parties (the resulting gains and losses of each; the implications for their future relationship to each other; and their reputation in the eyes of other interested individuals, groups, and organizations)[13]

Up to this point, we have learned about the role human needs play in the development of conflict, tangible and intangible sources of conflict, and some factors that affect conflict. Next we will examine how people approach conflict. Even though two people may have the same need, they may not view conflict the same way.

HOW PEOPLE APPROACH AND AVOID CONFLICT

Avoiding or approaching conflict varies with the individual and the specifics of the dispute.

Avoidance. People avoid conflict for many reasons. A person who feels anxious when confronted with a dispute may choose to avoid it all together. Or a person may decide that the disagreement is too insignificant to devote any resources to reaching a resolution.

Accommodation. Persons who employ this technique put the other parties' needs before their own. They may do this to avoid the conflict or because they do not view the outcome as important.

Compromise. When disputants use this method, they willingly give up something to get something in return. Sometimes the parties just "split the difference."

Cooperative/Collaborative. People using this technique work together to reach a settlement that will satisfy each side's interests and needs. They view the relationship as important and willingly make concessions.

Competitive. In this approach, winning is everything. A person's only objective is satisfying his needs. There is no concern about the relationship with the other party.

The tale about two sisters and an orange[14] illustrates these five approaches to conflict.

EXAMPLE

Two Sisters and an Orange

Photo by Katherine Ellis

Two sisters enter the kitchen simultaneously looking for an orange. Deanna needs the fruit for a recipe, and Kayla wants to make a glass of juice. When they find only one orange in the refrigerator, they begin to argue about who should get it.

Avoidance: The two sisters can't decide on who should get the orange, and so they do nothing.

Accommodation: Deanna tells Kayla that she can have the orange. Kayla says that she can't take it and wants Deanna to have it.

Compromise: Deanna and Kayla agree to cut the orange in half. Deanna now has her half for the recipe and Kayla has hers for a small glass of juice.

Cooperative/Collaborative: Kayla asks her sister what she plans to do with the orange. Deanna replies that she needs the rind for a recipe. Since Kayla needs only the edible fruit and not the rind, the sisters divide the orange, both receiving what they need.

Competitive: The sisters decide to flip a coin five times to determine who will get the orange. Kayla wins the orange, squeezes it, and drinks the juice. Of course, Deanna is not happy.

CONFLICT AVOIDANCE

People who try to avoid conflict altogether often fit into one of the following eight categories, according to Bernard Mayer.[15]

Aggressive Avoidance ("Don't Start with Me or You'll Regret It"). Aggressive behavior is a method of intimidation used to prevent the person from engaging in a conflict.

Passive Avoidance ("I Refuse to Tango"). This approach is avoiding conflict through inaction. For example, the person can refuse to speak, change the subject, physically leave the scene, or avoid the other person altogether.

Passive Aggressive Avoidance ("If You Are Angry at Me, That's Your Problem"). This behavior provokes others while avoiding any accountability.

Avoidance Through Hopelessness ("What's the Use?"). Here, the person sees the situation as not solvable or herself as powerless to change it. As a result, she concludes that there is no point in participating in the conflict.

Avoidance Through Surrogates ("Let You and Them Fight"). This tactic sidesteps conflict by allowing others to deal with the dispute while the avoider stays on the sidelines.

Avoidance Through Denial ("If I Close My Eyes, It Will Go Away"). By denying the existence of a conflict, the person hopes it goes away.

Avoidance Through Premature Problem Solving ("There's No Conflict; I Have Fixed Everything"). This method, which focuses on a solution, avoids an opportunity to understand the conflict and fails to allow for people to be heard and acknowledged.

Avoidance by Folding ("OK, We'll Do It Your Way; Now Can We Talk About Something Else?"). This approach avoids conflict by "giving in," by accepting more blameworthiness than is reasonable, or by yielding on all the issues.

We have learned that unmet or incompatible human needs lie at the core of all conflicts, that various factors affect conflict, and that people respond to conflict in different ways. Now we will explore a fundamental concept in conflict theory, "power." Power is the ability to get something done. Power differences between parties can make disagreements more difficult to resolve and affect the structure of the relationships and the nature of the outcomes. In the next section, we will learn about the exercise of power on people, where power comes from, context and power, and how power is used to influence people.

POWER AND CONFLICT

In 2002, Nigerians were in conflict with Chevron Texaco. They wanted more jobs and a commitment to social development. The Nigerian men, often using violence, had been unsuccessful. The Nigerian women then became involved.

"When several days had passed without success in negotiations, they threatened to take off their clothes if their demands were not met. In the culture of the Niger Delta, women bring great shame upon men by stripping naked in front of them."[16] Eventually, the oil company agreed to provide additional jobs and invest in the development of their communities. The Nigerian women used their power to end the conflict and bring about change. So, what is power, and how does power affect conflict?

"Power is the currency of conflict."[17] Power can be exercised deliberately or without even thinking about it. When we try to get something we want, we exercise power. How successful we are depends on how much power we have and how we use that power. Power can be used coercively or collaboratively.

In our culture, conflict is often linked with the use of force. From children's cartoons to television and movies, physical force is used to triumph over evil. As a result, we learn that force is the best way to get what we want. As we shall learn, exercising power may not be desirable. Coercive power can lead to alienation, which in turn can disempower the person exercising the power.

Let's begin our discussion by defining what power is. Power is "the ability to act, to influence an outcome, to get something to happen, or to overcome resistance."[18] A person has power "to the degree that he can satisfy the purposes (goals, desires, or wants) that he is attempting to fulfill in [a given] situation."[19] Although individual resources are important to understanding power, so too is how power is exercised, which is the focus of our next topic.

POWER AND PEOPLE

The following four themes on power help in understanding how people exercise and perceive power: "power over," "power with," "powerless," and "empowerment."

Power Over

Power over is the power of a person over another person or a group of people over another group of people. For example, a regional store manager tells a store manager to reorganize the layout of the merchandise. (The regional manager has power over the store manager.) The store manager then tells her head sales clerk (the manager has power over the head sales clerk), who in turn tells the sales staff (the head sales clerk has power over the sales staff). Power over is usually accomplished by coercion, which is discussed more fully below. Other examples of power over include military organizations, propagandists, cultists, and religious zealots.

Power With

Power over was the prevailing view in our society until the 1920s when Mary Parker Follett proposed the revolutionary idea that power could be developed jointly — **power with** — by combining the knowledge and experience of each individual. She called this "a co-active, not a coercive power."[20] The article that follows illustrates the co-active partnership developed between environmentalists and timber companies to preserve forests in northeast Washington.

Environmentalists, Loggers Push New Wilderness Deal in Northeast

Craig Welch, *Seattle Times*

After years of lawsuits and fights, environmentalists and timber companies are working together on proposals to preserve thousands of acres of forests in Northeast Washington — and an agreement to dramatically increase logging. The centerpiece is an initiative that will be unveiled Wednesday to add more than 180,000 acres of wilderness to Colville National Forest in Northeast Washington.

The rolling highlands of Northeast Washington are home to grape ferns, lady slipper orchids, burnt-orange flameflowers — and scratch-dry ponderosa pine that timber companies really want to log.

The wild country from the Kettle Range to the Selkirk Mountains offers a corridor linking Washington's elusive lynx with other carnivores in Montana. But it also offers uber-popular spots for riding dirt bikes, jeeps and all-terrain vehicles.

So after decades of lawsuits and arguments about this corner of the state, environmentalists and logging companies tried a different approach: They talked. And talked some more.

Eight years later they're putting forward something new: proposals to set aside tens of thousands of acres as wilderness.

Conservation Northwest, a Bellingham-based environmental group run by former EarthFirst! tree-sitter Mitch Friedman, will unveil an initiative Wednesday to add more than 180,000 acres of wilderness to Colville National Forest. The plan also calls for designating areas of the forest for recreation — from mountain bikes to dirt bikes — and raising up to $2 million from donors to put 2,200 acres of private land east of Republic, Ferry County, into a forest-conservation program. And it largely has timber-industry support.

The efforts still are being massaged, and all sides concede they're just getting started. But few dispute something remarkable has happened. Former enemies are working so well together that they're jointly trying to bring others along. . . .

Source: Craig Welch, Environmentalists, Loggers Push New Wilderness Deal in Northeast, Seattle Times, July 27, 2010, http://www.seattletimes.com/seattle-news/environmentalists-loggers-push-new-wilderness-deal-in-northeast-washington/.

Powerlessness

Powerlessness is "the expectancy or probability held by the individual that his own behavior cannot determine the occurrence of the outcomes . . . he seeks."[21] Powerful people are seen as being "in a position to impose their wills on others, or to make decisions on their own that may significantly affect the lives of others, or to do what they want to do at the expense of others without having to concern themselves with that expense. And, the powerless, on the other hand, are correspondingly understood to be those people who are not in such a position, but rather are the unfortunate 'others' who must endure such treatment."[22] An example is a victim of domestic violence. The victim feels helpless, alienated, angry, and resentful.

Surprisingly, sometimes powerlessness creates strength. Take the situation where the powerless conclude that because they have nothing to lose, they will challenge the powerful, which could make it costly for the stronger party. Or the position of the powerless may engender feelings of compassion and kindness in the more powerful.

Empowerment

The opposite of powerlessness is powerful, which gives rise to a feeling of independence or **empowerment**. Scholars refer to this as having "power to" or "power from," meaning that an individual has sufficient power to attain her objective, free from interference from other people or other things. Corporations and organizations that delegate authority or promote employee participation find that employees are less dependent on others and have enhanced senses of worth and self-assurance.[23]

"Daddy, Shoes"

One of the most evident ways that we are empowered is in how we care for ourselves. I can, for example, feed and dress myself. Training in this started at an early age.

As a child I wanted to run barefoot outside. My dad wanted me to wear shoes when I went outside. He was bigger than me. He had power over me such that, if I wanted to go outside, I had to have shoes on.

One day as I was playing outside with my shoes on, I discovered that one shoe was loose. I played with it and got it off. I played with the other one and got it off too. Then I took my socks off. Ah . . . barefoot in the grass. I ran and played and kicked the ball. I kicked the ball across the gravel drive but when I chased it, ouch, that hurts. It didn't feel that way when I had shoes on.

So I called out, "Daddy, shoes."

Continued >

> And he said to me, "Get your shoes and socks and bring them to me and I will put them on." And while I did, I realized that I hadn't had to bring him the shoes and socks before. He had always done that. Our relationship had changed. We had gone from power over to power with. Before he wanted me to have shoes on and I didn't but he was bigger than me so he got his way. Now we both wanted me to have my shoes on so we worked together to create what we both wanted. We both wanted Mark to have his shoes on.
>
> Over time I learned to find my shoes and socks, and then to put on my socks, and then my shoes (I had to know which one went on which foot), and then to tie them, and then to tie them so they stayed tied. Little by little over time I became empowered to put on my shoes and socks. But I did so by going from *power over* through *power with* to *empowerment*.
>
> *Source:* http://www.creativeconflictresolution.org/jc/maps-1/power-types.html (last visited June 20, 2015).

Now that we understand how people utilize power, let's find out where power comes from.

SOURCES OF POWER

Generally power comes from four sources: personal power, resource power, information power, and moral power. Personal power derives from the intrinsic traits of an individual, such as intelligence, determination, physical strength, confidence, wealth, appearance, affability, courage, respect, and communication skills. Resource power comes from the ability to control or access such things as money, property, oil, gas and other natural resources, people, and weapons. Information power means knowledge about facts and data. The more information a person has, the more power she can exert. Moral power comes from values, beliefs, and ethics. Acting with what a person believes to be a moral purpose helps her to be resolute and vigorous in her advocacy. Also, appealing to fairness or morality can overcome other sources of power such as wealth or physical strength. Knowing where power comes from is important, but we also need to be aware of the setting in which power is exercised.

POWER AND CONTEXT

Power is situation- or context-based. This means that the power a person has is affected by the particular circumstances and therefore, is never constant. Sometimes the most powerful people have no power in certain situations. For example, a supervisor has more power at the workplace than those she supervises, but outside this environment, say on a whitewater rafting trip, this power may not continue. A college president has no power over a police officer who stopped her for speeding. Thus a person's power is dependent upon the situation and the person's role in it. A change in the setting, no matter how small, may significantly affect the power dynamics.

THE APPLICATION OF POWER IN CONFLICT

We know that people acquire power from different sources and that situations affect power, but how are these powers used or applied to influence others? There are six primary ways in which people use power to sway or manipulate others.[24]

Coercive Power

The most recognizable type of power is the ability to force agreement. This is called **coercive power**. Examples are the threat to inflict physical punishment or financial consequences or the capability to harm a person's reputation or social status. For example, let's suppose Company A is the largest purchaser of Company B's product and anticipates increasing their purchases, which will result in a 100 percent increase in Company B's business. In exchange for this arrangement, Company A wants Company B to agree not to sell the product to anyone else. If it does not agree, Company A threatens to stop doing business altogether with Company B. Company A is using coercive power, i.e., the threat of financial consequences to force Company B to assent to its terms.

Reward or Exchange Power

Reward or **exchange power** is the flipside of coercive power. It offers something of value such as money, property, or recognition as a reward or exchange for what is wanted. Offering a child money in exchange for good grades in school is an example of reward or exchange power.

Ecological Power

Ecological power is the ability to control the environment. Manipulating or altering the environment may "persuade" the other person to behave or not behave in a certain way. In Maine, some years ago a large landowner had allowed the public to use her property to access various mountain trails. Unfortunately, some people began abusing this privilege by riding their snowmobiles and all-terrain vehicles on the land, causing environmental damage. Additionally, the landowner was constantly picking up trash left behind by the users. Frustrated, the landowner erected locked gates at various entry points, thereby preventing the public from accessing her land. By making this change the landowner used ecological power to change behavior, i.e., using other trails.

Normative Power

Normative power is the ability to convince others that what you are proposing is the correct thing to do and that they should act accordingly. It is the use of moral authority. For example, you are the owner of a company and believe in gender equality. An employee comes to you and points out that a coworker of the opposite gender who does the same work you do gets paid more. Because of your commitment to gender equality, you are persuaded to give the employee a raise.

Referent Power

Referent power is the power to influence others' desire to be like some person or group. The advertising industry frequently uses this type of power by having sports figures, singers, and other celebrities endorse products. Just look at television, the Internet, and magazines, and you will see well-known people hyping various consumer goods from soda to jeans to makeup. Advertisers hope that viewers will identify with the celebrity and buy the product.

Expert Power

Expert power comes from the superior knowledge or skill one person has over another. A lawyer, accountant, engineer, and real estate agent have more information and thus more power as it relates to matters within their fields of expertise. For example, a lawyer suing the builder of a home that caught fire due to an electrical problem will want an expert, in this case an electrician, to testify about the faulty workmanship, which caused the fire.

In addition to understanding the application of power, we must be aware of the potential for alienation by the person or group over whom the power is applied. This is what we will explore next.

POWER AND ALIENATION

Alienation can cause a person to be unfriendly, mistrustful, and even hateful. The six types of power discussed above can create more or less disaffection in a person subjected to the power. Coercive power is viewed as the most alienating, while expert and referent power the least. Alienation can also be expected when the power employed is viewed as illegitimate by the recipient.

When alienation occurs, the powerholder, in a sense, becomes powerless. The powerholder's options to employ other resources, normative, referent, expert, and reward, are greatly reduced or unavailable because the other party is no longer trusting and may even be hostile. Thus, the only option is to use coercion or ecological power, which may be effective in the short term but is not conducive to nurturing a long-term relationship.

Power is a complicated concept that can operate in contradictory ways. Power can increase or decrease a conflict. It can generate alienation or overcome it. People can use their power to encourage collaboration or to browbeat others into submission. We should be aware that there are different options when using power or responding to it.

CULTURE AND CONFLICT

Cultural norms, values, and conduct shape the way people approach disagreements. The objective in this brief discussion is to bring awareness of the impact that cultural differences have on conflict. Because "culture is the perception-shaping lens through which we experience conflict,"[25] recognizing the interplay between culture and conflict is important. Let's begin by looking at two definitions of culture:

1. Culture is "a common system of knowledge and experiences that result in a set of rules or standards; these rules and standards in turn result in behavior and beliefs that the group considers acceptable."[26]
2. Culture is "the socially transmitted values, beliefs and symbols that are more or less shared by members of a social group . . . through which members interpret and attribute meaning to both their own and others' experiences and behavior."[27]

Culture influences a person's perceptions, behaviors, decision making, and information processing. Not only can cultural differences create conflict, but they can also impact the resolution of the conflict.

Before we look at some examples of how culture affects disagreements, we need to know that individuals may belong to several groups and therefore possess attributes of multiple cultures. As a result, they may make use of more than one culture when interacting. Also, members of a group do not necessarily share the same culture in exactly the same way. Individuals can choose to accept or modify their cultural rules or beliefs. Therefore, stereotyping an individual based on his or her group affiliation should be avoided.

To help understand the impact of culture in disputes, we will look at what social scientists have termed "high-context" and "low-context" cultures and the distinctive communication patterns of each. In high-context cultures (e.g., Japanese, Chinese, and Vietnamese), the meaning of a message is revealed in what is not said: the nonverbal components of the communication such as tone of voice, eye contact, and facial expressions. This unspoken message is ingrained in the group's social and cultural knowledge. In low-context cultures (e.g., North American, German, and Scandinavian), what is said (the words) is the message. Here is an illustration:

> In . . . an organizational setting concerning the rejection of a sales proposal by a North American supervisor in the [low-context culture], a North American subordinate will probably view the conflict episode very differently than a Japanese subordinate. . . . The North American subordinate will probably enter

the conflict situation with a heated discussion and issue-oriented arguments [and] probably produce facts, figures, and graphs to illustrate his or her case. In contrast, the Japanese subordinate will probably be dumbfounded by the direct, outright rejection and will then proceed to analyze the conflict episode as a personal attack or a sign of mistrust. In fact, he or she will probably resign as soon as possible.[28]

Low-context individuals focus on the issue and not the person. They can be involved in a heated argument but still maintain a friendly relationship when the argument ends. They separate the people from the problem. The focus is on the verbal message that expresses thoughts, opinions, and feelings. In contrast, high-context individuals cannot separate the person from the conflict. Their expectations of the "proper" behavior from the person involved in the dispute are inseparable from the problem. Their attention is focused on the relationship, social norms, and roles of the parties. Low-context communication is seen in the following dispute between American neighbors:

Susan (knocks on her
neighbor's door):   Do you know what time it is? It's 11:45 in the evening and I can't get to sleep because you keep playing the piano. Please stop! I have to get up early for an important business meeting.

Ellen (unpleasantly):   Well, I have to practice because I have an audition in the morning. This is just as important as your business meeting.

Susan (irritated):   Look, you're being unreasonable. If you don't stop playing right now, I'm calling the police.

Ellen: Fine, go ahead. I'm not going to stop!

Contrast the above low-context interaction with the following high-context exchange. This scenario involves two Japanese mothers.

Mother 1:   Your son has been taking piano lessons. You must be very pleased. He is very talented. Maybe one day he will be famous. I admire his commitment. He practices for many hours even late at night.

Mother 2:   Oh thank you, but he is just beginning. Who knows what will happen in the future. We didn't know you could hear him. I am sorry that his practicing has been disturbing you.

In the first scenario, Susan and Ellen tell each other everything. Their conversation is direct and to the point. In contrast, Mother 1 expresses her concern about the noise indirectly. She wants to preserve the relationship with Mother 2 and therefore uses hints that allow Mother 1 to read between the lines.

Cultural conflicts often result from misunderstandings of nonverbal communication. Gestures, voice volume, facial expressions, and the use of interpersonal space or distance are some examples of nonverbal communication. Take the nonverbal OK sign. In the United States, it means success while in Brazil it is an insult (it is the equivalent of "giving the middle finger" in the United States), and in Japan it signifies money. Greeks, Italians, and Arabs tend to speak loudly and expressively when discussing important issues. When an Arab raises his voice and repeats himself to an American, he may appear angry. However, to an Arab he is just displaying concern for the subject of the discussion. Conversely, when an American speaks softly and does not repeat himself, the Arab may wonder if the American means what he just said.[29]

The use of interpersonal space is another variable among different cultures. What represents proper distance between people in one culture may be seen as crowding by another. Anthropologist Edward T. Hall posited that Americans communicate from "four distance zones."[30] From about 6 to 18 inches is considered intimate space and reserved for loved ones and close friends. Touching, whispering, and hugging usually take place in this area. Personal distance, between 1.5 to 4 feet, is reserved for friends and in which informal conversation takes place. Social distance is 4 feet to 12 feet and is common in informal social gatherings. Twelve feet and beyond is public space and where public interaction occurs. Examples are walking down the street or in a mall, listening to a public speaker, or watching a play. Keep in mind that these norms are unconscious.

Other cultures have different perceptions of space. For Arabs, the social conversation space is the same distance as the American intimate space (6 to 18 inches). So while an Arab and a Westerner are conversing, the Arab will tend to move closer while the American will move away. The American then concludes that the Arab is aggressive and rude, and the Arab concludes that the American is cold and standoffish. Because these norms are unconscious, the parties may not know why they feel uneasy. Think of the implications the treatment of space may have on a dispute.[31]

Cultural differences can be the source of conflict, and they can have a significant impact on attempts at resolving the conflict. Therefore, it is imperative that these cultural differences be understood and acknowledged.

PARALEGAL POINTERS

Your interactions with clients will not always be easy. Some clients may be frustrated with the process or confused about an issue. Depending on the subject matter of the representation, some clients may become very emotional. When these situations arise, the following may be helpful.

Effectively Dealing with Difficult Client Situations, Allison C. Shields, Esq., Legal Ease Consulting, Inc.

Let's face it — sometimes it's difficult dealing with clients, particularly when you have to tell them something you know they don't want to hear, or when a client has a complaint.

Often, conflicts arise because clients feel you don't understand their point of view. It's easy to forget that clients — even business clients — have an emotional

Continued >

investment in their legal matter. To you, it may be just another case. But to the client, it's their life, their livelihood, or their business.

When those difficult or uncomfortable client conversations arise, how can you handle them?

Mirror the client's thoughts. Let the client tell you what the issue is, and then reflect it back to the client. This way, the client knows they're being heard, and you ensure that you understand their issue.

Focus on the client. The key to resolution is concentrating on the client's *feelings* and the client's *desired outcome*, rather than focusing on yourself or on the work that you have to do. For example, if a client asks for something in a rush, respond by acknowledging the client's sense of urgency and how it affects their goals—not by telling them how much work you have to do or why what they're asking is impossible.

Work toward a resolution based on where you are now. Once the client is calmer and you've acknowledged them, you can begin to gather information that can help you to reach a solution. Offer the client options for resolution, even if you can't meet their specific demand.

Focus on the positive. Instead of saying no or telling a client what you can't do and why, tell them what you *can* do. Explain the options in terms of the client's goals (i.e. because I know that you don't want to drag this litigation out . . ." or "Since you want to keep costs down . . .").

Don't retreat or get defensive—it only escalates the confrontation.

Lay the groundwork for bad news—and go slowly. Resist the urge to just "get it over with" by blurting out the bad news all at once. When you know the client isn't going to be happy about what you have to tell them, start out by acknowledging the client's desired outcome or goals, introduce what you are going to discuss, or explain that there are a number of different strategies that can be employed to move forward with their matter. Be sure to give the client reasons for those options and for what occurred. After you've delivered the bad news, let the client know that you empathize with their position.

Know your boundaries and set limits. Often confrontations arise when the unexpected occurs. You can reduce many common difficult client situations by being prepared and setting boundaries at the outset of the engagement. Clients who can't abide by your processes or boundaries will often self-identify themselves, offering you the opportunity to explore the situation before a confrontation occurs or the chance to decline the representation. There's no reason to tolerate an abusive client!

CONSTRUCTIVE CONFLICT

As noted earlier in this chapter, not all conflict is bad. Disputes can lead to invention, creativity, and positive change. How conflict is managed is the key to its effectiveness. When parties focus on the issue and avoid focusing on people, they can disagree with ideas while confirming the other person's competence. This encourages information sharing and collaboration, which leads to conflict resolution. Here are some suggestions on how to engage in **constructive conflict**:[32]

- Question the idea, not the person.
- Do not take criticism of your suggestion as an attack on you personally.
- Remember that all parties have a stake in the conflict. Concentrate on finding the best resolution, not on victory.
- Encourage participation by all parties.
- Listen to each party even if your view differs.
- Recognize the other side's concerns.
- Identify differences and similarities, then see if these can be integrated.
- Do not hesitate to change your mind if the facts support a view different from yours.
- "Follow the golden rule of conflict: act toward opponents, as you would have them act toward you."[33] This means listen to their ideas, include their ideas in your thinking, and see the issue from their perspective.

Disagreeing in a manner that challenges the other person's competence will only strengthen commitment to their own ideas and the rejection of others'. Disagreeing while confirming the person's competence creates a closer relationship and a willingness to accept the other's views and information. The parties are then more likely to cooperate and reach an agreement.

Conclusion

This chapter discusses how conflict develops, how people approach and avoid conflict, the use of power, the effect of culture on disagreements, and the social utility of conflict. The legal system categorizes disputes in terms of rights, duties, and remedies. As a result, laws of legal responsibility, causation, and damages guide a lawyer's perspective of conflict. When lawyers disagree over these, they are trained to resolve the dispute by litigation. Chapter 2 discusses this traditional approach to resolving legal conflicts in our society.

Key Terms and Concepts

Alienation	Cultural norms
Coercive power	Ecological power
Conflict	Empowerment
Constructive conflict	Expert power

Human needs

Maslow's Hierarchy of Needs

Normative power

Powerlessness

Power over

Power with

Referent power

Reward or exchange power

Practice Test Questions

True/False

_____ 1. Some disputes can lead to invention, creativity, and change. How the conflict is managed is the key to its effectiveness.

_____ 2. Conflict can be described as a competition between people or groups who have incompatible interests (values, goals, and needs).

_____ 3. Cultural norms, values, and conduct shape the way people approach disagreements.

_____ 4. The power a person has is affected by the particular circumstances and, therefore, is never constant.

_____ 5. Conflict is counterproductive and should be avoided at all costs.

Multiple Choice

_____ 1. All of the following are considered a source of power *except*
   a. resource power.
   b. religious power.
   c. information power.
   d. personal power.

_____ 2. Conflict can arise from a dispute over
   a. resources.
   b. tangible objects.
   c. ineffective communication.
   d. all of the above.

_____ 3. Which of the following would *not* contribute to constructive conflict?
   a. questioning the person's integrity
   b. recognizing the other side's concerns
   c. identifying differences and similarities
   d. listening to the other party

_____ 4. All of the following are ways in which people try to sway or manipulate others *except*
   a. coercive power.
   b. ecological power.
   c. expert power.
   d. dominant power.

_____ 5. People approach and avoid conflict in all of the following ways *except*
   a. avoidance.
   b. compromise.
   c. cultural acceptance.
   d. accommodation.

Review Questions

1. The key to successful conflict resolution is to focus on the issue and not on the person. List and explain some methods that can help keep the parties focused on the issue and not on each other.
2. Conflicts can be attributed to a number of sources. List and explain the ones discussed in the chapter.
3. The chapter discusses five ways that people react to conflict. Name and discuss each of these concepts.
4. What are Maslow's Hierarchy of Needs? Explain each one.
5. How does a change in context affect a person's power?
6. Understanding the affect some variables have on a dispute is helpful when examining a particular conflict. List and discuss the factors that can influence a disagreement.
7. How does culture shape the way people approach conflict?
8. What is power, and how does power affect conflict?
9. Where does power come from? Explain each source.
10. What does "power over" people and "power with" people mean?
11. Explain each of the six primary ways in which people use power to manipulate other people.
12. How can the exercise of power alienate a person?

Application Questions

1. Consider the quotation from Mary Parker Follett near the beginning of the chapter. What do you think are some valuable attributes of conflict?
2. Conflicts can be both constructive and destructive. What are some of the distinctions between these two views? Have you experienced a situation in which conflict created a positive or constructive outcome? Would this result have happened without the conflict? Why?
3. All too often when a consumer complains to a store owner or service provider, she gets the brush-off. But when the consumer hires an attorney who calls or writes a letter to the same business about the dispute, he receives a prompt and polite response about the claim. Why the difference in treatment? What has changed?
4. Imagine that your job depends on the use of a specialized computer software. The version you have is quite old and slow. While attending a conference, you learn about new, faster software whose features will improve your company's productivity. You watch a demonstration and are persuaded that the company should purchase it. You talk with your supervisor and explain that this new software is more efficient but costs $10,000. Your supervisor emphatically says, "No." At the next department meeting, you ask the department head for authority to order the software. You explain the number of work hours that could be saved over the next six months and the reduction in the amount

of errors. Your request is approved, and the software is ordered. What power was used in the second scenario that was not in the first?

5. Culture affects how people approach conflict. What are the characteristic stereotypes of your culture? Do they apply to you? Why or why not?

Practice Exercises

1. Using the Internet, find a conflict that happened in your state. For example, it might be a dispute between environmentalists and developers, supporters and opponents of building a new school, or rezoning a piece of property. After you find it, describe and discuss the following:
   a. The nature of the conflict and how it developed
   b. The parties involved
   c. The source of the conflict
   d. The factors affecting the conflict
   e. How the conflict was resolved

2. Interview five people and ask each to tell you about a conflict they experienced. It could be something that happened at work, in school, in a restaurant or store, and so on. During your conversation, find out the following:
   a. The source of the conflict
   b. The factors that affected the conflict
   c. How the person approached or avoided the conflict
   d. How the conflict was resolved

   Be prepared to explain each interview to class. Your instructor may want you to write a paper in which you discuss each interview.

3. Research the Internet for information on how to resolve a conflict. Choose one approach and explain and discuss it.

Endnotes

1. James A. Schellenberg, *Conflict Resolution: Theory, Research, and Practice* 3-6 (State University of New York Press 1996).

2. *Id.* at 5.

3. *Id.*

4. Deborah M. Kolb, *The Love for Three Oranges Or: What Did We Miss About Ms. Follett in the Library*, 11 Neg. J. 339 (1995); Carrie Menkel-Meadow, *Mothers and Fathers of Invention: The Intellectual Founders of* ADR, 16 Ohio St. J. on Disp. Resol. 1 (2000).

5. *Dynamic Administration: The Collected Papers of Mary Parker Follett* 30-31 (Henry C. Metcalf & L. Urwick ed., Harper & Row 1941).

6. Morton Deutsch, *The Resolution of Conflict: Constructive and Destructive Processes* 8-9 (Yale University Press 1973).

7. Schellenberg, *supra* note 1, at 8.

8. Bernard Mayer, *The Dynamics of Conflict Resolution: A Practitioner's Guide* 3 (Jossey-Bass 2000).

9. *Dictionary of Conflict Resolution* 113 (1999).

10. Abraham Maslow, *Motivation and Personality* 35-47 (2d ed., Harper & Row 1954).

11. Christopher W. Moore, *The Mediation Process: Practical Strategies for Resolving Conflict* 37 (Jossey-Bass 1986); Christopher Moore, *The Mediation Process: Practical Strategies for Resolving Conflict* 71-72(2d ed., Jossey-Bass 1996); Christopher W. Moore, *The Mediation Process: Practical Strategies for Resolving Conflict* 75 (3d ed., Jossey-Bass 2003).

12. Deutsch, *supra* note 6, at 15.

13. Based on Deutsch, *supra* note 6.

14. Although Mary Parker Follett is frequently cited as the originator of this parable, I have been unable to locate a source citation. Professor Roy Lewicki, who has written numerous books on negotiation, believes that "Robert House, a well-known management professor, created a role play out of Mary Parker Follett's 'library window problem' and named it the Ugli Orange exercise. . . . In 1982, I [Lewicki] co-edited a book of classroom exercises, cases, etc. for use in Organizational Behavior [OB] courses. . . . Tim Hall [his colleague] did some kind of edited rewrite of House's activity . . . and we published it in the book, for use in classes in OB and negotiation." E-mail from Roy L. Lewicki, Professor Emeritus, Ohio State University, to author (Aug. 15, 2015, 14:55 EDST) (on file with author). The Ugli Orange exercise can be found in *Experiences in Management and Organizational Behavior* 82-84 (Douglas T. Hall, Donald D. Bowen, Roy J. Lewicki & Francine S. Hall eds., St. Clair Press 1982).

15. Bernard Mayer, *The Dynamics of Conflict Resolution* 44-46 (2d ed., John Wiley & Sons 2012).

16. *Nigerian Women Show Their Power,* news24.com (July 19, 2002), http://www.news24.com/Africa/Features/Nigerian-women-show-their-power-20020719.

17. Mayer, *supra*, note 8, at 50.

18. *Id.*

19. Deutsch, *supra*, note 6, at 84.

20. *Dynamic Administration, supra*, note 5, at 101.

21. Melvin Seeman, *On the Meaning of Alienation*, 24 Am. Soc. Rev. 783, 784 (1959).

22. *Major Social Issues: A Multidisciplinary View* 430 (Milton J. Yinger & Stephen J. Cutler eds., Free Press 1978).

23. *See The Handbook of Conflict Resolution: Theory and Practice* 111 (Morton Deutsch & Peter T. Coleman eds., Jossey-Bass 2000).

24. Deutsch, *supra* note 6, at 87.

25. Pat K. Chew, *The Pervasiveness of Culture in Conflict*, 54 J. Legal Educ. 60 (2004).

26. *Id.*

27. Kevin Avruch, *Culture as Context, Culture as Communication: Considerations for Humanitarian Negotiators*, 9 Harv. Negot. L. Rev. 391, 393 (2004).

28. Stella Ting-Toomey, *Toward a Theory of Conflict and Culture, in Communication, Culture, and Organizational Processes* 77 (William Gudykunst, Lea Stewart & Stella Ting-Toomey eds., Sage 1985).

29. Margaret K. (Omer) Nydell, *Understanding Arabs: A Guide for Modern Times* 125 (Nicholas Brealey 2005).

30. Edward T. Hall, *The Hidden Dimension* 109-120 (Doubleday 1966).

31. *Id.* at 147-159; Margaret K. Nydell, *Understanding Arabs: A Guide for Westerners* 54-56 (Intercultural Press 2002); Stella Ting-Toomey, *Communicating Across Cultures* 128 (Guilford Press 1999).

32. *See Handbook of Conflict Resolution, supra* note 23, at 70-71.

33. *Id.* at 71.

CHAPTER TWO

Litigation

Chapter Outline

Introduction
  Who Will Participate in the Process?
  What Are the Basic Stages of the Process from Beginning to Final Resolution?
  Where Will the Proceedings Occur?
  Which Claims and Issues Will Be Considered?
  What Information Will Be Considered, and How and When Will It Be Exchanged?
  Who Determines the Outcome?
  What Types of Outcomes Are Possible?
Advantages
  Ensures a Resolution
  Predictable Process
  Enforcement
  Precedent
  Discovery
  Due Process
  Openness of Process
  Appeals
  Interim Relief
  Parties Do Not Have to Deal with Each Other
  Provides Justice
Disadvantages
  Expensive and Costly
  Slow
  No Privacy
  Not Flexible
  Does Not Preserve Relationships
  Need for an Attorney
  Can't Choose the Decision Maker
Conclusion
Key Terms and Concepts
Practice Test Questions
Review Questions
Application Questions
Practice Exercises

It may be true that the law cannot make a man love me, but it can keep him from lynching me, and I think that's pretty important.

— MARTIN LUTHER KING

INTRODUCTION

More than 160 years ago Abraham Lincoln wrote: "Discourage litigation. Persuade your neighbors to compromise whenever you can. Point out to them how the nominal winner is often a real loser—in fees, expenses, and waste of time."[1]

While lawsuits can be costly, time-consuming, and stressful, we must not forget that they do resolve disputes and sometimes may be superior to other methods of dispute resolution. For example, litigation produces rules and precedents that provide society with a guide for future behavior, which in turn contributes to social stability.

Litigation has other benefits, along with detriments, but before we look at these, we need to discuss some basic characteristics of all dispute resolutions processes, including litigation. Jeffrey R. Seul suggests that

> any dispute resolution process must answer a number of fundamental questions:
> - Who will participate in the process?
> - What are the basic stages of the process from beginning to final resolution?
> - Where will the proceedings occur?
> - Which claims and issues will be considered?
> - What information will be considered and how and when will it be exchanged?
> - Who determines the outcome?
> - What types of outcomes are possible?[2]

Who Will Participate in the Process?

In a simple lawsuit, there is a **plaintiff** and **defendant**. The plaintiff is the party who initiates the lawsuit by asserting that the defendant caused a harm. The harm must be one that is recognized by law. Sometimes lawsuits involve multiple plaintiffs and multiple defendants. Other people involved may include attorneys for the disputants, their staffs, and private investigators.

If the case goes to trial, a jury or a trial judge participates by deciding the facts. The trial judge also applies the appropriate substantive and procedural laws. At trial, expert and lay witnesses may be called to testify for either party. Court personnel handle administrative functions such as assembling the jury pool, tracking and securing exhibits admitted into evidence, and managing the court calendar. If an appeal is filed, appellate court judges participate by deciding the issues on appeal. Finally, in a way, the general public is a participant. Unless the public or press is excluded from some or all of the trial, all court proceedings are open to the public and all court documents are available for inspection.

In other forms of dispute resolution, fewer people are involved. Mediation typically involves the disputants and a neutral third party and sometimes the parties' attorneys. Arbitration typically involves one arbitrator, the disputants, and their attorneys. Occasionally, witnesses may testify, but the substance of their testimony can be submitted in writing or presented orally by the respective attorneys.

What Are the Basic Stages of the Process from Beginning to Final Resolution?

A lawsuit begins with a formal written **complaint** prepared by the plaintiff, filed with a court and delivered to the defendant, along with a summons. The complaint is a summary of the plaintiff's claims and facts supporting the lawsuit and the relief plaintiff is seeking. (Examples of relief include money, return of property, and alimony.) The **summons** tells the defendant that he is being sued and in what court. It also warns the defendant that "[a] failure to appear and defend will result in a default judgment against . . . [him] . . . for the relief demanded in the complaint."[3] A default judgment is entered against a defendant who has failed to plead or defend against the plaintiff's claim.[4]

The defendant must **answer** the complaint or file a motion requesting that the court dismiss the lawsuit because the court lacks jurisdiction over the subject matter of the lawsuit or the defendant or it fails to state a claim recognized by law. Assuming that defendant's motion to dismiss is denied or she does not file a motion, she must answer the complaint. In this document, she admits or denies the allegations and asserts any defenses. The defendant can also sue the plaintiff by way of a counterclaim and other parties who may be liable.

Three stages in a lawsuit follow the summons and complaint: pretrial, trial, and posttrial. The pretrial phase involves a number of procedures designed to prepare the case for trial. The trial stage is where the case is presented to a judge or jury who render a decision. The posttrial phase is where the winner seeks to implement the judgment while the losing party can try to prevent it through the appeal process.

Other forms of dispute resolution can be less complex and faster. For example, arbitration does not require a summons and complaint. There is no or limited discovery and the dispute does not have to involve a claim established by law. Similarly, mediation eschews the necessity of formality. Disputants simply meet with a neutral third party; discuss their concerns and interests; and, with the guidance of the neutral, work toward reaching a mutually acceptable resolution.

PARALEGAL POINTERS

How Paralegals Help During Litigation

Paralegals are involved at many stages of litigation, including

- Preparing motions
- Explaining the litigation process to the client
- Writing memorandum of the facts underlying the dispute
- Performing legal research pertinent to the case
- Preparing subpoenas
- Preparing memoranda summarizing each witness's expected testimony
- Compiling a list of possible exhibits to be introduced
- Attending the proceeding and taking notes
- Preparing settlement agreements and other documents such as lien releases and personal property transfers

Chapter 11 explains these tasks in more detail.

Where Will the Proceedings Occur?

The simple answer is a courthouse. However, which courthouse depends on the **subject matter** of the dispute. For example, some states have a business court that hears only disputes between businesses; a family court that hears divorces or child custody and support issues; or a landlord tenant court. Some courts are limited to disputes of a certain monetary amount. Courts that are limited to hearing only certain subject matters are called courts of specific jurisdiction. Courts that can hear a variety of civil disputes are called courts of general jurisdiction. Additionally, courts are limited geographically. Litigation can also take place in federal courts. Just like state courts, federal jurisdiction depends on the subject matter, dollar amount in controversy, geographical location of the parties, and/or where the dispute arose. In other forms of dispute resolution, jurisdiction is not an issue and location could be anywhere, including on the Internet.

Which Claims and Issues Will Be Considered?

With few exceptions, courts typically are limited to deciding disputes involving rights and liabilities that are recognized under existing law. For example, in a case where a landlord seeks to evict a tenant, the court will look at the lease, if one exists, and/or applicable statutes, determine each party's rights and responsibilities, and decide whether the tenant can be legally evicted. The court will not consider any effect the eviction may have on the tenant or whether the rent is reasonable or excessive. These concerns could be addressed in one of the other dispute resolution methods such as mediation.

What Information Will Be Considered, and How and When Will It Be Exchanged?

In litigation, the information must be relevant to the issue and comply with the rules of evidence for the jurisdiction in which the case is being tried. In other forms of dispute resolution, the evidence does not have to conform to any evidentiary rule. So, for example, a witness could testify what he heard another person say. Under rules of evidence this would be hearsay and not admissible (with some exceptions). Another example is the evidentiary rule requiring that writings and photographs be authenticated by a qualified witness. In other forms of dispute resolution, this would not be necessary.

The **information exchange** takes place during the "discovery" period. The rules of civil procedure provide specific methods and procedures for this phase of a lawsuit. The rules provide that a party can use a deposition to question a witness and have the answers transcribed by a court reporter. Written questions can also be served upon the opposing party who must answer the questions under oath. And requests can be made on a party to produce certain documents or to allow examination of a physical piece of evidence. Other forms of dispute resolution are not as highly structured or formalized. In mediation, there is no discovery period. Arbitration may or may not include discovery or it may be very limited.

Who Determines the Outcome?

The outcome of a trial is decided by the **fact finder**, either a jury or judge. However, if a party appeals the decision, an appellate court will review the trial proceedings and either uphold or reverse the trial court's decision, send the case back for reconsideration, or order a new trial. As you will discover in the chapters on arbitration, under the Federal Arbitration Act and the Revised Uniform Arbitration Act, appeals are allowed only in limited circumstances. In mediation, the parties, with the help of the neutral, determine the resolution.

What Types of Outcomes Are Possible?

In civil litigation, there are two types of **remedies**: money damages and equitable relief. Monetary damages are the most common and include compensatory and punitive or exemplary damages. **Compensatory damages** are intended to compensate the plaintiff for the loss suffered by the wrongdoing of the defendant. **Punitive damages** are awarded to punish the defendant for conduct considered malicious, grossly reckless, or fraudulent.

Equitable relief is awarded in situations where a plaintiff wants the defendant to do, or to refrain from doing, a specified act. For example, in a divorce action where one party intends to move out of state and take certain antique furniture, the other party may request the court to issue an injunction prohibiting the removal of the antique furniture until there is a final divorce judgment. **Specific performance** is when a court orders a person to do a specified act. An example would be when a seller of property enters into a legally binding contract to sell a certain parcel of land to buyer but has a change of heart and refuses to complete the transaction. The buyer can request the court to order the seller to turn over the property to her. Other forms of dispute resolution may resolve the dispute, but either party may decide to renege. When this happens, the parties will have to seek redress in a court because only a court has enforcement powers.

Now let's look at the advantages and disadvantages of litigation over other forms of dispute resolution.

ADVANTAGES

Ensures a Resolution

A distinctive advantage of litigation is the ability to force others to respond to a disagreement. Unlike other forms of dispute resolution such as mediation and arbitration, litigation moves ahead even if the other party fails to participate.

Defendants who refuse to respond will be defaulted, and the court will enter a default judgment that grants the relief sought by plaintiff. Of course, the dispute has to be one recognized in the law.

Predictable Process

When compared to other dispute resolution methods, litigation is an extraordinarily structured and formalized process. There are rules and procedures that direct a lawsuit from its beginning to final appeal and enforcement of the judgment. The parties know or should know each step and associated deadlines.

Enforcement

Once a court has made its decision and any opportunity for appeal has ended, the parties are bound by the judgment and cannot relitigate the case. If the defendant refuses to comply with the decision, the prevailing party can seek help from courts and law enforcement agencies to enforce the judgment. For example, a court can order that defendant's property be seized and sold with the proceeds used to satisfy the judgment or order that the defendant's wages be garnished.[5]

Precedent

Litigation is desirable and necessary for some disputes. In situations where the law is unsettled or the issue is novel, a court resolution provides guidance about the probable result of similar disagreements in the future. This is what we refer to as **precedent**, which is central to the American legal system. Precedent requires judges to follow past decisions in similar cases. This practice provides certainty and predictability to our society. In *Aquila v. LaMalfa*, the court cited binding precedent as the reason for reversing the trial court's granting of summary judgment in favor of the defendant.

Aquila v. LaMalfa, **2007 WL 1125724 (Ohio Ct. App. Feb. 20, 2007):** Aquila and LaMalfa, adult male cousins, were roughhousing during a "sack race," a game in which players put their feet in a burlap or potato sack and race to the finish line by hopping. During this contest, LaMalfa collided with Aquila, causing Aquila to fall and break his hip. Aquila filed suit against LaMalfa alleging that LaMalfa's contact with him was negligent, reckless, or intentional. LaMalfa filed a motion for summary judgment arguing that there was no evidence that his action was reckless or intentional and that as a matter of law there is no negligence for injuries occurring during a recreational or sporting event. The trial court granted summary judgment on the negligence and intentional tort claims. The claim that LaMalfa acted recklessly was tried before a jury that rendered a verdict in favor of LaMalfa. Aquila appealed the court's grant of summary judgment on his negligence claim because it "refused to consider the application of binding precedent to underlying facts which would have supported such a negligence claim."

The appellate court agreed and reversed the trial court's decision granting summary judgment in favor of LaMalfa. The appellate court found that the "actual part of the activity" test in *Coblentz v. Peters*, No. 2004-T-0017, 2005-Ohio-1102 (Ct. App. 2005), is binding precedent that it must follow. In *Coblentz*, the plaintiff was struck and injured by a golf cart. The court found that because "a golf cart is not an actual part of the sport of golf and [that Coblentz] had no reason to assume that he would be struck and injured by a golf cart since it is not an ordinary risk of the game" the negligence standard is appropriate. The appellate court applied the "actual part of the activity" test and ruled that "sack racing does not include being intentionally tackled by an errant, although well-meaning, participant, and is not foreseeable conduct. Sack racing is not a contact sport or activity. In *Coblentz,* we held that a negligence standard should have been applied. We would find that to be the case in the instant matter as well." *Aquila* is an example of a court applying a ruling in a prior similar case as precedent in the present case.

Questions:
1. What "binding precedent" did the appellate court rule that the trial court had to follow?
2. What were the facts in *Coblentz*, and how did the court rule?
3. What were the facts in *Acquila*, and how did the appellate court apply the *Coblentz* test to the facts in *Acquila*?

Discovery

Discovery, used before trial, provides the parties with facts and information known only to their opponent. It helps both parties to better prepare and try their cases. "Discovery is used to disclose the real points of dispute between the parties and to afford an adequate factual basis in preparation for trial, discovery makes the trial 'less a game of blindman's buff and more a fair contest,' discovery is of great assistance in ascertaining the truth, and discovery makes evidence available at trial which might not otherwise be available or affordable."[6]

Discovery is not only useful in preparation for a hearing or trial, but it allows the parties to learn their opponent's strengths and their own case's weaknesses. Very often, this contributes to settlement of the dispute.

Due Process

When we think of **due process**, we usually think of the Fifth and Fourteenth Amendments to the U.S. Constitution, which prohibit the United States and state governments from depriving a person of "life, liberty or property without due process of law."[7] The minimum elements of due process include "notice of the charges or issue, the opportunity for a meaningful hearing, and an impartial decision maker."[8]

Various procedural safeguards in public litigation provide due process guarantees. Some of these include the notice to the defendant that he is being sued, the right to cross-examine witnesses, limitations on the admissibility of hearsay, and other rules of evidence.

Openness of Process

Unlike some forms of dispute resolution such as arbitration and mediation that can be conducted in secrecy, litigation is an open process from which the public benefits. It allows for oversight of the process and provides access to information about harmful or dangerous products in the marketplace[9] that could affect the public health, welfare, and safety.

The Firestone/Ford tire failures linked to numerous deaths and injuries[10] illustrate how the openness of litigation can warn the public about the dangerousness of a product, and deter or prevent companies from obscuring or hiding information. The recall of 6.5 million tires by Firestone in August 2000, and a congressional investigation this same year, "came eight years after the first of numerous product liability lawsuits concerning a tire that has now been linked to approximately 271 deaths (and many more injuries) in the United States alone. Many of those Firestone cases were confidentially settled, with discovery and court files concealed by agreed protective and sealing orders."[11] "It was the civil justice system that first prevented further tragedies. Initially, no one outside Firestone and Ford had publicly tracked incidents of tire tread separation, and those companies chose not to share that information with the public or the federal government. Without the lawsuits filed by victims, a pattern of crashes might never have emerged, the press might never have reported on the danger to consumers, and drivers might never have been alerted to these lethal hazards on the road."[12] The open process of litigation is another advantage of this dispute resolution method.

Appeals

Judges sometimes have difficulty deciding a case especially where the law is unclear or the facts are in dispute. However, in cases where the law is clear and the facts are not in dispute, judges can still make errors. For example, a judge may consider inadmissible evidence or may be predisposed to rule a certain way. Geoffrey P. Miller attributes bad judging to

(1) corrupt influence on judicial action; (2) questionable fiduciary appointments; (3) abuse of office for personal gain; (4) incompetence and neglect of duties;

(5) overstepping of authority; (6) interpersonal abuse; (7) bias, prejudice, and insensitivity; (8) personal misconduct reflecting adversely on fitness for office; (9) conflict of interest; (10) inappropriate behavior in a judicial capacity; (11) lack of candor; and (12) electioneering and purchase of office.[13]

Litigation provides an opportunity to correct judicial errors and for a party to appeal an adverse judgment. A losing party can ask a higher court to correct errors of law, bias, prejudice, or other perceived wrongs. This procedure is not available in other forms of dispute resolution.

Interim Relief

Interim relief is when a court makes a ruling on a temporary basis until a decision on the case is made. This is done when irreparable harm may befall one of the parties while waiting for trial.

The following are examples of situations in which interim relief might be granted:

- Jennifer files for divorce and seeks full custody of the children. She moves out of state with the children. Kevin, her husband, requests interim relief seeking to have the children returned to their home with him until the court decides the custody issue.
- A developer is planning to build condominiums on land that a conservation group wants to protect. The group seeks interim relief to prohibit the developer from beginning construction until after the court hears the case and issues a decision.
- A former employee plans to publish a "tell all" book about his former employer, who is a well-known celebrity. The famous person asks the court to issue interim relief to prohibit the writer from publishing the book until the court hears the case and determines whether he can legally reveal such material.

Interim relief is another advantage of litigation that is not available in other forms of dispute resolution.

Parties Do Not Have to Deal with Each Other

Litigation is an impersonal process for the parties. It is structured in a way that the litigants have no direct communication with each other. In the pretrial phases, they communicate through documents delivered to their attorneys and filed in the court. At trial, the parties speak to the jury or judge. In situations where the disputants are intensely alienated from one another or have no probability of future interaction, they may welcome the fact that litigation allows them to avoid direct communication.

Provides Justice

Adjudication is "a central part of our political life because adjudication is how we articulate public values"[14] and provide justice. It explains and "give[s] force to values in authoritative texts such as the Constitution and statutes: to interpret those values and to bring reality into accord with them."[15]

The value of litigation in providing justice can be illustrated with the landmark case *Brown v. Board of Education*.[16] In the 1950s, many states had laws that established separate schools for white and black students. This was permitted under the "separate but equal" doctrine handed down by the U.S. Supreme Court in 1896.[17] In the fall of 1951, a group of parents filed suit when the Topeka Board of Education denied an attempt to enroll their children in a school closest to their homes because the school was for white students only. The case eventually made it to the Supreme Court, which held that "in the field of public education, the doctrine of separate but equal has no place. Separate educational facilities are inherently unequal. Therefore, we hold that the plaintiffs and others similarly situated for whom the actions have been brought are, by reason of the segregation complained of, deprived of the equal protection of the laws guaranteed by the Fourteenth Amendment."[18] Had this case been settled by another form of dispute resolution, peace might have been obtained but not justice, meaning racial equality.

Just as there are advantages to litigating a dispute, there are also drawbacks. We now turn our discussion to the disadvantages of filing a lawsuit.

DISADVANTAGES

Expensive and Costly

Litigation is expensive. Remember the story in the Introduction about the governing board of a co-op housing unit in New York, which in 1988 sued a tenant for $909, the cost of installing window bars. When the case finally settled in 1993, the combined legal fees reached $100,000. Litigation is not only financially costly, but it can be time-consuming, emotionally draining, and damaging to the reputation of a person or business. Think about the effect a negligence lawsuit might have on the standing of a small-town business owner. Anyone who has been involved in a lawsuit can tell you about the emotional tolls associated with a lawsuit. "[L]itigation is not only stressful and frustrating but expensive and frequently unrewarding for litigants. A personal injury case, for example, diverts the claimant and entire families from their normal pursuits. Physicians increasingly take note of litigation neuroses in otherwise normal, well-adjusted people. This negative impact is not confined to litigants and lawyers. Lay and professional witnesses, chiefly the doctors who testify, are adversely affected."[19]

"You have a pretty good case, Mr. Pitkin. How much justice can you afford?"

Source: J.B. Handelsman/The New Yorker Collection/The Cartoon Bank

Cost of Litigation

According to a survey of Fortune 200 companies presented at the 2010 Conference on Civil Litigation at Duke Law School, litigation costs keep on rising.[20]

- The average outside litigation cost per respondent was nearly $115 million in 2008, up 73 percent from $66 million in 2000. This represents an average increase of 9 percent each year.
- For the 20 companies providing data on this issue for the full survey period, average outside litigation costs were $140 million in 2008, an increase of 112 percent from $66 million in 2000.
- Between 2000 and 2008, average annual litigation costs as a percent of revenues increased 78 percent for the 14 companies providing data on average litigation costs as a percent of revenues for the full survey period.
- Increases in hourly rates do not appear to be driving the increase in litigation costs, as the available data show relatively little change in outside legal fees over time.

(The amounts of judgments and settlements are not included in these figures.)

Slow

Litigation is often quite slow, in large part because of its complex and cumbersome procedures, strict adherence to formal rules of procedure, and availability of appeal. This prolonged time has a number of unintended consequences, including "an increase in litigation cost, . . . [the threat] to evidentiary quality as memories fade, evidence spoils, and witnesses and litigants die. Delays in the resolution of civil disputes erode public confidence in the civil justice system, disappoint and frustrate those seeking compensation through the legal system, and generate benefits for those with the financial ability to withstand delays or otherwise benefit from them. Such factors, individually and collectively, undermine public faith and confidence in the ability of our civil justice system to operate efficiently and, more importantly, equitably."[21]

No Privacy

Litigation is an open process, and cases filed in court are subject to public scrutiny. As a result, disclosure of wrongdoing could lead to additional lawsuits being filed. Adverse publicity could damage a company's reputation.[22] Proprietary information, business records, and other documents can be viewed by anyone, including competitors. Furthermore, because of the public nature of litigation, disclosure of certain facts could cause some embarrassment to the parties.

Not Flexible

Litigation is a formal, highly structured process. Numerous rules and procedures address almost every aspect of the process from the initiation of a lawsuit to final appeal to enforcement of the result. For example, the Federal Rules of Civil Procedure (Fed. R. Civ. P.)[23] has 86 rules with multiple parts that govern every conceivable aspect of a lawsuit. "Rule 2 Summons" has 14 subparts, and each subpart has multiple subparts. "Rule 6 Computing and Extending Time; Time for Motion Papers" has 4 subparts, each of which has subparts. All parties must adhere to these rules. Failure to do so could have negative consequences, including dismissal of the lawsuit.

Does Not Preserve Relationships

Litigation has been called a "scorched-earth, take no-prisoners, blow-'em-up style"[24] of dispute resolution. It usually ends with a winner and loser, "and whatever else we might say about it, litigation is not well suited for relationship building."[25] Litigation may resolve the legal issue but not the dispute, as the parties "will continue to seek rectification (appeal) or wreak vengeance or revenge on each other and so litigation continues the fighting and battles."[26]

Need for an Attorney

Navigating through litigation requires training and experience not only in court procedures, but also in the law. "[B]ecause of the procedural technicalities present in the American adversary system and compounded by complicated substantive laws, lawyers are needed to represent most litigants in American courts."[27] Rules of civil procedure must be strictly followed, and failing to do so could have dire consequences including the most drastic: dismissal of the lawsuit. Those parties without an attorney are unlikely to succeed. And depending on the subject matter of the lawsuit, the parties may need not just any attorney but one who concentrates her practice in a specific area of the law.

Can't Choose the Decision Maker

In litigation, the decision maker or fact finder is a judge or jury with little or no knowledge about the subject matter of the dispute. Thus, lawyers have to spend trial time educating them. Choosing a fact finder with appropriate knowledge or experience can not only save time, but may also help ensure a more just resolution of the dispute. This is particularly pertinent in business disputes because "an individual familiar with the commercial context of the dispute, including industry customs and vocabulary, is better suited to dispense justice than laypersons who might be hampered by their relative lack of business experience and understanding of trade practices."[28] Erwin N. Griswold, former dean of Harvard Law School, once said:

> Even in the best of cases trial by jury is the apotheosis of amateurs. How can anyone think that 12 people selected at random in twelve different ways with the only criterion being a complete lack of general qualification, would have special ability to decide on disputes between people?[29]

Now that we have discussed the advantages and disadvantages of litigation, we will turn our attention to how a lawsuit proceeds through the court system.

Conclusion

Alternatives to dispute resolution developed as substitutes for litigation. This view discounts the value litigation offers for certain disputes and parties. As we learned in this chapter, there are many advantages (and disadvantages) to using the traditional form of dispute resolution that must be considered carefully before dismissing it as unsuitable.

> The tradeoff inherent to alternative processes of dispute resolution is that what the parties gain in efficiency may be outweighed by society's losses. The settlement of a conflict achieves peace between the parties without taxing the court system. This peace, however, is obtained at the expense of a significant

purpose of adjudication. Courts not only aim to achieve peace between warring parties, but also to explicate and give force to the community's values, as they are embodied in their laws.[30]

Litigation is the traditional method of dispute resolution in the United States. Before learning about the nontraditional methods, we need to discuss negotiation in the next chapter. Why? Because negotiation is integral to every dispute resolution process. For example, parties will sometimes negotiate which dispute resolution method to use, where it will take place, who will be involved, and other aspects of the procedure. And during the actual process, the parties will often be involved in negotiation.

Key Terms and Concepts

Answer	Interim relief
Compensatory damages	Plaintiff
Complaint	Precedence
Defendant	Punitive damages
Discovery	Remedies
Due process	Specific performance
Equitable relief	Subject matter
Fact finder	Summons
Information exchange	

Practice Test Questions

True/False

____ 1. One advantage of litigating a dispute is that the court resolution will provide guidance for similar disagreements in the future.

____ 2. Litigation is not well suited to building relationships.

____ 3. In litigation, the decision maker or fact finder is a judge or jury with little or no knowledge about the subject matter of the dispute. Thus, lawyers have to spend trial time educating them.

____ 4. Similar to other dispute resolution methods, litigation does not ensure a resolution.

____ 5. Unlike some forms of dispute resolution, litigation is an open process from which the public benefits.

Multiple Choice

____ 1. Specific performance is a form of _____

    a. compensatory damages.

    b. equitable relief.

    c. punitive damages.

    d. money damages.

___ 2. Which of the following is *not* an advantage of litigation?
   a. Provides justice
   b. Predictable process
   c. Provides procedure for enforcing a judgment
   d. Privacy
___ 3. Courts typically are limited to deciding _____
   a. disputes as pled in the plaintiff's complaint.
   b. all disputes, including those not recognized under existing law.
   c. disputes involving rights and liabilities recognized under existing law.
   d. disputes where only equitable relief is sought.
___ 4. Litigation produces _____ that provide society with a guide for future behavior and in turn contribute to social stability.
   a. rules and precedents
   b. winners and losers
   c. predictable outcomes
   d. experienced attorneys
___ 5. Which of the following is *not* a disadvantage of litigation?
   a. Not flexible
   b. Provides for interim relief
   c. No privacy
   d. Need for an attorney

Review Questions

1. List and explain the advantages of litigation over other forms of dispute resolution.
2. List and explain the disadvantages of litigation over other forms of dispute resolution.
3. Explain how litigation provides justice.
4. If the jury decides in favor of the plaintiff, explain why this is not necessarily the end of the dispute.

Application Questions

1. Many people view lawsuits as expensive, frightening, annoying, degrading, and time-consuming. Over 160 years ago Abraham Lincoln wrote: "Discourage litigation. Persuade your neighbors to compromise whenever you can. Point out to them how the nominal winner is often a real loser—in fees, expenses, and waste of time." Do you agree or disagree with Lincoln's statement? Why? Include in your answer a hypothetical dispute to illustrate your position.
2. Eric Waterman, an employee with Whole Grocer, leaves his position in the IT department to work for another grocery chain of stores located in the same two states where Whole Grocer has stores. When Waterman was hired, he signed an employment contract that included a covenant not to compete. This

agreement prohibited Waterman from working in the same type of business in states where Whole Grocer does business. The competing company, Green Grocer, knows about the noncompete agreement but does not think it is enforceable, so they hired Waterman. Whole Grocer is concerned that Waterman may share some of its proprietary information. Do you think litigation is the appropriate dispute resolution mechanism? Why or why not?

3. Four partners own a furniture store. Over the years, disputes have arisen over such things as expansion plans, selecting vendors, and the hours each partner has been working or not working. Things came to a head when two partners, Roger and Greg, accused Richard and Dan of using corporate money for personal uses such as vacations and buying cars. Lines have been drawn and communication has broken down. Roger and Greg are not sure whether the best course of action is to file a lawsuit or use some other method of dispute resolution. After talking with them, you determine that litigation is more appropriate. Explain your reasoning.

4. Michelle and Jack have been married for 12 years and have two children. Allie is 3 and Sam is 8. Michelle wants to file a complaint for divorce.

According to Jack, he is the children's caregiver. He prepares their meals, bathes and dresses them, and provides for their medical and dental care. Jack claims that Michelle has been inconsistent in her care of the children. Although she takes care of Allie while he works and Sam is in school, when he gets home she leaves to party with her friends.

Although Michelle does not work, Jack claims he is the one who cleans the house and does the laundry. Jack believes that he is the one who provides clean clothes and a clean house for the children.

Michelle claims that she is a stay-at-home mother who has always cared for the children and home. Because Jack works 60 to 75 hours a week, six days a week, it is not possible for him to provide much care for the children. He does make breakfast for the children and puts them to bed at night, but this is the only daily contact he has with them.

Michelle says that Jack drinks too much and was recently arrested for drunk driving. She also states he is very controlling and possessive, and lately he has become threatening and scary.

Although state law requires that divorcing couples must file a lawsuit in court, considering what you have learned, is litigation the best dispute resolution mechanism for this divorce? Explain your answer.

Practice Exercises

1. Find a case in your jurisdiction in which the court awarded a form of equitable relief. Brief the case and be prepared to discuss it in class.

2. Find a case in your jurisdiction in which punitive damages was awarded. Brief the case and be prepared to discuss it in class.

3. Read one of the law review articles listed below and then prepare a written paper that should include
   a. a summary of the article, including the author's premise;
   b. a detailed discussion of the article; and
   c. whether you agree with the author (be sure to explain your position).

Stephanie Brenowitz, *Deadly Secrecy: The Erosion of Public Information Under Private Justice*, 19 Ohio St. J. on Disp. Resol. 679 (2004).

Lon L. Fuller, *The Forms and Limits of Adjudication*, 92 Harv. L. Rev. 353 (1978).

William M. Landes & Richard A. Posner, *Adjudication as a Private Good*, 8 J. Legal Stud. 235 (1979).

Geoffrey P. Miller, *Bad Judges*, 83 Tex. L. Rev. 431 (2004).

Carl F. Taeusch, *Extrajudicial Settlement of Controversies: The Business Man's Opinion: Trial at Law v. Nonjudicial Settlement*, 83 U. Pa. L. Rev. 147 (1934).

Endnotes

1. *The Oxford Dictionary of American Legal Quotation* 302 (1993).
2. Jeffrey R. Seul, *Litigation as a Dispute Resolution Alternative*, in *The Handbook of Dispute Resolution* 337-344 (Michael L. Moffitt & Robert C. Bordone eds., Jossey-Bass 2005).
3. Fed. R. Civ. P. 4(a)(1)(E).
4. *Black's Law Dictionary* 507 (Bryan A. Garner ed., 10th ed. 2014).
5. This is accomplished through a garnishment proceeding "in which the property, money, or credits of a debtor that are in the possession of another . . . are applied to the payment of a debt." 6 Am. Jur. 2d *Attachment and Garnishment* § 2 (2008). If a court orders a wage garnishment, then the employer must withhold a percentage of the judgment debtor's [the nonprevailing party's] wages and turn that amount over to the judgment creditor [the prevailing party].
6. Louis H. Willenken, *The Often Overlooked Use of Discovery in Aid of Arbitration and the Spread of the New York Rule to Federal Common Law*, 35 Bus. Law. 173, 181 (Nov. 1979).
7. U.S. Const. amends. V and XIV, § 1.
8. Erwin Chemerinsky, *Constitutional Law: Principles and Policies* 557 (2d ed., Aspen Law & Business 2002).
9. See Ralph Nader & Wesley J. Smith, *No Contest: Corporate Lawyers and the Perversion of Justice in America* 315-317 (Random House 1996), discussing cases in which litigation led to important safety improvements, including inflammable pajamas and football helmets.
10. Nat'l Hwy. Traffic Safety Admin., Press release (Oct. 4, 2001), http://www.nhtsa.gov/nhtsa/announce/press/Firestone/Update.html.
11. Laurie Kratky Dore, *Public Courts Versus Private Justice: It's Time to Let Some Sun Shine in on Alternative Dispute Resolution*, 81 Chi.-Kent L. Rev. 463, 465 n.5 (2006). "Similarly, in the beginning of 2002, the *Boston Globe* stunned the nation when it revealed that in the previous decade, the Archdiocese of Boston had quietly settled child molestation claims against at least seventy priests. *See* Stephanie S. Abrutyn, Commentary, *Courts Just as Guilty in Church Coverup*, Hartford Courant, May 26, 2002, at C1. Prior to these more recent scandals, similar lawsuits involving products like GM's side-mounted gas tanks, the Dalkon shield, the Shiley heart valve, BIC lighters . . . and prescription drugs like Zomax, Halcion, and the DTP vaccine, flew below public radar cloaked by confidentiality orders and agreements."
12. Roselyn Bonanti et al., *The Message of the Firestone/FordTragedy*, Trial, Apr. 2001, at 52.
13. Geoffrey P. Miller, *Bad Judges*, 83 Tex. L. Rev. 431, 432-433 (2004).
14. David Luban, *Settlements and the Erosion of the Public Realm*, 83 Geo. L. Rev. 2619, 2620 (1995).
15. Owen M. Fiss, *Against Settlement*, 93 Yale L. J. 1073, 1085 (1984).
16. 347 U.S. 483 (1954).
17. Plessy v. Ferguson, 163 U.S. 537 (1896).

18. 347 U.S. 483, 495 (1954).

19. Warren Burger, *Isn't There a Better Way*, 68 A.B.A. J. 274, 275 (1982).

20. *Litigation Cost Survey of Major Companies*, presented at the Committee on Rules of Practice and Procedure Judicial Conference of the United States at Duke Law School, May 10-11, 2010, http://www.uscourts.gov/file/document/litigation-cost-survey-major-companies.

21. Michael Heise, *Justice Delayed? An Empirical Analysis of Civil Case Disposition Time*, 50 Case W. Res. L. Rev. 813, 814-815 (2000).

22. Philip Rothman, *Pssst, Please Keep It Confidential: Arbitration Makes It Possible*, 49 J. Disp. Resol. J. 69, 69 (1994).

23. These can be found in title 28 of the United States Code (28 U.S.C.). There are similar rules of procedure for each state court.

24. Robert Gordon, *The Electronic Personality and Digital Self*, 56 APR Disp. Resol. J. 8, 9 (2001).

25. Michael Moffitt, *Three Things to be Against Settlement (Settlement Not Included)*, 78 Fordham L. Rev. 1203, 1214 (2009).

26. Carrie Menkel-Meadow, *And Now a Word About Secular Humanism, Spirituality, and the Practice of Justice and Conflict Resolution*, 28 Fordham Urb. L.J. 1073, 1084 (2001).

27. Stephen N. Subrin & Margaret Y.K. Woo, *Litigating in America: Civil Procedure in Context* 25 (Aspen 2006).

28. Thomas J. Stipanowich, *Rethinking American Arbitration*, 63 Ind. L.J. 425, 436 (1988).

29. Erwin N. Griswold, Harvard Law School, Dean's Report 5-6 (1962-1963), *reprinted in* Subrin & Woo, *supra* note 27, at 239.

30. Benjamin J.C. Wolf, *On-Line but Out of Touch*, 14 Cardozo J. Int'l & Comp. L. 281, 308-309 (2006).

Negotiation

Chapter Outline

Introduction

Negotiation Defined

Types of Legal Negotiations

    Transactions

    Civil Disputes

    Labor-Management Negotiations

    Criminal Cases

    Domestic Relations (Including Divorce and Child Custody)

    International Negotiations

The Lawyer and Client Relationship

Two Methods of Negotiation

    Distributive Negotiation

    Problem Solving

Negotiator Styles

    Competitive Negotiators

    Cooperative Negotiators

The Negotiation Process

    Preparation Stage: Setting Objectives and Limits

    Preliminary Stage

    Information/Positioning Stage

    Distributive/Competitive or Integrative/Collaborative Stage

    Reaching Agreement or Collapse Stage

Laws Affecting Negotiation and Settlement

    Promotion of Settlement

    Constraints Imposed by Contract and Tort Law

    Regulations for Specific Types of Negotiations

Ethical Constraints Affecting Negotiations

Conclusion

Key Terms and Concepts

Practice Test Questions

Review Questions

Application Questions

Practice Exercises

"Okay, so what number can we both be happy with?"

FAMILY CIRCUS ©2004 Bil Keane, Inc. Distributed by King Features Syndicate.

INTRODUCTION

Negotiation is something we learned to do as small children and continue to do every day. Much of our negotiating involves ordinary things like who will do the cooking and cleaning, where to vacation, which movie to see. Some negotiations will affect our lives in more serious ways like reaching an agreement about salary and benefits. Other negotiations involve long-term commitments such as purchasing a car or house.

Understanding what negotiation is and how it works is important for anyone involved in negotiations, especially lawyers. Whether practicing family, criminal, corporate, or real estate law, lawyers spend much of their time negotiating: resolving legal disputes, creating a legal relationship between their client and others, or assisting in transactions such as buying or selling real estate. A paralegal plays an integral part in this process too, as you will soon learn.

Legal negotiation, when successful, benefits clients in a number of ways. It avoids:

- the unknown outcome of trial;
- the stress and apprehension of trial;
- the costs and delays of a trial and possible appeal;
- any further damage to the relationship between the parties;
- ending the dispute with a "winner" and "loser";
- the limited range of court remedies in favor of a negotiated solution between the parties; and
- negative publicity.

Negotiation is an integral part of the various forms of alternative dispute resolution. Parties use negotiation to choose the ADR method and then use negotiation during the dispute resolution process. For example, the parties negotiate and decide to mediate their dispute. During the mediation, the parties use negotiation with the help of a third party, to reach a settlement. If the parties select either nonbinding arbitration, summary jury trial, or mini-trial they frequently discover the strengths and weaknesses of their case and then use this information to negotiate a resolution.

NEGOTIATION DEFINED

One definition of **negotiation** is "a process of potentially opportunistic interaction by which two or more parties, with some apparent conflict, seek to do better through jointly decided action than they could do otherwise.[1] Leonard Riskin defines negotiation as "an interpersonal process through which we make arrangements with others to resolve disputes or plan transactions, often by reconciling conflicting – or apparently conflicting – interests."[2] A federal court has defined negotiation as "a process of submission and consideration of offers until an acceptable offer is made, and accepted."[3]

No matter which definition you prefer, they all state that negotiation is a process in which two or more parties seek to move forward in their relationship. Therefore, the purpose of negotiation is to complete a transaction, resolve a controversy, or reach an agreement. Negotiation usually begins when the parties think that they have more to gain from the process or recognize the a risk for failing to negotiate.

American society and our system of jurisprudence encourage settlement negotiations. An intrinsic value in our democracy is the belief that people can determine what is in their best interests. Our courts encourage parties to settle disagreements, as reflected in the Federal Rules of Civil Procedure (FRCP) and similar rules in other U.S. jurisdictions. Rule 16(a)(5) allows the court to "order the attorneys and any unrepresented parties to appear for one or more pretrial conferences for facilitating settlement." The Advisory Committee Notes to Rule 16 also recommend that a request for a conference from a party willing to discuss settlement "should be honored, unless thought to be frivolous or dilatory."

Rule 16(c)(2)(I) permits the court to consider and take action on "settling the case and using special procedures to assist in resolving the dispute when authorized by statute or local rule." The Advisory Committee Notes to Rule 16 point out that parties should not be forced to participate in settlement negotiations, but "providing a neutral forum for discussing the subject might foster it."

Another way in which the FRCP encourage parties to settle is by imposing a monetary penalty if a party rejects a reasonable offer of settlement and, after trial, receives a lesser amount than the rejected offer. If this occurs, the plaintiff must pay "the costs incurred after the offer was made."

The Federal Rules of Evidence also promote the policy of reaching an agreement. Rule 408 bars the introduction of any settlement offers at trial, including any evidence that an offer was made, the amount of the offer, who made it, and any conduct or statements made about the claim in settlement negotiations. Without this prohibition, parties would be unlikely to offer to compromise for fear that this was tantamount to admitting liability.

Finally, because some state and federal statutes permit judges and juries to award prejudgment interest for certain damages, defendants have incentive to settle before a trial. Awarding prejudgment interest compensates an injured party for the loss of the use of money belonging to that party during the lawsuit. The danger of an award of substantial prejudgment interest can encourage the defendant to settle.

TYPES OF LEGAL NEGOTIATIONS

Before we discuss the types of negotiations, you need to be aware of three principles that apply to nearly all negotiations. First, each side has a point at which they will settle, and the negotiator's goal is to find it. For example, in a personal injury case, this could be the dollar amount the lawyer will accept for his client in order to avoid a trial. For a party purchasing real property, it is the maximum amount he will pay for the property. The second principle is that the negotiator should never reveal his settling point. And third, once the negotiator determines the opponent's settling point, he needs to persuade her that her case is worth less than that amount. Now let's look at the various approaches to negotiations.

Generally, there are six **types of negotiations**: transactions between parties, civil disputes, labor-management disputes, criminal cases, domestic relations (including divorce and child custody), and international transactions. To be effective, a negotiator must not only be proficient in negotiation skills, but she must have knowledge of the applicable law associated with the subject matter of the dispute.

Transactions

Transactions are voluntary agreements between parties that are mutually beneficial. Examples of transactions are sales of goods or services and real property purchases. Frequently, these exchanges are reduced to a writing called a contract. Negotiators in these situations must have a comprehensive understanding of the business facts associated with each category of transaction. Additionally, the negotiator must educate himself about the nature of the business, including the conventional industry standards, customs, and practices. Finally, transactions may be short or long term. Long-term agreements require continuing relations. Therefore, the parties will be concerned about avoiding discord and preserving harmony. This means the negotiators should avoid the adversarial approach, which could generate mistrust and antagonism, thus jeopardizing the cooperation between the parties.

Civil Disputes

In civil disputes, one or both parties claim that they have legal rights against the other and seek to enforce these rights in court. These disputes usually focus on some substantive law and an applicable remedy. The parties should consider the likelihood of prevailing, the cost, and the potential amount of recovery. Because the parties disagree on how the rules/law should be applied to the given facts, these types of negotiations have higher levels of aggressiveness and unreasonableness than would normally be accepted in the negotiation of consensual transactions.

In civil disputes, the parties must recognize that if they fail to negotiate an agreement, a court or other authorized person, such as an arbitrator, will decide the outcome, and the losing party will be compelled to comply with the decision.

Labor-Management Negotiations

Labor-management disputes have been ongoing for centuries. Until the twentieth century, workers were on their own to bargain for increased wages and benefits.

With the industrialization of our nation came the formation of unions whose primary function is to protect its members. The goals of unions are to acquire fair wages and good working conditions for their members. In the United States, labor-management relations are highly regulated. Federal law requires labor and management to bargain collectively:

> Obligation to bargain collectively. To bargain collectively is the performance of the mutual obligation of the employer and the representative of the employees to meet at reasonable times and confer in good faith with respect to wages, hours, and other terms and conditions of employment or the negotiation of an agreement, or any question arising there under, and the execution of a written contract incorporating any agreement reached if requested by either party, but such obligation does not compel either party to agree to a proposal or require the making of a concession.[4]

Although the parties are not required to reach an agreement, failure to do so could result in the assertion of laborer's power to strike and/or management imposing its power to close, relocate, or lock out workers. With these possibilities looming, there is increased pressure to reach a settlement.

Negotiations between labor and management have attributes of both transactions and civil disputes. They resemble transactions because the parties are seeking an agreeable contract, and they are involved in a continuing relationship. Because the parties have a legal duty to bargain, labor-management negotiations look like civil disputes. Just as in civil disputes, these negotiations can be highly adversarial.

Criminal Cases

Criminal law tells us what conduct is illegal and the prescribed punishment for the violation. Criminal law protects society from criminal acts and also protects defendants from overzealous or unlawful prosecution and punishment. The Sixth Amendment to the U.S. Constitution guarantees persons accused of committing crimes the right to the assistance of counsel. If they cannot afford one, one will be appointed by the court. Thus, in criminal cases, one party is the defendant and the other party the government or society.

Like civil cases, most criminal cases are settled before trial. The reasons are twofold. First, the government is frequently in the stronger position and, therefore, defendants are at a disadvantage by going to trial. Second, because of the volume of cases, if they all went to trial, the court would probably not be able to function. So lawyers for both sides try to settle. This is done in several different ways. One approach is the defense attorney may try to convince the prosecution not to bring charges against his client or the defense attorney may suggest that the case be deferred or adjourned for a predetermined period of time, sometimes with certain conditions imposed on the defendant during this period. Then, if the defendant complies with the condition and does not commit any new crime, the charge is dismissed. Another option might be the defendant agreeing to testify for the government in other criminal cases in return for immunity from prosecution. Finally, the parties could engage in plea negotiations. This may result in the defendant pleading guilty to some of the charges, with a dismissal of others, or to plead to lesser charges for a dismissal of the more serious charges. The negotiations could also involve how much time the defendant will spend in jail and/or on probation or parole.

The rules governing plea negotiations in federal courts are found in Rule 11(c) of the Federal Rules of Criminal Procedure. This rule provides that "an attorney for the government and the defendant's attorney, or the defendant when proceeding pro se, may discuss and reach a plea agreement." The rule includes the procedure for plea bargaining, disclosure of the agreement, judicial consideration and acceptance or rejection of the plea, the admissibility or inadmissibility of the discussions, and the recording of the proceedings.

Domestic Relations (Including Divorce and Child Custody)

This type of negotiation is intended to determine the rights and obligations of the parties in the future. Domestic relations disputes, which can involve children, are loaded with emotions and psychological impact that may interfere with agreeing to rational solutions.

International Negotiations

International negotiations involve transactions and disputes with unique characteristics not associated with the previous types. First are cultural barriers that could affect reaching an agreement. Second, there can be language differences, which could contribute to misunderstandings. Third, global politics must be considered.

THE LAWYER AND CLIENT RELATIONSHIP

A negotiator who is not acting on her own behalf acts for the benefit of another person. In essence, she represents her principal and is bound to act in accordance with the directives of the principal. She can, of course, and frequently does, counsel, advise, and make recommendations to the principal on what she thinks is a fair resolution of the dispute, but it is the client who has the ultimate say over whether to settle.

The legal relationship between a lawyer and client brings with it ethical and legal considerations. First, lawyers must provide competent representation. This means a lawyer must know the law, be prepared, perform services promptly, and keep her client informed.[5] Failure to exercise these obligations could result in legal malpractice and subject the attorney to a negligence lawsuit.[6]

Fundamental to settlement is the acquiescence of the client to the agreement. Because the case is the client's, the lawyer shall follow the client's decision on accepting a settlement offer.[7] An informed decision by the client requires the attorney to discuss all options. For example, the lawyer may tell the client about the feasibility of making a counteroffer or accepting a part of the offer and continuing to negotiate other areas of the dispute.

In the end, fully informed clients are more likely to be pleased with their decisions than clients who have not been updated during the negotiation process. Clients know how much risk they will accept, the stress they are under, the importance of preserving the relationship with the opposing party, and whether they just want their day in court.

TWO METHODS OF NEGOTIATION

Distributive Negotiation

Distributive negotiation is concerned with dividing limited resources. For example, many lawsuits involve the distribution of money. Sometimes the amount available is fixed, as in the maximum amount of insurance coverage. Other times the amount depends on the other party's resources. In either case, each side predetermines how much they pay or accept. The objective is to get the most possible from the other side.

Problem Solving

The other form of negotiation is commonly called interest-based or **problem solving**. Some negotiators refer to it as integrative, collaborative, or principled negotiation. Whichever name is used, the goal is the same: to reach a mutually satisfactory agreement. The negotiators work together to identify the interests and needs of each side in an effort to reach a fair settlement.

Choosing the method of negotiation, distributive or problem solving, frequently depends on the dispute. In money (or other fixed-resource) disputes, the parties are not concerned about an ongoing relationship. Each side only wants to get or keep as much of the resource as possible. When the parties have a common interest or desire to continue the relationship, the problem-solving or interest-based approach is appropriate.

NEGOTIATOR STYLES

Negotiator styles affect the bargaining environment (see Exhibit 3-1). Competitive negotiators typically raise the level of tension by using intimidation, manipulation, and threats. The goal is to achieve maximum tangible gains at the expense of the

Exhibit 3-1. IMPACT OF NEGOTIATOR STYLES

Cooperative Problem-Solving	Competitive Adversarial
Move Psychologically Toward Opponent	Move Psychologically Against Opponent
Try to Maximize Joint Returns	Try to Maximize Own Returns
Strive for Reasonable Results	Strive for Extreme Results
Courteous and Sincere	Adversarial and Disingenuous
Begin with Realistic Opening Positions	Begin with Unrealistic Opening Positions
Rely on Objective Standards	Focus on Positions Rather than Neutral
Rarely Resort to Threats	Standards
Maximize Information Disclosure	Frequently Resort to Threats
Open and Trusting	Minimize Information Disclosure
Work to Satisfy Underlying Opponent	Closed and Untrusting
Interests	Work to Satisfy Underlying Interests of
Willing to Make Unilateral Concessions	Own Side
Try to Reason with Opponents	Work to Induce Opponent to Make
	Unilateral Concessions
	Try to Manipulate Opponents

Source: Charles B. Carver, *The Impact of Negotiator Styles on Bargaining Interactions,* 35 Am. J. Trial Advoc. 1, 2 (2011).

other party. Cooperative negotiators are the exact opposite. They try to maximize both tangible and intangible gains for each side in a nonconfrontational manner. The goal is to reach a mutually agreeable resolution that is fair to both sides.

Competitive Negotiators

Competitive negotiators employ various tactics and ploys to pressure or mislead the other party into accepting their demands. The aim is to affect opposing counsel's confidence in himself and his case, lower expectations of what the opposing party had expected to gain, and cause him to settle for less than what had been demanded. Harry T. Edwards and James J. White list several tactics frequently linked with competitive negotiators.[8] Some of them are as follows:

1. **Anger, Feigned or Real**

    Negotiators use this technique for different reasons. The negotiator may be demonstrating his commitment or seek to convince the opposing party that he is committed.

    Sometimes the display of anger is used to show the client the negotiator's fervor for the case. Demonstrating anger may also force the opposing party to question his position or frighten and cower him. Of course the use of anger could have the opposite effect, causing the other side to become riled and oppose any attempt at settlement.

2. Aggressiveness

This tactic is sometimes used to force the other side to acknowledge a mistake or a defect in her position and make concessions. The aggressive negotiator must also recognize that this tactic could cause embarrassment and result in a strengthening of an opponent's determination to resist.

3. Inscrutability

Negotiators who exhibit this characteristic control how much talking they do and disguise their reactions. Too much talking could disclose too much information. Additionally, when talking, the negotiator is not listening and may miss information about the opponent's position. Sometimes a negotiator uses silence to create anxiety, hoping the opponent will answer the question instead.

4. First Offer, Large Demand

An almost universal truth in negotiations is to let the other side make the first offer. This approach helps avoid the mistake of under- or overvaluing your position. Consider the person buying an automobile. The dealer may ask the consumer how much she would be willing to pay for the car. If the buyer states her price, she risks paying more than what the dealer would have offered.

If custom in a particular negotiation calls for one party to make the first offer, he can offer an extreme number with the aim of just getting the negotiations started. This approach is regularly used in personal injury lawsuits where the lawyer makes an unreasonable demand knowing it will be rejected. In reality, the demand is made simply to start the negotiations.

5. Expose the Jugular

In the animal kingdom, when two males are fighting for control of the group and one is ready to end it, that animal will sometimes lie on his side or back, exposing his vulnerable underside and neck, signaling surrender. He is hoping this will cause his opponent to stop fighting. Negotiators who use this technique recognize the power of their opponent and seek sympathy by appealing to their morals or ethics and, in turn, hoping for a fair settlement.

6. Boulwareism or "Take-It-or-Leave-It"

This approach was named after Lemuel R. Boulware, who was a vice president and labor negotiator at General Electric from the late 1940s through the late 1960s. Before labor negotiations, GE would conduct its own research, then evaluate the union demands and make an offer it thought was right for the employees. The uniqueness of this approach was that the negotiations would begin with the final offer. This approach caused severe labor conflict because the labor unions saw it as demeaning and unfair.

This technique might be effective if the cost of negotiations would be greater than the cost of litigation or some other alternative. Negotiators who effectively make "take-it-or-leave-it" offers have gained reputations of making only one offer, but an offer that is fair and reasonable.

7. **Negotiator Without Authority**

   Negotiators using this ploy try to bind their opponents without actually obligating themselves. Once the other side commits to an agreement, they are more vulnerable to accepting counteroffers or concessions to preserve the agreement they think has been reached.

8. **Splitting the Difference**

   When the parties are close to an agreement, a frequent technique used is to split-the-difference. In negotiations where there have been numerous offers and counteroffers, the parties should be clear about which proposal is the subject of the split-the-difference suggestion.

9. **Draftsman**

   Drafting the agreement can be viewed as a continuation of the negotiations, and therefore the party who agrees to do this has a distinct advantage. She can shape the text of the agreement in a way most favorable to her client's interests. Ambiguous terms can be slanted in a way that favors her side. An array of boilerplate language can be inserted that addresses issues important to her client and for which she did not have to negotiate.

The competitive approach carries distinct disadvantages. Negotiators who use this style create stress and generate an atmosphere of mistrust. This could negatively affect the parties' relationship, making it difficult to continue. The competitive negotiator might be so focused on "winning" that she misses an opportunity to share information that may help her client. She also risks not recognizing solutions that could work to benefit both sides. There is a high possibility that the disputants will reach an impasse when competitive tactics are employed as compared to other approaches, resulting in the case going to trial.

Cooperative Negotiators

Cooperative negotiators approach the dispute as an opportunity to solve a problem or problems. They recognize that the parties have shared interests and values and openly exchange information in a search for common ground. A study by Professor Gerald R. Williams[9] found that effective cooperative negotiators

- are predominantly concerned with ethical conduct;
- seek to maximize settlement for their client;
- ensure that the settlement is fair;
- strive to meet their client's needs;
- avoid litigation; and
- maintain or establish good personal relationships with opponents.

When a dispute involves several issues and an assortment of possible results, cooperative negotiators search for and seek exchanges satisfactory to both sides.

For example, an insurance company may agree to a higher settlement amount if the payout is structured over a period of years as opposed to a lump-sum payment. Divorcing parties who live a great distance from each other may agree to longer summer visitations in lieu of fewer weekend visits.

Cooperative negotiators face risks that must be noted. The main disadvantage with this style is its susceptibility to exploitation. When negotiating with an aggressive/competitive negotiator, a cooperative negotiator may fail to recognize the absence of mutual cooperation and continue to share information, which is then used by the opposition to strengthen his position at the expense of the cooperative negotiator. By the time the cooperative negotiator recognizes that the negotiation is one-sided, if in fact he is able to do this, it is too late.

Another danger for the cooperative negotiator is the appearance of vulnerability. To competitive negotiators, people in positions of strength do not make concessions. Cooperation is viewed by opponents as a weakening of the cooperative negotiator's position and results in an increase in the competitive negotiator's demands, along with a higher expectation of what they will ultimately be able to gain.

THE NEGOTIATION PROCESS

Negotiation takes place in five steps that can occur in one or, more frequently, in multiple meetings: preparation, preliminary, information/positioning, distributive/competitive or integrative/collaborative, and agreement or collapse.

Preparation Stage: Setting Objectives and Limits

> If you know the enemy and know yourself, you need not fear the result of a hundred battles. If you know yourself but not the enemy, for every victory gained you will also suffer a defeat. If you know neither the enemy nor yourself, you will succumb in every battle.[10]

Negotiators who thoroughly prepare for bargaining sessions are more likely to achieve better results than those who do not. Knowledgeable negotiators display more confidence in their positions and thus weaken the opponent's valuation of his case and expectations of the outcome. With his confidence diminishing, the underprepared party makes more concessions.

Preparing for negotiations begins when the attorney meets with her client for the first time. At this conference, the attorney must elicit all relevant factual information and collect all pertinent documents. The attorney should then use the discovery process to gather information from the opposing party, witnesses, and all other persons who may have knowledge of the subject matter of the dispute. Once this stage is complete, the lawyer needs to know the pertinent legal doctrines, develop sound legal theories for her positions, and prepare for the opposing party's possible counterarguments.

Client Preparation

This is probably one of the most crucial steps in the negotiation process because it uncovers the real interests and goals of the client and in turn establishes the settlement parameters for the attorney. A client frequently approaches a dispute seeking only one particular remedy and fails to see the availability of other options. The lawyer must ascertain what the client really seeks to attain, not necessarily what he says he wants. For example, the client in a medical malpractice case may actually be happier if the doctor acknowledges his mistake and apologizes over being awarded a sum of money. A client with a permanent disability from an automobile accident may focus on a dollar amount when a structured settlement that guarantees lifetime healthcare might be just as or even more acceptable. Learning a client's underlying needs and interests can improve the bargaining position.

When determining the client's needs and interests, the lawyer should assign a weight to each item the client wants. Negotiators sometimes divide these into three categories: (1) essential; (2) important; and (3) desirable.[11] Essential needs are "must haves," that is, without these there will be little likelihood of a successful settlement. Important objectives are things the client would like to have but is willing to sacrifice for an essential item. Desirable wants carry less value, so that the client would willingly forgo them in exchange for essential or important items. Once the items are categorized, the lawyer must ascertain the client's preferences for each so she knows the ones to obtain and the ones that may be exchanged. This can be done by assigning a numerical value to each. For example, on a scale of 1 to 10, with 10 being most desirable, Item A might be assigned a "10," Item B a "9," Item C an "8," and so on.

Attorney Preparation

Once the attorney knows the relevant facts, legal theories, and doctrines and understands the client's needs and interests, she must establish the boundaries that cannot be crossed. This involves establishing "aspiration levels," "target points" or "goals," meaning what the party would like to attain, and the "bottom line" (sometimes referred to as the "reservation points" or "resistance points"), the place below which the party will not go. Establishing these points ensures that the negotiator will not enter into an agreement that would be worse than no agreement at all. Determining the reservation points (bottom line) requires the negotiator to identify alternatives to reaching a negotiated agreement and then decide which one is most appealing. Roger Fisher and William Ury call this the "Best Alternative to a Negotiated Agreement" (BATNA).[12] Once this is done, the lawyer must attempt to determine the other party's goals (aspiration levels) and reservation points (bottom line).

To help illustrate the process of setting goals and reservation points, we will use a dispute involving money. This type of negotiation is called "zero-sum" because a gain for one side is a corresponding loss for the other. Let's say Linda was involved in a car accident when Paul broadsided her car after failing to stop at a red light. The complaint filed in court by Linda's attorney seeks $1 million. Paul's insurance company has offered to pay $100,000. The reservation points are the minimum amount Linda will accept and the maximum amount Paul will pay. If Linda agrees to accept $500,000 to dismiss her lawsuit, this is her reservation point. If the insurance company is willing to pay on Paul's behalf up to $350,000 to settle, then this becomes Paul's reservation point. As in most cases involving money disputes, the parties share the same BATNA, litigating the case in court.

When determining goals, research suggests that negotiators with elevated aspirations usually achieve better results than negotiators who set lower targets.[13] However, the target must be realistically possible; otherwise the opponent may become discouraged and conclude that he will be unable to reach an agreement. In our example above, let's say that Linda's attorney has valued her case at $600,000. A realistic goal might be $700,000 to $750,000. The insurance company has computed the value of Linda's case at $450,000, and set its target at between $350,000 to $400,000.

The last task before the attorney is ready to negotiate is the formulation of an opening offer. When preparing the initial offer, the negotiator should create principled rationales to support her positions. In our above example, if Linda's attorney makes an initial offer to settle for $750,000, she must carefully demonstrate why Paul is liable. Next, she must compute the past and future medical expenses, prior and future lost earnings, and so on, and add a proper amount for pain and suffering. The lawyer should be able to explain in detail the specific basis for these requests. How was the value of past and anticipated future medical expenses determined? How was the amount for pain and suffering calculated? These amounts cannot be arbitrary because they can be too easily disputed. For example, while determining medical expenses is easy, since all one has to do is look at the medical bills, calculating pain and suffering is more difficult. Requesting a lump sum can be easily discounted by the insurance company. Instead, the lawyer should calculate the number of days, months, or years for which compensation for pain and suffering is proper and then assign a dollar amount per day to reach the amount requested.

Preparing for the negotiation is perhaps the most important phase of the process. Here, the facts, issues, interests, needs, goals, and objectives are uncovered and formulated into a strategy for negotiating a resolution of the dispute. Thorough preparation is essential, and failure to do so can have an adverse effect on the outcome.

PARALEGAL POINTERS

The Paralegal and Negotiation

The paralegal may be responsible for assisting the attorney in preparing for the negotiation. Because the attorney is negotiating on behalf of her client, "you" and "your" below refer to the client, not the attorney.

1. What do you want (i.e., your aspiration point)?
2. What is your resistance point (i.e., the lowest offer you will accept)?
3. What is your BATNA?
4. What does the opposing party want (i.e., his or her aspiration point)?
5. What is the opposing party's resistance point (i.e., the lowest offer he or she would accept)?
6. What is the opposing party's BATNA?
7. List the strengths and weaknesses of your position.
8. List the strengths and weaknesses of the opposing party's position.
9. What are the opposing party's needs and interests?
10. List information that you should not disclose.
11. Prepare an agenda.
12. Determine the opposing party's strategies and how to counter them.

Preliminary Stage

The Preliminary Stage is when the face-to-face negotiation session begins. The participants may or may not know one another. Lawyers who have interacted before know each other's negotiating styles and can begin more quickly. They should, however, devote time getting reacquainted to help establish a friendly environment. When the negotiators are not acquainted, the first part of the interaction will be devoted to establishing their identities and setting the tone for the discussions to follow. During this stage, the discussion should reveal how much each side knows about the facts of the case and the laws underlying the dispute.

The beginning segment of the negotiations is significant because the parties' initial interactions set the atmosphere for the ensuing bargaining sessions. Research has found that positive interactions between the participants produce more cooperation and are more likely to employ problem-solving methods to achieve mutual benefits. Conversely, when the mood is negative, the negotiation is more adversarial and there are fewer agreements. Additionally, negative mood negotiators are more prone to using questionable tactics and less likely to honor any agreement. In contrast, positive mood negotiators will more likely honor the settlement.[14]

Information/Positioning Stage

The Information or Positioning Stage is where the formal process of negotiation begins. Conversation now shifts from small talk to questions about the opponent's position (i.e., her needs and goals or what is "essential, important, and desirable"). This interaction should lead to identifying the items for distribution and the value placed on each by the other side. Establishing value means learning which items the opponent must have ("essential"), which she wants to get ("important"), and which she would like to obtain ("desirable"). The following questions may help reveal this information: Is Item A more or less significant than Item B and C? How much more valuable is Item A than Item B? Is Item B preferred over Item C? During this process the questioner compares his own rankings with those of the opponent's to identify items for mutual exchange. This interaction should result in expanding the overall pie or items to be divided and produce a more efficient interaction.

Distributive/Competitive or Integrative/Collaborative Stage

Distributive/Competitive

While the Information Stage is integral to the negotiation process, it is the Distributive/Competitive or Integrative/Collaborative Stage that reveals what each party finally receives. During the Information Stage, both sides focus on the needs and goals of their opponents. They try to uncover the various options that could meet their objectives. Practiced participants are usually adept at discovering the economic and noneconomic items available for distribution. Once this is accomplished, in the Distributive/Competitive Stage, the interaction shifts from what is desired to what the negotiators want for their own clients. This change is readily noticeable because the questions change from finding out about the other's situation to voicing their client's demands. The following illustrates this shift.

Information/Positioning Stage

1. What is your client seeking?
2. Why does your client want these items?
3. Are there any other alternatives?
4. Would your client be satisfied with _____?

Distributive/Competitive Stage

1. If we are to reach a mutually satisfying settlement, my client must get _____.
2. Your client must be willing to give us at least _____ or we will not be likely to reach a settlement.
3. No settlement will be possible if your client demands _____.
4. I am only authorized to offer you _____.
5. From the information I have, your client should not receive more than _____.

Some practitioners favor calling this part of the negotiations the "Distributive" Stage because this is where the participants allocate the items available for distribution. Others choose the term "Competitive" Stage because the parties are competing for the items. Whichever term is used, the negotiators seek to obtain as much as possible for their own clients. In the end, the central question is not did the party get everything he wanted or ended up with more or less than the other side, but given all of the circumstances, whether the party is satisfied with what he obtained.

Integrative/Collaborative

Typically, when parties engage in negotiations, they have underlying needs or goals – what they want to achieve and/or be compensated for as a consequence of a dispute or transaction. Although money is commonly the relief sought, it frequently is a substitute for more fundamental needs or objectives. If the parties can identify those underlying needs, they can then generate many and hopefully better solutions. This problem-solving approach presents an opportunity to meet more and varied needs and avoid a zero-sum fight.

To illustrate the problem-solving approach, let's look at a situation where Hotel A and Guest B are having a dispute over inferior lodging and food experienced while Guest B is staying at the hotel. B claims to have suffered emotional distress and food poisoning. Instead of paying B an amount of money, A can give B a written apology and free accommodations with meals at any of its hotels. With this resolution, B's complaint is acknowledged (the written apology), and he receives the equivalent of money (free lodgings and meals). The apology did not cost A any money, and the rooms may have been unused. Additionally, this solution encourages B to continue staying at A's hotels and allows A to reestablish the trust, goodwill, and future business of B.

Toward the end of the Integrative/Collaborative Stage, the parties either recognize that a mutual agreement is probable or they have reached an impasse. The negotiation now moves into the next stage.[15]

Reaching Agreement or Collapse Stage

In this stage, the negotiation faces two different paths. If an accord has been reached, the parties work out the details and finalize the agreement. If the negotiations have irretrievably broken down, the case goes to trial or the transaction is not completed.

Agreement

If the participants have reached a settlement, they now must work out the specifics and formalize the agreement. Because a settlement agreement is a type of contract, the rules of contract law apply. Offer, acceptance, and consideration requirements, along with the defenses and remedies available, affect these agreements.

Offer and Acceptance

A valid agreement must include an offer and acceptance. "An offer is a manifestation of willingness to enter into a bargain, so made as to justify another person in understanding that his assent to the bargain is invited and will conclude it."[16] Simply put, an offer is something that generates a power of acceptance.

"Acceptance of an offer is a manifestation of assent to the terms thereof made by the offeree in a manner invited or required by the offer."[17] In other words, the party to whom the offer was made agrees to accept it. An acceptance can be communicated in different ways. It can be verbal, written or implied. For example, a party who keeps a check tendered as full settlement of an obligation implies that he is satisfied with the offer.

Consideration

Legal consideration refers to something that is a benefit to one party or a detriment to the other party. As a general rule, unless a contract is supported by consideration, it will not be enforceable. So a settlement agreement can be supported by payment of money to one side in exchange for a release of all claims the party may have against the other side; the mutual requirement of the parties to do something for the benefit or each other; or the forbearance of a legal right. Looked at another way, consideration is what distinguishes a contract from a gift.

Writings and Formalities

When the parties reach settlement, documents formalizing the agreement need to be prepared. The documents could be releases, a structured settlement, deeds, a sale agreement, or conveyance of land. While agreements generally are not required to be written, there are two circumstances when a writing is necessary. First, local court rules and court procedure may mandate that to be enforceable, the agreement must be in writing. Second, if the subject matter of the settlement falls within the statute of frauds, a writing is required.[18]

Collapse

If the parties fail to reach a settlement and the negotiations are not resumed, the case goes to trial. In transactional settings, the parties look for others with whom to interact.

LAWS AFFECTING NEGOTIATION AND SETTLEMENT

Promotion of Settlement

The civil justice system generally favors settlement agreements because they lower the cost of legal expenses, save time for the disputants and the court, and encourage amicable and ongoing relations between the parties. "Public policy dictat[es] that courts should look with favor upon the compromise or settlement of law suits in the interest of efficiency and economical administration of justice and the lessening of friction and acrimony."[19]

Because settlement of disputes is encouraged, there are several procedural and evidentiary rules in both federal and state courts to foster this goal.

- Rule 16 of the Federal Rules of Civil Procedure promotes facilitating of settlements by the court.
- Rule 68 of the Federal Rules of Civil Procedure provides an opportunity for a defendant to make a settlement offer to the plaintiff. If the offer is rejected and the award at trial is less than the defendant's offer, the plaintiff must pay the defendant's costs incurred after the offer was made.
- Rule 408 of the Federal Rules of Evidence generally prohibits settlement discussions from being introduced at trial.

Constraints Imposed by Contract and Tort Law

The negotiating behavior of lawyers and their clients is restrained by tort and contract law and by specific statutes and regulations. The following is a discussion of these legal protections.

Misrepresentation and Fraud

When parties reach a negotiated settlement that resulted from false statements made during the bargaining process, negotiators may be liable for damages or the agreement may be subject to rescission. Common law of torts and contracts requires truthfulness during negotiations. However, not all lying is prohibited. Only false statements when justifiably relied upon by the opposing party are subject to these common law prohibitions.

> One who fraudulently makes a misrepresentation of fact, opinion, intention or law for the purpose of inducing another to act or to refrain from action in reliance upon it, is subject to liability to the other in deceit for pecuniary loss caused to him by his justifiable reliance upon the misrepresentation.[20]
>
> A fact is material if it is important to a reasonable person in deciding whether or not to do something. So, false statements that are material and justifiably relied upon, could make the speaker liable. For example, a person buys a used car because the salesman said that the car has only been driven 35,000 miles. A week later the buyer learns that the car had 95,000 miles on the odometer when it was sold to the dealer by the previous owner. This is a misrepresentation.[21]

Duty to Disclose

Generally, the law requires that a party disclose a misrepresentation when he knows

(a) . . . that disclosure of the fact is necessary to prevent some previous assertion from being a misrepresentation or from being fraudulent or material.

(b) . . . that disclosure of the fact would correct a mistake of the other party as to a basic assumption on which that party is making the contract and if nondisclosure of the fact amounts to a failure to act in good faith and in accordance with reasonable standards of fair dealing.

(c) . . . that disclosure of the fact would correct a mistake of the other party as to the contents or effect of a writing, evidencing or embodying an agreement in whole or in part.

(d) . . . the other person is entitled to know the fact because of a relation of trust and confidence between them.[22]

To be binding, the parties must knowingly and voluntarily enter into the settlement agreement. An agreement induced by misrepresentations is not entered into knowingly and therefore may not be binding.[23]

The following case illustrates the concept of misrepresentation and the duty to disclose.

Fire Insurance Exchange v. Bell
643 N.E.2d 310 (Ind. 1994)

. . . On May 28, 1985, sixteen-month-old Jason Bell was severely burned in a fire at the Indianapolis home of Joseph Moore (Moore), Jason's grandfather. Gasoline had leaked onto the floor of Moore's utility room and was ignited by a water heater. The fire department cited Moore for the careless storage of gasoline. The carrier for Moore's homeowner's policy was Farmer's, whose claims manager was Dennis Shank (Shank) and whose attorney was Scaletta. Jason's mother, Ruby Bell (Bell), retained attorney Robert Collins to represent Jason regarding his claims for injuries sustained in the fire. Collins communicated with Scaletta and Shank on many occasions in an effort to obtain information regarding the insurance policy limits. By October, 1985, Farmers informed Scaletta that Moore's policy limits were $300,000. In February, 1986, Scaletta told Collins that he did not know the policy limits, even though Farmers had already provided Scaletta with this information. Collins claimed that Scaletta and Shank told him on separate occasions that Moore had a $100,000 policy limit. Scaletta confirmed his misrepresentation to Collins in a letter he wrote to Shank on February 14, 1986. When Jason's condition stabilized, Shank and Scaletta each represented to Collins that Farmers would pay the $100,000 policy limit. As a result of these conversations, Collins advised Bell to settle. The agreement was approved by the probate court, and after settling with Farmers, Bell filed a products liability action against the manufacturer of Moore's water heater. Through negotiations with the water heater company, Collins learned that Moore's homeowner's policy limits were actually $300,000. Collins informed Bell that he had been deceived and advised her to seek independent counsel to assert claims against Farmers and Ice Miller. Bell filed a complaint against the appellants, alleging among other claims the fraudulent misrepresentation of the insurance policy limits.

Ice Miller and Scaletta each contend that they were entitled to summary judgment because of the absence of the right to rely, a component of the reliance element required to prove fraud. They contend that Bell's attorney had, as a matter of law, no right to rely on the alleged misrepresentations because he was a trained professional involved in adversarial settlement negotiation and had access to the relevant facts. . . .

. . . This Court has a particular constitutional responsibility with respect to the supervision of the practice of law. The reliability and trustworthiness of attorney representations constitute an important component of the efficient administration of justice. A lawyer's representations have long been accorded a particular expectation of honesty and trustworthiness.

Commitment to these values begins with the oath taken by every Indiana lawyer; it is formally embodied in rules of professional conduct, the violation of which may result in the imposition of severe sanctions; and it is repeatedly emphasized and reinforced by professional associations and organizations. . . . The Preamble of the Standards for Professional Conduct within the Seventh Federal Judicial Circuit begins with the following statement:

> A lawyer's conduct should be characterized at all times by personal courtesy and professional integrity in the fullest sense of those terms. In fulfilling our duty to represent a client vigorously as lawyers, we will be mindful of our obligations to the administration of justice, which is a truth-seeking process designed to resolve human and societal problems in a rational, peaceful, and efficient manner.

143 F.R.D. 441, 448 (1992). The Seventh Circuit standards expressly include the following duty of lawyers to other counsel: "We will adhere to all express promises and to agreements with other counsel, whether oral or in writing. . . ." *Id.* at 449. Similarly, the Tenets of Professional Courtesy adopted by the Indianapolis Bar Association declare, "A lawyer should never knowingly deceive another lawyer or the court," and "A lawyer should honor promises or commitments to other lawyers and to the court, and should always act pursuant to the maxim, 'My word is my bond.'" *Tenets of Professional Courtesy,* Indianapolis Bar Association (1989). The International Association of Defense Counsel likewise emphasizes that "[w]e will honor all promises or commitments, whether oral or in writing, and strive to build a reputation for dignity, honesty and integrity." *See, e.g.,* 60 Def. Coun. J. 190 (1993).

Ice Miller and Scaletta contend that the plaintiff's attorney "had no right to rely on the representations he claims because he had the means to ascertain relevant facts, was in an adverse position, was educated, sophisticated and not involved in any dominant-subordinate relationship." Brief of Appellants Ice Miller Donadio & Ryan and Scaletta in Support of Petition to Transfer at 18-19. They further argue "that the relationship was adverse, the negotiations were protracted and that both sides were at all times represented by counsel," *id.* at 19, and emphasize that policy limits information was available to Bell's attorney from a variety of sources, including the rules of discovery.

We decline to require attorneys to burden unnecessarily the courts and litigation process with discovery to verify the truthfulness of material representations made by opposing counsel. The reliability of lawyers' representations is an integral component of the fair and efficient administration of justice. The law should promote lawyers' care in making statements that are accurate and trustworthy and should foster the reliance upon such statements by others.

We therefore reject the assertion of Ice Miller and Scaletta that Bell's attorney was, as a matter of law, not entitled to rely upon their representations. However, rather than finding this to be an issue of fact for determination at trial, as did our Court of Appeals, we hold that Bell's attorney's right to rely upon any material misrepresentations that may have been made by opposing counsel is established as a matter of law. The resolution of the questions of what representations were actually made and the extent of reliance thereon are, along with any other remaining elements of plaintiff's case, issues of fact which must be determined at trial. . . .

SHEPARD, C.J., and DeBRULER, and SULLIVAN, JJ., concur.
GIVAN, J., concurs in result.

Questions:
1. How did Bell learn about the misrepresentation of the insurance policy limits?
2. What defense did Ice Miller and Scaletta assert? Did the court agree with them? Why? Why not?
3. What was the court's decision? Do you agree? Disagree?

Regulations for Specific Types of Negotiations

Some negotiations, because of their subject matter, have additional legal restrictions. For example, the National Labor Relations Act requires that the parties involved in collective bargaining bargain in "good faith." Although there are no clear parameters of what constitutes good faith, a number of behaviors are prohibited. For example, the parties must be prepared for negotiations, should be willing to offer counterproposals, and should not present take-it-or-leave it offers.

In some negotiations, the law requires the disclosure of certain information even when it is not requested. In residential real estate transactions, many states impose a duty on the seller to disclose a variety of information such as malfunctions of the water supply system, the presence or prior removal of hazardous materials, and any known defects.

Finally, in bargaining situations where a party is subject to exploitation, the law steps in to provide protection. For example, in divorce actions, most states require court approval of divorce agreements. Also, many jurisdictions give consumers several days to rescind an agreement made with door-to-door salespersons or telemarketers.

ETHICAL CONSTRAINTS AFFECTING NEGOTIATIONS

A number of ethical rules provide guidelines for lawyers involved in negotiations. Paralegals who work under the supervision of an attorney are subject to these same rules in addition to rules governing paralegal behavior. Other professions may also have ethical guidelines, but this section focuses on those that apply to attorneys. Many states have adopted the American Bar Association's (ABA) Model Rules of Professional Conduct or have similar rules. One rule requires lawyers to be truthful when communicating with third persons. This has been interpreted to mean that lawyers shall not be untruthful when making statements about the substance of the negotiation or the law.[24]

The rule refers to factual statements significant to negotiations. Statements such as "this is a good deal" or "this car is a cream puff" are considered puffing or embellishment and not significant. Therefore, these would not be considered ethical violations.

There are other ethical obligations imposed upon lawyers. As we learned earlier in this chapter, a lawyer must keep her client informed about any settlement offers. *Covington v. Continental General Tire, Inc.* discusses what happens when a lawyer settles a case without the consent of her client.

Covington v. Continental General Tire, Inc.
381 F.3d 216 (3d Cir. 2004)

. . . Plaintiffs Emma Jean Williams, Jamie Williams, Mary Lou Covington, Richard Abrams, and Sheila Abrams were passengers in a car that was involved in an accident allegedly caused by a defective tire manufactured by Continental General Tire, Inc. Plaintiffs subsequently retained Carl R. Schiffman, Esq. to bring suit against Continental, as well as Sears and Roebuck. As part of the retainer agreement, plaintiffs executed a power of attorney in favor of Schiffman, that stated in relevant part that: Schiffman, "shall not make any settlements without [clients'] consent."

During the ensuing discovery, Schiffman engaged tire expert Gary A. Derian who prepared a report and provided deposition testimony. However, Derian's testimony turned out to be problematic for plaintiffs. Schiffman concluded that Derian's testimony seriously weakened his case against Continental, and he decided to enter into settlement discussions with Clem Trischler, counsel for Continental. Plaintiffs and Schiffman disagree about whether Schiffman ever informed them of those negotiations. However, it is undisputed that Schiffman eventually represented to Trischler that plaintiffs were willing to settle their case against Continental and proceed only against Sears. Schiffman and Trischler then reached an agreement whereby plaintiffs would dismiss their action against Continental and pursue only Sears in return for Continental's agreement to provide its expert for plaintiffs to use against Sears. Upon learning of the purported settlement, plaintiffs told Schiffman they would not sign the agreement and stipulated dismissal.

When Schiffman informed Trischler that plaintiffs would not execute the settlement documents, Continental filed the instant motion to enforce the agreement. The District Court granted the motion based upon the Magistrate Judge's Report and Recommendation. This appeal followed. . . .

Plaintiffs contend that they are not bound by Schiffman's representation of settlement authority because they never expressly agreed to settle their claims, which they argue is required under Pennsylvania law before an attorney can settle his/her client's case. Defendants, on the other hand, argue that Pennsylvania recognizes an attorney's apparent authority to bind a client to a settlement, and that Schiffman's apparent authority to act on behalf of his clients in this instance was sufficient to compel enforcement of the settlement agreement.

Although the Pennsylvania Supreme Court has not recently addressed this issue, our analysis is informed by our own decision in *Farris v. JC Penney Co., Inc.*, 176 F.3d 706 (3d Cir. 1999), as well as early decisions of the Pennsylvania Supreme Court, which we examined in reaching our decision in *Farris*.

In *Farris*, plaintiff's attorney represented in open court that plaintiffs had agreed to a settlement with defendant. However, plaintiffs never actually agreed to settle the case and, in fact, had told their attorney that they would not settle until medical treatment was completed. Although plaintiffs were in court when the agreement was read into the record, they did not understand what was happening until after the proceeding was over. Upon realizing the nature of the settlement, plaintiffs expressed their displeasure to their attorney and told opposing counsel they had not authorized the settlement that had just been presented to the court. Nevertheless, the District Court entered an order dismissing the suit under Federal Rule of Civil Procedure 41(b). Plaintiffs subsequently obtained new counsel and filed a motion for relief from the dismissal pursuant to Federal Rule of Civil Procedure 60(b). The District Court denied the motion and plaintiffs appealed.

We reversed the District Court's decision based largely upon the Pennsylvania Supreme Court's decision in *Starling v. West Erie Bldg. & Loan Ass'n*, 333 Pa.

124, 3 A.2d 387 (1939). In *Starling,* the court had stated that "[w]ithout express authority [an attorney] cannot compromise or settle his client's claim. . . ." *Id.* at 388. Although the court recognized that the authority granted an attorney by virtue of his/her office is broad and includes the authority to "bind his/her clients by admissions and acts in the course of suit or in the management of the regular course of litigation," it cautioned that "such apparent or implied authority does not extend to unauthorized acts which will result in the surrender of any substantial right of the client, or the imposition of new liabilities or burdens upon him." *Id.* . . .

[W]e rule that an attorney has to have an express authority to settle a client's claims therefore, we will reverse.

Questions:
1. Why did Schiffman decide to settle with Continental?
2. Continental filed a motion to enforcement the settlement agreement with plaintiffs. What was their argument?
3. What did plaintiffs argue?
4. How did the court rule? What was the court's rationale?

Conclusion

Negotiation is usually the first method parties try to settle a dispute. When this fails, the disputants may negotiate the use of another ADR process. If they agree on one, the parties then negotiate on the selection of a third-party neutral and the rules and procedures to be followed. As you continue to read this book, you will learn about the fundamental role negotiation plays in the various ADR processes.

Key Terms and Concepts

Competitive negotiators
Cooperative negotiators
Distributive negotiation
Five stages of negotiation

Negotiation
Problem-solving negotiation
Types of legal negotiations

Practice Test Questions

True/False

____ 1. The purpose of negotiation is to complete a transaction, resolve a controversy, or reach an agreement.

____ 2. Distributive negotiation is concerned with dividing limited resources.

____ 3. The civil justice system generally favors settlement agreements because they lower legal costs, save time, and contribute to ongoing relations between the parties.

____ 4. There are no ethical rules guiding a lawyer's behavior during negotiations.

____ 5. To be effective, a negotiator must not only be proficient in negotiation skills but she must have knowledge of the applicable law associated with the subject matter of the dispute.

Multiple Choice

____ 1. The five stages in negotiation are
  a. preparation, preliminary, disclosure, information/positioning, agreement.
  b. preparation, preliminary, information/positioning, distributive/competitive or integrative/collaborative, agreement or collapse.
  c. preliminary, disclosure, distributive/competitive or integrative/collaborative, promotion, agreement.
  d. preparation, promotion, distributive/competitive or integrative/collaborative, promotion, agreement.

____ 2. When parties reach a negotiated settlement that resulted from false statements that were material and justifiably relied upon, negotiators may be liable for damages or the agreement may be subject to rescission. Which of the following statements could be considered false:
  a. "This car is a cream puff."
  b. "This car drives like a dream."
  c. "This car has never been involved in an accident."
  d. "Everyone who owns one of these cars loves it."

____ 3. From a client's perspective, successful negotiation is beneficial because it avoids all of the following *except*
  a. negative publicity.
  b. the likelihood that a judge's decision would be no different than the negotiated settlement.
  c. the costs and delays of a trial.
  d. any further damage to the parties' relationship.

____ 4. Effective cooperative negotiators are concerned with all of the following *except*
  a. ethical conduct.
  b. avoiding litigation.
  c. a fair settlement.
  d. winning.

____ 5. A client's needs and interests can be divided into which of the following categories?
  a. essential, important, and desirable
  b. predictable, essential, and important

    c. disposable, important, and desirable

    d. essential, fungible, and desirable

Review Questions

1. Name and explain each of the six types of negotiations.
2. What are the characteristics of a competitive negotiator?
3. Name the tactics frequently associated with competitive negotiators. Explain the purpose of each.
4. What are the characteristics of a cooperative negotiation?
5. Explain the risks cooperative negotiators face.
6. Name and discuss the ethical constraints affecting negotiations.
7. Negotiation is a process with several different stages. List and explain these segments in order of occurrence.
8. There are several procedural and evidentiary rules and laws that affect negotiation and settlement. List and discuss these legal restraints.
9. A negotiator who acts on behalf of another person is bound to act in accordance with the directives of the principal. When a lawyer negotiates on behalf of a client, there are additional obligations. Discuss these requirements.

Application Questions

1. **The stages of negotiation.** Consider the following scenario. You and your spouse are looking to buy a new house. After much searching, you find one that meets your requirements, and the price is fair based on your research of the value of houses in the area. The listed price is $375,000, but the real estate broker thinks the seller will take less so you offer $355,000. The owner's real estate broker does not reply to the offer and wants you to see the house again. While there, the broker points out the expanded family room and new wood floors. He also shows you the finished basement with a guest bedroom. You tell him that the roof will need replacing soon and the furnace is old and a new one will be needed. When you inquire about your offer he says that the owners' counteroffer is $370,000. Knowing that the house has been on the market for a year, you counteroffer with $360,000 and indicate that this is your final offer. The owners accept. Using the five stages discussed in the chapter, at which point does each stage begin in the above scenario? What issues are left for stage five?
2. **Is negotiation like a sport?** Why do many negotiators (or people involved in negotiations) think of negotiation like a sport or war? Why is negotiation not like this?
3. **Misrepresentation.** Misrepresentation includes an intentional untruth. Uncorrected mistakes are also considered a knowing misrepresentation. Read the following case and then discuss the questions that follow.

State v. Tate

21 Cal. App 3d 432 (1971)

The agreement in question was signed by both parties on February 21, 1968. . . .

In the negotiations both sides apparently agreed that the community property was to be evenly divided. They did not agree, however, on the value of certain items and on the community property status of certain stocks that stood in the husband's name alone.

These disagreements centered principally on items which, it was understood, were to be retained by the husband. . . .

In January 1968, Joan's attorney prepared a document entitled "Second Proposal for a Basis of Settlement — Tate v. Tate" which, among other things, arrived at a suggested figure of $70,081.85 for the value of Joan's share in the Holt property. This value was arrived at by a computation set forth in the proposal. It is copied in the footnote.[25]

It is obvious that Joan's attorney arrived at the figure of $70,081.85 for the community equity in the property only by making two substantial errors. First, the net value after deducting the encumbrances from the asserted gross value of $550,000 is $241.637.01, not $141,637.01; second, one-half of $141,637.01 is substantially more than $70,081.85. The correct figure for the equity should have been $120,818.50 or, roughly $50,000 more.

The mistake did not escape Tim's accountant who discovered it while helping Tim's attorney in preparing a counteroffer. He brought it to the attention of the attorney who, in his own words, reacted as follows:

> I told him that I have been arguing with [the wife's attorney] to use the value that was on the real property tax statement, but I knew that that was low and [he] would never go for it, that the appraisal had been $425,000.00 when the building had been purchased by said owners, and I thought that until we got it, that we would use something like a $450,000.00 value, and he said, "Fine." It is my recollection that I said to him, "You know, you might as well use the figure that Walker has there because his mistake is a hundred thousand dollars and we value it as a hundred thousand dollars less, so it is basically the same thing, so give it a $70,000.00 equity," and that is what he did and that is how it came about.

A counteroffer was then submitted to Joan and her lawyer. It lists all of the community assets, with the property in question being valued at $70,082.00, rounding up the erroneous figure in Joan's offer to the nearest dollar. There can be no reasonable doubt that the counteroffer was prepared in a way designed to minimize the danger that Joan or her attorney would discover the mistake. . . .

On February 16, 1968, the parties and their attorneys had a settlement conference. The counteroffer was the basis for the discussion. There was no mention that the figure of $70,082 for the equity in the Holt property was based on an agreed value of $550,000 or any other figure. . . .

The mistake might never have come to light had not Tim desired to have that exquisite last word. A few days after Joan had obtained the divorce he mailed her a copy of the offer which contained the errant computation. On top of the page he wrote with evident satisfaction: "PLEASE NOTE $100,000.00 MISTAKE IN YOUR FIGURES. . . ." The present action was filed exactly one month later. . . .

   a. After reading Tim's note on the copy of the offer he mailed to her, Joan notified her attorney, who promptly filed a motion seeking that the judgment be reversed. Based on the Restatement (Second) of Contracts §§ 161 and 164, should the court grant her motion? Why or why not?
   b. What should Tim and his lawyer have done about the mistake?
   c. What do you think should happen if Tim intentionally avoided knowing the truth? Same result?
   d. There are rules and regulations about what a party must disclose during negotiations. However, if negotiations take place in private, how will the other party or a court find out if someone is withholding information that must be disclosed? Should a court review all settlement agreements for fairness or full disclosure? How would this affect negotiations?

4. **Material facts.** Remember from your reading of the chapter that some "puffing" and "embellishment" are acceptable in negotiations. However, when the exaggeration is about a material fact, it could be considered a fraud. Judge Learned Hand's decision in *Vulcan Metals Co. v. Simmons Manufacturing Co.*[26] explains how courts evaluate sales promises.

Simmons Manufacturing Company was in the furniture business and had begun to manufacture vacuum cleaners. After making about 15,000 of them, the company decided that selling vacuum cleaners was not compatible with the furniture business and decided to sell. Vulcan Metals Company purchased "all the tools, dies, and equipment owned by [Simmons Manufacturing] for the manufacture of . . . vacuum cleaning machines, all manufactured machines and unassembled parts, . . . and all inventions, applications, and letters patent owned by the Simmons Company in vacuum cleaners, together with certain proposed improvements to be made thereon."[27]

Not long after the purchase, Vulcan Metals discontinued manufacturing the vacuum cleaners because "they proved to be ineffective and of little or no value"[28] and sued Simmons Manufacturing Company for deceit. Vulcan Metals alleged "that the officers and agents of the Simmons Manufacturing Company made false representations as to the character of the vacuum cleaners so sold and the extent to which they had been used upon the market, to which Vulcan Metals Company, Incorporated, acted to its prejudice, because the machines and patents were totally inefficient and unmarketable."[29] The court directed a verdict for

Simmons Manufacturing Company on the deceit claim. The appeals court reversed and ordered a new trial.

Judge Hand wrote at length about when "puffing" or "dealers' talk" becomes a misrepresentation.

> The first question is of the misrepresentations touching the quality and powers of the patented machine. These were general commendations, or, in so far as they included any specific facts were not disproved; e.g. that the cleaner would produce 18 inches of vacuum with 25 pounds water pressure. They raise, therefore, the question of law how far general "puffing" or "dealers' talk" can be the basis of an action for deceit.

The conceded exception in such cases has generally rested upon the distinction between "opinion" and "fact"; but that distinction has not escaped the criticism it deserves. An opinion is a fact, and it may be a very relevant fact; the expression of an opinion is the assertion of a belief, and any rule which condones the expression of a consciously false opinion condones a consciously false statement of fact. When the parties are so situated that the buyer may reasonably rely upon the expression of the seller's opinion, it is no excuse to give a false one. And so it makes much difference whether the parties stand "on an equality." For example, we should treat very differently the expressed opinion of a chemist to a layman about the properties of a composition from the same opinion between chemist and chemist, when the buyer had full opportunity to examine. The reason of the rule lies, we think, in this: There are some kinds of talk which no sensible man takes seriously, and if he does he suffers from his credulity. If we were all scrupulously honest, it would not be so; but, as it is, neither party usually believes what the seller says about his own opinions, and each knows it. Such statements, like the claims of campaign managers before election, are rather designed to allay the suspicion which would attend their absence than to be understood as having any relation to objective truth. It is quite true that they induce a compliant temper in the buyer, but it is by a much more subtle process than through the acceptance of his claims for his wares. . . .

In the case at bar, since the buyer was allowed full opportunity to examine the cleaner and to test it out, we put the parties upon an equality. It seems to us that general statements as to what the cleaner would do, even though consciously false, were not of a kind to be taken literally by the buyer. As between manufacturer and customer, it may not be so; but this was the case of taking over a business, after ample chance to investigate. Such a buyer, who the seller rightly expects will undertake an independent and adequate inquiry into the actual merits of what he gets, has no right to treat as material in his determination statements like these. . . . We therefore think that the District Court was right in disregarding all these misrepresentations.

As respects the representation that the cleaners had never been put upon the market or offered for sale, the rule does not apply; nor can we agree that such representations could not have been material to Freeman's decision to accept the contract. The actual test of experience in their sale might well be of critical consequence in his decision to buy the business, and the jury would certainly have the right to accept his statement that his reliance upon these representations was determinative of his final decision. . . .

    a. Was the lie about whether the vacuum cleaners had been marketed puffing? Embellishment? Sales talk? Exaggeration? Material?

    b. Do you agree or disagree with the court?

    c. What did the court say about these types of lies?

    d. Was the lie about the performance of the vacuum cleaners puffing? Embellishment? Sales talk? Exaggeration? Material?

    e. What did the court say about these types of lies? What was the court's reasoning? Do you agree or disagree?

Practice Exercises

1. Rule 408 of the Federal Rules of Evidence generally prohibits settlement discussions from being introduced at trial.

    a. What do you think is the rationale for this exclusion? Do you agree or disagree?

    b. Does Rule 408 have any exceptions to the general prohibition? What are they?

    c. Does your state have a similar evidence rule? What is the citation? If your state does not have this rule, find a nearby state that has adopted it. What is the citation?

    d. Find a case (in your state if there is a rule similar to Rule 408; otherwise look at a nearby state) and explain the rationale for both the prohibitions and exceptions. Do you agree with the court's rationale? Why or why not?

2. Some negotiations that result in a settlement agreement prohibit the parties from revealing any of the settlement terms.

    a. Do courts in your jurisdiction (or nearby jurisdiction) support confidentiality of settlements agreements?

    b. Are there any instances where the court would order the record to be unsealed?

    c. What is the court's rationale for making the record available?

3. In *Beavers v. Lamplighters Realty, Inc.*, 556 P.2d 1328 (Okla. App. 1976), a purchaser of a home sued the realtor for fraud. When the realtor told the purchaser that another person was going to buy the house for $37,000, the purchaser offered $37,250. After moving into the house, purchaser learned that there had not been an offer to buy the house for $37,000.

    Plaintiff argued that the realtor knew his statement about the $37,000 offer was false and that it was made it to induce him to purchase the property. The defendant asserted that his statement was mere "puffing."

Read the case and answer the following questions:

a. By arguing that his statement was nothing more than "puffing," the defendant was asserting the doctrine of caveat emptor. Did the court agree? Why or why not?

b. Did the court find that the defendant's statement about an existing offer was a fraudulent inducement? What did the court say? What was the court's rationale?

c. In whose favor did the court rule?

d. What was the court's decision?

Endnotes

1. David A. Law & James K. Sebenius, *The Manager as Negotiator: Bargaining for Cooperation and Competitive Gain* 11 (Free Press 1986).

2. Leonard L. Riskins, James E. Westbrook, Chris Gutherie, Timothy J. Heinsz, Richard C. Reuben & Jennifer K. Robbennolt, *Dispute Resolution and Lawyers* 98 (abr. 3d ed., West 1988).

3. Gainey v. Bhd. of Railay & Steamship Clerks, Freight Handlers, Express & Station Emps., 275 F. Supp. 292, 300 (E.D. Pa. 1967).

4. 29 U.S.C. § 158(d) (2012).

5. Model Rules of Prof'l Conduct R. 1.1, 1.4.

6. *See, e.g.*, Wilcox v. Ex'rs of Kemp Plummer, 29 U.S. 172, 181 (1830); Butler v. Mooers, 771 A.2d 1034 (Me. 2001); Paterek v. Petersen & Ibold, 890 N.E.2d 316, 321 (Ohio 2008).

7. Model Rules of Prof'l Conduct R. 1.2.

8. Harry T. Edwards & James J. White, *The Lawyer as a Negotiator* 113-121 (West 1977).

9. Gerald R. Williams, *Legal Negotiation and Settlement* 20-21 (West 1983).

10. Sun Tzu, *The Art of War* 18 (James Clavell ed., Dell 1983).

11. Herb Cohen, *Negotiate This* 127-128 (Warner Business 2003); Edward Brunet, Charles B. Craver & Ellen E. Deason, *Alternative Dispute Resolution: The Advocate's Perspective Cases and Materials* 73 (3d ed., Lexis-Nexis 2006).

12. Roger Fisher & William Ury, *Getting to Yes* 98-106 (Penguin 1991).

13. Russell Korobkin, *Aspirations and Settlement*, 88 Cornell L. Rev. 1, 19-30 (2002).

14. *Id.*; Clark Freshman, Adele Hayes & Greg Feldman, *The Lawyer-Negotiation as Mood Scientist: What We Know and Don't Know About How Mood Relates to Successful Negotiation*, 2002 J. Disp. Resol. 1, 15.

15. According to Carrie Menkel-Meadow, the concept of "integrative" solutions originated with Mary Parker Follett, who was an early contributor to the development of constructive conflict. *See* Carrie Menkel-Meadow, *Mothers and Fathers of invention: The Intellectual Founders of ADR*, 16 Ohio St. J. on Disp. Resol. 1 (2000).

16. Restatement (Second) of Contracts § 24 (1981).

17. *Id.* § 50.

18. The statute of frauds refers to statutes that require certain agreements to be in writing and signed by the party to be charged or against whom enforcement is sought. The statute of frauds was first adopted in England in 1677, and every state in the United States has enacted a similar law. Some examples of agreements required by the statute of frauds to be in writing are contracts for the sale of land, agreements not to be performed within one year, and agreements made on consideration of marriage.

19. Long v. State, 807 A.2d 1, 8 (Md. 2002). "Under California law settlement of disputes is a strongly favored public policy, for settlement reduces costs for all parties, conserves judicial and private resources, and promotes good will." Neary v. Regents of the Univ. of Cal., 834 P.2d 119, 121 (Cal. 1992). "The law of this Commonwealth establishes that an agreement to settle legal disputes between parties is favored. There is a strong judicial policy in favor of voluntarily settling lawsuits because it reduces the burden on the courts and expedites the transfer of money into the hands of the complainant." Step Plan Servs., Inc. v. Koresko, 12 A.3d 401, 409 (Pa. Super. 2010).

20. Restatement (Second) of Torts § 525 (1977).

21. *Id.*

22. *Id.* § 161.

23. *Id.* § 164.

24. Model Rules of Prof'l Conduct R. 4.1.

25. "888 East Holt Avenue, Pomona
(Note: value as per previous offer)

Total value	$550,000.00
Less encumbrance	308,362.99
Net value	$141,637.01
One-half community	$70,081.85"

26. 248 F. 853 (2d Cir. 1918).

27. *Id.* at 854.

28. *Id.* at 855.

29. *Id.* at 854-855. There was evidence that some agents of Simmons Manufacturing Co. had not been able to sell any of the vacuum cleaners.

CHAPTER FOUR

Mediation

Chapter Outline

Introduction

What Is Mediation?

A Brief History of Mediation

  The Pound Conference

  The Uniform Mediation Act

The Advantages and Disadvantages of Mediation

  Advantages

  Disadvantages

The Mediation Process

  Stages of Mediation

The Role of the Mediator

  Educating the Parties

  Organizing the Sessions

  Developing and Maintaining Communication

  Managing Emotions

  Maintaining Interest

Generating Solutions and Reaching Agreement

Caucuses

Mediation Forms

  Evaluative Mediation

  Facilitative Mediation

  Transformative Mediation

Mediator Qualifications

Mediator Skills

Ethical Issues in Mediation

  Standards of Conduct for Mediators

Med-Arb (Mediation-Arbitration)

Conclusion

Key Terms and Concepts

Practice Test Questions

Review Questions

Application Questions

Practice Exercises

> Discourage litigation. Persuade your neighbors to comprise wherever you can. Point out to them how the nominal winner is often a real loser — in fees, expenses and waste of time. As a peacemaker, the lawyer has a superior opportunity of being a good man.
>
> — ABRAHAM LINCOLN

INTRODUCTION

Two farmers each claimed to own a certain cow. While one farmer pulled on the cow's head and the other farmer pulled on her tail, the cow was milked simultaneously by the farmers' lawyers.

    Another pair of farmers each claimed to own another cow. One farmer pulled on the cow's head and the other pulled on her tail. When they realized that their efforts were accomplishing nothing and that the cow's milk was going to waste, they decided to find a neutral third party to help mediate their dispute.

With the mediator's assistance, the farmers agreed to milk the cow on alternating days and split the meat when it came time to butcher her. These farmers' dispute was resolved quickly and it cost them each less milk and (more importantly) time. Meanwhile, the first pair of farmers eventually agreed to sell the cow to pay their legal fees.[1]

Mediation is another approach for resolving disputes. It improves on negotiation by introducing a neutral third party[2] to help facilitate the discussions, manage the emotions that may surface, encourage the creation of new options, and work with the parties to reach agreement. As we will see, the process differs from other dispute resolution alternatives in a number of ways. However, the paramount distinction is that mediation honors the participants' right to self-determination.

WHAT IS MEDIATION?

"**Mediation** involves the assistance of a neutral third party, the mediator, in attempting to resolve the dispute. The mediator's function is to assist the parties in their negotiations, by helping the parties define the issues, overcome barriers to communication, and explore different methods of resolving their dispute."[3] It is a process wherein a neutral party "attempt[s] to systematically isolate points of agreement and disagreement, explore alternative solutions, and consider compromises for the purpose of reaching a consensual settlement of the issues relating to their conflict."[4] Simply put, mediation is negotiation but with the help of a neutral third party. The parties decide the outcome but have the benefit of guidance by a person knowledgeable about the mediation process and often the subject matter of the dispute. Of all the various forms of alternative dispute resolution (ADR), mediation gives the parties the most control over the process and the outcome. The disputants, not attorneys, judges, or mediators, decide the rules and the outcome.

Depending on the issue and the mediator's style, mediation is either "rights-based" or "interest-based." Each has its own approach to addressing the dispute. **Rights-based** or **evaluative mediation** centers on the legal rights of the disputants, such as the contract, the accounting principles involved, industry practice, or the applicable law. The mediator evaluates the dispute and suggests an appropriate resolution.

Interest-based or **facilitative mediation** centers on the needs of the parties. The mediator "facilitates communications, promotes understanding, focuses the parties on their interests, and seeks creative problem solving to enable the parties to reach their own agreement."[5]

Mediation is growing faster than other forms of alternative dispute resolution and is used in a variety of disagreements including neighbors' conflicts, small claims actions, divorce, and disputes between large corporations involving millions of dollars.[6] The use of mediation in business disputes can save thousands of dollars in litigation costs and preserve the ongoing relationship between the parties. Mediation can help neighbors learn to be good neighbors and divorced parents to cooperate in raising their children.

A BRIEF HISTORY OF MEDIATION

Mediation in the United States has its roots in the colonial period. The early colonists had a strong need to avoid any conflict that would undermine the stability of their community.

> Expulsion and criminal prosecution aside, the only alternative consistent with group harmony was mediation, which turned disputants toward each other in reconciliation, not away from each other in acrimonious pursuit of self-interest. The colonists understood that legal disputation, with its adversarial imperatives, was destructive of the group solidarity upon which they depended for the fulfillment of their mission in the New World.[7]

Mediation was also favored by early immigrant groups to shield them from an unfamiliar legal system.

In the late 1800s, the growing unrest between labor and management in the railway industry forced the federal government to intervene. Congress first passed the Arbitration Act of 1888, which provided for mediation and arbitration of railway labor disputes. The Erdman Act of 1898 followed in an attempt to strengthen the Arbitration Act. The Newlands Act of 1913 created the Board of Mediation and Conciliation, and in 1926, Congress passed the Railway Labor Act, which created the Board of Mediation, later renamed the National Mediation Board. In 1947, the Taft-Hartley Act created the Federal Mediation and Conciliation Service "to prevent or minimize interruptions in the free flow of commerce growing out of labor disputes, to assist parties to labor disputes in industries affecting commerce, to settle such disputes through conciliation mediation."[8]

The late 1960s and early 1970s saw the creation of mediation programs for resolving community disputes. The Community Relations Service, a federal program created through the Civil Rights Act of 1964, used mediators to help neighborhoods create peaceful ways to deal with racial conflict. In the mid-1970s, the federal government gave support to six Neighborhood Justice Centers that used mediation in an array of interpersonal disagreements.

The Pound Conference

The genesis of mediation in the courts began in 1906, when Roscoe Pound, a lawyer, judge, law school professor, and dean of Harvard Law School, spoke at the American Bar Association about the need to improve the administration of the courts. His lecture, "The Causes of Popular Dissatisfaction with the Administration of Justice," was and remains a landmark statement on the need for an efficient and fair judicial system.

In 1976, lawyers, judges, law professors, and court administrators came together to study problems in the legal establishment in a conference titled "The National Conference on the Causes of Popular Dissatisfaction with the Administration of Justice." The Pound Conference,[9] as it is now commonly called, is recognized as the start of the modern mediation movement. Two important concepts originated at this symposium. The first was the creation of the Neighborhood Justice Centers that laid the foundation for the creation of community dispute resolution centers throughout the United States. The second was the "multi-door courthouse" approach to resolving disputes. Harvard Professor Frank E.A. Sander addressed the increased demands on courts throughout the United States and suggested that courthouses could offer multiple dispute resolution "doors" or programs. The process would begin with an evaluation of the case, after which it could be sent for resolution by mediation, conciliation, arbitration, litigation, or some other program inside or outside of the courthouse. Sander's model is now in use throughout the United States, and courts offering various ADR programs are called "multi-door courthouses."[10]

The Uniform Mediation Act

Since the Pound Conference in 1976, mediation has become a vital branch of dispute resolution in courts, businesses, government agencies, and community programs. States have written statutes establishing mediation programs in courts, and some have created state agencies to promote and support the use of mediation. The Uniform Mediation Act (see Appendix A), a four-year effort by scholars, practitioners, and lawyers, was written to provide a model law to promote uniformity of mediation throughout the states.

Uniform Mediation Act, Prefatory Note

The Drafters intend for the Act to be applied and construed in a way to promote uniformity . . . and also in such manner as to:

- promote candor of parties through confidentiality of the mediation process, subject only to the need for disclosure to accommodate specific and compelling societal interests;
- encourage the policy of fostering prompt, economical, and amicable resolution of disputes in accordance with principles of integrity of the mediation process, active party involvement, and informed self-determination by the parties; and
- advance the policy that the decision-making authority in the mediation process rests with the parties.

Source: Uniform Mediation Act (2003) Prefatory Note. © Uniform Law Commission. Reprinted with permission.

Mediation is well established in our society as an effective method for resolving many disputes. The next section discusses the advantages and disadvantages of using this method of ADR.

THE ADVANTAGES AND DISADVANTAGES OF MEDIATION

Advantages

Faster, Cheaper, and Procedurally Easier

The driving forces behind the adoption of mediation as an alternative to litigation were the increasing costs of a lawsuit, the length of time it took to get to trial, and the increasing number of cases filed in courts. Because mediation avoids the need for discovery, filing of motions, court hearings, and compliance with the rules of evidence, it is a less expensive and quicker process. Additionally, when the disputants mediate without lawyers, they realize additional savings in legal fees. Exhibit 4-1 compares the costs of mediation to those of litigation.

Privacy

When a lawsuit is filed, the dispute becomes public. Because courthouses are open to any person, all the details of the disagreement then become available for anyone to view. In contrast, mediation takes place behind closed doors, and the discussions are confidential. Disputants may be more comfortable discussing issues in a private setting instead of a public courtroom. Additionally, mediators are not permitted to disclose any information to anyone, including a court, unless the parties consent or required by law. Confidentiality encourages more open discussion. What happens when a mediator violates confidentiality by submitting a report on the mediation to the court? The following case shows how a California court decided this issue.

***Foxgate Homeowners' Association, Inc. v. Bramalea California, Inc.*, 25 P.3d 1117 (Cal. 2001):** This case involved construction defects allegedly caused by the defendants, developer Bramalea and various subcontractors. The plaintiff was a Culver City, California, homeowners' association composed of the owners of a 65-unit condominium complex. During the pendency of the lawsuit, the trial court ordered the parties to participate in mediation and appointed retired judge Peter Smith as mediator. Judge Smith scheduled a five-day period for mediation and ordered the parties to bring their experts and claims representatives. On the first day, plaintiff's attorney and their nine experts appeared. Bramalea's attorney, Ivan Stevenson, appeared late and did not have any experts. The mediator cancelled the mediation, concluding that it could not proceed without defense experts.

Two days after the terminated mediation session, Judge Smith filed a report that stated, among other things:

> "Mr. Stevenson has spent the vast majority of his time trying to derail the mediations. . . ."

> ". . . Mr. Stevenson arrived 30 minutes late" to the mediation session.

83

Exhibit 4-1. COMPARISON OF COSTS TO MEDIATE VS. LITIGATE

Costs to Mediate:	
Initial 2-hour consultation:	$250.00 - $500.00
Follow up meeting: 4 hours at $300.00/hour, or	$1,200.00
Preparation of Mediated Settlement Agreement:	$500.00
Preparation of additional documents, such as Parenting Plan, Child support Worksheet, and/or Dissolution filings (if necessary):	$500.00
Approximate Total Cost of Mediation*:	**$500.00 - $2,500.00**
Costs to Litigate:	
Initial Consultation:	$250.00 - $500/hour
Retainer:	$2,500 - $5,000.00
Filing Initial Pleadings (Summons and Initial Petition):	$1,000.00
Serving Discovery:	$500.00
Responding to Discovery:	$750.00
Preparing Financial Affidavit and Mandatory Disclosure Compliance:	$1,800.00
Preparing Motions:	$750.00
Preparing Motion for Attorneys' Fees:	$750.00
Responding to Motions:	$750.00
Hiring Experts:	$2,000.00
Hearings/Court Appearances:	$4,500.00
Mediation (Court-Ordered):	$1,200.00
Co-Parenting Classes and Preparation of Parenting Plan:	$500.00
Trial:	$7,500 - $10,000
Appear:	$5,000.00
Approximate Total Cost of Litigation*:	**$32,700.00+**

*These are approximations and are contingent upon complexities of each individual case and time involved with the parties.
Used with permission of author Diane L. Danois, J.D.

". . . Mr. Stevenson refused to bring his experts to the mediation.

"Mr. Stevenson stated on several occasions that he did not need experts because of his vast knowledge in the field of construction defect litigation."

Toward the end of the first mediation session, "it became apparent that Mr. Stevenson's real agenda was to delay the mediation process so he can file a Motion for Summary Judgment. Mr. Stevenson asserted that he has a valid Statute of Limitations defense to plaintiff's entire claim. Mr. Stevenson wants to open discovery in order to bolster his position."

"The [mediator] has no idea whether Mr. Stevenson's Statute of Limitation contention is valid. However, it has been the experience of the mediator, in past mediations, that this tactic can be used to cut the amount of plaintiff's claims."

"Mr. Stevenson has had adequate time to file a Motion for Summary Judgment. . . ."

"As a result of Mr. Stevenson's obstructive bad faith tactics, the remainder of the mediation sessions were canceled at a substantial cost to all parties. . . ."[11]

The report also recommended, inter alia, that Bramalea/Stevenson be ordered to reimburse all parties for expenses incurred as result of the canceled mediation sessions.

Plaintiff's first motion for sanctions was denied without prejudice because Bramelea, Ltd., was then in a Canadian bankruptcy proceeding. Plaintiff eventually filed a new motion for sanctions, citing as support Judge Smith's report and statements made during the mediation. Bramalea/Stevenson opposed the motion and objected to the submission of Judge Smith's report because it violated the mediation confidentiality statute, which provides: "Neither a mediator nor anyone else may submit to a court . . . and a court . . . may not consider, any report, assessment, evaluation, recommendation, or finding of any kind by the mediator concerning a mediation conducted by the mediator, other than a report that is mandated by court rule or other law. . . ."[12]

The trial court, after considering Judge Smith's report and a declaration by plaintiff's counsel reciting statements made during the mediation session, granted plaintiff's second motion for sanctions. Bramalea/Stevenson appealed to the court of appeal and argued that the court "violated the confidentiality of mediation when the judge considered the report of the mediator in assessing the events and communications that occurred during the [mediation session]."[13] The court of appeal disagreed and reasoned that "immunity from sanctions, shielding parties to court-ordered mediation who disobey valid orders governing their participation in the mediation process, thereby intentionally thwarting the process to pursue other litigation tactics" was not the intent of the legislature.

Bramalea/Stevenson appealed to the California Supreme Court claiming "that any exception that permits reporting to the court and sanctioning a party on the basis of a mediator's report of conduct or statements allegedly undertaken in bad faith during mediation violates the statutes that guaranty confidentiality of mediation."[14] The California Supreme Court agreed and found that the legislative intent of the statute was clear and that "the purpose of confidentiality is to promote 'a candid and informal exchange regarding events in the past. . . . This frank exchange is achieved only if the participants know that what is said in the mediation will not be used to their detriment through later court proceedings and other adjudicatory processes.'"[15] The court reasoned that "confidentiality is essential to effective mediation, a form of alternative dispute resolution encouraged and, in some cases required by, the Legislature."[16]

In a footnote, the court recognized that "[t]he conflict between the policy of preserving confidentiality of mediation in order to encourage resolution of disputes and the interest of the state in enforcing professional responsibility to protect the integrity of the judiciary and to protect the public against incompetent and/or unscrupulous attorneys has not gone unrecognized. . . . [H]owever, any resolution of the competing policies is a matter for legislative, not judicial, action."[17]

Questions:
1. Did the California Supreme Court express its concern about the conflict between confidentiality of mediation and the behavior of attorneys? What did the court say?
2. Do you agree with the court? Why? Why not?

Permits Exploration of the Relationship Between the Parties

Often, the disputing parties need to continue their relationship after the dispute has been settled. For example, divorcing parents still need to parent their children, neighbors may continue to live near each other, buyers and sellers involved in a long-term contract will continue doing business, and landlords and tenants may carry on their interactions. Mediation is uniquely suited to preserving these relationships by helping the parties understand the origin of the dispute and generating ways to prevent a reoccurrence. Additionally, the participants have an opportunity to understand and acknowledge the other's point of view in a neutral and nonthreatening environment. This new perception can lead to better future conflict avoidance or resolution.

Empowers the Parties

Unlike a trial, where court rules dictate the procedure and a judge or jury determines the winner, mediation allows the parties to control the process and decide the outcome. As a result, parties are more likely to be satisfied with the outcome and less likely to violate the agreement.

Allows for More Creativity and Flexibility of Remedies

Litigation usually ends with one party winning and the other losing. Frequently, the remedy is monetary, which may not be what the "winning" party was seeking. Sometimes an apology, an acknowledgment of feelings, or an acceptance of responsibility can provide the closure sought. In child custody cases, visitation schedules written by the parties can address the unique needs of each parent whereas a judge-ordered plan may not be as flexible. Unlike litigation, mediation allows the disputants to craft a solution uniquely suited to their needs and concerns.

Improves Communication and Builds Trust

An effective mediator, because she is impartial, can neutralize anger and facilitate dialogue between parties whose communication has become strained.

The parties may accept a mediator's observation more readily than one made by a disputant. An impartial mediator's comment can foster open communication and promote discussion. Mediators can also reframe the parties' views of each other, help each to validate the other, and, in the process, encourage shared trust and improved relations.

Disadvantages

Unequal Bargaining Power

In situations where one party has greater bargaining ability because of legal knowledge, a better understanding of the facts, or greater economic or emotional power, the other party is disadvantaged, and any resolution may not be fair or appear fair. This disparity can occur in a divorce and custody case where one spouse has been the object of verbal and physical abuse. The victim may be scared or feel threatened in the presence of the abuser and therefore reluctant to participate. Another example is a dispute between a business owner and a consumer. The consumer may be disadvantaged by not having the knowledge, education, and/or experience of the business owner. In these situations, the mediator's role is crucial. An incompetent mediator could favor the party with the power while a good mediator will recognize the power imbalance and work to ensure fairness.

Does Not Create Legal Precedent

A settlement reached in mediation does not set any legal precedent, which a disputant could use to resolve other similar cases. Much of the legal reform in our country is the result of litigation and review by an appellate court. Civil rights, consumer product safety, and workers' rights are only a few examples of disputes settled by courts that resulted in far-reaching changes to our society. If these cases had been mediated, any settlement reached would have been limited to the disputing parties.

Abuse of the Process

There is always the possibility that one of the disputants can abuse the process of mediation. For example, one party may be participating only to use it as an informal method of discovery, a fishing expedition—that is, an opportunity to uncover information that might help in the litigation process. Another example is when one party sends a representative to the mediation, and the representative has no authority to enter into any agreement.

No Guarantee of Settlement

Mediation does not always lead to a settlement; in such cases, the parties will be forced to either pursue another form of ADR or litigate the dispute. In contrast, when the parties litigate, a resolution is a certainty.

Clearly, there are advantages and disadvantages to using mediation as an alternative to litigation. The parties need to evaluate these before deciding whether the dispute should be mediated. The next section looks at the procedure when using mediation.

THE MEDIATION PROCESS

The process of mediation is simple, even in complicated disputes. Each party has an opportunity to express feelings and tell his or her account of the disagreement. The mediator then encourages them to share information, perhaps not previously disclosed, and listen with an open mind. The parties thus are able to "achieve a new and shared perception of their relationship, a perception that will redirect their attitudes and dispositions toward one another,"[18] creating an opportunity to work together and generate new ideas for resolving the dispute.

PARALEGAL POINTERS

How Paralegals Help During Mediation

Paralegals play an important role assisting the attorney and client in mediation. The following are some paralegal tasks:

- Preparing motions
- Writing a memorandum of the underlying facts
- Performing legal research
- Researching the mediator
- Explaining the process to the client
- Attending the mediation session and taking notes
- Preparing settlement agreements and other necessary documents

These tasks are more fully discussed in Chapter 11.

There are numerous models of the stages of mediation. Jay Grenig summarizes the stages as "preliminary arrangements, mediator's introduction, parties' opening statements, information gathering, issue identification and agenda setting, option generation, negotiation, agreement, closure."[19] Below is a generic model of the mediation process. Keep in mind that stages often overlap rather than occur as distinct and static stages.

Stages of Mediation

1. **Agreement or Requirement to Mediate** Mediation usually takes place because the parties have a written agreement to mediate disputes, a dispute arises and the parties decide to mediate, or mediation is court

ordered. An example of a written mediation agreement is found in Appendix B.

2. **Selection of the Mediator** When the dispute does not involve a court, the parties usually choose the mediator and incorporate the choice into the written agreement. In court-ordered mediation, the mediator is usually selected by the court, although the parties may be able to choose from a list of court-approved mediators.

3. **Mediator's Opening Remarks and Instructions** Here the mediator describes the process and the rules. She explains that the procedure is informal and consensual, that she is impartial and that the parties are responsible for determining their own solutions. The mediator then tells them that each disputant will have an opportunity to give uninterrupted, opening statements, after which there will be a discussion of the issues. The parties will also be told that the mediator may, from time to time, meet privately with each disputant. This private meeting is called caucusing and can be helpful in providing an opportunity for each side to tell the mediator their feelings about a particular problem. The discussions are private unless permission is given to share them with the other party.

   The mediator next lays out the ground rules, such as not interrupting the other party when he is speaking, not using abusive language, the need to attend all sessions on time, bathroom breaks, and coffee and lunch breaks. Finally, the mediator discusses confidentiality. She tells the parties that anything said or learned during the mediation will be confidential and cannot be used at a trial in the event a settlement is not reached. The confidentiality rules include a provision that the mediator is prohibited from revealing anything from the session.

4. **Parties' Opening Statements** This is the opportunity for the disputants to present, uninterrupted, their view of the dispute. They usually raise issues and make suggestions on how they think the disagreement should be resolved. Remember, in mediation, the parties are the ones who identify the issues and set the agenda. The mediator's role is to assist them. The opening statement is also a time for venting feelings such as anger or frustration. Although this process can be constructive, the mediator must ensure that it does not become abusive and derail the discussions.

5. **Identification of Issues and Interests** This is the stage where the parties, with the guidance of the mediator, explore the conflict, identify the needs and interests of each, and develop an agenda for discussing the issues.

   Mediators use various techniques to encourage a full exchange of information between the disputants. Two of these are open-ended questions and summarization. For example, when a mediator believes a party may have more to say, he might encourage that person to continue speaking by asking open-ended questions such as "What do you mean?" "How do you feel about that?" "What happened as a result?" "How about . . . ?"

Mediators use summarization to show their understanding of what has been stated. When a mediator summarizes an exchange without its emotional content, disputants may be more apt to listen, which could generate more communication.

6. **Generation of Options for Resolution** Once the issues have been identified, the participants express their proposal for resolving the dispute and together develop new alternatives that may be acceptable to each. A useful tool for creating new ideas is brainstorming, a method for generating a large number of ideas for resolving a problem. Once options are generated, the parties, with the help of the mediator, discuss and analyze each and agree to either accept or reject them. The mediator, either with both parties present or in a private caucus, may discuss any unrealistic alternative in an effort to move the parties toward agreement. Often the choices are reduced to a small number, and the mediator will guide the participants through principled negotiation leading to resolution acceptable to both.

7. **Reaching Agreement** When a resolution of the dispute or perhaps a part of the dispute is achieved, the agreement will be put in writing. If the negotiations are unsuccessful, the mediator will tell the parties the areas of agreement and the possibility for settlement.

8. **Putting the Agreement in Writing** The written agreement can be prepared by the mediator, a party, or a lawyer. The writing may include a clause that requires the parties to return to mediation if a dispute arises in the future.

THE ROLE OF THE MEDIATOR

The mediator's role includes the following:

- Educating the Parties
- Organizing the Sessions
- Developing and Maintaining Communication
- Managing Emotions
- Maintaining Interest
- Generating Solutions and Reaching Agreement

Educating the Parties

Mediators educate the disputants on various areas. At the opening session, the mediator explains the process and ground rules. She may also discuss the advantages of mediation and alternative forms of dispute resolution. Mediators also educate by exhibiting appropriate behavior such as listening actively, not interrupting, and avoiding name calling.

Organizing the Sessions

The parties' opening statements, the dispute itself, or a combination of both may reveal the issues and the order in which they should be discussed. Sometimes, the mediator may suggest the order. Setting an agenda helps to keep the parties focused. Of course, as the mediation progresses, the agenda may be subject to revision.

Developing and Maintaining Communication

Communication is the glue that holds the mediation together. Through conversation the parties identify issues, clarify misunderstandings, discuss solutions, and reach agreement. The mediator's role is to encourage dialogue. One method often used to do this is active or emphatic listening, which is a style of listening and responding that advances understanding, trust, and respect. It allows the parties to express their feelings, which reduces tension, encourages the disclosure of more information, and creates an environment that promotes collaborative problem solving.

Managing Emotions

Frequently, emotions run high during mediation, and managing these is important. When emotions surface, mediators encourage participants to recognize the other party's feelings. This validation can advance positive feelings and collaboration.

Maintaining Interest

Mediation can sometimes be distasteful for the disputants. After all, what brought the parties to mediation in the first place was conflict, and conflict is often unpleasant. The issues that confront them are difficult and sometimes mediation hits an obstacle. When this happens, the disputants may feel resigned to end the mediation. An effective mediator must encourage the parties to continue with the process. Reviewing areas of agreement, reminding the parties of the progress made, pointing out the gloomy alternatives to settlement and the benefits of ongoing discussions are tactics mediators use to keep the parties motivated.

Generating Solutions and Reaching Agreement

The mediator identifies areas of agreement and encourages the parties to offer suggestions for a solution. When a settlement is reached, the mediator typically puts it in writing.[20]

CAUCUSES

Caucuses play an important part in mediation and deserve special mention. As previously stated, **caucuses** are private meetings with one party and the mediator that take place during mediation. They are useful in a number of ways. If emotions are escalating, caucusing allows venting and a period for cooling off. When one party becomes threatening or intimidating, caucusing separates the parties for a brief period of time. Caucusing encourages parties to be open and discuss the heart of the disagreement. The parties can also review or clarify an issue and learn information that may generate new solutions. Caucusing also provides an opportunity for both sides to evaluate their positions to see whether they are realistic.

MEDIATION FORMS

The type of dispute and the mediator's style determine the mediation approach. The most common forms are "evaluative" (sometimes referred to as "bargain-based"), "facilitative" (sometimes called "therapeutic"), and transformative, a term created by Robert Baruch-Bush and Joseph P. Folger.[21] Evaluative mediation is frequently used in commercial and tort disputes, while facilitative mediation is found in family and divorce conflicts. Transformative mediation is effective for workplace disagreements. It is a method suitable for those who, having a need to continue their association, can examine their differences with an aim toward restoring the relationship.

Some mediators believe that all mediation should be facilitative, pointing out that a hallmark of mediation is self-determination, and evaluation mediation could pressure one party into adopting a specific solution. Other mediators believe that the evaluative approach is appropriate for certain kinds of disputes. Many mediators are now accepting the idea that some evaluation is necessary for mediation to succeed. Let's look more closely at each form: evaluative, facilitative, and transformative.

Evaluative Mediation

Evaluative mediation is the most prevalent style used in court-ordered mediation for civil disputes (commercial, construction, and personal injury lawsuits). Mediators are frequently lawyers with an expertise in the subject matter of the disagreement. They use their experience to explain to the parties the strengths and weaknesses of their case, make predictions about the outcome of a trial, and offer suggestions for settlement. With this knowledge, the parties are better able to assess their positions and determine whether a negotiated settlement is more favorable than litigating the case in court.

In a typical session, the parties meet jointly with the mediator and explain their positions and interests, after which the mediator caucuses with each and searches for areas of agreement that may lead to a compromise. The mediator also looks for information that could help in his assessment of the disagreement. Here is what the mediation may look like:

> Fred Spaulding built a house for Steve Caulder. Before making final payment, Steve hired an inspector to examine the home. The inspector found numerous defects and recommended that they be fixed before Steve made final payment. Fred made some corrections but disputed the need to make others. Steve insisted that the disputed defects be fixed and also felt that the corrections made were not acceptable. He refused to make final payment. Fred hired an attorney and filed suit. Steve also retained an attorney. The court ordered the parties to participate in mediation.
>
> The parties hired Alyssa Madison, a civil litigator with experience in construction cases, to be the mediator. At the first session, the lawyers and the parties presented their view of the disagreement and then met privately with the mediator. During the confidential sessions, Alyssa assessed each party's position and shared her prediction on a likely outcome in the event the case went to trial. She discussed the bottom line for each party and searched for opportunities to compromise such as hiring an independent inspector, agreed to by the parties, or making partial payment with the remainder being used to make any corrections suggested by the independent inspector. After two joint sessions and a meeting with just Alyssa and the attorneys, an agreement was reached.

Facilitative Mediation

The underlying premise in facilitative mediation is that the parties are better able to resolve their dispute than mediators, lawyers, judges, and juries; they just need a neutral third party to guide the negotiation. The facilitative mediator does this by helping the parties to identify the issues and to understand each other's needs and interests, and by assisting them in creating and evaluating a resolution. Emphasis is placed on improving communication by encouraging the parties to be respectful and to express feelings in a nonthreatening way. The ultimate goal is for the disputants to produce their own agreement.

In a typical session, the parties meet jointly with the mediator and explain their positions and interests, after which the mediator caucuses with each and searches for areas of agreement that may lead to a compromise. The mediator also looks for information that could help in his assessment of the disagreement. Here is what the mediation may look like:

> Dan and Bruce were partners in a food business called Provisions. In addition to offering creative sandwiches, the business sold deli meats; cheeses, including a homemade cheese spread; wine; beer; and other food items. Provisions also provided catering services, which was a growing part of the business. The two partners had reached an impasse over whether to concentrate on catering or marketing their cheese spread.
>
> The dispute had reached a point where they were considering ending the partnership when their lawyer suggested mediation and recommended Roberto

Hernandez as the mediator. Roberto met with Dan and Bruce in a half-dozen 90-minute sessions. At the first meeting, Roberto explained the process of mediation and asked each partner to explain his goals and plans for the future of the business. Dan and Bruce explained their desires and expressed hope that the business would continue. During the sessions, Roberto helped the two list the goals they shared and the goals they did not share. The mediation then focused on various ways to meet the goals.

At times, Dan or Bruce became discouraged and wanted to end mediation and the partnership. Roberto reviewed with them the accomplishments they had achieved together, the progress they had made in mediation, and the desire of both to keep the business operating. Eventually, mediation succeeded. The men agreed to hire a person to help with the catering business, which would allow Bruce to concentrate on marketing the cheese spread. They also agreed to return to mediation if further disputes arose.

Transformative Mediation

Transformative mediation focuses on "empowering" each party to make decisions and to gain the ability to recognize each other's perspectives (i.e., needs, interests, values, and points of view). Unlike facilitative mediation where the goal is reaching a resolution, transformative mediation focuses on improving the relationship between the parties, thus enabling them to address any issues that may occur in the future.

Transformative mediation is different from facilitative mediation in that the parties, not the mediator, structure the process and the outcome. The mediator is there to create an environment that lets the parties reach a resolution. Rather than giving her opinion or recommendation, she asks questions designed to validate each party's point of view and uncover common interests. The mediator also assists the parties in finding and analyzing options for settlement.

Here is an example of a transformative mediation:

Brian and Debbie are neighbors. Brian is married and has two small children, ages 4 and 2. Debbie is a single parent with two children, Michael, a freshman in college, and Sarah, a junior in high school. Brian and Debbie would frequently get into arguments in the street about Debbie's kids and their friends playing music loudly at night, driving fast on the street, and, in nice weather, camping out in their yard. Brian was upset because his kids couldn't get to sleep or would be awakened in the middle of the night. Debbie didn't understand why Brian just didn't close the windows or, if it was a hot evening, use an air conditioner. She also didn't like Brian calling the police. Their neighbors, who were sick of the two arguing, convinced Brian and Debbie to meet with a mediator.

Amy Hall, who practices transformative mediation, met with the pair for three, $2\frac{1}{2}$ hour sessions. She helped them to understand and validate each other's viewpoint and to improve their empowerment. Eventually, the parties agreed that after 8:00 p.m. during weekdays and 9:00 p.m. on weekends,

Debbie's kids and their friends would turn the music down and talk quietly. If there were a problem, Brian would call Debbie instead of the police. Debbie, along with other neighbors, would monitor the kid's driving and if any were speeding, Debbie would ask the police to talk with the offender. Both parties agreed to return to mediation if needed.

MEDIATOR QUALIFICATIONS

The use of mediation has received widespread acceptance in courts throughout the United States. As a result, some states have created commissions or committees to advance the use of ADR and set qualifications for mediators (see Exhibit 4-2). For example, the Arkansas Alternative Dispute Resolution Commission promotes the use of ADR and educates courts, government agencies, and the public on the methods, advantages, and applications of ADR. It also establishes standards for the regulation of mediators.[22] In Maine, mediators must meet certain minimum requirements to be included on the court roster of mediators. The Court Alternative Dispute Resolution Service (CADRES) Committee was established to oversee the selection and evaluation of CADRES ADR providers.[23] Although there are no uniform requirements for education, training, and experience for mediators, many states have developed similar criteria.

MEDIATOR SKILLS

A mediator must master a number of skills to be effective in helping parties reach a resolution. Some of these are communicating, listening, restating, reframing, questioning, and controlling emotions.

Communicating is the essence of mediation. Disputes frequently arise because the parties have not effectively communicated or failed to communicate at all. Mediators help the disputants talk with each other. She assists them in identifying issues, creating solutions, and, when necessary, venting emotions.

By *listening* to the parties' discussions, the mediator can help them listen to each other by ensuring that they do not talk at the same time and checking to be sure that the listener understands what has just been said. Sometimes parties may be encouraged to participate more actively knowing that someone is listening to their account of the dispute. For some, this may be the first time somebody has actually listened to them.

The ability to *restate* a message and *reframe* issues are other essential skills a mediator needs. Sometimes things can be stated in such a negative way that the party only hears the emotional aspect and misses the content of the

Exhibit 4-2. MINIMUM REQUIREMENTS FOR MEDIATORS IN ARKANSAS
AND MAINE

ARKANSAS

Requirements for inclusion on the voluntary Roster of Mediators:

Civil Division

Training
1. Have completed a minimum of 40 hours in a mediation training approved by the Commission;
2. Applicants who complete a mediation training course outside of Arkansas must also complete the Commission's course on Arkansas Law for Mediators.

Education
1. Have master's level degree or higher; or
2. Have a bachelor's degree plus a graduate level certificate in conflict resolution or mediation from an accredited college, university, or law school that has been approved by the Commission; or
3. Have a juris doctorate or equivalent; or
4. Have a substantial, demonstrated, and satisfactory knowledge, skills, abilities, and experience as a mediator in the applicable field of mediation.

Practical Experience
1. Have observed, mediated, or co-mediated two mediations involving issues that would be heard in circuit court, other than domestic relations or juvenile matters;
2. Observations and co-mediations must be of a case that is, or would be, filed in the civil division of the Arkansas Circuit Courts. Observations and co-mediations must be completed with a mediator who is certified by the Arkansas ADR Commission.

Ethics
1. Be of good moral character; and
2. Accept and follow the Arkansas Alternative Dispute Resolution Commission's *Requirements for the Conduct of Mediation and Mediators.*

Examination
1. Prior to granting certification, the Commission may require applicants to successfully complete an examination on mediation concepts, ethics, and other topics relevant to mediation in the Arkansas Circuit Court system.

Domestic Relations

Training
1. Have completed a minimum of 40 hours in a family mediation training program approved by the Commission; or
2. Have completed 40 hours of basic mediation training with an additional 20 hours of family mediation training in a program devoted entirely to family or parenting mediation which is approved by the Commission;
3. Applicants who complete a basic or family mediation training course outside of Arkansas must also complete the Commission's course on Arkansas Law for Mediators.

Continued >

Education

1. Have a bachelor's level degree with at least two years work experience in family and marriage issues; or
2. Have a master's degree or higher; or
3. Have a bachelor's degree plus a graduate level certificate in conflict resolution from an accredited college, university, or law school that has been approved by the Commission; or
4. Have a juris doctorate or equivalent; or
5. Have substantial, demonstrated, and satisfactory knowledge, skills, abilities, and experience as a mediator in the applicable field of mediation.

Practical Experience

1. Have observed, mediated, or co-mediated two domestic relations mediations;
2. Observations and co-mediations must be of a case that is, or would be, filed in the domestic relations division of the Arkansas Circuit Courts. Observations and co-mediations must be completed with a mediator who is certified by the Arkansas ADR Commission.

Ethics

1. Be of good moral character; and
2. Accept and follow the Arkansas Alternative Dispute Resolution Commission's *Requirements for the Conduct of Mediation and Mediators.*

Examination

1. Prior to granting certification, the Commission may require applicants to successfully complete an examination on mediation concepts, ethics, and other topics relevant to mediation in the Arkansas Circuit Court system.

MAINE

The Court Alternative Dispute Resolution Service (CADRES) of the Maine Judicial Branch maintains Mediation Rosters. Court referrals must be made from the appropriate roster. (The CADRES Director may waive qualification criteria for a particular applicant.)

Qualifications for General Civil Litigation Roster

Have a combination of 100 hours of training and experience including;

1. a minimum of 40 hours mediation process training (15 hours within 2 yrs of application), involving lectures, role plays and mediation theory;
2. at least 20 hours experience as mediator or co-mediator; and
3. 10 hours of training or experience in general civil law and court procedure; and
4. 15 hours annual continuing education in specified areas.

Qualifications for Domestic Relations Roster

1. a minimum of 40 hours mediation process training (15 hours within 2 yrs of application), involving lectures, role plays and mediation theory;
2. at least 20 hours experience as mediator or co-mediator; and
3. 10 hours of training or experience in the substance of domestic relations law; and
4. at least 8 hours of training relating to domestic abuse issues.
5. 15 hours annual continuing education in specified areas.

Source: Arkansas Judiciary, *Standards for Inclusion on Roster of Certified Mediators,* https://courts.arkansas .gov/sites/default/files/tree/CERTIFICATION%26DISCIPLINE2012_1.pdf (last visited Mar. 19, 2017).

Source: State of Maine Judicial Branch, *Becoming a Mediator or ADR Neutral,* http://www.courts.maine .gov/maine_courts/adr/become_neutral.html (last visited Mar. 19, 2017).

message. This obviously impedes communication. A mediator must recognize when this happens and be able to restate what the person said in a neutral fashion. For example:

Speaker: I just want him to turn his damn stereo off after 9:00 in the evening.

Mediator: It's important for you to have quiet time, especially in the evening?

Speaker: He should bring the children home when he is supposed to because I have things to do.

Mediator: You need to be able to plan your day so you will be home for the children.

Reframing is when a mediator suggests that the parties look at the problem from a different perspective. This may unearth possible solutions that had not previously surfaced. For example, in a dispute over child visitation, instead of the parties talking about when they want to have the child, they focus on what's best for the child. This new perspective could lead to different ideas for resolving the visitation issue.

Questioning is the way a mediator gathers information from the parties. It can also refocus the dialogue and assist the parties in reality testing. Sometimes a party's proposal is unrealistic. By posing questions, a party may realize that the proposal is not workable. Suggesting that the neighbor just get rid of her barking dog is not realistic. Through questioning, the mediator might be able to get the party to realize that the idea is not reasonable, and this could lead to the generation of other alternatives.

Not infrequently, mediation sessions get emotional. Emotions likely fueled the dispute and may have caused the negotiation process to break down. Skilled mediators must *control the emotions* of the parties and not let them impede the discussion. At the same time, the emotions should not be suppressed or dampened because this may cause resentment and a breakdown of the process. One effective method for dealing with emotional outbursts is allowing the party to vent his feelings. Once a party feels heard, he is more likely to move on to the substantive issue or issues and work toward an agreement.

ETHICAL ISSUES IN MEDIATION

Standards of Conduct for Mediators

The success of mediation depends in large part on the trust the public has in the process. Ethical standards of conduct are designed to promote public confidence and to serve as a guide for mediators. Accordingly, many organizations and courts have developed standards of practice. The American Arbitration Association, American Bar Association, and the Association for Conflict Resolution collaborated to develop the Model Standards of Conduct for Mediators. These standards were adopted by all three organizations in 2005.

Remember that a mediator's role is to assist the parties in reaching a voluntary agreement resolving their dispute. The following are some of the ethical principles required of mediators:

1. **Self-determination.** The authority for resolving a dispute rests with the parties. A mediator's purpose is to assist them in the process by facilitating communication, aiding in identifying issues and solutions, and reaching an agreement. The ultimate control is always with the disputants, and the mediator must respect this important principle.

2. **Impartiality.** A mediator must always remain neutral and manage the process in an even-handed manner. If at some point a mediator cannot remain impartial, she must withdraw.

3. **Competency.** A mediator should be qualified to mediate. This includes being knowledgeable about the process and the subject matter. She must be able to lead and guide the discussions and manage any problems that may arise.

4. **Conflict of interest**. Any connection with the subject matter of the dispute or relationship with a party that might create an appearance of possible bias must be made known by the mediator. After disclosure, the mediator cannot continue serving without the consent of the parties. Examples of conflicts of interest are a mediator and party who both serve on the same board of directors for a nonprofit organization; a mediator who has a business relationship with one of the parties; a lawyer-mediator who has represented one of the disputants. In some situations, even with consent of the parties, a mediator should decline to participate because the nature of the conflict has the appearance of affecting the mediator's impartiality.

5. **Confidentiality.** A mediator shall not disclose anything learned during a private session either to the other party or any third party (including a court) without permission, unless required by law. Information about child abuse or a plan to commit a crime are examples of disclosures required by law.

6. **Advertising.** A mediator's advertising shall not be misleading or deceptive. Mediators shall not make promises or guarantee results.

7. **Fees.** Before mediation begins, the mediator must inform the parties about all fees, costs, and charges for her services. The fee arrangement should be in writing. A mediator may not charge a fee contingent upon the results.

MED-ARB (MEDIATION-ARBITRATION)

Mixed or hybrid processes are sometimes used to resolve disputes.[24] **Med-arb** is a combination of mediation and arbitration. In this process, the third-party neutral tries to mediate the party's dispute. If mediation fails, the neutral acts as the arbitrator and issues a binding decision. Chapters 5 and 6 provide detailed treatment of arbitration.

Conclusion

Mediation is negotiation with the assistance of a neutral third party, called a mediator. The disputants retain full control of the process while the mediator works to facilitate communication, manage emotions, and encourage solutions. Mediation is confidential, and rules have been enacted to preserve this essential characteristic. Because mediation is used in the courts, workplaces, schools, and neighborhoods, states and professional organizations have set certain minimum qualifications for mediators that include education and practical experience.

Key Terms and Concepts

Advantages/disadvantages of
  mediation
Caucuses
Evaluative mediation
Facilitative mediation

Interest-based mediation
Med-arb
Mediation
Rights-based mediation
Transformative mediation

Practice Test Questions

True/False

_____ 1. Some desirable mediator skills are communicating, listening, restating, reframing, questioning, and controlling emotions.

_____ 2. The Pound Conference is recognized as the start of the modern mediation movement.

_____ 3. Self-determination is the core principle of mediation.

_____ 4. A mediator must be impartial, competent, avoid the appearance of any conflict of interest, and preserve confidentiality.

_____ 5. Caucuses are private meetings with the attorney and mediator.

Multiple Choice

_____ 1. "I can't trust him. Every time he makes a promise to me, he breaks it."

"You are worried that because prior agreements haven't gone well this agreement might also fail."

The above is an example of

a. questioning.

b. organizing.

c. maintaining interest.

d. reframing.

____ 2. The most prevalent style of mediation used in court-ordered mediation for civil disputes is
    a. transformative.
    b. evaluative.
    c. facilitative.
    d. therapeutic.

____ 3. Which of the following is *not* a role of the mediator?
    a. Maintaining interest
    b. Offering solutions
    c. Educating the parties
    d. Managing emotions

____ 4. All of the following are advantages of mediation *except*
    a. does not create legal precedent.
    b. privacy.
    c. empowers the parties.
    d. builds trust.

____ 5. Mediation improves on negotiation by
    a. permitting the parties to attend along with their attorneys.
    b. requiring the parties to offer solutions.
    c. bringing the parties to a neutral zone.
    d. introducing a neutral third party.

Review Questions

1. What is the difference between negotiation and mediation?
2. Explain the focus of rights-based and interest-based mediation.
3. Explain the concept of self-determination.
4. What are the stages of mediation? Briefly provide an explanation of each.
5. What are the differences between evaluative, facilitative, and transformative mediation?
6. Why are there standards of conduct for mediators? List and explain each standard of conduct.
7. List the advantages of mediation and explain each.
8. List the disadvantages of mediation and explain each.
9. Why is confidentiality and mediator impartiality so important to mediation?
10. Explain the role a mediator plays in mediation.
11. What qualifications are necessary to become a mediator?
12. What skills are needed to be a mediator?

Application Questions

1. You are a paralegal and work in the litigation department of a law firm. Over the past 20 years you have assisted attorneys in hundreds of tort cases. Recently, you signed up with the local court to mediate civil actions.

A judge has assigned a case for you to mediate. The dispute involves a man whose car was rear-ended while stopped at a red light. The other driver said she was distracted by her infant son's crying in the back seat. In addition to the damaged car, the man injured his neck and head. Both sides have elected to use mediation and want you to tell them what would be the likely result if the case went to trial. Are there any problems with you participating as an evaluative mediator?

2. Brenda and Mike get into a minor fender bender while in the drive-through lane at a fast-food restaurant. Brenda claims Mike backed into her while Mike claims Brenda hit his car. Brenda sued him in small claims court, and Mike countersued. The judge sends them to mediation. At the first session, Brenda and Mike tell their stories. Mike shows the mediator and Brenda some papers including an estimate for repairs. Included with the documents is a letter from Mike's insurance company offering to pay for the damage, but in an amount much less than the repair estimate. Mediation is unsuccessful, and the judge assigns a date for trial. Can Brenda testify about the repair estimate? Can Mike? Is the insurance letter admissible at trial? Provide support for your answers.

3. In mediation, disputants have an opportunity to tell their side of the story in a nonadversarial setting. Their opinions are valued, and they are treated respectfully. Some believe that this contributes to each party accepting the outcome even if it is less favorable to one of them. How is this different from litigation? What skills must a mediator employ to ensure that the parties feel that they were heard, and treated fairly and respectfully?

4. Plaintiffs, 50 homeowners whose wells were polluted with fuel that leaked from a nearby storage tank owned by the defendant, have subpoenaed the mediator to appear as a witness at a hearing on plaintiffs' motion to enforce a settlement that they claim was reached at the end of mediation. Plaintiffs contend that the mediation resulted in a binding settlement agreement and want to call the mediator to ask whether a document drafted at the end of mediation contains all of the terms agreed to by the parties. Assume that the defendant objects on the ground that mediation is confidential and, therefore, the mediator is prohibited from testifying. Do you agree or disagree? Why? Cite any sources that support your position. What if both parties agree that the mediator can testify, but the mediator refuses, asserting that he cannot reveal anything that took place during mediation because disclosure would violate his ethical responsibilities? Do you agree or disagree? Cite sources to support your position. Should parties be allowed to waive confidentiality? What does such a waiver do to the confidentiality protection of mediation?

5. The facilitative mediator helps the disputants make their own decisions. He acts as a neutral and assists the parties in communicating with each other, focuses them on their interests, and promotes creative problem solving and creative solutions. The evaluative mediator, on the other hand, takes a more

active role. He listens to each side, determines the facts, weighs credibility, applies relevant law or rules, and gives his opinion.

Which style do you prefer and why? Do you think that the choice of facilitation or evaluation depends on the subject matter of the dispute, the preference of the mediator, or both? Provide one example of a dispute where you think facilitation is better and explain why. Provide one example where you think evaluation is more appropriate and explain why.

If a basic tenant of mediation is neutrality, does the evaluation approach undermine this principle? Why? Why not?

6. Eric Miller and David Porter were close friends. Miller is married to Emily, Porter's sister. As a result of growing problems between Miller and Emily's family, the friendship between Miller and Porter ended. At some point, friends told Porter that Miller was spreading rumors about him. Porter left threatening and vulgar messages on Miller's voicemail. Miller heard the messages and drove to Porter's house to confront him. He banged on the door and a window, waking Porter, his wife Maggie, and Maggie's brother Carl. Porter went outside, and he and Miller began arguing. According to Porter, Miller walked to his car parked out front, opened the trunk, and pulled out a sword. Miller swung the sword at Porter and cut Miller's right arm. The two continued to fight and fell onto some broken glass on the ground. When Maggie yelled that she called the police, Miller got into his car and drove away. After police arrived, they talked with Porter and Maggie. They also found a scabbard (protective cover for a sword) on the ground where the two were fighting. Police went to Miller's apartment where he was arrested. Police found a sword under Miller's bed. Police charged him with felony assault and possession of a dangerous weapon.

Miller filed a protection from harassment complaint against Porter alleging that Porter was harassing him by leaving phone messages. Pursuant to court rules, the parties were required to attend mediation, which was unsuccessful. The mediator, Richard Harris, referred the matter back to court.

At trial, Miller sought court permission to call the mediator as a witness to bolster his claim of self-defense. Out of the presence of the jury, the mediator said that the mediation was chaotic, with both Miller and Porter talking at the same time. The mediator told the judge that at one point it sounded like Porter said he picked up a baseball bat but didn't hit anyone. He also said he didn't recall hearing anything about a sword.

The state in which this happened has adopted the Uniform Mediation Act. Pursuant to the UMA, can a mediator testify in a criminal trial about statements made during mediation? Why or why not? Your answer should include reference to the appropriate section or sections of the UMA.

The Sixth Amendment to the U.S. Constitution entitles a defendant to call and cross-examine witnesses. The UMA protects the confidentiality of mediation unless the defendant can show the following:

1. The mediation communication is needed in a criminal trial; and
2. The need for the mediator's testimony is greater than the interest in protecting confidentiality; and
3. The evidence is not available except through the mediator's testimony.

   Should the court allow the mediator to testify in Miller's criminal trial? Why or why not?

Practice Exercises

1. Does your state offer court-annexed mediation? In which types of courts is it used? Is it mandatory in these courts? Do these courts have a list of approved mediators?

   Who selects the mediator?
2. Find five mediators in your area and provide the following information:
   a. Name
   b. Background
   c. Experience
   d. Cost
   e. Types of conflicts mediated
3. Are there any educational or training requirements for mediators in your state? What are they?
4. Do the courts in your jurisdiction have a list of approved mediators? What are the requirements for mediators to be listed?
5. Assume you are a mediator. Prepare an opening statement and then present it to the class.
6. On the Internet, find a video of a mediation and watch it. When finished, prepare a written paper in which you provide the following:
   a. A description of the conflict.
   b. An explanation of the skills used by the mediator.
   c. A description of the result of the mediation.
7. This exercise provides you with an opportunity to be a mediator. "The Angry Neighbours" is an interactive animation about a dispute between two neighbors and can be found at http://www.sfhgroup.com/global_docs/the-angry-nieghbours.htm. The video allows you to stop it at any point and interject yourself into the dispute. Directions are provided. When you finish, prepare a paper explaining what you learned.

Endnotes

1. Douglas Noll, *Peacemaking: Practicing at the Intersection of Law and Human Conflict* 80 (Cascadia 2003).
2. A neutral third party means that the person "should be free from bias." Kimberlee K. Kovach, *Mediation*, in *The Handbook of Dispute Resolution* 311-312 (Michael L. Moffitt & Robert C. Bordone eds., Jossey-Bass 2005).
3. 1 Jay E. Grenig, *Alternative Dispute Resolution* 27 (3d ed., Thomson/West 2005).
4. Joyce W. Chang, *Non-adversarial Representation: Rule 2.2 and Divorce Mediation*, in *A Study of Barriers to the Use of Alternative Methods of Dispute Resolution* 112 (Vermont Law School 1984).

5. John Feerick et al., *Standards of Professional Conduct in Alternative Dispute Resolution*, 1995 J. Disp. Resol. 95, 123.

6. Patricia A. Garcia, *Road Maps, Alternative Dispute Resolution: Alternatives to Litigation* 10 (ABA 2000).

7. Jerold S. Auerback, *Justice Without Law?* 20 (Oxford University Press 1983).

8. 29 U.S.C. § 173(a) (2012).

9. The Pound Conference was named for Roscoe Pound, reforming dean of Harvard Law School from 1916 to 1936.

10. *See The Multi-Door Experience, Dispute Resolution and the Courthouse of the Future* (Larry Ray & Prue Kestner eds., ABA 1988).

11. Foxgate Homeowners' Ass'n, Inc. v. Bramalea Cal., Inc., 25 P.3d 1117, 1121 (Cal. 2001).

12. *Id.* at 1122.

13. *Id.*

14. *Id.* at 1123.

15. *Id.* at 1126.

16. *Id.*

17. *Id.* at 1128 n.13.

18. Lon L. Fuller, *Mediation—Its Forms and Functions*, 44 S. Cal. L. Rev. 305, 325 (1971).

19. Grenig, *supra* note 3, at 93.

20. For a good discussion on creative problem solving, see 2 John W. Cooley, *Generic Strategies for Creative Problem Solving, in The Creative Problem Solver's Handbook for Negotiators and Mediators: A Pracademic Approach* (ABA Sec. of Disp. Res. 2005).

21. Robert A. Baruch Bush & Joseph P. Folger, *The Promise of Mediation: Responding to Conflict Through Empowerment and Recognition* (Jossey-Bass 1994).

22. Ark. Code Ann. § 16-7-101 (repl. 2005).

23. 4 M.R.S.A. § 18-(6) (2016); Me. R. Civ. P. 16B.

24. Barry C. Bartel, *Med-Arb as a Distinct Method of Dispute Resolution: History, Analysis, and Potential*, 27 Willamette L. Rev. 661 (1991).

CHAPTER FIVE

Arbitration: An Overview

Chapter Outline

Introduction
A Brief History of Arbitration
  Biblical Times
  Greeks and Romans
  Middle Ages
  The United States
Arbitration vs. Litigation
Advantages of Arbitration over
  Litigation
  Speed and Cost
  Privacy
  No Precedent
  Finality
  Informal Atmosphere
  Flexibility
  The Parties Choose the Decision
    Maker

Preservation of Relationship
Disadvantages of Arbitration over
  Litigation
  No Due Process
  No Appeal/Finality
  No Discovery
  Absence of Record and Reasoned
    Opinions
  Too Much Like Litigation
  May Not Be Fast or Inexpensive
  Arbitrator Bias
Conclusion
Key Terms and Concepts
Practice Test Questions
Review Questions
Application Questions
Practice Exercises

> The arbitrator sees equity, the juror the law; indeed that is why an
> arbitrator is found — that equity might prevail.
>
> — ARISTOTLE

INTRODUCTION

Arbitration is "intended to avoid the formalities, the delay, the expense, and vexation of ordinary litigation."[1] It is a dispute resolution process in which the parties present evidence and argument, to one or more third-party neutrals, who then issue a judgment, or **award**. Unlike negotiation or mediation where the parties resolve the outcome, in arbitration, a neutral party called an **arbitrator** decides the dispute. Thus, arbitration is similar to litigation but less formal, and, by agreement, the parties select the arbitrator or "judge," and the procedural and evidentiary rules. Commonly, an agreement to arbitrate includes a provision making the award mutually binding, called "binding arbitration," and enforceable in a court of law. As explained a little later, overturning an award is very difficult.

The use of arbitration has grown as court dockets have become more crowded. Traditionally, arbitration was used to settle labor, employment, and commercial disputes. Businesses favored arbitration because of its speed, lower cost, and privacy. Today, arbitration clauses are ubiquitous and can be found in many consumer transactions such as credit card agreements, online transactions, and consumer purchases and service agreements. If a dispute arises, these arbitration clauses subject the consumer to mandatory arbitration, where frequently the rules and procedures are one-sided in favor of the business. Although courts have become receptive to consumer claims that binding arbitration clauses should not be enforced, the U.S. Supreme Court continues to favor arbitration agreements, even when they appear to be unconscionable.

Disputes that have been subject to arbitration are numerous and as varied, as the following examples illustrate:

- A dispute involving the construction of a Major League Baseball stadium
- A challenge by a runner banned from competing in the Olympics because of his carbon fiber prosthetic limbs
- A claim for employment discrimination against an employer
- A controversy between a customer and the bank that issued a credit card
- A dispute over a trademark infringement
- A claim of fraud by an investor against a securities broker
- A boundary line dispute between Egypt and Israel
- A dispute between a speedskater and U.S. Speedskating, the governing body for the sport of speedskating in the United States

The chapter begins with a brief history of arbitration, followed by a comparison of arbitration and litigation. Finally, we look at the advantages and disadvantages of arbitration over litigation.

A BRIEF HISTORY OF ARBITRATION

Arbitration has an ancient history reaching back to biblical times and continuing through the centuries. The Greeks and Romans used arbitration and spread it throughout Europe up to the Middle Ages, where it was employed by traveling merchants and English guilds to resolve disputes quickly. The early English settlers brought arbitration to the "new land," what became the United States.

Biblical Times

The oldest known use of arbitration is found in the Bible, chapter 18 of the book of Exodus. During the 40 years when the Israelites roamed the wilderness,

their population grew into the millions. Along with their travels came the inevitable increase in disputes and the resulting burden on Moses to resolve them.
Recognizing the stress on Moses, his father-in-law Jethro suggested that Moses
select some trustworthy and able men to act as arbitrators to decide the smaller or
routine cases. Moses was then able to devote his time to resolving the more serious matters.

> Moses' father-in-law said to him, "What you are doing is not good. You will surely
> wear yourself out, both you and these people with you. For the task is too heavy
> for you; you cannot do it alone. Now listen to me. I will give you counsel, and God
> be with you! You should represent the people before God, and you should bring
> their cases before God; teach them the statutes and instructions and make
> known to them the way they are to go and the things they are to do. You should
> also look for able men among all the people, men who fear God, are trustworthy,
> and hate dishonest gain; set such men over them as officers over thousands,
> hundreds, fifties, and tens. Let them sit as judges for the people at all times; let
> them bring every important case to you, but decide every minor case themselves.
> So it will be easier for you, and they will bear the burden with you. If you do this,
> and God so commands you, then you will be able to endure, and all these people
> will go to their home in peace."[2]

Greeks and Romans

Both the ancient Greeks and Romans practiced arbitration. The Greeks had
public and private arbiters:

> The private arbiter seems to resemble more closely, in character and functions,
> the arbiter of later times. He was selected by the parties themselves; his powers
> in each case were limited by the contract of the parties and he took an oath to
> decide the case in question impartially. At the same time the parties bound
> themselves to abide by the award and could make no appeal to any court of law.[3]

The use of arbitration appears in the laws of the Twelve Tables, the earliest
legislation enacted by the Romans in the fifth century BCE, and in the Pandects,
the code of Roman law compiled by Justinian I in the sixth century CE.[4]

> Whether one obtained a *iudex* [a judge] in some cases, an *arbiter* with his
> wider discretion in others, or whether an appointee had functions both of judging
> and of assessing is unknown and greatly disputed. The process may well,
> however, mark the first introduction of arbitration as distinct from strict judging
> in Roman law.[5]

Middle Ages

Arbitration in medieval England was the preferred method for resolving disputes among guild merchants.[6] By royal charter, men of various towns were
granted broad rights and privileges to sell and trade their wares. These chartered

guilds helped to protect and regulate trade and arbitrate disputes between members. "[W]e may notice the institution known as the Guild Merchant, which seemingly was an association for the purpose, amongst others, of mutual arbitration. Members of the same guild were bound to bring their disputes before the gild before litigating the matter elsewhere."[7]

Until the late nineteenth century, arbitration was a private matter in England "for which there was no authority except the personal authority of the parties to the agreement, and for the enforcement of whose awards there was no machinery except the regular actions of the common law which every subject had for the settlement of his private affairs."[8] Although suit could be brought for breaching an agreement to arbitrate, the only remedy offered by the court was damages that would be difficult to prove. The courts refused to force a party to submit to arbitration because at common law, an agreement for "submission to arbitration was revocable. . . . The courts in fact held that they would give only nominal damages on the theory that there could be no actual injury in forcing people to litigate in the King's own courts of justice."[9] The courts believed that arbitration agreements were against public policy because they ousted the courts of jurisdiction. The origins of this hostility toward arbitration are unknown, but one scholar suggests that it may have stemmed from the dependence of judges on their income derived from hearing cases and/or the courts effort to establish their legitimacy.[10]

In 1698, Parliament responded to the common law judges' repugnance to arbitration by passing the first arbitration act, which made arbitration agreements irrevocable, and gave the courts authority to enforce these agreements through the courts' contempt powers. However, these agreements could still be revoked before the issuance of an award. Recognizing this, Parliament continued to pass legislation that reinforced the 1698 statute until passage of the Arbitration Act of 1889, which made all agreements to arbitrate irrevocable.

The United States

When the Pilgrims landed at Plymouth Rock, they carried with them many of their traditions and institutions. Two of these were English common law and arbitration. As their descendants spread out and started new communities, arbitration came with them. Many of these colonies had laws and statutes that allowed arbitration for specific causes. For example, in Pennsylvania, a law dated April 2, 1664, in the Duke of Yorke's Books of Laws, permitted arbitration for debt and trespass actions. And both the Massachusetts Colony, in 1646, and South Carolina, in 1694, had laws permitting arbitration for trespass disputes.

Probably the earliest law on commercial arbitration in the colonies was passed by the Town of New Amsterdam in 1647. The ordinance declared:

> Whereas in consequence of the increase of the Inhabitants, Lawsuits and disputes which parties bring against each other, are multiplied, and also divers questions and quarrels of trifling moment, which can be determined and disposed of by Arbitrators, but, in consequence of matters of greater importance, frequently

Exhibit 5-1. GEORGE WASHINGTONS WILL

George Washington recognized the value of arbitration and wrote the following in his will:

> But having endeavoured to be plain, and explicit in all Devises — even at the expence of prolixity, perhaps of tautology, I hope, and trust, that no disputes will arise concerning them; but if, contrary to expectation, the case should be otherwise from the want of legal expression, or the usual technical terms, or because too much or too little has been said on any of the Devises to be consonant with law, My Will and direction expressly is, that all disputes (if unhappily any should arise) shall be decided by three impartial and intelligent men, known for their probity and good understanding; two to be chosen by the disputants — each having the choice of one — and the third by those two. Which three men thus chosen, shall, unfettered by Law, or legal constructions, declare their sense of the Testators intention; and such decision is, to all intents and purposes to be as binding on the Parties as if it had been given in the Supreme Court of the United States.

remain over and undecided, to the prejudice and injury of this place and the good people thereof, and also to the great expence, loss of time and vexation of the contending parties . . . , three out of those chosen as arbitrators are required to attend "once a week, on Thursday, the usual Burgher Court Day to our General Council," and further provided that "parties referred, being judged shall remain bound to submit without opposition to the pronounced decision."[11]

Despite the extensive use of arbitration in the colonies (see Exhibit 5-1 for one well-known example), the common law remained opposed to agreements to arbitrate future disputes. Judges ruled that these agreements were not enforceable because they interfered with the courts' jurisdiction over these disputes.

The English **ouster of jurisdiction** concept was followed by the courts in this country during the nineteenth century: Courts would not grant specific performance or a stay of court proceedings for executory agreements. An **executory arbitration agreement** means that the parties have agreed to arbitrate any dispute that may arise in the future. In 1874, the U.S. Supreme Court held that "agreements in advance to oust the courts of the jurisdiction conferred by law are illegal and void."[12]

American courts were also concerned about the protection of the parties' rights to a fair and equitable hearing.

Now we all know, that arbitrators, at the common law, possess no authority whatsoever, even to administer an oath, or to compel the attendance of witnesses. They cannot compel the production of documents, and papers and books of account, or insist upon a discovery of facts from the parties under oath. They are not ordinarily well enough acquainted with the principles of law or equity, to administer either effectually, in complicated cases; and hence it has often been said, that the judgment of arbitrators is but rusticum judicium [rough justice]. Ought then a court of equity to compel a resort to such a tribunal, by which, however honest and intelligent, it can in no case be clear that the real legal or equitable rights of the parties can be fully ascertained or perfectly protected?[13]

In the early 1900s, although judges' bias against enforcement of arbitration agreements began to change, they were reluctant to move toward supporting arbitration because of the need to follow precedent.

> [T]he final question for determination under these motions is whether the law as laid down by the Supreme Court of the United States permits the enforcement as a remedy of the arbitration clause contained in a contract, assuming that such clause (as here) is intended to oust the court and all courts of their jurisdiction.
>
> I think the decisions cited show beyond question that the Supreme Court has laid down the rule that such a complete ouster of jurisdiction as is shown by the clause quoted from the charter parties is void in a federal forum. It was within the power of that tribunal to make this rule. Inferior courts may fail to find convincing reasons for it; but the rule must be obeyed, and these motions be severally denied.[14]

During the latter part of the 1800s and early 1900s, commercial entities viewed courts as "the most indirect, inexact, inefficient, uneconomical and unintegrated instrumentality in the modern state. . . ."[15] Businessmen were willing to "settle for fifty per cent of the amount in dispute, rather than be subjected to a lawsuit, even in a court which has been considered peculiarly the business man's court in the metropolis."[16] Businessmen began to see arbitration as a sensible answer to the expense and delay of litigation. Recognizing that the courts would not enforce agreements to arbitrate future disputes, the business community, joined by lawyers, turned to the states and federal government for legislation that would require these agreements' enforcement. The first attempt resulted in the passage of the New York Arbitration Act (1920), which provided that agreements to arbitrate future controversies were irrevocable and enforceable.

With the passage of New York's arbitration law, reformers turned their attention to the federal courts. After heavy lobbying, the American Bar Association (ABA) drafted an arbitration bill, which was modeled after New York's statute. In 1925, Congress enacted the United States Arbitration Act, later renamed the Federal Arbitration Act. In 1955, after considerable effort, the National Conference of Commissioners on State Laws propounded the Uniform Arbitration Act, which served as a model for many state statutes.

ARBITRATION VS. LITIGATION

Arbitration is an adversarial adjudicatory process, similar to litigation except that it is **private adjudication** while litigation is **government adjudication** (see

Exhibit 5.2. COMPARISON OF TYPICAL FEATURES OF ARBITRATION
AND LITIGATION

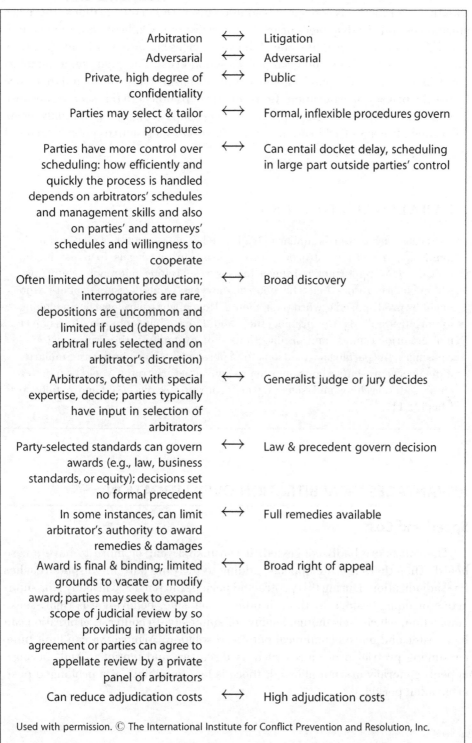

Arbitration	⟷	Litigation
Adversarial	⟷	Adversarial
Private, high degree of confidentiality	⟷	Public
Parties may select & tailor procedures	⟷	Formal, inflexible procedures govern
Parties have more control over scheduling: how efficiently and quickly the process is handled depends on arbitrators' schedules and management skills and also on parties' and attorneys' schedules and willingness to cooperate	⟷	Can entail docket delay, scheduling in large part outside parties' control
Often limited document production; interrogatories are rare, depositions are uncommon and limited if used (depends on arbitral rules selected and on arbitrator's discretion)	⟷	Broad discovery
Arbitrators, often with special expertise, decide; parties typically have input in selection of arbitrators	⟷	Generalist judge or jury decides
Party-selected standards can govern awards (e.g., law, business standards, or equity); decisions set no formal precedent	⟷	Law & precedent govern decision
In some instances, can limit arbitrator's authority to award remedies & damages	⟷	Full remedies available
Award is final & binding; limited grounds to vacate or modify award; parties may seek to expand scope of judicial review by so providing in arbitration agreement or parties can agree to appellate review by a private panel of arbitrators	⟷	Broad right of appeal
Can reduce adjudication costs	⟷	High adjudication costs

Exhibit 5-2). The nonparty decision maker in arbitration is one or more arbitrators. In litigation, the court (a judge and sometimes a jury) makes the decision. As with the other methods of dispute resolution discussed in this textbook, there are advantages and disadvantages of arbitrating a dispute. While reading this section, you will probably notice that some of the advantages are also disadvantages. How they are viewed depends on each party's self-interest. For example, a manufacturer does not want the public to know about its hazardous product and therefore favors the privacy of arbitration. Consumer groups object to this secrecy because it shields the public from learning about and perhaps avoiding a potentially harmful product. Privacy of arbitration can also thwart any legislative action in terms of regulation.

PARALEGAL POINTERS

Because arbitration is similar to traditional litigation and thus more complex than, say, mediation, attorneys rely heavily on paralegals to assist in the process. One important paralegal task is researching potential arbitrators. Although arbitrators must be neutral, lawyers want decision makers who might be predisposed toward their clients. How might a paralegal begin looking for arbitrators? By researching the candidate's philosophy on the subject matter, prior rulings, and predilections. For example, if the firm represents a business, the paralegal would look for a person who is pro-business. Similarly, if the firm represents a consumer, a pro-consumer arbitrator would be a better choice. Researching and selecting an arbitrator is discussed more fully in Chapter 11.

ADVANTAGES OF ARBITRATION OVER LITIGATION

Speed and Cost

The courts are badly congested. It can take a year or more to have a case heard. Then there are the appeals, adding to the time until the dispute reaches final adjudication. During this protracted period, the parties will likely stop interacting or doing business with each other. Each side, believing it is right, seeks vindication, which fuels mutual feelings of animosity. In contrast, arbitration can be a faster and more economical path to resolution. Arbitration can limit time-consuming pretrial procedures such as discovery and motions. And, because appeals generally are not allowed, there is less possibility of a prolonged post-arbitration period.

Privacy

Arbitration is a private process not open to the public. Its confidential nature is probably the most important advantage over litigation. Many companies and well-known individuals use arbitration to avoid the media spotlight that could cast them in a bad light. Additionally, parties do not want the disclosure of proprietary information, business records, or documents.

No Precedent

The privacy of the proceedings also means that awards are not made public and, with the exception of certain areas such as labor and domain name disputes, there are no written decisions. Therefore, awards do not create **precedent** that could affect other pending or future disputes.

Finality

The "essence" of arbitration is **finality**. When the arbitrator issues an award, the dispute is over. Parties choosing arbitration want finality. They desire to resolve their dispute quickly, avoid protracted litigation, and eliminate numerous **appeals**. "The theory of arbitral finality posits that the signatories to an arbitration contract seek a result that is informal, prompt and fair and one not associated with the delays or formalities of appellate justice; the parties have a preference for a final decision instead of an appellate court's second-guess."[17]

Finality can be advantageous for consumers with limited resources. For example, consumers who purchase low-cost items on the Internet want a resolution but do not have the financial ability to bring a lawsuit and perhaps an appeal. The following case illustrates the importance of finality, even when the parties agreed that an arbitration award could be set aside.

***Saika v. Gold*, 49 Cal. App. 4th 1074 (1996):** Plaintiff Carol Lynn Saika sued Dr. Robert Gold claiming she was severely burned as a result of a face peel he performed. After answering the complaint, Gold filed a motion to compel arbitration claiming Saika had executed an arbitration agreement. The court granted his request. Arbitration resulted in an award of $325,000 in favor of Saika. Following this, Gold filed a request for a trial de novo pursuant to the arbitration agreement. Saika filed a motion to strike Gold's request and a petition to confirm the award. The trial court granted Gold's request and denied Saika's motion to strike and her petition to confirm.

The trial de novo clause read as follows:

> In the event that an arbitration award made pursuant to the terms of this agreement is equal to or greater than Twenty Five Thousand Dollars ($25,000.00), either the Doctor or myself [sic] may request a "trial de novo," which means new trial, by filing a civil action with sixty (60) days from the date of the arbitration award in a court of law having jurisdiction. Upon the filing of a

civil action, the arbitration award that was made under the terms of the Patient-Physician Arbitration Agreement will be null and void and may not be used for any purpose thereafter. An award which is equal to or greater than Twenty Five Thousand Dollars ($25,000.00) shall become binding sixty (60) days after such award is made, provided neither party has filed suit as provided herein, within sixty (60) days. Neither party to this agreement shall move to have such an arbitration award confirmed by a court of law until the sixty (60) day time period has elapsed.[18]

The appeals court overturned the trial court finding that "the trial de novo clause here contravenes the strong public policy in favor of arbitration. . . ."[19] Citing a litany of cases, the court pointed out that "[a]rbitration has become highly favored as an economical, efficient alternative to traditional litigation in law courts."[20] Arbitration is also desired when the parties seek finality.

> By choosing arbitration, parties avoid the palaver of procedural challenges that lend, at least for a time, uncertainty to any judgment rendered in the courts. With only very narrow exceptions, an arbitrator's decision cannot be reviewed for error of fact or law; the parties do not get to appeal an adverse decision. "Conclusiveness is expected; the essence of the arbitration process is that an arbitral award shall put the dispute to rest." . . .
>
> [T]he practical effect of the [trial de novo] clause is to tilt the playing field in favor of the doctor. By making arbitration virtually illusory as far as one side is concerned, the clause contravenes the strong public policy favoring arbitrations. Accordingly, we conclude the trial de novo clause is not enforceable in equity. It was error for the trial court to deny the patient's petition to confirm the arbitration award in this case.[21]

Questions:
1. On what grounds did Gold file a request for a trial de novo?
2. Explain the trial de novo clause in the arbitration agreement between Saika and Gold.
3. What were the court's reasons for setting aside the trial de novo clause?

Informal Atmosphere

Because arbitration is a contract between the parties, they design the process, which may be informal or have characteristics of litigation. Parties opting for informality can avoid protracted discovery and pretrial motions. They can elect to have a hearing or submit evidence in writing. Hearings can be scheduled at convenient times at agreed-to places. Frequently, arbitration occurs in an attorney's conference room or other meeting space, not a courtroom. The atmosphere is less formal and intimidating and may help to maintain business relationships between the parties.

Flexibility

By agreeing to arbitrate, the parties have chosen to opt out of the legal system and its substantive rules. Not surprisingly, then, courts have permitted arbitrators to hear any evidence presented by the parties. Arbitrators do not have to follow the formal rules of evidence or procedure, and they alone decide on the admissibility and relevance of the evidence.

In *Commercial Arbitration at Its Best, Successful Strategies for Business Users*, the CPR Commission on the Future of Arbitration noted that "many business users regard control over the process — the flexibility to make arbitration what you want it to be — as the single most important advantage of binding arbitration. . . ." [22] Arbitrators have substantial flexibility in deciding remedies. Unconstrained by the law, they often apply principles of equity. "He may do justice as he sees it, applying his own sense of law and equity to the facts as he finds them to be and making an award reflecting the spirit rather than the letter of the agreement, even though the award exceeds the remedy requested by the parties." [23] Thus, an arbitrator can create a remedy that meets the parties' needs.

The Parties Choose the Decision Maker

"Selecting an arbitrator is the most critical step in arbitration." [24] Unlike litigation, where a judge is assigned to preside over the trial, in arbitration the parties can select the decision maker. Thus, the parties are more likely to follow the arbitrator's decision and lessen the chance of an appeal.

The parties may choose a person who is well informed about the practices, customs, and vocabulary of their particular business. A knowledgeable arbitrator is better able to identify key issues and focus the hearing on those issues, thus saving time and money. Relying on their own experience, arbitrators can create an equitable resolution in lieu of a strict interpretation of the law that could result in an unjust award. "It is often said that the parties do not expect the arbitrators to make their decision according to rules but rather, especially when the arbitrators are not lawyers, on the basis of their experience, knowledge of the customs of the trade, and fair and good sense for equitable relief." [25] One of our country's most respected jurists, Justice Learned Hand, said this about arbitrators:

> If they were of the trade, they were justified in resorting to their personal acquaintance with its prices. In trade disputes one of the chief advantages of arbitration is that arbitrators can be chosen who are familiar with the practices and customs of the calling, and with just such matters as what are current prices, what is merchantable quality, what are the terms of sale, and the like. [26]

Preservation of Relationship

In many commercial arbitrations, the primary concern of the parties is preserving their relationship and reputations. Therefore, they want to resolve their dispute amicably and quickly. In advocating for arbitration, the American Arbitration Association (AAA) points to the value of arbitration in maintaining ongoing business dealings:

> People want to do business, not argue about it. In the world of trade and commerce, however, disputes are inevitable. Parties might disagree as to their individual rights and obligations no matter how carefully a contract is written. This can lead to delayed shipments, complaints about the quality of merchandise, claims of nonperformance of contracts, and similar misunderstandings and, even with the best of intentions, parties often perform less than they promise.
>
> Those disputes seldom involve great legal issues. On the contrary, they concern the same evaluation of facts and interpretation of contract terms that business persons and their attorneys are accustomed to handling every day. Consequently, when differences arise from day-to-day commercial affairs, parties often prefer to settle them privately and informally, in the businesslike kind of way that encourages continued business relationships. That is the function of commercial arbitration.[27]

So, where the parties are interested in repeat or future business, they are willing to settle a dispute without resorting to litigation. Preserving the relationship is more important than a particular result.

We have examined the advantages of arbitration over litigation; now let's look at the downside.

DISADVANTAGES OF ARBITRATION OVER LITIGATION

"When viewed critically, arbitration's advantages seldom stack up against its disadvantages."[28] As one court cautioned, arbitration is "an inferior system of justice, structured without due process, rules of evidence, accountability of judgment and rules of law."[29] Another court warned that "[a]rbitration provides neither the procedural protections nor the assurance of the proper application of substantive law offered by the judicial system. . . . One choosing arbitration should not expect the full panoply of procedural and substantive protection offered by a court of law."[30]

Even the U.S. Supreme Court acknowledged that arbitration is not comparable to litigating a case in court.

> Moreover, the factfinding process in arbitration usually is not equivalent to judicial factfinding. The record of the arbitration proceedings is not as complete; the usual rules of evidence do not apply; and rights and procedures common to civil trials, such as discovery, compulsory process, cross-examination, and testimony under oath, are often severely limited or unavailable. And . . . arbitrators have no obligation to the court to give their reasons for an award.[31]

In fact, one jurist compared arbitration to the kudzu vine,[32] a notoriously invasive weed:

> The consumer has little choice: give up constitutional rights long held precious to Western legal systems or give up access to the marketplace. When introduced as a method to control soil erosion, kudzu was hailed as an asset to agriculture, but it has become a creeping monster. Arbitration was innocuous when limited to negotiated commercial contracts, but it developed sinister characteristics when it became ubiquitous.[33]

So what are some distinct disadvantages of using arbitration in place of litigation?

No Due Process

As the chapter on litigation explains, the concept of **due process**, found in the Fifth and Fourteenth Amendments to the U.S. Constitution, prohibit the United States and state governments from depriving a person of "life, liberty or property without due process of law."[34] The minimum elements of due process include "notice of the charges or issue, the opportunity for a meaningful hearing, and an impartial decision maker."[35] Arbitration not only does not guarantee these rights, it also deemphasizes them. For example, formal rules of evidence do not apply, and discovery, if permitted at all, is usually very limited. "Because arbitrators are not constrained by legal rules, constitutional protections have little or no impact within an arbitration proceeding. An arbitrator may listen to an argument that a constitutional right has been breached, but will not be required to apply any aspect of substantive law, including civil liberties, to remedy that breach."[36] One critic posits that the absence of legal standards can translate into gross substantive and procedural injustices, particularly when there are severe power imbalances between the parties, and the absence of substantive judicial review worsens the situation by making capricious awards essentially uncorrectable. This problem is exacerbated by the fact that arbitrators, unlike judges, have economic incentives with respect to their case loads that can affect their judgment in individual cases, making them perhaps more favorably disposed toward repeat players than one-shotters.[37]

Repeat players refer to parties that have more experience with arbitration and with certain arbitrators. By contrast, one-shot players refer to parties that may be participating in arbitration for the first time.[38]

No Appeal/Finality

While finality is attractive to parties looking to put a dispute behind them and move forward in their business relationship, finality can be a grave disadvantage to a party unhappy with an award or with the process. Even when an arbitrator makes a mistake of fact or law, there is no right to appeal. (There are limited grounds for appealing an award. For example, 9 U.S.C. § 10(a) allows awards to be vacated because of "fraud, corruption or undue means.") The California Supreme Court ruled that awards are not reviewable for errors of law notwithstanding that, as Justice Kennard wrote in her dissent, the result is to tolerate substantial injustice.[39] As a result, finality may actually deter parties from choosing arbitration.

No Discovery

The reasoning underlying the prohibition of **discovery** in arbitration proceedings is that by choosing to arbitrate, the parties wanted to limit the cost and time associated with court actions including the discovery process. Critics, however, often cite the lack of discovery as a reason to avoid arbitration because parties might not have a complete understanding of the case without this process. Absent discovery, "a party comes to the hearings without a complete understanding of the character of the opposition's case, let alone knowledge of what documents are to be relied upon or what witnesses are to be called. In such cases, arbitration threatens to become trial by surprise. . . ."

Discovery is not only useful in preparation for a hearing or trial, but the disputants often learn the adverse party's strengths and their own case's weaknesses. Very often, this contributes to settlement of the dispute.

Absence of Record and Reasoned Opinions

Stare decisis, Latin for "to stand by things decided," is a bedrock principle of American jurisprudence. It "is the doctrine that judicial decisions stand as precedents for cases arising in the future."[40] This principle is important because "it promotes the evenhanded, predictable, and consistent development of legal principles, fosters reliance on judicial decisions, and contributes to the actual and perceived integrity of the judicial process."[41] However, an arbitrator is not bound to follow prior decisions, and his decisions are not reviewable. An arbitrator is free "to do justice as he sees it, applying his own sense of law and equity to the facts as he finds them to be and making an award reflecting the spirit rather than the letter of the agreement. . . ."[42] The absence of precedent "hurts society because rules and precedents are used to guide future actions of citizens and impose order where uncertainty would otherwise chill people's behavior. Arbitration, therefore deprives courts of the occasion to render an interpretation of society's values and laws"[43] and "may deny the public access to information regarding issues affecting health, safety, and other important policies."[44] Criticizing the lack of a written record, one unhappy judge wrote:

> [A]fter four years and sixty-four days, the arbitrators simply awarded $14 million to Sands without any explanation whatsoever other than a finding that Perini had

"failed to properly perform its obligations as construction manager pursuant to the contract. . . ." There are no reasons, no findings of fact, no conclusions of law, nothing other than the foregoing. For all we know, the arbitrators concluded that the sun rises in the west, the earth is flat, and damages have nothing to do with the intentions of the parties or the foreseeability of the consequences of a breach.[45]

Too Much Like Litigation

At one time disputants turned to arbitration because it was a faster and cheaper way for resolving disputes. Unlike litigation, there was minimal or no discovery, no motions, and no appeals. "By the beginning of the twenty-first century, however, it was common to speak of U.S. business arbitration in terms similar to civil litigation—judicialized, formal, costly, time-consuming, and subject to hardball advocacy."[46] This change is attributable to the diversity and complexity of cases brought to arbitration. The result is that arbitration has become longer and lawyers use the same approach they employ in litigation. The increase in the use of motions and discovery is seen as contributing to the growing expense and longer time for resolving disputes in arbitration. Thus, arbitration has become too similar to litigation.

May Not Be Fast or Inexpensive

In 1985, then AAA president Robert Coulson said, "people used to promote arbitration (for its speed, economy, and justice) . . . like religious zealots . . . I don't think any of those words are entirely accurate."[47] Twenty-seven years later, this was still the case. In 2012, Alan Dabdoub and Trey Cox published the results of a study comparing the cost and speed of arbitration with litigation, which showed arbitration costs more and is slower than litigation.[48] Noted scholar Thomas Stipanowich calls contemporary arbitration, the new litigation: "[T]he arbitration experience has become increasingly like the civil procedures they were designed to supplant, including prehearing discovery and motion practice."[49] Business lawyers also lament that arbitration is not faster or less expensive than litigation. According to one corporate general counsel: "[W]e found arbitration generally is as expensive [as litigation,] . . . less predictable, and not appealable. Arbitration is often unsatisfactory because litigators have . . . run it exactly like a piece of litigation."[50]

Arbitrator Bias

Choosing an arbitrator is perhaps the most significant step in arbitration. As you have already learned, an arbitrator can decide a case based on her concept of fairness, and not the law. If bias or prejudice affects an arbitration proceeding, injustice will likely result. According to scholar Thomas J. Stipanowich, "[r]elatively few issues in arbitration have generated more legal activity than concerns about arbitrator conflict of interest. A host of legal decisions have considered motions to vacate based on an arbitrator's failure to disclose a connection to the case or participants."[51]

David R. Karon divides bias into two types: personal and contextual. **Personal bias** refers to the arbitrator's class-based prejudices and includes race and ethnicity. **Contextual bias** refers to the relationship between the arbitrator and one of the parties. The following are examples of contextual bias:

1. The arbitrator is the attorney for one of the parties in another matter.
2. The arbitrator has been previously employed by one of the parties.
3. The arbitrator or a member of the arbitrator's firm has previously acted as co-counsel with one of the attorneys.
4. The arbitrator acts as an advocate for one of the parties.
5. The arbitrator has a financial or personal interest in the outcome of the dispute.
6. A party's attorney has represented the arbitrator or the arbitrator's employer in another matter.
7. The arbitrator has a familial relationship with one of the parties.
8. The arbitrator expresses an opinion before the award is rendered.

Personal bias is harder to identify than contextual bias because it is psychological. Contextual bias is factually based and therefore easier to discover.[52]

In the following case, the court found that the designated arbitrator was biased and could not hear the dispute.

***Erving v. Virginia Squires Basketball Club*, 468 F.2d 1064 (2d Cir. 1972):** Julius Erving played in the National Basketball Association (NBA) from 1976 to 1987. Well known for "slam dunking," Erving won three championships and was voted most valuable player four times. In 1993, he was inducted into the Basketball Hall of Fame. Erving began his professional career playing for the American Basketball Association (ABA) team the Virginia Squires. (In 1976, the ABA merged with the NBA.) He agreed to play with the team for four years. After his first year, he signed a contract worth a lot more money with an NBA team. He then sued the Squires to rescind the contract, claiming fraud. The Squires counterclaimed seeking enforcement of the arbitration clause in the contract and seeking an injunction to prohibit Erving from playing basketball with any other professional team. The U.S. district court found the arbitration clause enforceable and issued the injunction. The court also ruled that although the contract required disputes to be heard before the commissioner of the ABA, because the commissioner was a partner of the law firm representing the defendant, a neutral arbitrator should be appointed to hear the case. Erving then appealed to the circuit court.

Circuit Judge Medina began his opinion by commenting on the staggering salaries of professional sports players.

This case presents another chapter in the history of contract jumping by famous American athletes. As usual the amounts paid by the competing teams are fantastic. Julius W. Erving, we are told, was playing a remarkable game of basketball as an undergraduate at University of Massachusetts when, after his junior year, he agreed to turn professional and he signed a contract with the Virginia Squires to play exclusively for the Squires for four years commencing October 1, 1971 for $500,000. He made an extraordinary record in his first year as a pro, but he seems, for one reason or another, to have defected and in April 1972 he signed a contract to play for the Atlanta Hawks. This contract with the Hawks is not before us but we were informed on the oral argument that it called for payments to Erving, or "Dr. J." as he was generally called by the fans, aggregating $1,500,000.00 or more.[53]

Judge Medina went on to say,

In view of the large sums of money involved, and the publicity generated by the reputation of Dr. J. as a highly talented basketball player with a brilliant future, we need not be surprised at the amount of perhaps pardonable exaggeration and bombast in the claims of the respective parties. On the one hand we are assured that Dr. J. was, as stated in the opinion below, for all practical purposes the Squires' whole team, that he was featured in the Squires' advertisements as fabulous and that the fans were deserting in droves when told that Dr. J. had switched to the Hawks. On the other hand we are told that there is no showing of irreparable harm to the Squires if Dr. J. plays with the Hawks, and the charge of fraud in inducing this innocent collegian to leave college and play for the Squires for four years for the inadequate sum of $500,000 is repeated ad nauseam.[54]

Judge Medina found the arbitration clause valid and ruled that "the fraud issues are for the arbitrator to decide."[55] He also upheld the district court's disqualification of the commissioner as arbitrator.

Questions:
1. Who was the designated arbitrator agreed to in the contract between Julius Irving and the Virginia Squires?
2. What was the arbitrator's relationship to the parties?
3. What was the district court's finding about the arbitrator's bias? What was the court's rationale?
4. Do you agree or disagree with the court's finding? Explain your answer.

Conclusion

In this chapter, you learned about the evolution of arbitration, compared arbitration with litigation, and looked at the advantages and disadvantages of arbitration compared with traditional dispute resolution. The next chapter discusses the Federal Arbitration Act, its development and content, and federal policy favoring its use. You will also learn what arbitrability means, what an adhesive arbitration agreement is, the process of an arbitration proceeding, and the grounds for vacating an arbitration award.

Key Terms and Concepts

Appeal	Finality
Arbitrator	Government adjudication
Award	Ouster of jurisdiction
Contextual bias	Personal bias
Discovery	Precedent
Due process	Private adjudication
Executory arbitration agreement	

Practice Test Questions

True/False

____ 1. Arbitration is a dispute resolution process in which the parties present evidence and argument to one or more third-party neutrals, who then issue an award.

____ 2. Arbitration is an adversarial adjudicatory process, similar to litigation except that it is private adjudication.

____ 3. In arbitration, the parties do not select the decision maker.

____ 4. An arbitrator is required to follow prior decisions and therefore cannot apply his own sense of law and equity to the facts.

____ 5. Arbitration is preferable to litigation when the parties are interested in repeat or future business.

Multiple Choice

____ 1. In arbitration, the dispute is decided by
   a. a mediator.
   b. the parties.
   c. the lawyers.
   d. a neutral party.

____ 2. All of the following are advantages of using arbitration *except*
   a. privacy.
   b. flexibility.
   c. provides due process.
   d. finality.

____ 3. An executory arbitration agreement means that the parties have agreed
   a. to arbitrate any dispute that may arise in the future.
   b. that any future dispute may be subject to arbitration.
   c. in advance to the selection of an arbitrator.
   d. to mediation followed by arbitration.

____ 4. An arbitrator's decision is called a/an
   a. ruling.
   b. finding.
   c. decree.
   d. award.
____ 5. All of the following are disadvantages of arbitration *except*
   a. no discovery.
   b. informal atmosphere.
   c. too much like litigation.
   d. arbitrator bias.

Review Questions

1. Explain how arbitration is similar to litigation. How is it different?
2. In the nineteenth century, American courts followed the English "ouster of jurisdiction" view. Why?
3. What were the reasons that businesses in the late 1800s and early 1900s were critical of the courts?
4. List and explain the advantages of arbitration over litigation.
5. List and explain the disadvantages of arbitration over litigation.

Application Questions

1. Parties expect that an arbitrator will be fair and unbiased. The AAA requires arbitrators to disclose "any interest or relationship likely to affect impartiality or which might create an appearance of partiality." The Code of Ethics for Arbitrators in Commercial Disputes, Canon II (2004). Two years ago, Alyssa Hoffman had cosmetic lip surgery that was performed by a medical doctor, Charles Wentworth. After the procedure, Hoffman experienced complications, including stiffness and numbness in her lips and an asymmetrical smile. These symptoms persisted and after a year, when they did not improve, she filed a lawsuit against Wentworth alleging battery and medical malpractice. Based upon an arbitration agreement, the parties stipulated to binding arbitration of Hoffman's claims. That agreement provided for a panel of arbitrators composed of one arbitrator selected by each party and a neutral arbitrator jointly chosen in turn by those two arbitrators.

   Both parties agreed to the appointment of a retired superior court judge, Walter Haley, as the neutral arbitrator. In his disclosure statement required by Canon II, Haley stated that he had been involved in legal proceedings with other members of defense counsel's firm, but had no other information to report.

   At the arbitration hearing, Hoffman, who previously had undergone several other cosmetic surgeries performed by various physicians, contended that she had not consented to the particular surgical procedure employed by Wentworth, that the use of that procedure fell below the standard of care, and that the procedure had caused her numerous complications. The panel, in a split decision authored by Haley, issued its award in favor of Wentworth.

Two months later, Hoffman learned that Haley, who was appointed to the trial bench in 1988, had been publicly censured by this court for engaging in "conduct prejudicial to the administration of justice that brings the judicial office into disrepute." Specifically, during a two-year period, Haley on several occasions made sexually suggestive remarks to and asked sexually explicit questions of female staff members; referred to a staff member using crude and demeaning names and descriptions and an ethnic slur; referred to a fellow jurist's physical attributes in a demeaning manner, and mailed a sexually suggestive postcard to a staff member addressed to her at the courthouse. None of the conduct occurred while court was in session or while the judge was on the bench conducting the business of the court.

Canon II requires that in any arbitration pursuant to an arbitration agreement, when a person is to serve as a neutral arbitrator, the proposed neutral arbitrator shall disclose all matters that could cause a person aware of the fact to reasonably entertain a doubt that the proposed neutral arbitrator would be able to be impartial.

Was Haley required to disclose to the parties the circumstance that years earlier, he received a public censure based upon his conduct toward and statements to court employees, which together created "an overall courtroom environment where discussion of sex and improper ethnic and racial comments were customary"? Why or why not?

2. Millworks Cabinets entered into a subcontract with Saltwater Construction, the general contractor, to assemble and install simulated wood grain cabinets in the kitchens and bathrooms of a 32-unit apartment complex that Saltwater was building for the owner, Bay Properties, Inc.

The cabinets were assembled with components supplied to Millworks by other companies and included fiberboard, paper, adhesives, and foil. Not long after Millworks installed the cabinets, they became stained and discolored. Testing showed that the paper covering the fiberboard permitted foreign substances (cleaning solutions and food) to leak onto the adhesive causing a chemical reaction that resulted in staining and discoloring.

What are the advantages to using arbitration for Millworks?

3. Dan Wing worked for Rockaway Auto, Inc. as a mechanic before becoming the service manager. After three years in this position, he was demoted back to a mechanic and eventually terminated. He claims the demotion and termination were the result of his investigating and reporting warrant fraud. He sued defendant for wrongful termination. In addition to compensatory and punitive damages, Dan wants the public to know about Rockaway Auto's warranty fraud actions.

What are the disadvantages to using arbitration for Dan?

4. Dr. Alexandra Littlefield is being sued for medical malpractice for failing to remove a surgical sponge from a patient's abdomen, which was discovered five months after the surgery. As a result, the patient had to have additional surgeries to remove the sponge, treat an abscess, and heal the wound.

   What are the advantages for using arbitration to Dr. Littlefield?

Practice Exercises

1. Go to the AAA website (https://www.adr.org) and explain how to file and manage a business dispute. Be sure to include the AAA fee, how an arbitrator is selected, the arbitrator's fee, and which party pays this fee.

2. The Judicial Arbitration and Mediation Services (JAMS) offers services similar to the AAA. Go to the JAMS website (https://www.jamsadr.com) and explain how to file and manage a business dispute. Be sure to include the JAMS fee, how an arbitrator is selected, the arbitrator's fee, and which party pays this fee.

3. Has your state adopted the Revised Uniform Arbitration Act (RUAA)? If yes, which version? Find a case in your state where the RUAA is cited. In a written paper, summarize the facts of the case, any issue involving arbitration, and the court's decision and rationale. If your state has not adopted the RUAA, find a state that has and do the above.

Endnotes

1. In re Curtis, 30 A. 769, 770 (Conn. 1894).

2. *The New Oxford Annotated Bible with the Apocryphal/Deuterocanonical, Augumented* 109 (3d ed., Michael D. Coogan, Marc Z. Brettler, Carol A. Newsom & Pheme Perkins eds., Oxford University Press 2007).

3. Sabra A. Jones, *Historical Development of Commercial Arbitration in the United States*, 12 Minn. L. Rev. 240, 242-243 (1927-1928).

4. *Id.* at 243. The Twelve Tables are "[t]he earliest surviving legislation enacted by the Romans, written on 12 tablets in the 5th century B.C. The Tables set out many rights and duties of Roman citizens, including debtors' rights, family law, wills, torts, civil procedure, and some public law. They substituted a written body of laws, easily accessible and binding on all citizens of Rome, for an unwritten usage accessible to only a few." *Black's Law Dictionary* 1659 (9th ed., West 2009). The Pandects are "[t]he 50 books constituting Justinian's Digest (one of the four works making up the *Corpus Juris Civilis*), first published in A.D. 533." *Id.* at 1219. *Corpus Juris Civilis* refers to "[t]he body of the civil law, compiled and codified under the direction of the Roman emperor Justinian in A.D. 528-556." *Id.* at 395.

5. A.M. Prichard, *Private Roman Law* 438 (3d ed., MacMillan 1961).

6. Merchant guilds were "an incorporated society of merchants having exclusive trading rights within a town." *Black's Law Dictionary* 758 (9th ed. 2009).

7. A.T. Carter, *A History of English Legal Institutions* 269 (3d ed., Butterworth 1906).

8. Paul L. Sayre, *Development of Commercial Arbitration Law*, 37 Yale L.J. 595, 598 (1927-1928).

9. *Id.* at 604. Additionally, proving "expectation damages—compensation for not receiving the gains of promised arbitration—would be virtually impossible to prove." Ian R. MacNeil, *American Arbitration Law* 20 n.39 (Oxford University Press 1992).

10. "Although the precise reasons for the development of a common-law bias against arbitration are obscure, it is possible to understand better the English experience with arbitration by considering the common-law judiciary in its historical context. In 1856 Lord Campbell speculated that the rule against arbitration probably originated with English judges' almost total dependence on fees from cases for income. Another contributing factor might have been the centuries-long struggle of the early law courts for

jurisdiction." John R. Allison, *Arbitration Agreements and Antitrust Claims: The Need for Enhanced Accommodation of Conflicting Public Policies*, 64 N.C. L. Rev. 219, 224 (1986).

11. Julius Henry Cohen, *Commercial Arbitration and the Law* 5-6 (D. Appleton 1918).

12. Home Ins. Co. of N.Y. v. Morse, 87 U.S. (20 Wall.) 445, 451 (1874).

13. Tobey v. County of Bristol, 23 Fed. Cas. 1313, 1321 (C.C.D. Mass. 1845).

14. U.S. Asphalt Refining Co. v. Trinidad Petroleum Co., 222 F. 1006, 1011-1012 (S.D.N.Y 1915).

15. William L. Ranson, *The Layman's Demand for Improved Judicial Machinery*, 73 Annals Am. Acad. Pol. & Soc. Sci. 132, 148 (1917); see Christine B. Harrington, *Shadow Justice: The Ideology and Institutionalization of Alternatives to Court* 15-23 (Greenwood Press 1985).

16. Ranson, *supra* note 15, at 147.

17. *See* Office of Supply, Gov't of the Republic of Korea v. N.Y. Navigation Co., 469 F.2d 377, 379 (2d Cir. 1972) ("[I]t is settled that upon judicial review of an arbitrators' award the court's function in . . . vacating an arbitration award is severely limited."); Int'l Standard Elec. Corp. v. Bridas Sociedad Anonima Petrolera, Industrial y Comercial, 745 F. Supp. 172, 178 (S.D.N.Y. 1990) ("The whole point of arbitration is that the merits of the dispute will not be reviewed in the courts, wherever they be located."); Edward Brunet, Charles B. Carver & Ellen E. Deason, *Alternative Dispute Resolution: The Advocate's Perspective, Cases and Materials* 431 (LexisNexis 2006); Richard Speidel, *Arbitration of Statutory Rights Under the Federal Arbitration Act: The Case for Reform*, 4 Ohio St. J. on Disp. Resol. 157, 159 (1989) ("Unlike the judicial process there is no review of the merits of this primary decision by the arbitrator. In the absence of fraud, bias, or process defects, the court is empowered to confirm and enforce the award as if it were a final judgment.").

18. Saika v. Gold, 49 Cal. App. 4th 1074, 1077 (1996).

19. *Id.* at 1182.

20. *Id.* at 1176.

21. *Id.* at 1176-1177 (quoting Moncharsh v. Heily & Blasé, 3 Cal. 4th 1, 10 (1992)).

22. *Commercial Arbitration at Its Best, Successful Strategies for Business Users* xxiii (Thomas J. Stipanowick & Peter H. Kaskell eds., ABA & CPR Inst. for Disp. Resol. 2001).

23. In re Arbitration Between Silverman & Benmor Coats, Inc., 461 N.E.2d 1261, 1266 (N.Y. 1984).

24. Robert Coulson, *Arbitration in the Eighties: How to Make Arbitration Work for You*, 17 Forum 673, 673 (1982).

25. Martin Domke, *Domke on Commercial Arbitration: The Law and Practice of Commercial Arbitration* § 30:2 (Larry E. Edmonson ed., 3d ed., West 2009).

26. Am. Almond Prods. Co. v. Consolidated Pecan Sales, 144 F.2d 448, 450 (2d Cir. 1944).

27. Am. Arbitration Ass'n, *A Guide to Arbitration for Business People*, in Sarah Rudolph Cole, *Incentives and Arbitration: The Case Against Enforcement of Executory Arbitration Agreements Between Employers and Employees*, 64 UMKC L. Rev. 449, 458 (1996).

28. Richard S. Bayer & Harlan S. Abrahams, *The Trouble with Arbitration*, 11 Litig. 30, 31 (Winter 1985).

29. Stroh Container Co. v. Delphi Indus., Inc., 783 F.2d 743, 751 n.12 (8th Cir. 1985).

30. Bowles Fin. Grp., Inc. v. Stifel, Nicolaus & Co., 22 F.2d 1010, 1011 (10th Cir. 1994).

31. Alexander v. Gardner-Denver Co., 415 U.S. 36, 57-58 (1974).

32. "A Japanese vine, with compound leaves and reddish-purple flower clusters, grown for fodder and forage and for containment of erosion." *Webster's II New College Dictionary* 612 (Houghton Mifflin 1999).

33. In re Knepp, 229 B.R. 821, 828 (N.D. Ala. 1999).

34. U.S. Const. amends. V & XIV, § 1.

35. Erwin Chemerinsky, *Constitutional Law: Principles and Policies* 557 (2d ed., Aspen 2002).

36. Edward Brunet, *Arbitration and Constitutional Rights*, 71 N.C. L. Rev. 81, 88-89 (1992).

37. Richard C. Reuben, *First Options, Consent to Arbitration, and the Demise of Separability: Restoring Access to Justice for Contracts with Arbitration Provisions*, 56 S.M.U. L. Rev. 819, 823 (2003).

38. Cole, *supra* note 23, at 452-453.

39. Moncharsh v. Heily & Blase, 832 P.2d 899, 919-920 (Cal. 1992).

40. Jonathan S. Lynton, *Ballentine's Legal Dictionary and Thesaurus* 633 (Delmar 1995).

41. Payne v. Tennessee, 501 U.S. 808, 827 (1991).

42. In re Silverman (Benmor Coats), 61 N.Y.2d 299, 308 (1984).

43. Benjamin J.C. Wolf, *On-line but Out of Touch: Analyzing International Dispute Resolution Through the Lens of the Internet*, 14 Cardozo J. Int'l & Comp. L. 281, 309 (2006).

44. Amy J. Schmitz, *Curing Consumer Warranty Woes Through Regulated Arbitration*, 23 Ohio St. J. on Disp. Resol. 627, 630 (2008).

45. Perini Corp. v. Greate Bay Hotel & Casino, Inc., 610 A.2d 364, 392 (N.J. 1992).

46. Thomas J. Stipanowich, *Arbitration: The New Litigation*, 2010 U. Ill. L. Rev. 1, 8.

47. James Lyons, *Arbitration: The Slower, More Expensive Alternative?* Am. Law., Jan.-Feb. 1985, at 107.

48. Alan Dabdoub & Trey Cox, *Which Costs Less: Arbitration or Litigation? A Case Study Shows That When It Comes to Expenditures and Resolution Time, Litigation Is Cheaper and Faster,* Inside Counsel, Dec. 6, 2012, http://www.insidecounsel.com/2012/12/06/which-costs-less-arbitration-or-litigation.

49. Stipanowich, *supra* note 42, at 9.

50. Thomas J. Stipanowich, *ADR and the Vanishing Trial: The Growth and Impact of Alternative Dispute Resolution*, 1 J. Empirical Legal Stud. 843, 895 (2004).

51. Stipanowich, *supra* note 42, at 19-20.

52. Daniel R. Karon, *Kicking Our Gift Horse in the Mouth – Arbitration and Arbitrator Bias: Its Sources, Symptoms, and Solutions*, 7 Ohio St. J. on Disp. Resol. 315, 325-332 (1992).

53. Erving v. Va. Squires Basketball Club, 468 F.2d 1064, 1065-1066 (2d Cir. 1972).

54. *Id.* at 1066-1067.

55. *Id.* at 1067.

CHAPTER SIX

Settling Disputes with Arbitration

Chapter Outline

Introduction
The Federal Arbitration Act
Revised Uniform Arbitration
  Act
Agreements to Arbitrate and
  Arbitrability
Consent and Fairness: Adhesive
  Arbitration Agreements
    Supporters of Adhesive
      Arbitration Agreements
Common Types of Arbitration
    Labor and Employment
      Arbitration
    Consumer Arbitration
    Securities Arbitration
      (Investor/Broker Disputes)
    Commercial Arbitration
    International Commercial
      Arbitration
The Arbitration Process

Filing a Demand for Arbitration
Selection of Arbitrators
Preliminary Meeting
Prehearing Conference
Exchange of Information and
  Discovery
The Hearing
The Award
Judicial Enforcement of Awards
  Manifest Disregard of the Law
  Arbitrary and Capricious
  Irrationality
  Violates Public Policy
Conclusion
Key Terms and Concepts
Practice Test Questions
Review Questions
Application Questions
Practice Exercises

INTRODUCTION

Chapter 5 discussed the history of arbitration, its evolvement into a judicially favored method for dispute resolution, and the advantages and disadvantages of arbitration compared to litigation. In this chapter, we look at the mechanics of arbitration, including when arbitration can take place, what makes a dispute arbitrable, the judicial support for arbitration, the arbitration process, and the limited grounds available for vacating an award. Let's begin with looking at the Federal Arbitration Act.

THE FEDERAL ARBITRATION ACT

In 1925, the U.S. Congress enacted the United States Arbitration Act, which was codified in 1947 as the **Federal Arbitration Act (FAA)**. The FAA, which ended judicial hostility to arbitration, provides a legal framework for managing arbitrations and applies to all maritime transactions and interstate or foreign commerce. It does not apply to employment disputes. The key provisions of the FAA are:

§ **2:** A written agreement to arbitrate is "valid, irrevocable, and enforceable, save upon such grounds as exist at law or in equity for the revocation of any contract."

§ **3:** If a suit is filed in federal court and the court finds that there is a valid arbitration agreement, the court shall stay the trial (i.e., the court proceedings) "until such arbitration has been had in accordance with the terms of the agreement. . . ."

§ **4:** If a party refuses to arbitrate, the opposing party "may petition any United States district court . . . for an order directing that such arbitration proceed in the manner provided for in such agreement." After hearing, if the court determines that there is a valid arbitration agreement, and that there is no issue about the failure to participate, "the court shall make an order directing the parties to proceed to arbitration in accordance with the terms of the agreement."

§ **5:** If the arbitration agreement makes provision for a method of naming an arbitrator or arbitrators, "such method shall be followed; but if no method be provided therein" or if there is a "lapse in the naming of an arbitrator or arbitrators . . . the court shall designate and appoint an arbitrator or arbitrators."

§ **7:** Authorizes arbitrators to summon witnesses to appear and testify and to bring documents, if requested. If the witness refuses to appear, the parties can petition the court to compel attendance.

§ **9:** If the parties have agreed, the court shall enter the arbitration award as a court judgment.

§ **10:** This section provides the grounds for which courts can vacate arbitration awards. [FAA Grounds for Vacating Arbitration Awards.] They are as follows:

§ **10(a)(1):** "corruption, fraud, or undue means";

§ **10(a)(2):** "evident partiality or corruption in the arbitrators";

§ **10(a)(3):** "misconduct in refusing to postpone the hearing . . . or . . . refusing to hear evidence pertinent and material to the controversy; or of any other misbehavior by which the rights of any party have been prejudiced";

§ **10(a)(4):** "where the arbitrators exceeded their powers, or so imperfectly executed them that a mutual, final, and definite award . . . was not made."

§ **11:** Authorizes a court to "modify" or "correct" an award if there was "an evident material miscalculation of figures or an evident material mistake in the description of any person, thing, or property referred to in the award" or where the arbitrator's award applies to "a matter not submitted to them."

To summarize, the FAA recognizes and supports a private adjudicatory method through which parties can agree, by contract, to resolve their dispute. The Act provides a legal framework for the courts to manage the process and enforce awards. *Allied-Bruce Terminix Cos. v. Dobson* is a case in which the U.S. Supreme Court was called upon to address judicial hostility to arbitration agreements.

Allied-Bruce Terminix Cos. v. Dobson
513 U.S. 265 (1995)

. . . In August 1987, Steven Gwin, a respondent who owned a house in Birmingham, Alabama, bought a lifetime "Termite Protection Plan" (Plan) from the local office of Allied-Bruce Terminix Companies, a franchise of Terminix International Company. In the Plan, Allied-Bruce promised "to protect" Gwin's house "against the attack of subterranean termites," to reinspect periodically, to provide any "further treatment found necessary," and to repair, up to $100,000, damage caused by new termite infestations. App. 69. Terminix International "guarantee[d] the fulfillment of the terms" of the Plan. *Ibid.* The Plan's contract document provided in writing that "*any controversy or claim* . . . arising out of or relating to the interpretation, performance or breach of any provision of this agreement *shall be settled exclusively by arbitration.*" *Id.,* at 70 (emphasis added).

In the spring of 1991, Mr. and Mrs. Gwin, wishing to sell their house to Mr. and Mrs. Dobson, had Allied-Bruce reinspect the house. They obtained a clean bill of health. But no sooner had they sold the house and transferred the Plan to Mr. and Mrs. Dobson than the Dobsons found the house swarming with termites. Allied-Bruce attempted to treat and repair the house, but the Dobsons found Allied-Bruce's efforts inadequate. They therefore sued the Gwins, and (along with the Gwins, who cross-claimed) also sued Allied-Bruce and Terminix in Alabama state court. Allied-Bruce and Terminix, pointing to the Plan's arbitration clause and § 2 of the Federal Arbitration Act, immediately asked the court for a stay, to allow arbitration to proceed. The court denied the stay. Allied-Bruce and Terminix appealed.

The Supreme Court of Alabama upheld the denial of the stay on the basis of a state statute, . . . making written, predispute arbitration agreements invalid and "unenforceable." To reach this conclusion, the court had to find that the Federal Arbitration Act, which pre-empts conflicting state law, did not apply to the termite contract. To reach this conclusion, the court had to find that the Federal Arbitration Act, which pre-empts conflicting state law, did not apply to the termite contract. It made just that finding. The court considered the federal Act inapplicable because the connection between the termite contract and interstate commerce was too slight. In the court's view, the Act applies to a contract only if "'at the time [the parties entered into the contract] and accepted the arbitration clause, they *contemplated* substantial interstate activity.'" *Ibid.* (emphasis in original). Despite some interstate activities . . . the court found that the parties "contemplated" a transaction that was primarily local and not "substantially" interstate. . . .

We therefore proceed to the basic interpretive questions aware that we are interpreting an Act that seeks broadly to overcome judicial hostility to arbitration agreements and that applies in both federal and state courts. We must decide in this case whether that Act used language about interstate commerce that nonetheless limits the Act's application, thereby carving out an important statutory niche in which a State remains free to apply its antiarbitration law or policy. We conclude that it does not. . . .

For these reasons, we accept the "commerce in fact" interpretation, reading the Act's language as insisting that the "transaction" in fact "involve[e]" interstate commerce, even if the parties did not contemplate an interstate commerce connection. . . .

The parties do not contest that the transaction in this case, in fact, involved interstate commerce. In addition to the multistate nature of Terminix and Allied-Bruce, the termite-treating and house-repairing material used by Allied-Bruce in its (allegedly inadequate) efforts to carry out the terms of the Plan, came from outside Alabama.

Consequently, the judgment of the Supreme Court of Alabama is reversed, and the case is remanded for further proceedings not inconsistent with this opinion.

Questions:
1. What was the Alabama Supreme Court's rationale for upholding the denial of the stay?
2. What was the issue before the U.S. Supreme Court?
3. How did the U.S. Supreme Court rule?

REVISED UNIFORM ARBITRATION ACT

As you just learned, the FAA applies only to interstate commerce. Recognizing this, in 1955, the National Conference of Commissioners on Uniform State Laws promulgated the Uniform Arbitration Act (UAA). Revised in 2000, the **Revised Uniform Arbitration Act (RUAA)** has been adopted, in whole or part, by well over half the states. Functioning much like the FAA, the RUAA governs enforcement of arbitration awards, the appointment of arbitrators, the procedure for arbitration hearings, methods for compelling testimony and evidence at the hearing, and the reviewability of awards.

The RUAA "modernized outdated UAA provisions, added entirely new sections, resolved issues ambiguous or unanswered under the old statute, and codified case law developments." Some new provisions include:

> § 1: Definitions
>> § 1(6): "Record" now includes information "that is stored in an electronic or other medium."

§ 6: Validity of Agreement to Arbitrate

  (b) "The court shall decide whether an agreement to arbitrate exists or a controversy is subject to an agreement to arbitrate."

  (c) "An arbitrator shall decide whether a condition precedent to arbitrability has been fulfilled and whether a contract containing a valid agreement to arbitrate is enforceable."

§§ 8, 18: Provide for provisional remedies and enforcement by the court.

§ 12: Disclosure by Arbitrator

  (1) Arbitrators must disclose a "financial or personal interest in the outcome of the arbitration proceeding" and

  (2) "an existing or past relationship with any of the parties to the agreement to arbitrate or the arbitration proceeding, their counsel or representatives, a witness, or other arbitrators."

§ 14: Immunity of Arbitrator

  (a) "An arbitrator or an arbitration organization acting in that capacity is immune from civil liability to the same extent as a judge of a court. . . ."

§ 15: Arbitration Process

  (a) Confers on the arbitrator the power to order prehearing conferences "and, among other matters, determine the admissibility, relevance, materiality and weight of any evidence," and

  (b) if agreed to by the parties, "an arbitrator may decide a request for summary disposition of a claim or particular issue."

§ 17: Witnesses; Subpoenas; Depositions

  (a) An arbitrator can issue subpoenas for witnesses and for the production of records and other evidence.

  (b) An arbitrator can allow the deposition of a witness.

  (c) An arbitrator may allow discovery.

  (d) An arbitrator may order a party to comply with discovery.

  (e) The court can enforce discovery orders.

§ 18: Judicial Enforcement of Pre-award Ruling by Arbitrator

  Permits a pre-award ruling to be incorporated into an award.

§ 21: Remedies; Fees and Expenses of Arbitration Proceeding

  Permits an arbitrator to award punitive damages, attorney's fees, and other expenses related to the arbitration.

§ 25: Judgment on Award; Attorney's Fees and Litigation Expenses

  Authorizes the court to order reasonable attorney's fees and other expenses of litigation incurred in a judicial proceeding after the award is made. . . ."

The RUAA retains the fundamental principles of the UAA while permitting the use of present technology, like the Internet and video conferencing.

AGREEMENTS TO ARBITRATE AND ARBITRABILITY

Arbitration takes place when the parties have inserted into their contract an **arbitral clause**, which binds them to arbitrate future disputes (**predispute**

agreement). Parties can also agree to arbitrate a present dispute. This is called a **submission agreement** (see Exhibit 6.1).

Arbitration occurs when the parties have an agreement. However, sometimes the agreement is unclear about which disputes the parties intended to arbitrate. Whether there was an agreement to arbitrate and the extent of the agreement is called **arbitrability**. The following questions are useful when deciding arbitrability:

1. Whether the parties entered into an agreement to arbitrate (and who decides);
2. Whether a specific issue or dispute is included within the scope of the arbitration agreement (and who decides);
3. Whether any conditions that might be necessary to trigger the contractual duty to arbitrate have been satisfied (and who decides).[1]

Agreements to arbitrate are not always voluntary. Mandatory arbitration clauses are commonplace in a broad range of consumer transactions and can be found in cell phone contracts, gym membership agreements, employment contracts, healthcare and health insurance agreements, mortgages, construction agreements, automobile leases and automobile purchases, and credit card agreements. These forced agreements, called adhesion contracts, have been the subject of much academic, judicial, legislative, and regulatory debate about fairness. Let's look more closely at these "take-it-or-leave-it contracts."

CONSENT AND FAIRNESS: ADHESIVE ARBITRATION AGREEMENTS

A **contract of adhesion** is "a standardized contract, which, imposed and drafted by the party of superior bargaining strength, relegates to the subscribing party

Exhibit 6.1. AGREEMENTS TO ARBITRATE AND ARBITRABILITY
(SUBMISSION AGREEMENT)

ARBITRATION CLAUSE FOR FUTURE DISPUTES:

Any controversy or claim arising out of or relating to this contract, or the breach thereof, shall be settled by arbitration administered by the American Arbitration Association in accordance with its Commercial [or other] Arbitration Rules, and judgment on the award rendered by the arbitrator(s) may be entered in any court having jurisdiction thereof.

ARBITRATION AGREEMENT FOR EXISTING DISPUTES:

We, the undersigned parties, hereby agree to submit to arbitration administered by the American Arbitration Association under its Commercial [or other] Arbitration Rules the following controversy: [describe briefly]. We further agree that a judgment of any court having jurisdiction may be entered upon the award.

Used with permission. © American Arbitration Association, Inc.

---

only the opportunity to adhere to the contract or reject it."[2] To be more specific, an adhesion contract is "(1) a standardized (typed or printed) form document (2) drafted by, or on behalf of, one party which (3) participates routinely in numerous like transactions and (4) presents the form to the other, adhering party on a take-it-or-leave-it basis; (5) the adhering party enters into few transactions of the type in question, and (6) the adhering party signs the form after dickering over the few terms, if any, that are open to bargaining."[3] Exhibit 6.2 is an example of an **adhesive arbitration agreement**. If the consumer wants the computer, she has no choice but to accept the terms and conditions of the purchase as written by the manufacturer, which includes mandatory arbitration of any "dispute, claim, or controversy" that arises between the parties.

Exhibit 6.2. MANDATORY ARBITRATION AGREEMENT

PLEASE READ THIS DOCUMENT CAREFULLY! IT CONTAINS VERY IMPORTANT INFORMATION ABOUT YOUR RIGHTS AND OBLIGATIONS, AS WELL AS LIMITATIONS AND EXCLUSIONS THAT MAY APPLY TO YOU. THIS DOCUMENT CONTAINS A DISPUTE RESOLUTION CLAUSE.

This Agreement contains the terms and conditions that apply to purchases by Home, Home Office, and Small Business customers from the Dell entity named on the invoice ("*Dell*") that will be provided to you ("*Customer*") on orders for computer systems and/or related products sold in the United States. You agree to be bound by and accept this agreement as applicable to your purchase of product(s) or service(s) from Dell. By accepting delivery of the computer systems and/or other products described on that invoice, Customer agrees to be bound by and accepts these terms and conditions . . . .

12. **Binding Arbitration.** ANY CLAIM, DISPUTE, OR CONTROVERSY (WHETHER IN CONTRACT, TORT, OR OTHERWISE, WHETHER PREEXISTING, PRESENT[,] OR FUTURE, AND INCLUDING STATUTORY, COMMON LAW, INTENTIONAL TORT[,] AND EQUITABLE CLAIMS) AGAINST DELL, its agents, employees, successors, assigns[,] or affiliates (collectively for purposes of this paragraph, "*Dell*"[ ),] arising from or relating to this Agreement, its interpretation, or the breach, termination[,] or validity thereof, the relationships which result from this Agreement (including, to the full extent permitted by applicable law, relationships with third parties who are not signatories to this Agreement), Dell's advertising, or any related purchase SHALL BE RESOLVED EXCLUSIVELY AND FINALLY BY BINDING ARBITRATION ADMINISTERED BY THE NATIONAL ARBITRATION FORUM (NAF) under its Code of Procedure then in effect (available via the Internet at **http:// www.arb-forum.com**[,] or via telephone at 1–800–474–2371). The arbitration will be conducted before a single arbitrator and will be limited solely to the dispute or controversy between Customer and Dell. The arbitration shall be held in a mutually agreed upon location in person, by telephone, or online. Any award of the arbitrator(s) shall be final and binding on each of the parties[ ] and may be entered as a judgment in any court of competent jurisdiction. Information may be obtained and claims may be filed at any office of the NAF or at P.O. Box 50191, Minneapolis, MN 55405.[4]

Eat Burger, Waive Right to Sue

Mandatory arbitration agreements forcing people to give up their rights to sue are now standard fare in everything from cell phone contracts to Hooters' employment agreements. But the owner of an East Texas Whataburger has apparently taken arbitration mania to a new level. Every public entrance to the burger franchise displays a sign informing people that simply setting foot

Continued >

on the premises means that they are giving up their right to sue the company for any reason, even if, for instance, they get a little *e coli* along with their fries. Instead, customers will be forced to arbitrate their claims before the American Mediation Association, an organization that seems to consist of three lawyers in Dallas hired by the Whataburger (part of a 58-year-old fast food chain deemed a "Texas treasure" by the state legislature).

Attorney Dan Sorey spotted the sign in early January while in Kilgore investigating the scene of a motorcycle crash for a case. The Whataburger offered an ideal vantage point to study the intersection where the crash happened. Sorey says when he went in, he told a befuddled cashier that he didn't think that the arbitration notice was enforceable, that anyway he wasn't agreeing to it, and, "I need a taquito and a coffee." He says he sat down, watched some traffic, and ate his taquito. "I didn't choke, I didn't burn myself, and I didn't sue 'em," he reports. Sadly, while we suspect there is a good story behind the signs, the Whataburger franchise owner did not respond to requests for an interview. We'll just have to assume that the signs are the product of one too many late-night talk-show jokes about McDonalds' coffee lawsuits.

Source: Stephanie Mencimer, Mother Jones, Jan. 31, 2008,
http://www.motherjones.com/mojo/2008/01/eat-burger-waive-right-sue.

Those critical of predispute arbitration provisions in consumer transactions and employment contracts point to the unfairness in the procedures and remedies. (You may want to review the disadvantages to arbitration that you learned about in Chapter 5.) However, unless the consumer can show that the arbitration agreement was procured by fraud or duress, or the terms are unconscionable, courts will likely enforce the agreement. The reason is § 2 of the FAA, which requires courts to enforce arbitration agreements "save upon such grounds as exist at law or in equity for the revocation of any contract." In *Doctor's Associates, Inc. v. Casarotto*, the Supreme Court reinforced this provision.

[G]enerally applicable contract defenses, such as fraud, duress or unconscionability, may be applied to invalidate arbitration agreements without contravening § 2 [of the FAA]. Courts may not, however, invalidate arbitration agreements under state laws applicable only to arbitration provisions. By enacting § 2, we have several times said, Congress precluded States from singling out arbitration provisions for suspect status, requiring instead that such provisions be placed upon the same footing as other contracts.[5]

So parties objecting to enforcement of arbitration agreements must successfully assert one of the recognized contract defenses (fraud, duress, and unconscionability). Employment and consumer protection laws, and other state statutes, are inapplicable.

Fraud means "a knowing misrepresentation of the truth or concealment of a material fact to induce another to act to his or her detriment."[6] In 2009, Amber Duick successfully argued that her agreement to mandatory arbitration was procured by fraud. Duick sued Toyota and its advertising company when she became an unwitting participant in a prank, which subjected her to frightening and disturbing messages, as part of Toyota's ad campaign for the Matrix. Toyota sought to compel arbitration, citing the terms and conditions Duick agreed to when she clicked a box beside the sentence: "I have read and agree to the terms and conditions"[7] that included the following arbitration provision: "You agree that . . . any and all disputes, claims, and causes of action arising out of, or connected with, Your Other You . . . shall be resolved individually, without resort to any form of class action, and exclusively by arbitration to be held solely in Los Angeles, California under the auspices of the American Arbitration Association and pursuant to its Commercial Dispute Resolution Rules and Procedures."[8]

The court agreed with Duick and found that the contract, including the arbitration clause, was void and unenforceable because it was obtained by fraud. The court reasoned that

> if a misrepresentation as to the character or essential terms of a proposed contract induces conduct that appears to be a manifestation of assent by one who neither knows nor has a reasonable opportunity to know of the character or essential terms of the proposed contract, his conduct is not effective as a manifestation of assent. . . . The contract is consequently void because of fraud in the inception, and every part of it is therefore unenforceable, including the arbitration provision.[9]

So Duick was thereby able to sue Toyota.

The second contract defense is duress, which means that a party did not freely and voluntarily enter into the agreement. In a South Carolina divorce case, the wife argued that because she was forced to enter the property and separation agreement, the court should vacate the judgment. The court ultimately found that the wife did not introduce sufficient evidence to prove duress and denied her motion. In its decision, the court explained that "[f]reedom of will is fundamental to the validity of an agreement. A party claiming duress can prevail if she shows that she has been the victim of a wrongful act or threat that deprives her of free will, with the result that she was compelled to make a disproportionate exchange of values."[10] The court then explained three factors that must be proved to demonstrate that a contact was obtained through duress: "(1) that the person was coerced to enter into the contract; (2) that the person was put in such fear that he was bereft of the quality of mind essential to the making of a contract; and (3) that the contract was thereby obtained as a result of this state of mind."[11]

Unconscionability is the contract defense on which courts frequently rely in refusing to enforce adhesive arbitration agreements. A finding that an arbitration clause (or any contract clause) is unconscionable "requires 'a "procedural" and a "substantive" element, the former focusing on "oppression" or "surprise" due to unequal bargaining power, the latter on "overly harsh" or "one-sided" results."[12] "Oppression arises from an inequality of bargaining power which results in no real negotiation and an absence of meaningful choice. . . . Surprise involves the extent to which the supposedly agreed-upon terms of the bargain are hidden in a prolix [wordy] printed form drafted by the party seeking to enforce the disputed terms. . . . Characteristically, the form contract is drafted by the party with the superior bargaining position."[13]

When determining **procedural unconscionability**, Florida courts look at the following:

> (1) the manner in which the contract was entered into; (2) the relative bargaining power of the parties and whether the complaining party had a meaningful choice at the time the contract was entered into; (3) whether the terms were merely presented on a "take-it-or-leave-it" basis; and (4) the complaining party's ability and opportunity to understand the disputed terms of the contract.[14]

When determining the substantive element, Florida courts "focus on the terms of the agreement itself and whether the terms of the contract are unreasonable and unfair. . . . Florida generally defines **substantive unconscionability** in reference to an agreement "no man in his senses and not under delusion would make on the one hand, and as no honest and fair man would accept on the other."[15] *Hooters of America, Inc. v. Phillips* is a case in which the Fourth Circuit Court of Appeals found the mandatory arbitration agreement unconscionable and void for reasons of public policy.

Hooters of America, Inc. v. Phillips
173 F.3d 933 (4th Cir. 1999)

[Annette R. Phillips alleged that she was sexually harassed while working at a Hooters restaurant. After quitting her job, she threatened to sue Hooters. Hooters claimed that Phillips had agreed to arbitrate employment-related disputes and filed suit to compel arbitration. The federal district court found the agreement unconscionable and void for reasons of public policy and refused to compel arbitration.]

OPINION

WILKINSON, Chief Judge:

Annette R. Phillips worked as a bartender at a Hooters restaurant in Myrtle Beach, South Carolina. She was employed since 1989. . . .

Phillips alleges that in June 1996, Gerald Brooks, a Hooters official and the brother of . . . [the] principal owner, sexually harassed her by grabbing and slapping her buttocks. After appealing to her manager for help and being told to "let it go," she quit her job. Phillips then contacted Hooters through an attorney claiming that the attack and the restaurant's failure to address it violated her Title VII rights. Hooters responded that she was required to submit her claims to arbitration according to a binding agreement to arbitrate between the parties.

141

. . . The [arbitration] agreement provides that Hooters and the employee each agree to arbitrate all disputes arising out of employment, including "any claim of discrimination, sexual harassment, retaliation, or wrongful discharge, whether arising under federal or state law." The agreement further states that ". . . any claims [will be resolved according to the company's rules and procedures which will be provided] upon written request of the employee.

The employees . . . were . . . given a copy of this agreement . . . [but not] a copy of Hooters' arbitration rules and procedures. Phillips signed the agreement on November 25, 1994 [and again] [w]hen her personnel file was updated. . . .

The Hooters rules . . . are so one-sided that their only possible purpose is to undermine the neutrality of the proceeding. The rules require the employee to provide the company notice of her claim at the outset . . . [but not Hooters]. . . . Additionally, at the time of filing this notice, the employee must provide the company with a list of all fact witnesses with a brief summary of the facts known to each. The company, however, is not required to reciprocate.

The Hooters rules also provide a mechanism for selecting a panel of three arbitrators that is crafted to ensure a biased decisionmaker. . . . This gives Hooters control over the entire panel and places no limits whatsoever on whom Hooters can put on the list. . . .

In addition, the rules provide that upon 30 days notice Hooters, but not the employee, may cancel the agreement to arbitrate. Moreover, Hooters reserves the right to modify the rules, "in whole or in part," whenever it wishes and "without notice" to the employee. Nothing in the rules even prohibits Hooters from changing the rules in the middle of an arbitration proceeding. . . .

We hold that the promulgation of so many biased rules — especially the scheme whereby one party to the proceeding so controls the arbitral panel — breaches the contract entered into by the parties. . . . By creating a sham system unworthy even of the name of arbitration, Hooters completely failed in performing its contractual duty. . . . Thus we conclude that the Hooters rules also violate the contractual obligation of good faith. . . . We therefore permit Phillips to cancel the agreement and thus Hooters' suit to compel arbitration must fail. . . .

By promulgating this system of warped rules, Hooters so skewed the process in its favor that Phillips has been denied arbitration in any meaningful sense of the word. To uphold the promulgation of this aberrational scheme under the heading of arbitration would undermine, not advance, the federal policy favoring alternative dispute resolution. This we refuse to do. . . .

Questions:
1. What were Hooters' arbitration rules?
2. What did the court say about these rules?
3. What was the court's holding?
4. What did the court conclude?

Congress has considered a number of bills that would restrict the enforcement of predispute arbitration agreements in consumer transactions. The most sweeping of these is the Arbitration Fairness Act (see Appendix C), which has been introduced in Congress a number of times but has never passed. The Arbitration Fairness Act of 2013 is aimed at eliminating mandatory predispute arbitration clauses in employment, consumer, antitrust, and civil rights disputes, thereby allowing such individuals to decide whether to engage in arbitration once a dispute arises.

Supporters of Adhesive Arbitration Agreements

While adhesive agreements to arbitrate receive more criticism from scholars than support, those defending these contracts argue that "general enforcement is socially desirable and that it benefits most consumers, employees, and other adhering parties . . . [because they lower businesses' dispute resolution costs and] . . . this benefit to businesses is also a benefit to consumers. That is because whatever lowers costs to businesses tends over time to lower prices to consumers."[16]

The majority of state and federal courts actively endorse mandatory arbitration and follow the U.S. Supreme Court's ruling that "in enacting § 2 of the federal Act [the FAA], Congress declared a national policy favoring arbitration and withdrew the power of the states to require a judicial forum for the resolution of claims which the contracting parties agreed to resolve by arbitration."[17] The Supreme Court applied this view in striking down a California Supreme Court decision that struck down a mandatory arbitration clause. In *AT&T Mobility LLC v. Concepcion*, the Court reaffirmed the supremacy of the FAA and found that the FAA preempted the application of California's unconscionability rule to the arbitration clause in a consumer cell phone contract. The Court explained that "[t]he overarching purpose of the FAA, evident in the text of §§ 2, 3, and 4, is to ensure the enforcement of arbitration agreements according to their terms so as to facilitate streamlined proceedings. . . . The 'principal purpose' of the FAA is to 'ensure that private arbitration agreements are enforced according to their terms.'"[18]

Mandatory arbitration agreements conceivably help in reducing overcrowded court dockets and may be economically efficient. And, unless adhesive arbitration agreements "shock the conscience," perhaps they should be enforced. Because these points rest on value judgments, they will continue to be debated not only in academia but also in the political arena.

COMMON TYPES OF ARBITRATION

This section examines five common types of arbitration, each with its own legal footing. The first of these involves employers and workers. When unions are involved, arbitration is governed by § 301 of the National Labor Relations (Taft-Hartley) Act, 29 U.S.C. § 185 (2000). For nonunion employees, the FAA applies. The second category is **consumer arbitration**, which involves contracts between businesses and consumers. The third type, securities arbitration, focuses on disputes between investors and brokers and is overseen by the Financial Industry Regulatory Authority. Commercial arbitration, the fourth category, deals with business-to-business disputes and is governed by the FAA. International arbitration, the last type, is regulated by the 1958 U.N. Convention on the Recognition and Enforcement of Foreign Arbitral Awards as adopted by Congress in 9 U.S.C. § 201 et seq. (2000).

Labor and Employment Arbitration

Labor arbitration involves job-related disputes between unions and employers. Over 95 percent of collective bargaining agreements require the use of arbitration when grievances occur. **Employment arbitration** differs from labor arbitration in that it applies to non-union employees. Labor arbitration involves rights-based arbitration and interest or grievance arbitration. Rights-based arbitration arises when a party to the existing collective agreement alleges a violation or misinterpretation of a particular section of the agreement. Interest or contract arbitration is used to establish the new terms and conditions under a collective bargaining agreement. For example, a new agreement covering autoworkers may break down over certain provisions. These disputed matters would then be decided by one or more arbitrators.

Unlike most types of arbitration, labor arbitration is governed by § 301 of the Labor Management Relations Act of 1947, not the FAA. A series of landmark cases known as the *Steelworkers Trilogy*[19] explain the federal policy on labor arbitration. They also establish arbitration as the method for resolving disputes in collective bargaining agreements between labor unions and management.

In *AT&T Technologies v. Communications Workers of America*,[20] the U.S. Supreme Court summarized the judicial policy on labor arbitration:

> The principles necessary to decide this case are not new. They were set out by this Court over 25 years ago in a series of cases known as the *Steelworkers Trilogy*. . . . These precepts have served the industrial relations community well, and have led to continued reliance on arbitration, rather than strikes or lockouts, as the preferred method of resolving disputes arising during the term of a collective-bargaining agreement. We see no reason either to question their continuing validity, or to eviscerate their meaning by creating an exception to their general applicability.
>
> The first principle gleaned from the *Trilogy* is that arbitration is a matter of contract and a party cannot be required to submit to arbitration any dispute which he has not agreed so to submit. . . . This axiom recognizes the fact that arbitrators derive their authority to resolve disputes only because the parties have agreed in advance to submit such grievances to arbitration. . . .

The second rule, which follows inexorably from the first, is that the question of arbitrability—whether a collective-bargaining agreement creates a duty of the parties to arbitrate the particular grievance—is undeniably an issue for judicial determination. Unless the parties clearly and unmistakably provide otherwise, the question of whether the parties agreed to arbitrate is to be decided by the court, not the arbitrator. . . .

The third principle derived from our prior cases is that, in deciding whether the parties have agreed to submit a particular grievance to arbitration, a court is not to rule on the potential merits of the underlying claims. Whether arguable or not, indeed even if it appears to the court to be frivolous, the union's claim that the employer has violated the collective-bargaining agreement is to be decided, not by the court asked to order arbitration, but as the parties have agreed, by the arbitrator. . . .

Finally, it has been established that where the contract contains an arbitration clause, there is a presumption of arbitrability in the sense that an order to arbitrate the particular grievance should not be denied unless it may be said with positive assurance that the arbitration clause is not susceptible of an interpretation that covers the asserted dispute. Doubts should be resolved in favor of coverage. . . .

This presumption of arbitrability for labor disputes recognizes the greater institutional competence of arbitrators in interpreting collective-bargaining agreements, furthers the national labor policy of peaceful resolution of labor disputes and thus best accords with the parties' presumed objectives in pursuing collective bargaining. . . . [21]

The federal policy favoring arbitration of employment disputes began in 1991, with the U.S. Supreme Court decision in *Gilmer v. Interstate/Johnson Lane Corp.*[22] Prior to this case, the Court was unwilling to enforce mandatory arbitration of discriminatory employment practices. *Gilmer* changed that and opened the door to the use of predispute arbitration agreements in employment contracts.

Gilmer involved an age discrimination claim under the Age Discrimination in Employment Act of 1967 (ADEA). Interstate hired Robert Gilmer as a manager of financial services. A condition of his employment was that he register as a securities representative with several stock exchanges, including the New York Stock Exchange (NYSE). His registration application provided that he agree to arbitrate "any dispute, claim or controversy" arising between him and his employer. Interstate terminated Gilmer's employment in 1987, at which time Gilmer was 62 years of age. Gilmer filed an action in federal court alleging age discrimination under the ADEA. Interstate filed a motion to compel arbitration pursuant to the NYSE rules and the FAA. The Supreme Court held that arbitration should be compelled. The Court reasoned that "by agreeing to arbitrate a statutory claim, a party does not forgo the substantive rights afforded by the statute; it only submits to their resolution in an arbitral, rather than a judicial, forum."[23] The Court found that "[m]ere inequality in bargaining power . . . is not a sufficient reason to hold that arbitration agreements are never enforceable in the employment context."[24]

After *Gilmer*, there was still uncertainty as to whether the FAA applied to all employment contracts because the FAA excludes from its coverage "contracts of employment of seamen, railroad employees or any other class of workers engaged in foreign or interstate commerce."[25] In 2001, the Supreme Court resolved the issue in *Circuit City Stores, Inc. v. Adams*,[26] holding that the exception applied only to "contracts of employment of transportation workers."[27]

Legal challenges to employment disputes will continue, and court rulings and perhaps legislation will influence the enforceability of certain arbitration agreements. For now, however, federal policy favors arbitration of employment claims. The prevailing view is that arbitration is a faster process than litigation and only changes the forum for resolving disputes, not employees' substantive rights.

Consumer Arbitration

Many contracts between a consumer and a business for the sale or lease of goods and services include an arbitration clause. Consumers, however, are usually unaware that they have agreed to arbitrate any future dispute that may arise. The mandatory arbitration clause can usually be found on a form included with a product or on the reverse side of a service agreement. The consumer probably does not understand the language of the clause or its implications. Nonetheless, with few exceptions,[28] courts will enforce the arbitration agreement. This is because of the judicial attitude that favors arbitration over litigation.

The FAA provides that "[a] written provision . . . in a contract evidencing a transaction involving commerce to settle by arbitration a controversy thereafter arising out of such contract . . . shall be valid, irrevocable, and enforceable, save upon such grounds as exist at law or in equity for the revocation of any contract."[29] The Supreme Court has interpreted this provision to apply to consumer contracts. In *Allied-Bruce Terminix Cos. v. Dobson*, the Court broadly construed the words "involving commerce" to be "the functional equivalent of affecting [commerce] . . . and embodies Congress' intent to provide for the enforcement of arbitration agreements within the full reach of the Commerce Clause."[30] *Allied-Bruce* effectively eliminates state laws that protect consumers from mandatory arbitration by ruling that the FAA preempts state anti-arbitration policies.

Securities Arbitration (Investor/Broker Disputes)

The stock market crash in 1929 led to the federal regulation of the securities industry. The Securities Act of 1933 and the Securities Exchange Act of 1934 were designed to protect investors from the problems that caused the crash, specifically, fraud and the lack of information about securities transactions. Both federal securities laws specifically provide that disputes must be brought in a judicial forum. Section 22(a) of the Securities Act gives federal and state courts concurrent jurisdiction. Section 27 of the Exchange Act authorizes only federal court jurisdiction. Both of these securities laws, enacted after the adoption of the FAA in 1925, contravene the federal policy found in the FAA that favors arbitration. This clash between the FAA and the two securities acts was first addressed by the U.S. Supreme Court in 1953 in *Wilko v. Swan*.[31]

Wilko v. Swan arose from a lawsuit filed by a customer/investor against an investment firm. The investor claimed the firm fraudulently induced him to buy 1,600 shares of common stock of Air Associates, Inc. The investor brought suit pursuant to the Securities Act of 1933. Prior to the lawsuit, the investor had signed a brokerage contract with the firm that included a predispute arbitration agreement clause. The investor sought to have his claim resolved in a judicial forum as provided in the Securities Act. The firm moved to stay the judicial proceeding and argued that the agreement to arbitrate should be enforced. The U.S. Supreme Court acknowledged the federal policy favoring arbitration; however, it ruled that the arbitration agreement was unenforceable. The Court reasoned that the arbitration clause contradicted the express policy of the Securities Act, which prohibited the waiver of any provision, specifically in this case, the right to bring suit in a federal or state court.

> Two policies, not easily reconcilable, are involved in this case. Congress has afforded participants in transactions subject to its legislative power an opportunity generally to secure prompt, economical and adequate solution of controversies through arbitration if the parties are willing to accept less certainty of legally correct adjustment. On the other hand, it has enacted the Securities Act to protect the rights of investors and has forbidden a waiver of any of those rights. Recognizing the advantages that prior agreements for arbitration may provide for the solution of commercial controversies, we decide that the intention of Congress concerning the sale of securities is better carried out by holding invalid such an agreement for arbitration of issues arising under the Act.[32]

Remember that the plaintiff in *Wilko v. Swan* filed suit under the Securities Act of 1933. The Supreme Court's decision, therefore, did not apply to the Securities Exchange Act of 1934. In 1987, 34 years after *Wilko*, the Court finally addressed the enforceability of arbitration agreements under the Securities Exchange Act in *Shearson/American Express, Inc. v. McMahon*.[33] This case involved Eugene and Julia McMahon, who jointly held various pension and profit-sharing accounts with Shearson/American Express Inc., a brokerage firm. The McMahons filed suit against Shearson claiming that, with Shearson's knowledge, the registered representative who handled their accounts "had violated § 10(b) of the Exchange Act . . . by engaging in fraudulent, excessive trading on [their] accounts and by making false statements and omitting material facts from the advice given to [them]."[34] They also alleged violations under the Racketeer Influenced and Corruption Organization Acts (RICO).

The Court referred to earlier cases, in which it declared that the FAA "establish[ed] a federal policy favoring arbitration . . . requiring that we rigorously enforce agreements to arbitrate."[35] The Court then declared that "to defeat application of the Arbitration Act . . . the McMahons must demonstrate that Congress intended to make an exception to the Arbitration Act for claims arising under RICO and the Exchange Act, an intention discernible from the text, history, or purposes of the statute."[36] Finding that the McMahons did not meet this burden, the Court held agreements to arbitrate claims enforceable.[37] While the Court did not overrule *Wilko*, it limited *Wilko*'s application to the Security Act, not the Exchange Act.

Following the *McMahon* decision, lower courts were split over the continued validity of *Wilko*. Some circuits believed that although *McMahon* questioned *Wilko*, *Wilko* was still precedent. Other courts thought *McMahon* negated the rationale of *Wilko*. In 1989, the Supreme Court resolved the quandary in *Rodriguez de Quijas v. Shearson/American Express, Inc.*[38]

The petitioners in *Rodriguez* used Shearson as their broker and invested about $400,000 in securities. The standard customer agreement included a binding arbitration clause. The investments did poorly, and petitioners filed suit under the Securities Act of 1934. They alleged that their losses occurred as a result of unauthorized and fraudulent transactions by the broker-agent in charge. The Court ruled that alleged violations of the Securities Act were arbitrable, thereby overruling *Wilko*. The Court found that the aversion to arbitration in *Wilko* was imbued with "the old judicial hostility to arbitration"[39] and "[t]o the extent that *Wilko* rested on suspicion of arbitration as a method of weakening the protections afforded in the substantive law to would-be complaints, it has fallen far out of step with our current strong endorsement of the federal statutes favoring this method of resolving disputes."[40] The Court also decided that the Securities Act and Exchange Act "should be construed harmoniously because they constitute interrelated components of the federal regulatory scheme governing transactions in securities."[41] Additionally, the Court reasoned that "the inconsistency between *Wilko* and *McMahon* undermines the essential rationale for a harmonious construction of the two statutes, which is to discourage litigants from manipulating their allegations merely to cast their claims under one of the securities laws rather than another."[42]

After the decisions in *McMahon* and *Rodriguez*, investors have been required to arbitrate disputes with brokerage firms. The process of securities arbitration is now overseen by the quasi-governmental administrative body called the Financial Industry Regulatory Authority (FINRA).

Commercial Arbitration

Commercial arbitration is believed to have originated in England with the merchant guilds.[43] It was brought to the United States by the early settlers. In 1768, according to scholar Fred I. Kent, "the first committee ever to be appointed in this country for the settlement of commercial disputes outside of the courts" was created by the State of New York Chamber of Commerce on

May 3. The use of arbitration by chambers of commerce was then adopted by trade groups such as the Silk Association of America, the Grain and Feed Dealers' National Association, the National Hay Association, and the American Spice Trade Association, to name some.

Commercial arbitration involves a dispute between two businesses. Examples are disputes between buyers of a particular product and the suppliers, franchisees and franchisors, and builders and subcontractors. Unlike a consumer dispute, the parties in commercial arbitration know each other and have long-term relationships; therefore, arbitration can help to preserve these business relationships. The parties in business disputes are familiar with the arbitration process and have equal bargaining power. They frequently favor arbitration because of its speed and the concern that protracted litigation can interrupt business, cost lost revenue, and derail a project.

International Commercial Arbitration

International arbitration is analogous to arbitration in the United States in many respects. Both require the agreement of the disputing parties, are normally a private process, and occasionally need the assistance of courts. Because of these similarities and the breadth of the field, our discussion about international arbitration will be brief.

While many of the advantages of arbitration discussed in the previous chapter apply, the motivating force for international arbitration has been the parties' concern about litigating a dispute in a foreign judicial forum. Parties are concerned that their unfamiliarity with the language, laws, and court procedures, and perhaps foreign judicial bias, will put them at a disadvantage. Additionally, there is the issue of enforcement of judicial awards. However, by agreeing to arbitrate, businesses can submit their disagreement to an international arbitration provider whose rules are satisfactory to both parties. And because nearly all countries are signatories to the Convention on the Recognition and Enforcement of Foreign Arbitral Awards (commonly known as the New York Convention), there is an enforcement mechanism for foreign arbitral awards.

The growth of international arbitration is attributable to the increase of international trade and commerce after World War II. "By the mid-1980s, at least, it had become recognized that arbitration was the *normal* way of settlement of international commercial disputes."[44] As international commerce continues to expand, so likely will international arbitration.

THE ARBITRATION PROCESS

Typically, arbitration occurs in several steps. Keep in mind, however, that the parties, by agreement, can design their own procedure. What follows are the main steps in an arbitration.

Filing a Demand for Arbitration

The arbitration process begins with the complaining party filing a demand for arbitration or "notice of intention to arbitrate." The notice must include the name of the parties, the arbitration clause from the parties' agreement, a brief statement of facts, and the relief sought. The manner for serving the demand may or may not be included in the arbitration clause. Any method of service for initiating a court action will generally be acceptable.

Selection of Arbitrators

Arbitrators may be selected by different methods that include appointment pursuant to the rules of an organization administering the arbitration, directly by the parties, or by a court. In cases that use a tribunal of arbitrators, frequently three, each party appoints an arbitrator, with the third arbitrator being selected by the two arbitrators appointed by the parties.

Preliminary Meeting

This meeting is between the arbitrator, the parties, and their lawyers, if any. The purpose is to discuss the issues of the dispute and procedural matters. Some specific topics could include the procedures for obtaining information, the actual exchange of information, identification of witnesses and the exchange of witness statements, and the date, time, and location of the hearing.

Prehearing Conference

The prehearing conference can be extremely helpful in expediting the hearing. The purpose is to fully discuss and plan the conduct of the arbitration hearing.

> The prehearing conference . . . provides an opportunity to address the full range of procedural matters, including (1) clarifying the contractual basis of the arbitration and the issues presented, the rules governing arbitration, and the location of the hearings; (2) specifying approved methods of communication; (3) identifying jurisdictional issues; (4) establishing a framework for addressing motions for interim or provisional relief, and for dispositive motions; (5) establishing a timetable or schedule for the process; (6) developing a framework for information exchange and discovery; (7) setting specific ground rules for the hearing; (8) considering protections for confidential information; and (9) setting parameters for the arbitration award.[45]

Exchange of Information and Discovery

Parties often choose arbitration because it is faster and less expensive than an adversarial court proceeding. Discovery, associated with conventional litigation, can be time consuming and expensive, so parties frequently agree to exchange information. Although for many years discovery was not allowed, today the arbitrator can order that it take place. Discovery is frequently limited to information relevant to the main issues in the dispute. Requests for admission and interrogatories, available under the civil procedure discovery rules, are uncommon in arbitration. And, unless by agreement of the parties, taking of depositions requires a showing of good cause before an arbitrator will consent.

The Hearing

Arbitration hearings are commonly less formal than a trial and can take place in an office at a conference table, a meeting room, or any place agreed to by the parties or designated by the arbitrator. At the hearing, each side makes an opening statement followed by questioning of witnesses through direct and cross-examination, the submission of any documents, and closing statements and arguments. The formal rules of evidence do not apply unless agreed to by the parties. Thus, evidence inadmissible in court, such as hearsay, may be considered by the arbitrator.

The length of the hearing depends on the complexity of the dispute and the number of disputants involved. A hearing could be completed in a day or could be prolonged over an extended period of time.

PARALEGAL POINTERS

Preparing Exhibits

Large complex cases can involve numerous documents that have to be reviewed to determine which ones will be presented at the arbitration hearing. Paralegals are often responsible for analyzing and organizing these documents and preparing them as exhibits to be introduced as evidence. This will ensure an efficient and effective presentation by the attorney. There are many software programs and forms available to help with assembling and introducing exhibits at the hearing. Preparing exhibits is more fully discussed in Chapter 11.

The Award

After considering all of the information, the arbitrator issues a decision and **award**. The arbitrator has considerable discretion in fashioning the award. The American Arbitration Association Rules permit "any remedy or relief that the arbitrator deems just and equitable and within the scope of the agreement of the parties, including, but not limited to, specific performance of a contract."[46]

Traditionally, arbitrators do not provide written explanations for their awards because this could provide grounds for appeal by a party unhappy with the outcome and thus undermine the advantage of the finality of arbitration awards. Of course, if requested by the parties or agreed to in the arbitration clause, a written explanation will be issued. In labor relations, written awards with the arbitrator's rationale for the decision have been common practice for many years.

JUDICIAL ENFORCEMENT OF AWARDS

Once an award is rendered, a number of things can happen. The losing party can abide by the terms of the award, which then obviates the need for enforcement action. If there is no voluntary compliance, an action to confirm or vacate the award can be filed in the court. The court can confirm or remand (send back) the award, requesting the arbitrator to clarify any alleged uncertainty or confusion. Finally, either party can file an action with the court to modify or correct clerical mistakes.

The general rule is that arbitral awards are nonreviewable, and exceptions are very limited. Judicial deference in supporting enforcement of awards is important to the viability of arbitration as a method for resolving disputes. The appellate court in *Remmey v. PaineWebber, Inc.*[47] provided an excellent explanation for why review of awards should be extremely limited.

> We must underscore at the outset the limited scope of review that courts are permitted to exercise over arbitral decisions. Limited judicial review is necessary to encourage the use of arbitration as an alternative to formal litigation. This policy is widely recognized, and the Supreme Court has often found occasion to approve it. . . .
>
> A policy favoring arbitration would mean little, of course, if arbitration were merely the prologue to prolonged litigation. If such were the case, one would hardly achieve the twin goals of arbitration, namely, settling disputes efficiently and avoiding long and expensive litigation. . . . Opening up arbitral awards to myriad legal challenges would eventually reduce arbitral proceedings to the status of preliminary hearings. Parties would cease to utilize a process that no longer had finality. To avoid this result, courts have resisted temptations to redo arbitral decisions. As the Seventh Circuit put it, "[a]rbitrators do not act as junior varsity trial courts where subsequent appellate review is readily available to the losing party."
>
> Thus, in reviewing arbitral awards, a district or appellate court is limited to determining whether the arbitrators did the job they were told to do—not whether they did it well, or correctly, or reasonably, but simply whether they did it. . . . Courts are not free to overturn an arbitral result because they would have reached a different conclusion if presented with the same facts.[48]

Apart from § 10 of the FAA, reprinted earlier in this chapter, there are four judicially created grounds for vacating an arbitration award: manifest disregard of the law (similar to arbitrators exceeding their powers under the FAA), arbitrary and capricious, irrationality, and violates public policy.

Manifest Disregard of the Law

While the precise definition of "manifest disregard of the law" is uncertain, "it clearly means more than error or misunderstanding with respect to the law."[49] To show that an arbitrator manifestly disregarded the law, a challenger must establish "(1) that the error is so obvious that it would be readily and instantly perceived by a typical arbitrator, and (2) that the arbitrator was subjectively aware of the proper legal standard but proceeded to disregard it in fashioning the award. Furthermore, the knowing disregard of the law must be apparent on the face of the record."[50] Challengers will have a difficult time establishing manifest disregard of the law because awards are seldom accompanied by a written statement of the applicable law, and usually, there are no transcripts of the proceedings.

Arbitrary and Capricious

For an arbitral award to be considered arbitrary and capricious, there must be a showing beyond an error of law or interpretation. An award will be considered arbitrary and capricious "only if a ground for the arbitrator's decision cannot be inferred from the facts of the case."[51] Provided that there is a rational basis for the arbitrator's decision, the award will stand. Because arbitrators rarely provide reasons for an award, meeting the arbitrary and capricious standard is difficult.

Irrationality

A New York court explained that "as long as [arbitrators] remain within their . . . [authority] and do not reach an irrational result, they may fashion the law to fit the facts before them."[52] Again, because written opinions and transcripts of the proceedings are rare, proving an award was irrational is extremely difficult.

Violates Public Policy

The public policy exception is based on the common law principle that courts can refuse to enforce contracts when the cause of action is derived from an immoral or illegal act.[53] Courts recognize the public's concern that, because it is not a party, its views may be unrepresented and any public interest could be harmed. The U.S. Supreme Court has stated that the public policy "must be well defined and dominant, and is to be ascertained by reference to the laws and legal precedents and not from general considerations of supposed public interests."[54] If a public policy is established, then the court must determine whether the arbitration award violates it.

A violation of public policy will be found when the award

(1) endangers the public; (2) compels illegal acts; (3) involves the use of drugs in a safety sensitive position or in a position involving the operation of dangerous machinery; (4) violates a no drugs policy issued by the employer; (5) exceeds the

maximum amount of recovery allowed by law; (6) contravenes arbitration; or (7) violates a prohibition against waiver of arbitration.[55]

Conclusion

Arbitration, once relegated to disputes between businesses, has become a judicially sanctioned remedy for a wide array of civil disagreements including consumer transactions, employment, and securities disputes. According to one scholar, this expansive role is making arbitration more like litigation and in turn alienating business users.

> Today, for example, proceedings under standard arbitration rules are likely to include prehearing motion practice and extensive discovery. Hearings may go on for extended periods of time in order to avoid charges of procedural injustice, and there is evidence that the much-vaunted finality of arbitral awards is eroding. The higher costs associated with these developments is a leading cause for complaint about arbitration among business users. At the same time, paradoxically, it appears that an increasing number of lawyers are seeking ways of eliminating the remaining differences between arbitration and court trial, most notably through contractual provisions for expanded judicial review of arbitration awards.[56]

Scholars have also been critical of the Supreme Court's decisions favoring binding arbitration in consumer and employment agreements and have put forth suggestions for reform. In addition, members of Congress have proposed mandating fairness in arbitration for employees and consumers. (See Appendix C, "Proposed Arbitration Fairness Act of 2013.")

For the foreseeable future, arbitration will remain a viable option to traditional litigation, along with the other methods of dispute resolution. The key is to understand what it is and how it functions. With this knowledge, a party and a party's representative can decide whether arbitration is the appropriate format for resolving the dispute.

Key Terms and Concepts

Adhesive arbitration agreements	Labor arbitration
Arbitrability	Predispute agreement
Arbitral clause	Procedural unconscionability
Award	Revised Uniform Arbitration
Commercial arbitration	Act (RUAA)
Consumer arbitration	Securities arbitration
Contract of adhesion	Submission agreement
Employment arbitration	Substantive unconscionability
Federal Arbitration Act (FAA)	Unconscionability

Practice Test Questions

True/False

___ 1. The FAA provides a legal framework for managing arbitrations and applies to all maritime transactions and interstate or foreign commerce.

___ 2. The general rule is that arbitral awards are reviewable.

___ 3. Unconscionability is the contract defense on which courts frequently rely in refusing to enforce adhesive arbitration agreements.

___ 4. An agreement to arbitrate a present dispute is called a submission agreement.

___ 5. At a minimum, arbitrators are required to follow the rules of evidence during hearings.

Multiple Choice

___ 1. Arbitrators may be selected by all of the following methods *except*
   a. Directly by the parties
   b. By two arbitrators selected by the parties
   c. By a court
   d. By one party

___ 2. What are the four judicially created grounds for vacating an arbitration award?
   a. Manifest disregard of the law, arbitrary and capricious, irresponsibility, and violates common sense
   b. Manifest disregard of the law, arbitrary and capricious, irrationality, and violates precedent
   c. Manifest necessity, selective enforcement, irrationality, and violates public policy
   d. Manifest disregard of the law, arbitrary and capricious, irrationality, and violates public policy

___ 3. Which of the following are *not* grounds for vacating arbitration awards under the FAA?
   a. Arbitrator incorrectly applied the law
   b. Corruption, fraud, undue means
   c. Evident partiality in the arbitrators
   d. Arbitrators exceeded their powers

___ 4. A contract of adhesion is
   a. a contract, agreed to and entered into willingly by the parties.
   b. a contract, drafted by the more experienced party, forcing the other party to accept or reject it.
   c. a mutually bargained-for agreement.
   d. without legal force.

___ 5. Whether there was an agreement to arbitrate and the extent of the agreement is called

  a. a meeting of the minds
  b. reciprocal burdens
  c. arbitrability
  d. mutual consideration

Review Questions

1. What is an arbitral clause? What makes an arbitral clause adhesive?
2. What is the difference between predispute agreements and submission agreements?
3. Explain the concept of unconscionability and provide an example of an agreement that is unconscionable. Be sure to include procedural unconscionability and substantive unconscionability.
4. What does "arbitrability" mean? How do you decide whether a particular dispute is arbitrable under an arbitration agreement?
5. What is the difference between labor and employment arbitration? Provide an example of each.
6. Why are courts reluctant to strike down mandatory arbitration agreements?
7. What criteria did a Florida court use to determine whether a mandatory arbitration agreement was unconscionable?
8. List and explain the FAA's defenses to an arbitration award.
9. Name and explain the judicially created defenses to an arbitration award discussed in the chapter.
10. List and explain each step in the arbitration process.

Application Questions

1. If you owned a business that sold consumer goods such as computers, cell phones, or televisions, why would you want mandatory arbitration?
2. From a consumer perspective, why are mandatory agreements to arbitrate a bad idea?
3. Applying the Florida court's criteria for unconscionability discussed in the chapter, determine whether the arbitration agreement in *Vazquez v. Liberty Wireless* unconscionable. If your answer is "yes," is it procedural or substantive unconscionability? Be sure to provide sufficient reasoning for your answer.

Vazquez v. Liberty Wireless

Facts:

Liberty Wireless is a retail store and the exclusive provider for the new Snap phone. A person who signs up for the Snap must do so for a minimum of two years. The Snap's battery, although rechargeable, may not last that long. Replacing the battery requires that the user send the phone to Snap and pay a $95.00

service fee plus shipping charges, and an additional fee if he wants to use a loaner Snap phone. The only option for the user is to cancel his service before the two-year term ends, which results in a substantial early termination fee.

Liberty Wireless began marketing and promoting the Snap phone because it was available for sale. No mention was made of the limited life of the battery and what would be required to replace it.

Isabella Vazquez, intrigued by the new phone and wanting to be one of the first to own it, purchased it the day it went on sale at Liberty Wireless. retail store. The sales receipt noted that she could return the phone by June 28 but would be charged a fee of $50 if the box in which the phone was sold had been opened.

Vazquez learned about the battery issue after buying the phone and sued Liberty Wireless and Snap in state court, alleging that the need to purchase a battery before the two-year minimum service term ended amounts to a de facto annual maintenance and/or service charge. She alleged that in marketing the phone, Liberty Wireless and Snap hid information about the phone's limited battery life and the information of the replacement program until after the phone went on sale. Vazquez claimed common law fraud, breach of contract, implied warranty, unjust enrichment, and violation of the state's consumer fraud act.

Liberty Wireless and Snap removed the case to federal court and filed a motion to compel arbitration. Vazquez argues that the arbitration agreement was hidden from her prior to or at the time of her purchase. She asserts that she did not see and did not have access to a paper copy of any documents explaining or referencing Liberty Wireless's terms of service. Liberty Wireless asserts that paper copies are available at their retail stores but cannot offer any evidence substantiating this claim. Liberty Wireless also claims that the terms of service are available online and all one has to do is use the "search" tool and type in an appropriate query, such as "terms of service," "agreement," or "conditions." Liberty Wireless did admit that the service agreement available online was obsolete and not valid for Vazquez's purchase.

4. Arbitration occurs when the parties have an agreement. However, sometimes the agreement is unclear about which disputes the parties intended to arbitrate. Determining whether there was an agreement to arbitrate is called arbitrability. In the following hypotheticals, decide whether the parties had an agreement to arbitrate the dispute.

a. **Kayla v. Get Fit**

Kayla is a former sales representative for Get Fit fitness center. When her employment ended, she filed suit alleging Get Fit failed to pay her overtime wages in violation of the FLSA (Fair Labor Standards Act). During her employment, Get Fit issued an employee handbook that, among other things, required that all employment-related disputes, whether commenced by an employee or Get Fit, would be decided only by an arbitrator through final and binding arbitration.

Disagreements under the Fair Labor Standards Act were included in matters subject to mandatory arbitration. The handbook also provided that the FAA would govern the arbitration. Kayla signed the following acknowledgment:

> I agree that if there is a dispute involving my employment, I will submit it to binding and final arbitration. I also understand that Get Fit retains the right to revise, delete, or add to the employee handbook. Any changes to the handbook will be communicated through official written notices approved by the President of Get Fit or her designee. All changes must be in writing.

b. Deanna v. Sinclair Investments

Deanna, a sophomore in college, inherited some money from a rich relative when she was a young child. The money was held in a custodial account with Sincair Investments. When she turned eighteen, she changed the customer account from a custodial account to one in her own name. She signed a customer agreement that included a predispute arbitration clause as follows:

ARBITRATION

1. Arbitration is final and binding on all parties.
2. The parties waive their right to seek any remedies in court, including the right to a jury trial.
3. Pre-arbitration discovery is limited.
4. The arbitrator is not required to provide factual findings or legal reasoning.
5. Any right to appeal or to request modification of any arbitrator ruling is limited.
6. The panel of arbitrators will include a minority of arbitrators who were or presently are involved in securities industry.

Above Deanna's signature line the following was written:

THIS IS A BINDING CONTRACT. I HAVE READ IT CAREFULLY BEFORE SIGNING.

The signature page also indicated that Deanna had received a copy of the document.

Over the next two years, Deanna used the money for living expenses and college tuition. During those two years, her account suffered significant losses. She sued Sinclair Investments for breach of contract, fraud, and breach of fiduciary duty for mishandling and losing her investments.

Sinclair Investments filed a motion to compel arbitration. Deanna claims that she had not agreed to arbitration and she signed the document only to change the account name.

Is there a valid binding arbitration agreement?

Practice Exercises

1. There are many considerations when drafting an arbitration clause. For example: Do you want a single arbitrator or a panel? Should the arbitrator prepare a written decision? Is confidentiality important? Will the award be binding?

   The attorney you work for, Daniel Flores, represents Randy's Flooring, Inc., which is owned by Randy Thomas. Randy's Flooring is a retail business that sells and installs all types of flooring, including carpet, laminate, hardwood, vinyl, and tile. Randy recently had some problems with a customer who sued him for negligence. Although the case was eventually settled, it was expensive and time consuming. Randy has decided that he now wants to include an arbitration clause in his contracts. Attorney Flores has asked you to research various arbitration clauses and prepare a memo explaining each clause along with your opinion on whether the clause should be included in the contract. For help preparing the arbitration agreement, you may want to look at https://www.clausebuilder.org.

2. Locate six private arbitrators in your state and discuss their credentials, areas of expertise, and fees.

3. Choose three topics discussed in this chapter and find court cases in your jurisdiction (federal or state court) that discuss the issues. Prepare a written brief for each case.

Endnotes

1. Richard C. Reuben, *First Options, Consent to Arbitration, and the Demise of Separability: Restoring Access to Justice for Contracts with Arbitration Provisions*, 56 S.M.U. L. Rev. 819, 833 (2003).

2. Neal v. State Farm Ins. Cos., 10 Cal. Rptr. 781, 784 (Ct. App. 1961).

3. David S. Schwartz, *Enforcing Small Print to Protect Big Business: Employee and Consumer Rights Claims in an Age of Compelled Arbitration*, 1997 Wis. L. Rev. 33, 55.

4. Hubert v. Dell Corp., 835 N.E.2d 113, 118-119 (Ill. App. Ct. 2005) (emphasis in original).

5. Doctor's Assocs., Inc. v. Casarotto , 517 U.S. 681, 687 (1996).

6. *Black's Law Dictionary* 731 (9th ed., Thomson Reuters 2009).

7. "Your Other You" was the name of the advertising campaign and "consisted of sending an unwitting recipient emails from an unknown individual." Duick v. Toyota Sales, U.S.A., Inc., 198 Cal. App. 4th 1316, 1318-1319 (2011).

8. *Id.*

9. *Id.*

10. Gainey v. Gainey, 675 S.E.2d 792, 799 (S.C. Ct. App. 2009).

11. *Id.*

12. AT&T Mobility v. Concepcion, 563 U.S. 333, 340 (2011).

13. A&M Produce Co. v. FMC Corp., 135 Cal. App. 3d 473, 486 (1982).

14. Pendergast v. Sprint Nextel Corp., 592 F.3d 1119, 1135 (3d Cir. 2010).

15. *Id.* at 1139.

16. Stephen J. Ware, *The Case for Enforcing Adhesive Arbitration Agreements — with Particular Consideration of Class Actions and Arbitration Fees*, 5 J. Am. Arbitration 251, 255 n.5 (2006).

17. Southland v. Keating, 465 U.S. 1, 10 (1984).

18. AT&T Mobility LLC v. Concepcion, 563 U.S. 333, 344 (2011).

19. Steelworkers v. Am. Mfg. Co., 363 U.S. 564 (1960); Steelworkers v. Warrior & Gulf Navigation Co., 363 U.S. 574 (1960); Steelworkers v. Enterprise Wheel & Car Corp., 363 U.S. 593 (1960).

20. 475 U.S. 643 (1986).

21. *Id.* at 648-650.

22. 500 U.S. 20 (1991).

23. *Id.* at 26.

24. *Id.* at 33.

25. 9 U.S.C. § 1 (1947).

26. 532 U.S. 105 (2001).

27. *Id.* at 119.

28. The exceptions are those grounds that "exist at law or in equity for the revocation of any contract." 9 U.S.C. § 2.

29. 9 U.S.C. § 2.

30. 513 U.S. 265, 273-274 (1995).

31. 346 U.S. 427 (1953).

32. *Id.* at 438.

33. 482 U.S. 220 (1987).

34. *Id.* at 223.

35. *Id.* at 226.

36. *Id.* at 227.

37. The Court also held that "the McMahons, having made the bargain to arbitrate, will be held to their bargain. Their RICO claim is arbitrable under the terms of the Arbitration Act." *Id.* at 242.

38. 490 U.S. 477 (1989).

39. *Id.* at 480.

40. *Id.* at 481.

41. *Id.* at 484-485.

42. *Id.* at 485.

43. *See* the section in Chapter 5 titled "A Brief History of Arbitration"; *see also* Earl Wolaver, *The Historical Background of Commercial Arbitration*, 83 U. Pa. L. Rev. 132, 133 (1934).

44. W. Laurence Craig, *Some Trends and Developments in the Laws and Practice of International Commercial Arbitration*, 30 Tex. Int'l L.J. 1, 2 (1995).

45. Jay Folberg, Dwight Golann, Thomas J. Stipanowich & Lisa A. Kloppenberg, *Resolving Disputes: Theory, Practice, and Law* 587 (Aspen 2010).

46. *Commercial Arbitration Rules and Mediation Procedures*, R-47 Scope of Award (Am. Arbitration Ass'n 2013).

47. 32 F.3d 143 (4th Cir. 1994).

48. *Id.* at 146.

49. Merrill Lynch, Pierce, Fenner & Smith, Inc. v. Bobker, 808 F.2d 930, 933 (2d Cir. 1986).

50. Raiford v. Merrill Lynch, Pierce, Fenner & Smith, Inc., 903 F.2d 1410, 1412-1413 (11th Cir. 1990).

51. *Id.* at 1413.

52. Exercycle Corp. v. Maratta, 174 N.E.2d 463, 466 (N.Y. 1961).

53. United Paperworkers Int'l Union, AFJ-CIO, v. Misco, Inc., 484 U.S. 29, 42 (1987).

54. W.R. Grace & Co. v. Local Union 759, Int'l Union of the United Rubber, Cork, Linoleum & Plastic Workers of Am., 461 U.S. 757, 766 (1983).

55. Martin Domke, *Domke on Commercial Arbitration: The Law and Practice of Commercial Arbitration* § 39:9 (Larry E. Edmonson ed., 3d ed., West 2009).

56. Thomas J. Stipanowich, *Arbitration: The New Litigation*, 2010 U. Ill. L. Rev. 1, 5-6.

CHAPTER SEVEN

Online Dispute Resolution: The Beginnings

Chapter Outline

Introduction

What Is ODR, and How Does It Work?

The Evolution of ODR

    First Period: Pre-1995

    Second Period: 1995-1998

    Third Period: 1998-2000

Conclusion

Key Terms and Concepts

Practice Test Questions

Review Questions

Application Questions

Practice Exercises

> Cyberspace is an active place, a creative place and, for some, a
> lucrative place. It is not, however, a harmonious place.
>
> — ETHAN KATSH[1]

As you read this chapter and the next, keep in mind that technology changes so rapidly that what you study today may become antiquated two or three years from now. Additionally, some of the companies mentioned in this chapter that offer dispute resolution services may not exist in the future, but almost certainly new ones will appear.

INTRODUCTION

In the 1990s, many people were not convinced of the necessity or possibilities of **online dispute resolution (ODR)**. Not so today.

A growing number of cases are being resolved by online tools, and sometimes lawyers and judges are not even involved. Impartial web-based systems apply computation, algorithms, and cryptographic technology to bring about resolution quickly and inexpensively. A growing stable of private sector companies are beginning to compete with the judicial system for "customers" and are also changing the face of traditional Alternate Dispute Resolution or ADR, which has typically included mediation, arbitration, and other alternatives to the courts.[2]

In 2012, General Electric's oil and gas division began testing Cybersettle in its Italian offices to reduce time and money spent on lawyers for simple disputes.[3] Cybersettle is a double-blind ODR system that collects the parties' confidential settlement offers and demands and determines whether the parties should settle and for what amount. (More information about Cybersettle appears later in this chapter.) The system was designed to handle disagreements of about $65,000 (approximately €50,000) in value or less. According to GE, the cost for arbitrating a settlement, $12,962 (€10,000) for each side is not cost-effective. According to general counsel of GE Oil & Gas, Kenneth Resnick, "we get a large number of claims that are simply about money and they can take up a lot of attorney time and costs."[4] Using Cybersettle "allows a cheap — and, most important, fast — way of solving them."[5]

New York City began using Cybersettle in February 2004 to settle personal injury and property damage claims. According to the city comptroller, during approximately four years, the city settled 3047 claims that saved taxpayers $33.4 million. The average settlement amount using Cybersettle was close to $11,000, compared to $28,000 before using it. Additionally, claims that would take about four years to settle were resolved in six months to one year.[6] In the middle of 2011, the city's new comptroller decided not to use Cybersettle, claiming that it's cheaper to use in-house claims adjusters.

PayPal and eBay resolve more than 60 million disputes every year.[7] Colin Rule, who served as PayPal's and eBay's first director of ODR from 2003-2011, created and directed the programs. EBay continues to resolve disputes online.

In May 2012, British Columbia passed a law promoting ODR. It provides for nonfacilitated and facilitated dispute resolution with the final stage being a tribunal hearing, which could occur online.

The European Union (EU) launched its Online Dispute Resolution platform on February 15, 2016. One year later the platform has handled more than 24,000 cases. "More than a third of the complaints concerned cross-border purchases within the EU. Most complaints were about clothing and footwear, airline tickets and information and communication technology goods."[8]

The Better Business Bureau (BBB) recognizes the growth of business conducted over the Internet, or e-commerce, and requires its members with online shopping sites to use its dispute resolution services.[9] Before resorting to the BBB, a consumer must attempt to resolve the dispute with the merchant. If this is unsuccessful, she then files a complaint on BBBOnline. The BBB contacts the business and tries to settle the dispute using conciliation, mediation, or arbitration.

Online sales "reached $394.86 billion [in 2016], a 15.6% increase compared with $341.70 billion in 2015. That's the highest growth rate since 2013, when online sales grew 16.5% over 2012."[10]

If you are still not convinced that ODR is relevant and will continue to be so, remember that "the children of today [the digital natives] soon will be the adults, and therefore the clients, of tomorrow . . . [and they have been] . . . immersed far more deeply in technology than those who were raised in a less technology-saturated world [the digital immigrants]."[11]

> Members of the younger generation, in particular, have become reliant on technology in almost every area of their lives. Not only do they use technology throughout their workdays, they've become comfortable using it in many of their most intimate personal relationships. As such, when a dispute arises, many people now expect to be able to use the same kinds of tools to address issues quickly and effectively. Technology is built into our daily lives so thoroughly that, for many people, *not* using computer-mediated communication to address a workplace dispute would seem weird. Yet many mediators and ombudsmen remain skeptical.[12]

We will begin our exploration of ODR with a brief explanation of what it is, followed by a discussion on the creation of the Internet. The chapter then provides a historical overview of ODR, from its beginnings in the early 1990s to about 2000. You will probably be surprised to learn that virtual communities began in the 1990s but were all text based. Participants directed characters by typing in textual commands. These early virtual worlds did not have images, graphics, video, or sound. Every scene and every movement had to be described or directed textually. Wait until you read a sample dialogue from one of these early places. Virtual reality has come a long way.

One famous cyberspace dispute, which you will read about later in the chapter, led to the recognition of the need for an ODR system. The incident caused such outrage that the online community almost disbanded. After a lot of discussion among members, they acknowledged the need for a formal method to handle disputes that arise among participants.

The development of **Internet Service Providers (ISPs)** and the lifting of the ban on commercial Internet activities increased the number of both Internet users and online disputes. A number of people involved in the Internet recognized the need for an online system to resolve disputes. Several experimental ODR projects, funded by a private foundation, showed the feasibility of ODR programs, and this stirred the interest of for-profit enterprises. Using sophisticated technology, various companies created online programs for dispute resolution. This chapter discusses some of the early experiments and commercial enterprises that developed and offered ODR services.

WHAT IS ODR, AND HOW DOES IT WORK?

One of the pioneers in the field, Colin Rule, defines ODR as "[a]ny use of technology to complement, support, or administer a dispute resolution process. . . ."[13] ODR expands on ADR forms (negotiation, mediation, and arbitration) in that it adds the use of technology to these traditional methods. This technology is sometimes referred to as the "fourth party."[14] (ADR typically involves three parties: the two disputants and the neutral party (e.g., a mediator or arbitrator).) As technology progresses, ODR will also be used in summary jury trials, mini-trials, and early neutral evaluation. For now, we will look briefly at how technology is used in three common types of ADR.

Traditionally, negotiation involves two parties who work to reach agreement about a disputed matter. In ODR, technology "assists" (or enhances) the negotiation, hence we call it "assisted negotiation." The technology used can serve as the communication medium through which the negotiation takes place, or it can be software, which can present the parties with alternative solutions and help them determine and evaluate what exchanges they are willing to offer. Noninteractive forms use technology in place of human beings. This approach is called "automated negotiation." The most common form of automated negotiation is "blind bidding"; it is frequently used when the dispute involves only money and the parties cannot agree on a settlement amount. In blind bidding, the parties submit offers and a computer determines whether a settlement can be reached.

Online mediation mirrors much of what takes place in offline mediation. There are opening statements by the mediator and parties, discussions about interests and concerns, and various settlement options. Private caucuses between the mediator and one or both of the parties are available. In the beginning, online mediation used e-mail to exchange information. This progressed to posting information on secure bulletin boards. With the creation and availability of video conferencing, mediation moved from strictly textual to face-to-face communication. The next improvement, at the time of writing this textbook, appears to be the use of holography and perhaps robots and avatars.[15] Chapter 8 discusses these topics more fully.

Arbitration, as we learned, is the use of one or more neutral third parties to determine the outcome from the evidence submitted by the disputing parties. Online arbitration is simple when the evidence consists of only written documents. The parties submit these through the Internet, and the arbitrator renders a decision. If there are live witnesses, the parties can use the technology available to present their testimony. At the time of writing this chapter, the existing technological platforms included audio and video conferencing.

Now that you have a basic understanding of ODR and how it is applied to negotiation, mediation, and arbitration, let us turn to the development of ODR. First is a discussion of the creation of the Internet and the growth of Internet users. Next you will learn about the inevitable occurrence of online disputes. This is followed by a discussion of the experiments in ODR programs and the involvement of commercial enterprise in ODR.

THE EVOLUTION OF ODR

The Internet as we know it today began in 1969, when it was developed as a way for the Department of Defense "to ensure the availability of computer communication between the government and government funded research-ers."[16] Up until the early 1990s, the only people who could access the Internet were those associated with the military and universities. This changed when college students brought personal computers to campus and were able to access the Internet through their universities' mainframes. As a result, the Internet population grew, and along with this, so did disputes, largely involving students. The National Science Foundation's decision in 1992 to lift its ban on commercial activity on the Internet also contributed to a rise in the number of disputes. One of the pioneers of ODR, Ethan Katsh, recognized in 1996 that along with the growth of the Internet would come an increase in the number of disputes and the need for "online places that can be employed to reduce and resolve conflict."[17]

Ethan Katsh and Janet Rifkin divide the history of ODR into three time periods.[18] The first, lasting until approximately 1995, was a period in which disputes arose and dispute resolution was applied informally and in particular contexts. The second period, from 1995 to 1998, corresponded with the growth of the Internet, especially in commerce. With this came an increasing awareness of the need for online institutions to handle online disputes. The third period from 1998 to 2001, when the Katsh and Rifkin book was published, saw commercial enterprise involvement in ODR. From 2001 through 2012, interest in ODR continued to grow; however, it has been slowed by a need for more sophisticated technology. For example, mediation, perhaps the most ubiquitous of the ADR methods, is most effective when conducted face to face. The promise of videoconferencing and the development of Skype have not met expectations. Perhaps holography—three-dimensional images—holds the key. (Chapter 8 includes a discussion of the use of holography in ODR.)

First Period: Pre-1995

Before 1995, eBay, Amazon, and Google were not in our lexicon. Mosaic, later called Netscape, did not offer its IPO (initial public offering) until August 1995. Only a few corporations recognized the potential value of domain names, and ICANN (the Internet Corporation for Assigned Names and Numbers) did not exist. In April 1994, the first spam case arose, and the Federal Trade Commission prosecuted its first Internet fraud case. Individual conflicts erupted in **flamewars** on **listservs** and in **virtual worlds**. "A virtual world is a computer-simulated environment inhabited by users who interact through their on-screen avatars. Social life in the virtual world is depicted by multiple users appearing together in three-dimensional graphical scenes. The world being simulated has real-world physical characteristics such as gravity, topography, locomotion, real-time actions, and communication.[19] As a result, people began to recognize the need for some method for resolving these disputes. Let's look more closely at these flamewars and virtual worlds' conflicts.

In the early 1990s, listservs were the forum through which most discussions took place. Topics included everything from politics to fantasy games to book clubs. Anyone visiting could read and respond to posted messages; however, there was usually some type of preregistration requirement. The responses were then automatically forwarded to all subscribers.

While most discussions followed established norms of good behavior called "netiquette,"[20] many disagreements escalated into "flaming," a term meaning "gratuitous insults and any other unnecessarily inflammatory responses."[21] The following is an example of flaming:

User A: How stupid can you be? That makes absolutely no sense. Any troglodyte knows that can't be done.

User B: Hey, I'm entitled to my opinion and I'm not the only one who takes that position.

User A: Well, then you and your friends are all morons!

These attacks usually attracted others who were not involved in the earlier discussions. Because these rude exchanges began to affect the majority of subscribers, moderators intervened and tried, through private communication with the offender, to explain how the way he was communicating affected the quality of the discussion. Another approach was to encourage other participants not to respond and hope that the miscreant would go away. Of course, the board owner had the power to unsubscribe the offender; however, this potentially would create a new dispute about the abuse of authority and interference with free speech. Additionally, the unsubscribed person had the option to resubscribe using a different name or address. Sometimes a specific area was created where users could continue to vent their anger.

The virtual worlds in the 1990s did not look anything like they do today. Everything was text based. There were no visible characters, rooms, or objects, only words and computer commands. Exhibit 7-1 is an example of a room depiction and dialogue.

One famous dispute that occurred in cyberspace involved a text-based virtual world called LambdaMOO. The house in this fantasy community accommodated as many people as visited it. People could also put objects in any room and make them do whatever they desired.

On a night in March 1993, a player known as Mr. Bungle, "a fat, oleaginous, Bisquick-faced clown,"[22] made a voodoo doll, placed it in the living room, and used it to force "legba, a Haitian trickster spirit of indeterminate gender" to sexually service him.[23] Mr. Bungle was ejected from the room but could still use the voodoo doll to coerce legba into violent sexual acts with other individuals. Eventually "someone summoned Zippy, a wise and trusted old-timer who brought with him a gun of near wizardly powers, a gun that didn't kill but enveloped its targets in a cage impermeable even to a voodoo doll's powers. Zippy fired this gun at Mr. Bungle, thwarting the doll at last and silencing the evil, distant laughter."[24]

Exhibit 7-1.   TEXT-BASED VIRTUAL WORLD

The Entrance Hall (#19)

This small foyer is the hub of the currently occupied
portion of the house. To the north are the double doors
forming the main entrance to the house. There is a mirror
at about head height on the east wall, just to the right
of a corridor leading off into the bedroom area. The south
wall is all rough stonework, the back of the living room
fireplace; at the west end of the wall is the opening
leading south into the living room and southwest into the
kitchen. Finally, to the west is an open archway leading
into the dining room. You see a mirror at about head height,
a globe, and Edgar the Footman here.

Script 10. LambdaMOO room description.

This is what dialogue would look like:

Prof says, "hello"
Albert [to Prof]: Hi there! I'm the local tour-guide robot.
To start a tour type 'follow <botname>'. When you want to
stop, type 'unfollow <botname>'. Cheers!
Prof says, "who are you?"
Albert looks around, confused.
Prof says, "Brad?"
Albert [to Prof]: Brad? Oh, yes. I know him . . .
Prof jumps up and down
Prof pushes Albert.
Albert is at your service.
Prof . o O (I wonder why you said that)
Albert [to Prof]: Well why not?
Prof looks confused.
Prof smiles.
Albert grins wildly.

Script 4. Dialogue between a user and a bot

Used with permission. Anna (Cicognani) Cico, A Linguistic Characterisation of Design in Text-Based Virtual
Worlds (Sept. 1998) (unpublished Ph.D. dissertation, University of Sydney) (on file with the author).

This incident deeply concerned the residents of LambdaMOO. After lengthy
discussions about what acts Mr. Bungle performed, whether these caused actual
harm and what type of place was this fantasy world, Mr. Bungle was deleted from
the system. The LambdaMOO community recognized a need for some formal
method to handle conflicts arising in their society. Because outside online dispute
programs were nonexistent at this time, LambdaMOO had to create its own
method to resolve disputes and settled on arbitration. The LambdaMOO inhabi-
tants became the arbitrators who settled issues and handed out any necessary
punishment.

While the early users of the Internet were connected with academia, this soon changed and in a big way. In 1992, two things happened that created a surge in the numbers of people with Internet access and the way in which the Internet was used. One was that private ISPs began making the Internet accessible to people not affiliated with colleges and universities. For a monthly fee, anyone with a computer and a telephone was able to connect to the Internet via private companies. The second was when the National Science Foundation's Acceptable Use Policy team, which was managing the Internet at the time, lifted its ban on commercial activity on the Internet. As the numbers of Internet users increased, so did the number and range of conflicts. For example, in the mid-1990s, disputes arose with ISPs. Some of these revolved around the ISPs' rights and responsibilities, such as: When could an ISP terminate a subscriber? Was the ISP responsible for ensuring that a user did not engage in illegal activity? Were they liable in any way when a subscriber distributed copyrighted material? Sensing a need for addressing Internet conflict, a group of people met in Washington, D.C., in late 1995 to explore the development of an online system to resolve these disputes. Thus began the second period in the evolution of ODR.

Second Period: 1995-1998

In early 1996, the National Center for Automated Information Research (NCAIR), a private foundation, provided grants for the development of three pilot projects intended to create a practicable online system for settling disputes. These three experiments were the Virtual Magistrate Project, Online Ombuds Office, and Maryland Family Mediation Project. Each project focused on different kinds of disputes and employed different methods for resolution. All of these formed the framework for further research, experimentation, and development of future ODR programs. Let's look at each of these experiments in more detail.

Virtual Magistrate Project

The Virtual Magistrate Project (VPM) was an online arbitration program focused on "disputes between users of online systems, system operators, and those who claim to be harmed by wrongful messages, postings, or files. These disagreements can consist of complaints about alleged copyright or trademark infringement, misappropriation of trade secrets, defamation, fraud, deceptive trade practices, inappropriate materials, invasion of privacy, and other wrongful content."[25]

The first and only case submitted to the VMP, *Tierney v. American Online (In re Email America)*, involved a subscriber's complaint about an advertisement offering for sale a large list of AOL subscribers and their e-mail addresses for use in bulk e-mailings.[26] Tierney posted his complaint with the VMP and indicated that he wanted AOL to remove the posting because

> (1) the advertisement promotes bulk—e-mailing, which is a practice that is against sound public policy and is not in the interest of Internet users, (2) bulk—e-mailing

is a violation of America Online's long-standing rules prohibiting such practices, (3) the advertisement is a potential invasion of privacy and would damper use of the Internet, and (4) the advertisement was deceptive and was, in effect, false advertising.[27]

VMP sent the complaint over the Internet to the American Arbitration Association (AAA), the entity chosen to administer cases for the program. The AAA assigned a magistrate who ultimately rendered a decision. American Online was notified, via e-mail and telephone, of the complaint by Tierney, and it submitted a response supporting Tierney. When VMP's attempts to notify Email America went unanswered, Email America was defaulted, and the magistrate posted his decision that America Online should remove Email's advertisement.[28]

Although the VMP had lofty goals, it is now defunct. Some scholars attribute the failure to the lack of public awareness, absence of recognition by businesses, and inability of the magistrate to force participation or enforce decisions.[29]

Online Ombuds Office

The second project funded by NCAIR, the Online Ombuds Office (OOO),[30] was established in 1996. It was developed by Ethan Katsh and Janet Rifkin at the University of Massachusetts and operated like a typical ombudsperson, an independent investigator of people's complaints,[31] except that the office resided in cyberspace. The OOO provided users with two services. First, users could access extensive materials to help manage their disputes. Second, they could ask for the assistance of an online ombudsperson.

The procedure at OOO was as follows: a user completed an electronic form explaining his dispute. An ombudsperson would reply via e-mail and possibly pose some questions. If another party was involved and wanted to cooperate, the ombudsperson would mediate the dispute. If not, the ombudsperson would offer some suggestions.

The first case for OOO involved an individual living in the Midwest who had developed a website that provided news and information.[32] Robert Gray sent an e-mail to OOO complaining that a local newspaper, the *Hampshire County News*, threatened to sue him for copyright violations. The newspaper claimed that Gray was using its copyrighted material and posting it verbatim onto his website. OOO's ombudsperson responded to Gray via e-mail and requested more information. The ombudsperson then e-mailed the complaint to the newspaper. A number of e-mails were exchanged between the parties over the course of about one month. The newspaper explained that it was not threatening to sue Gray but was only concerned about the origin of his news. When the newspaper learned that Gray consulted various sources for his stories, the newspaper was satisfied and the dispute ended.

In December 1998, eBay approached OOO about developing a dispute resolution program for its company. The pilot project was launched in early 1999. We will discuss this experiment in more detail in the section below titled "Third

Period: 1999 to 2000." The OOO continues today as part of the Center for Information Technology and Dispute Resolution at the University of Massachusetts.

Maryland Family Mediation Project

Funded by NCAIR, the University of Maryland Online Mediation Project (Mediate-net) was launched in 1996. The purpose of this experiment was to determine the feasibility of using the Internet for resolving "two types of disputes: domestic disputes such as custody, visitation, child support and property division; and health care disputes between either consumers and insurance companies, or consumers and health care device manufacturers."[33] The hope was to show that mediating family and health disputes online would be less expensive, be effective in facilitating agreements, and create a foundation for postdivorce conflict resolution. The objectives were to

- provide a clearinghouse for information regarding online mediation and negotiation;
- create an environment for online mediation and negotiation, first in the State of Maryland and then in other jurisdictions, as needs and interests developed;
- undertake research into the effectiveness of online mediation and the communication technologies that facilitate it; and
- train alternative dispute settlement professionals in online mediation and negotiation techniques.[34]

The project used e-mail, electronic conferencing, real time, and private online chats and videoconferencing. If requested, face-to-face meetings would be arranged.

There were four stages in the program. In Stage 1, the participants made their first contact with the project and learned about the process and basic rules for mediation. In Stage 2, the parties met online with the mediator. This could be in synchronous or asynchronous time. Asynchronous time is when parties are not communicating at the same time. Examples are e-mail or web-based communication. Synchronous communication is "real-time" communication; after one party finishes commenting, the other party responds. Examples are face-to-face interaction and communication over the telephone. When these discussions concluded, the mediation moved into Stage 3 where the mediator, through a memorandum, suggested a resolution and provided a rationale for her conclusion. In the final part, the mediator worked with the disputants to reach consensus. If the parties were in accord, they would each sign the agreement.

Failing to attract many cases, the Maryland Project closed during 2001. Perhaps it needed more publicity and marketing, or maybe it was just ahead of its time. No matter what the reason, the project played a vital part in the evolution of ODR. In fact, the three projects funded by NCAIR demonstrated the need and merit of ODR not only for online disputes, but for those occurring offline. They provided the opportunity to experiment with technological systems and collect data on ODR methods with the aim of developing a framework on which to build and grow the field.

The second period of ODR was a time of experimentation. The pioneers in the field believed that as the World Wide Web developed, so would the need for ODR programs. Their experiments laid the groundwork for the future. As we shall see in the next section, commercial activity began to flourish on the Internet and along with it, the development of for-profit ODR programs. The government also acknowledged and supported the expansion of e-commerce and recognized the need for dispute resolution systems if e-commerce were to succeed.

Third Period: 1999-2000

The third period saw significant growth in e-commerce and an increase in disputes. This created a flurry of entrepreneurial activity in the development of profitable ODR programs. Katsh called the period of 1999-2000 the "Internet bubble" because of the many ODR businesses that emerged and disappeared.[35]

The government also became involved in ODR during these years. Various agencies saw the potential of e-commerce and understood the importance of instilling consumer confidence for its success. As a result, the government sponsored workshops where interested parties could discuss the emergence of online commerce.

The auction site eBay is generally credited with launching the first commercial ODR program during the third period. What began as an experiment eventually evolved into eBay's method for resolving disagreements between sellers and users. Although there were many startup commercial companies during this time frame, we will discuss three of the most successful: SquareTrade, which became eBay's dispute resolution provider until 2008;[36] Cybersettle; and SmartSettle, the latter two still in existence at the time of writing this book.

eBay

In 1999, eBay asked the Center for Information Technology and Dispute Resolution (the "Center") at the University of Massachusetts, which created the OOO discussed previously, if it was interested in developing a dispute resolution program for eBay users. The Center agreed, and beginning in mid-March 1999, eBay informed users that they could get assistance with transaction disputes by clicking on a link and completing a complaint form. The program used a single mediator and the process was as follows:

- Upon receiving a complaint, the mediator e-mailed the other disputant information about the process of mediation and the project developed by the Center. The mediator also solicited basic information about the dispute and inquired about the party's willingness to mediate.
- Each party then had an opportunity to present his narrative and make claims, demands, and what they were seeking.
- The mediator attempted to distill the basic issues and problems of the disagreement. This sometimes required repeated communication exchanges with disputants, allowing the mediator to refine the stories and posit certain facts and conditions.

- At some point during the exchange of e-mails with the mediator, one or both parties had to give in or compromise. Sometimes it took numerous exchanges; at other times the decisional point presented itself at the outset. The mediator facilitated the information exchanges by providing a buffer, soliciting discussion and responses, and reformulating not only the dispute but also the claims of each party in search of that ground where a deal might be constructed.
- If the parties could not agree, the mediation concluded and the dispute was considered at an impasse. The parties were then left to their own devices for settling the disagreement.[37]

During the two-week period of the project, 225 users filed complaints.[38] One hundred and eight of these complaints were mediated with 46 percent being resolved satisfactorily and 54 percent reaching an impasse.[39]

The success of the eBay program led to the creation of SquareTrade, an independent company that launched its website in March 2000. SquareTrade became eBay's preferred dispute resolution provider until 2008.[40] SquareTrade offered two services: a free web-based program where parties could attempt to negotiate their own settlement or use a professional mediator. In its first year of operation, SquareTrade handled in excess of 100,000 complaints with most coming from eBay.[41] From 2000 to about 2005, SquareTrade handled close to six million disputes.[42]

SquareTrade

The first stage of SquareTrade's automated system began with the complainant filling out an online complaint form that asked questions about the dispute. The complainant could check a box that described the problem or explain the dispute in an open-space box. The complainant was also prompted to choose one or more solutions she would be willing to accept or could write her own solution. SquareTrade then e-mailed the other party with information about the complaint and the services offered by SquareTrade. The system also encouraged the respondent to select a solution from a list of suggestions or to propose an alternative. If each side chose the same remedy, the program would recommend that the parties adopt that proposal. If the parties did not reach an agreement, they could then enter into direct negotiations with each other using e-mail. If they were still unsuccessful, the dispute would enter stage two with the involvement of an online mediator for which there was a nominal fee. The mediator did what an offline mediator would do: manage the discussions, determine the parties' needs and interests, and guide the parties toward an acceptable remedy. Unlike traditional mediation where the parties and mediator meet face-to-face, communication online was conducted in writing, by e-mail, and separately with each party.

In early 2008, SquareTrade discontinued its ODR service. It now provides protection plans for cell phones, computers, tablets, and other consumer electronics and appliances.

Cybersettle

Cybersettle was an automated double-blind bidding process for settling uncontested economic issues. The disputants or their attorneys submitted monetary offers and demands to a computer. If the offer was equal to or greater than the demand, the case was settled. If the offer and demand were within a certain range of each other, agreed to ahead of time, the computer splits the difference and the dispute was settled. When the offers were outside the range, the parties could continue to negotiate or request the help of a facilitator. The offers were never revealed to the opposing party.

The idea for Cybersettle germinated when two attorneys, involved in settlement negotiations, used a blind-bid process to reach agreement:

> Cybersettle grew out of a 1995 encounter between seasoned trial attorneys Charles Brofman and James Burchetta who were representing opposing sides in attempting to settle an insurance claim. Jim, who in this case was representing the plaintiff, had demanded tens of thousands of dollars more than the amount Charlie, the defense counsel, was willing to offer. Both parties were well aware of what amount would eventually settle this case, but neither wanted to compromise his bargaining position—so on to court they went. In the courthouse, they agreed to secretly write down their bottom line numbers and hand them to a court clerk, who was instructed to give them a "thumbs-up" if they were within a few thousand dollars of each other. If the case didn't settle, the clerk would destroy the papers and never reveal the figures. He flashed a "thumbs-up." The amounts were within $1,000 of each other. They split the difference and settled the case within minutes.[43]

Cybersettle worked this way: The complainant went to the online website, opened an account, provided information about the opposing party, and briefly explained the claim. The user then entered three settlement offers for each of the three rounds. This amount was kept confidential. Cybersettle notified the opposing party by fax, e-mail, or telephone. The opposing party could review the claim on Cybersettle's website and enter three blind settlement offers. The system compared the corresponding offers for each round. No numbers were ever revealed. If during any round the offers were within a predetermined range, agreed to by both sides, the program would end the dispute by splitting the difference. If an agreement was not reached, the parties could begin again by submitting new offers. The parties also had the option of requesting a "live" facilitator.[44]

Cybersettle, was effective for resolving uncontested monetary disputes. Unfortunately, it was no longer operating at the time of writing this book. Cases involving multiple issues are not compatible with the automated blind-bid process. These disputes require the use of more enhanced software such as that created by Smartsettle.

Smartsettle

Smartsettle, developed by Ernest M. Thiessen, is a sophisticated negotiation software that can involve any number of parties and unlimited quantitative and/or qualitative issues. It is the outcome of Theissen's experience as a volunteer water resources engineer in Nepal, working on a rural development project and trying to determine how to share irrigation benefits with non-landowners. In 1993, this issue became his Ph.D. dissertation and led to a method to solve complex negotiation problems with the use of a computer.

The software developed by Theissen uses patented optimization algorithms to reach fair and efficient results. The negotiation process is designed to help the disputants through each step by comparing input from all the parties. The software looks for common language about the disagreement, identifies issues and options where the parties agree, and leads the parties to fair solutions.

The program lets the parties negotiate at any time through asynchronous communications using e-mail and an alert system that notifies participants when a response has been posted on Smartsettle's secure server. This allows the disputants to negotiate with or without the assistance of a third-party facilitator.

PARALEGAL POINTERS

Online Dispute Resolution

More and more people are using technology and social networks. Online commerce is booming. Disputes are inevitable, and today individuals prefer to reach a settlement from the comfort of their homes rather than a courthouse. ODR makes this choice possible and is often faster and cheaper than litigation. And it is the wave of the future. Paralegals should familiarize themselves with the platforms and websites offered on the Internet. All of the traditional forms of ADR (negotiation, mediation, and arbitration) are available along with other modes such as summary jury trial, med-arb, and early neutral evaluation.

Government and ODR

Recognizing the increase of online commercial activity and acknowledging the potential for continuing and rapid growth, governmental agencies sponsored a two-day workshop in 1999 and again in 2000. The focus was on how ODR could be implemented to help consumers with problems resulting from online purchases.

The first workshop was held on June 8-9, 1999. The premise for the gathering was that the growth in e-commerce might be slowed "until consumers develop confidence in commercial activities conducted over global networks and businesses are assured of a stable and predictable commercial environment. Accordingly, the present challenge is to encourage the development of a global marketplace that offers safety, transparency, and legal certainty."[45] The intent of the meeting was to create some objectives essential for the success of online commercial transactions.

Workshop participants included "all the stakeholders — industry members, consumer advocates, academics, government officials, and international representatives [and] generated broad support . . . for several key general principles":

- Online consumers should be afforded the same level of protection as offline consumers.
- Stakeholders should work toward international consensus as to core protections for consumers in e-commerce.
- Everyone benefits from business practices and initiatives that foster informed decision-making and build consumer confidence in e-commerce.
- Stakeholders should strive to facilitate cooperation and information sharing among consumer protection law enforcement agencies and the private sector internationally; and
- Achieving effective protection for consumers in the global electronic marketplace will require a combination of government law enforcement, private sector initiatives, and international cooperation.[46]

On June 6-7, 2000, the Federal Trade Commission and Department of Commerce jointly sponsored a public workshop to explore the use of ADR for online transactions. Representatives from academia, consumer groups, industry, and government "examined existing and developing ADR programs, incentives and disincentives to use ADR, how to make ADR fair and effective, and the roles of stakeholders, including consumers, businesses and governments, in developing and implementing ADR programs."[47]

Participants agreed that cooperation among all stakeholders must continue. Specifically, they recommended cooperation in the following areas:

- Finding global solutions to address global transactions
- Pursuing technological innovation
- Pursuing multiple ADR programs
- Ensuring fairness and effectiveness of ADR programs
- Consumer and business education
- Action against fraudulent and deceptive practices related to ADR[48]

In the third period, ODR moved beyond being an experiment to recognition and acceptance by businesses and consumers. The efficacy of using technology to resolve disagreements was clearly established. However, unlike the private sector, government did not yet understand the value of the Internet for resolving disputes between the various government agencies and its citizens. It took another ten or so years for this to begin to happen.

Conclusion

Until the early 1990s, the only people with access to the Internet were those involved in research and associated with the military and universities. Internet providers did not exist. Eventually, college students gained access through their school's mainframes, and online disputes began to appear. In 1992, ISPs emerged, making the Internet available to anyone with a computer and a modem. In this same year, the ban on commercial activity ended. These two events contributed to the increase of online disputes. As a result, attention began to focus on finding online methods for resolving online disagreements. Private foundations provided the early funding for experimentation that led to the eventual entry of for-profit ventures and the creation of ODR services.

From the end of the third period to the time this is written, in the summer of 2017, interest in ODR and its applications has continued to grow. Government agencies in the United States are now using ODR for resolving issues with citizens. The United Nations is working on procedures for cross-border e-commerce disputes. There is more software now available for ODR. The feasibility of ODR has been successfully demonstrated and will continue to expand and develop.

> [In 1996], many were skeptical of the need and potential of ODR; today, it is well understood. Most importantly, ODR is no longer solely focused on disputes related to online activities, and it is now employed in some offline disputes. Rather than finding disputes that can utilize ODR, the new challenge is finding tools that can deliver trust, convenience, and expertise for many different kinds of conflicts.[49]

In the next chapter, we continue our discussion of ODR by learning about the different types of online communication, the process, how the three traditional forms of ADR are implemented in cyberspace, the advantages and disadvantages of ODR, and cutting-edge technology and its application to ODR.

Key Terms and Concepts

Blind bidding
Flamewars
Internet service provider (ISP)

Listserv
Online dispute resolution (ODR)
Virtual world

Practice Test Questions

True/False

_____ 1. The development of ISPs and the lifting of the ban on commercial activities on the Internet led to increased numbers of Internet users and online disputes.

_____ 2. The second period of ODR was a time of experimentation.

_____ 3. Cybersettle was effective for resolving uncontested monetary disputes.

_____ 4. In the early 1990s, listservs were the forum through which most discussions took place on the Internet.

_____ 5. ODR is defined as the use of technology to complement, support, or administer a dispute resolution process.

Multiple Choice

___ 1. The most common form of automated negotiation is called _____
   a. blind negotiation.
   b. assisted bidding.
   c. negotiated bidding.
   d. blind bidding.

___ 2. ODR technology is sometimes referred to as
   a. an additional participant.
   b. the fourth party.
   c. an outside participant.
   d. the neutral party.

___ 3. In 1992, _____ emerged, making the Internet available to anyone with a computer and a modem.
   a. computers
   b. ISPs
   c. improved technology
   d. college courses

___ 4. _____ is real-time communication.
   a. Synchronous communication
   b. Asynchronous communication
   c. Simultaneous translation
   d. Automated exchange

___ 5. "Digital native" refers to those who _____
   a. were raised in a less technology-saturated world.
   b. are studying technology.
   c. were raised in a technology-saturated world.
   d. are not technology savvy.

Review Questions

1. What is ODR? How does it work?
2. Explain the two occurrences that contributed to a surge in the growth of the Internet.
3. During the second period in the development of ODR, the National Center for Automated Information Research provided grants for three pilot projects. Name and describe each one.
4. In 1999 the Center for Information Technology and Dispute Resolution at the University of Massachusetts developed a dispute resolution program for eBay. Explain how the program worked.
5. Cybersettle was an automated double-blind bidding process for resolving uncontested economic issues. Describe how the program operated.
6. In 1999, the government sponsored a workshop focused on how ODR could be used to promote the growth of e-commerce. What principles did the participants agree were important for the success of online commercial transactions?

Application Questions

1. Does ODR decrease the risk for consumers in online commercial transactions? Why or why not?
2. Is ODR a better way to resolve offline disputes? Why or why not?
3. How does technology change the process of ADR?
4. Have you had difficulty with an online commercial business? If the answer is no, find someone who has encountered a problem with an online commercial transaction. Explain the dispute. How did the business handle the problem? Did the business have an ODR program? If yes, describe the process. Were you or the person you know satisfied with the outcome? Why or why not?

Practice Exercises

1. Online sites frequently contain forum selection and/or choice-of-law clauses. Go to a popular website, click on its "terms of use," and find the forum selection and/or choice-of-law clauses. Copy and paste these into a word-processing document. Identify the website and summarize the clauses for your instructor and/or class discussion.
2. Find an ODR services provider, review its site, and answer the following questions:
   a. What are the procedures for the service?
   b. What are the synchronous and/or asynchronous forms of online communication that the service provider offers to the parties?
   c. What types of disputes do you think would be appropriate for this provider?
   d. What are the benefits and limitations of using this service?
3. A trustmark is a badge, image, or logo displayed on online business websites to indicate that the website has been determined to be trustworthy by the issuing organization. Some common trustmarks include those for the Better Business Bureau (BBB), Norton, McAfee, and TRUSTe. Visit a website for an online business that displays a trustmark on its homepage. What form of ADR/ODR does the trustmark program use to resolve conflicts between the customer and business? Does the trustmark organization post any actual decisions that were rendered? Is there any statistical data about the program? Prepare a summary of the process.

Endnotes

1. Ethan Katsh, *Dispute Resolution Without Borders: Some Implications for the Emergence of Law in Cyberspace*, First Monday, Feb. 5, 2006, http://firstmonday.org/ojs/index.php/fm/article/view/1313/1233.
2. Christy Burke, *Web-based Dispute Resolution Systems Gain Traction as Court Delays and Low Value Disputes Surge*, Legal IT Professionals (May 15, 2012), https://www.legalitprofessionals.com/legal-it-columns/christy-burke/4236-web-based-dispute-resolution-systems-gain-traction-as-court-delays-and-low-value-disputes-surge.
3. Vanessa O'Connell, *At GE, Robo-Lawyers: Oil-and-Gas Unit Tests Online Resolution to Control Costs*, Wall St. J., Oct. 10, 2011, Business Technology.

4. *Id.*

5. *Id.*

6. Sally Goldenburg, *Settling Suits Online Is Net Gain for City*, N.Y. Post, Aug. 4, 2008, at 2.

7. Colin Rule, *Technology and the Future of Dispute Resolution*, 21 Disp. Resol. Mag. 4 (2015).

8. Press release, Buying online and solving disputes online: 24,000 consumers used new European platform in first year (March 24, 2017), http://europa.eu/rapid/press-release_IP-17-727_en.htm.

9. Better Business Bureau, http://www.bbb.org/us/bbb-online-business (last visited Mar. 30, 2017).

10. Stefany Zaroban, *US e-Commerce Sales Grow 15.6% in 2016* (Feb. 17, 2017), https://www.digital commerce360.com/2017/02/17/us-e-commerce-sales-grow-156-2016/

11. David Allen Larson, *Brother, Can You Spare a Dime? Technology Can Reduce Dispute Resolution Costs When Times Are Tough and Improve Outcomes*, 11 Nev. L.J. 523, 527 (2011). The terms "digital natives" and "digital immigrants" was coined by Mark Prensky, *Digital Game-Based Learning* (MCB Univ. Press 2001).

12. Rule, *supra* note 7.

13. Colin Rule, *Online Dispute Resolution for Business* 44 (Jossey-Bass 2002).

14. Ethan Katsh & Janet Rifkin, *Online Dispute Resolution: Resolving Conflicts in Cyberspace* 93 (Jossey-Bass 2001).

15. *See* Susan Nauss Exon, *The Next Generation of Online Dispute Resolution: The Significance of Holography to Enhance and Transform Dispute Resolution*, 12 Cardozo J. Conflict Resol. 19 (2010); David Allen Larson, *Artificial Intelligence: Robots, Avatars, and the Demise of the Human Mediator*, 25 Ohio St. J. on Disp. Resol. 105 (2010).

16. Maureen A. O'Rourker, *Fencing Cyberspace: Drawing Borders in a Virtual World*, 82 Minn. L. Rev. 609, 615-616 (1998).

17. Ethan Katsh, *Dispute Resolution in Cyberspace*, 28 Conn. L. Rev. 953, 960, 964 (1996).

18. Katsh & Rifkin, *supra* note 14.

19. Space Today Online, http://www.spacetoday.org/SpcStns/SecondLife/SL_ISS.html (last visited Apr. 12, 2017).

20. *See* Virginia Shea, *Netiquette* (Albion 1994).

21. Ian Macduff, *Flames on the Wires: Mediating from an Electronic Cottage*, 10 Negot. J. 5, 6 (1994).

22. Julien Dibbell, *A Rape in Cyberspace: How an Evil Clown, a Haitian Trickster Spirit, Two Wizards, and a Cast of Dozens Turned a Database into a Society*, Village Voice, Oct. 18, 2005, at 36-42, http://www.villagevoice.com/news/a-rape-in-cyberspace-6401665.

23. *Id.*

24. *Id.*

25. George H. Friedman, *Alternative Dispute Resolution and Emerging Online Technologies: Challenges and Opportunities*, 19 Hastings Comm. & Ent. L.J. 695, 702 (1997).

26. Frank A. Cona, *Application of Online Systems in Alternative Dispute* Resolution, 45 Buff. L. Rev. 975, 995 (1997).

27. *Id.*

28. *Id.* at 996-997; Victoria C. Crawford, *A Proposal to Use Alternative Dispute Resolution as a Foundation to Build an Independent Global Cyberlaw Jurisdiction Using Business to Consumer Transactions as a Model*, 25 Hastings Int'l & Comp. L. Rev. 383, 391-392 (2002).

29. *See* Alejandro E. Almaguer & Roland W. Baggott III, *Shaping New Legal Frontiers: Dispute Resolution for the Internet*, 13 Ohio St. J. on Disp. Resol. 711, 730-736 (1998); Cona, *supra* note 26, at 998-999; Lucille M. Pointe, *Boosting Consumer Confidence in E-Business: Recommendations for Establishing Fair and Effective Dispute Resolution Programs for B2C Online Transactions*, 12 Alb. L.J. Sci. & Tech. 441, 458-461 (2002).

30. *See* Cona, *supra* note 26, at 988-989.

31. "An ombudsman is an independent, objective investigator of people's complaints against government agencies and other organizations, both public and private sectors. After a fair, thorough review, the ombudsman decides if the complaint is justified and makes recommendations to the organization in order to resolve the problem." *Online Dispute Resolution: Theory and Practice, A Treatise on Technology and Dispute Resolution* 328-329 (Mohamed S. Abdel Wahab, Ethan Katsh & Daniel Rainey eds., Eleven Int'l 2012).

32. Lan Q. Hang, *Online Dispute Resolution Systems: The Future of Cyberspace Law*, 41 Santa Clara L. Rev. 837, 847 (2001).

33. Richard S. Granat, *Creating an Environment for Mediating Disputes on the Internet: A Working Paper for the NCAIR Conference on Online Dispute Resolution*, Washington, DC, May 22, 1996.

34. Norman Solovay & Cynthia Reed, *The Internet and Dispute Resolution: Untangling the Web* 2-11 (Law Journal Press 2003).

35. *Online Dispute Resolution, supra* note 31, at 27.

36. "Due to eBay's change to its feedback system in May 2008, SquareTrade decided to discontinue its ODR program. . . ." Thomas J. Stipanowich, *Arbitration: "The New Litigation,"* 2010 U. Ill. L. Rev. 1, 29, n. 199.

37. Ethan Katsh, Janet Rifkin & Alan Gaitenby, *E-Commerce, E-Disputes, and E-Dispute Resolution: In the Shadow of eBay Law,* 15 Ohio St. J. on Disp. Resol. 705, 710 (2000).

38. *Id.* at 709.

39. *Id.* at 711.

40. As of the date of writing this book, eBay handles disputes on its own website at the Resolution Center.

41. Rule, *supra* note 13, at 104.

42. Ethan Katsh & Leah Wing, *Ten Years of Online Dispute Resolution (ODR): Looking at the Past and Constructing the Future,* 38 U. Tol. L. Rev. 19, 26 (2006).

43. Cybersettle, http://www.cybersettle.com/pub/home/demo.aspx (last visited Mar. 30, 2017).

44. *Id.*

45. Public Workshop: U.S. Perspectives on Consumer Protection in the Global Electronic Marketplace, 63 Fed. Reg. 69289, 69290 (Dec. 16, 1998), http://www.cptech.org/ecom/ftc-dec1998.html.

46. Fed. Trade Comm'n, *Consumer Protection in the Global Electronic Marketplace: Summary of Federal Trade Commission Public Workshop, June 8-9, 1999,* at 1-2, https://www.ftc.gov/system/files/documents/reports/consumer-protection-global-electronic-marketplace-looking-ahead/appa.pdf.

47. *Summary of Public ADR Workshop,* http://www.mediate.com/articles/ftc1.cfm (last visited Apr. 12, 2017).

48. *Id.*

49. Katsh & Wing, *supra* note 42, at 21.

CHAPTER EIGHT

Online Dispute Resolution: Settling Disputes

Chapter Outline

Introduction
eNegotiation
    Assisted eNegotiation
    Automated "Blind-Bid"
        eNegotiation
eMediation
eArbitration
    American Arbitration Association
    Virtual Courthouse
Advantages of ODR
    Convenient
    Saves Money and Time
    Speed
    No Physical Presence
    Avoids Jurisdictional Issues
    Data Storage and Retrieval

Disadvantages of ODR
    No Face-to-Face Contact
    Confidentiality
    Deception
    Lack of Trust and Confidence
    Enforcement of Agreement
    Access to and Proficiency in
        Technology
What's Next? Holography and
    Artificial Intelligence
Conclusion
Key Terms and Concepts
Practice Test Questions
Review Questions
Application Questions
Practice Exercises

> If my predictions are correct, online resolution of issues will become the new normal.
>
> — COLIN RULE[1]

INTRODUCTION

The major objective of alternative dispute resolution (ADR) is to resolve disputes without going to court. As discussed in Chapter 7, online dispute resolution (ODR) applies technology to the ADR methods. The technology can be anything from using e-mail to videoconferencing to artificial intelligence. These options give greater flexibility to the third-party neutral when determining the ODR platform. The neutral must choose the type of online communication that best complements the disputants' needs and supports the process. For example, e-mail might be appropriate for mediation when the parties have a history of hostility. Videoconferencing, because it allows face-to-face contact, might be the appropriate communication method for disputants who desire to reestablish trust so as to maintain an ongoing relationship.

There are two basic communication modes: **synchronous** and **asynchronous**. Synchronous communication is "real-time" communication, meaning that after one party finishes talking, the other party responds. Examples are face-to-face interaction and communication over the telephone. Asynchronous communication is when parties are not communicating at the same time. Examples are e-mail or other web-based communication.

Chapter 7 introduced using online technology for settling online e-commerce disputes. Increasingly, ODR is being used for offline disputes as well. All of the traditional forms of alternative dispute resolution (negotiation, mediation, and arbitration) are now offered online. Even other forms (e.g., summary jury trial, med-arb, early neutral evaluation) can take place on the Internet. (Exhibit 8-1 summarizes the ODR process.)

We will begin this chapter with a look at eNegotiation, both assisted and automated. Then we discuss online mediation and arbitration. Finally, we will briefly look at the cutting-edge technology that will shape the future of ODR.

Exhibit 8-1. THE ODR PROCESS

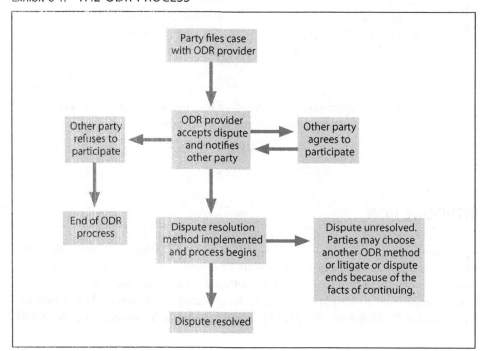

eNEGOTIATION

Chapter 3 described negotiation as a process in which two or more parties seek to resolve a conflict by making offers and counteroffers until they reach a mutually agreed-upon outcome. **eNegotiation** (electronic negotiation) is negotiation with the use of computers or other electronic communications. eNegotiation can be either assisted or automated.

Assisted eNegotiation

In **assisted eNegotiation**, computer software is used to set up the communication between the parties, facilitate with developing agendas, identify possible solutions, and help with writing agreements. Although there are a number of negotiation support systems available, Smartsettle, originally called OneAccord, is the precursor of this system. Smartsettle can be used in disputes that are simple or complex, comprise one issue or multiple issues, and involve two parties or multiple parties. The Smartsettle Infinity[2] system works by having the parties move through a series of six steps that clarify the issues, determine the importance of each issue, and outline the range of acceptable outcomes.

There are no limits on time or the number of proposals that may be exchanged. The parties are in complete control and may terminate the negotiation at any time. If they reach an impasse, they can agree to submit the case to arbitration or just end the case. Once a party removes himself from the system, any information on the neutral site is no longer accessible. However, before removal, the parties can export their private information to their own computers. (Smartsettle One users can have information transferred to them.)

The Smartsettle website provides very tight security. Each party's information is completely confidential and available only by access codes. Even Smartsettle staff cannot view the data. The Smartsettle server functions are located within a virtual private network controlled by ICAN Systems Inc. (the maker of Smartsettle), and all communication between the server and clients is encrypted.

Automated "Blind-Bid" eNegotiation

Blind bidding systems, primarily designed to resolve monetary disputes, use an automated algorithm to evaluate dollar settlement offers ("bids") submitted by the disputants. If these bids fall with a certain range (e.g., 15 percent) of each other, then the parties agree to settle for the median. If the case does not settle, the offers are destroyed, and neither side will be able to learn what the other proposed. Before the process begins, both parties are informed about how the program operates, and they agree to abide by the resolution, if one is reached. Cybersettle, one of the first ODR systems to offer automated blind bidding, went online in 1998. Unfortunately, at the time of writing this book Cybersettle does not appear to be up and running. According to Cybersettle's website when it was available, it had facilitated more than $1.8 billion in settlements and had 150,000 attorneys and 10,000 insurance claims professionals who were registered users. Approximately 30,000 attorneys had used the system to settle client's cases. If the negotiation was unsuccessful, the parties could have agreed to use mediation.

eMEDIATION

Chapter 4 described mediation as negotiation with the assistance of a third party. The mediator's role is to help identify the issues, create and maintain dialogue between the parties, and assist the parties in reaching an agreeable resolution. In the United States, mediation is the most often used ADR method in state and federal courts.[3] "In online mediation, parties negotiate with one another under the auspices of the mediator via e-mail or on specially designed Internet sites that provide virtual 'rooms' in which the parties congregate electronically."[4]

While mediation is recognized as one of the traditional forms of ADR, it is not as closely associated with ODR. Noam Ebner suggests that

> this may be due to the multiple influences informing the rapid evolution of the ODR field. Additionally, the two best-known success stories of the field, cited in just about every paper written on ODR, involve online arbitration . . . and assisted negotiation. . . . Finally, it may be that there are things inherent to the online environment that are more conducive to other processes, and Fourth Party[5] functions [are] better suited for assisting processes other than mediation. For example, automation functions may be powerful tools in automated and assisted negotiation, allowing dealing with large volumes of similar-type cases/claims—but less helpful in e-mediation. It might be that the Fourth Party provides enough support or assistance on its own in some cases, allowing parties to work things out without involving a human mediator.[6]

Nonetheless, **eMediation** is offered by a number of companies and, in this author's opinion, will become an increasingly valuable platform for resolving both online and offline disputes. One organization that has been promoting eMediation is the Association of Conflict Resolution-Hawaii (ACR Hawaii). In November 2011, ACR Hawaii launched the Virtual Mediation Lab Project. Created by mediator Giuseppe Leone, the goal was to demonstrate how eMediation, via Skype, could be used by mediators to practice and advance their mediation skills. After more than 100 online mediations of various types of disputes, the project revealed the following:

- Online mediators need to master the software/platform they use
- Mediation skills and experience are much more important than [the use of] online mediation technology
- A mediator's learning process can be considerably accelerated
- Mediation by video, phone, email and face-to-face are not mutually exclusive
- Online mediation can open up new market opportunities[7]

ACR Hawaii continues to support eMediation and offers a number of training videos on its website (http://www.virtualmediationlab.com).

Online mediation divides into three categories:[8]

1. Programs that use computer communication to facilitate the administration of physical-presence (traditional) mediation. Mediation is not conducted online.
2. Hybrid-mediation programs in which the mediator may use both online and in-person mediation.
3. Virtual-mediation programs where mediation takes place entirely online or a computer program is used as the mediator.

The preferred mode of eMediation, at least at the time of writing this book, has been text-based, asynchronous communication (e.g., e-mail). However, some critics argue that because "physical presence . . . is the *sine qua non* [meaning] of mediation,"[9] asynchronous mediation is not effective. These critics argue that body language (e.g., facial expressions and gestures) and verbal cues (e.g., tone of voice and word choice) convey messages important to the mediation process because they can build rapport between the parties.

PARALEGAL POINTERS

Paralegals' Role in Online Dispute Resolution

Paralegals perform a number of tasks in traditional ADR. With ODR, they have additional responsibilities. For example, the attorney may ask you to determine whether the dispute is appropriate for online resolution. If it is, there are questions that need to be answered. For example, what websites offer ODR, and how do they operate? What is the cost and who pays? If the attorney and client decide that ODR is suitable, you will be in charge of explaining to the client the process and the applicable rules and regulations. Entering all of the required information into the website and monitoring the progress are additional paralegal responsibilities.

eARBITRATION

The third traditional form of ADR, arbitration, is ideally suited to ODR because, unlike mediation, it focuses on the information (evidence) submitted to the arbitrator, not on dialogue between the parties; therefore, the technology needed is less complicated. (The challenge for online arbitration is enforceability, which we will not discuss.)

Generally, the **eArbitration** process begins by filing a request for arbitration. If the case is accepted, the opposing party is notified and must agree to participate. The parties then select an arbitrator and submit evidence. Next are hearings, either text based, audio only, or audio/video. After deliberation, the arbitrator issues her decision.

Let's look at two providers of online arbitration: the American Arbitration Association and Virtual Courthouse.

American Arbitration Association

The American Arbitration Association (AAA) was formed on January 29, 1926, as a result of the merger of several arbitration organizations. The process for ODR with the AAA is as follows.

Filing and Initiation

The AAA generally commences administration of an arbitration case when one party submits a Demand for Arbitration, a copy of the arbitration provision, and the appropriate filing fee. From there, the respondent is notified by the AAA, and a deadline is set for an answer and/or counterclaim. Cases also may commence with a Submission to Dispute Resolution, the appropriate filing fee to the AAA, and the consent of all parties if no arbitration agreement exists or the AAA is not named as the resolution provider in the arbitration agreement.

Arbitrator Selection

Following the respondent's answer, the AAA works with the parties to identify and select arbitrators from its roster of neutrals. The parties' criteria are used to identify neutrals with qualifications that match the needs of the case. Once parties agree on the neutral, the arbitration proceedings begin.

Preliminary Hearing

This meeting, conducted by the arbitrator, is the first opportunity for the parties and the arbitrator to discuss directly the substantive issues of the case. At this point, procedural matters such as the exchange of information and witness lists also will be discussed.

Information Exchange and Preparation

Parties make ready their presentations, and the arbitrator can address any impasses or challenges related to information sharing. The goal of this stage is to arrive at the point where evidence and arguments may be presented in the hearings.

Hearings

At this stage, parties have an opportunity to present testimony and evidence to the arbitrator in order to arrive at a resolution.

Post-hearing Submissions

This phase of the process provides parties with an opportunity to submit additional documentation, if allowed by the arbitrator. If this stage is necessary, it usually occurs shortly after the hearings.

The Award

The arbitrator closes the record regarding the case and issues a decision, inclusive of an award.

Virtual Courthouse

"Virtualcourthouse.com is an Internet-based service that enables parties to submit disputed claims, responses and supporting material in digital form for resolution by a neutral. . . ."[10] The services include arbitration, mediation, neutral case evaluation, and settlement conferences. It was developed in 2001 by Judge Monty Ahalt, who served for 15 years on the Circuit Court for Prince George's County in Maryland, retiring in 1999.

ADR Case Filing

The parties and representatives start a case with a brief description. Then they select three or more mediators/arbitrators, rank them, and send them to the opposing party, along with an invitation to participate in an ADR process through VirtualCourthouse.com. The parties present their case online, schedule a meeting or videoconference, and use the Virtual Courthouse Secure Confidential asynchronous messaging system.

Virtual Courthouse Rules of Arbitration

- Rules. The rules of arbitration or mediation are what the parties agree. The neutral will ask the parties if they have agreed upon rules. If the parties cannot agree on the rules or disagree on specific rules, then they will be as the neutral determines appropriate for the parties.
- Neutral Selection. The neutral (arbitrator, mediator) will be determined by the agreement of the parties. The parties by agreement may request Virtual Courthouse to designate a neutral. Before Virtual Courthouse designates a neutral, Virtual Courthouse will consult with the parties. If the parties cannot agree, then either party may petition a court of competent jurisdiction to appoint a neutral.
- Case Initiation. A case will be initiated by a party filing a new case with VirtualCourthouse.com®, and by VirtualCourthouse.com® notifying the other party or parties that the case has been started.
- The Neutral will be notified that the case presentation is complete and will review the evidence and render a decision. The parties will then be notified by e-mail when the decision is filed.

Used with permission. ©Virtualcourthouse.com®

You have now learned that ODR communication is either synchronous or asynchronous and looked at the three traditional forms of ADR available online: eNegotiation, eMediation, and eArbitration. The next logical topic for discussion is what are the advantages and disadvantages of resolving a dispute online.

ADVANTAGES OF ODR

Convenient

Since disputes, whether online or offline, can occur between people separated by great distances, different time zones, and even countries. As a result, at least one party will be forced to travel. ODR obviates the necessity of traveling because the disputants can participate in the process from anywhere with Internet access. Additionally, because traveling is eliminated, participants save valuable time for work or other matters. Finally, with text-based communication, parties can participate at their convenience, thus eliminating scheduling issues.

Saves Money and Time

ODR can save money and time in a number of ways. Because communication takes place in cyberspace, there is no need to spend money on travel, food, and accommodations. ODR eliminates lost productivity and business disruptions incurred when executives, their advisers, legal counsel, accountants, and support staff have to divert their attention from company business to attend a scheduled negotiation or mediation. ODR also makes it unnecessary to rent a neutral facility for meetings. The disputants may not need to hire attorneys, thus saving money on legal fees. Finally, the cost for the neutral party may be considerably less.

Additionally, text-based communication saves time. In traditional in-person ADR, one party must sit and wait while the neutral meets with the other participant, thus wasting the idle party's time. In asynchronous communication, the party not caucusing avoids having to needlessly sit around and wait.

Speed

People have come to expect that things will happen quickly, and the Internet excels at meeting this expectation. ODR is available instantly and accessible twenty-four hours a day, seven days a week. ODR eliminates finding a mediator, coordinating all the participants' schedules, arranging travel, and finding a space to meet. In cyberspace, a neutral can be employed from anywhere in the world. A meeting room can be accessed instantaneously, and scheduling and traveling are eliminated.

No Physical Presence

Many ADR neutrals, especially mediators, argue that disputants need to sit face-to-face (F2F) with each other and the neutral. Other neutrals point out that when the dispute is extremely contentious and emotions are high, text-based electronic communication has advantages. In this section, we will focus on disputes in which the participants are better served with asynchronous communication.

Less Hostility

Sometimes, with F2F mediation, the communication can turn hostile and result in accusations, name calling, and threatening gestures. The impersonal nature of text-based communication can lessen tensions where the parties have a history of antagonism or the dispute is extremely emotional. A text-based environment eliminates the possibility of any negative body language that could derail the process. Instead of focusing on the other party's physical presence, the parties are forced to concentrate on the substantive issues and evaluate the dispute in a dispassionate way.

Clearer and Focused Communication

In F2F mediation, participants must reply immediately. However, a first response might not be the best response. Because asynchronous communication does not take place in "real time," the participants have time to reflect on the discussion, conduct research, talk with others, consider options, and reply in a more thoughtful and impassive manner.

A Great Equalizer

The text-based environment levels the playing field for the disputants. The anonymity of the parties eliminates equality and bias issues and power imbalances. A party does not have to be concerned about characteristics such as gender, race, age, and social status, along with any preconceived notions usually associated with these, which can stifle meaningful discussions. Similarly, physically attractiveness and the ability to dominate F2F discussions are diminished in text-based communication. "Technology can protect parties from uncomfortable or threatening face to face confrontations and offer vulnerable individuals a place where their communications can appear as forceful as the statements of someone who is physically much larger and louder."[11] However, there is a risk of cyberbullying.[12]

Avoids Jurisdictional Issues

A fundamental tenet in our legal system is that a court must have jurisdiction before it can decide a case. Jurisdiction is the power of a court to hear a dispute and render a binding, enforceable judgment. Jurisdiction is found either at the place where a person or business "resides" or the location where the event that is the subject of the dispute took place. Most lawyers and law students will tell you that determining jurisdiction is not always easy. Resolving disputes online avoids the jurisdictional issues because the parties create their own solutions and can agree that the resolution is binding.

Data Storage and Retrieval

The use of computer technology puts all relevant information at the fingertips of all participants. E-mails, settlement proposals, memoranda, photographs, diagrams, audio, and video can be archived at secure designated sites and made available for access. Agreement drafts can be downloaded quickly, edited, and uploaded to the storage site for review by the other party. Additionally, because all the submissions are saved, a third-party neutral can more effectively manage the case, and the disputants can learn the status of their dispute at any time.

DISADVANTAGES OF ODR

No Face-to-Face Contact

As discussed above, there is a rift between proponents of text-based and synchronous communication. Here we will discuss the benefits of F2F ODR. In the early years of the development of ODR, some commentators suggested that online mediation would not gain wider acceptance "until technology replicating face-to-face interaction [was] available universally at a low cost and well understood by all those who would participate."[13] We now have videoconferencing technology, and while some sing its praises,[14] others argue that "videoconferencing is not the panacea that many legal mediators assume[d] that it would be."[15] Some proponents argue that videoconferencing allows disputants to hear and see the subtleties of nonverbal communication such as the party's sarcastic tone of voice, a facial smile, or a nod of the head showing agreement. However, videoconferencing can present problems, for example, a delay or loss of the digital signal; poor transmission of images, which diminishes the ability to see body language; and the awkwardness of having to look into a camera when speaking.

Developers of telepresence, the current cutting-edge technology, claim it improves videoconferencing to the point where it appears the parties are in the same room. Telepresence is defined as "visual collaboration solutions that address the human factors of participants and attempt to replicate, as closely as possible, an in-person experience."[16] Through the use of screen projections, it lets "users feel as if they are 'present' in the same physical space with others who might be thousands of miles away."[17] The participants appear life-sized; their motions are fluid; skin tones are precise; eye contact is accurate; the video, light-ing, and acoustics are studio quality; and the technology remains hidden.[18]

So how does F2F contact help dispute resolution? It helps in a number of ways, beginning with fostering the development of trust between the disputants and, in the case of mediation, between the disputants and the mediator.

> The existence of trust between individuals makes conflict resolution easier and more effective. This point is obvious to anybody who has been in a conflict. A party who trusts another is likely to believe the other's words, assume that the other will act out of good intentions, and probably look for productive ways to resolve a conflict should one occur. [T]he level of trust or distrust in a relationship therefore definitively shapes emergent conflict dynamics.[19]

Research has shown, however, that building trust where there is a physical distance between parties is not as effective as F2F communication.

> [R]esearch [has] made clear that people communicating at a distance through technological means are likely to experience low levels of interpersonal trust and higher rates of disruption and deterioration than those engaged in face-to-face dialogue.[20]

F2F fosters interpersonal rapport, which encourages trust and cooperation. For example, "eye contact has been shown to be a cue . . . for friendliness, for approval, . . . for romantic love, for status relationships, and for speech synchro-nization."[21] So if trust is important to conflict resolution and trust is developed through interpersonal contact, then F2F communication would appear to be the appropriate ODR platform.

Mediation is often valued as much for helping the parties understand the cause of the dispute and generating ways to avoid a reoccurrence as it is for reaching an agreement. It can open communication between the participants in a safe and nonthreatening environment, thereby allowing one party to share and acknowl-edge the other's point of view. Trying to do this through e-mail, instant messaging, or a chat room, suggests Joel Eisen, is as practical "as a therapist forgoing face-to-face evaluation and treating a patient by reading her journal."[22]

For many parties, mediation is about expressing their perspectives and emo-tions ("venting"). "The opportunity to tell one's version of the case directly to the opposing party and to express accompanying emotions can be cathartic for mediation participants."[23] This process is better suited to F2F than e-mail. The emotional effect of expressing feelings is hampered when technology separates the disputants.

Finally, F2F helps the third-party neutral manage tempers and emotions and maintain control. With asynchronous communication, this is more difficult because e-mails are not always received quickly, thus delaying intervention. Also, one or both parties could ignore the mediator's e-mail or delay sending a response.

Confidentiality

An attractive feature of ADR is confidentiality. In litigation, everything is open to the public. Anyone can view documents filed with the court and attend court hearings. ADR is generally private and confidential. In mediation, rules prohibit the disclosure of discussions in most circumstances. ODR cannot guarantee identical security.[24] Too frequently, we learn about hackers breaking into businesses' computers and accessing financial information about the company and its customers. Not only can hackers read and use the information, but they can also modify it.

Deception

"On the Internet, nobody knows you're a dog."

Trust is the foundation on which ADR, especially mediation, both online and F2F, rests. The disputants must have sufficient trust in the neutral to share personal and sometimes confidential information. Additionally, they must trust that the third party will remain neutral. The parties also have to trust each other, or the process will fail. Unfortunately, not everyone can be trusted. Worse, lying is sometimes acceptable behavior: "Lying (or deception) is acknowledged [among legal professionals] as a necessary and standard negotiation practice."[25] According to one scholar on dishonesty, "[l]ying is not exceptional; it is normal, and more often spontaneous and unconscious than cynical and coldly analytical. Our minds and bodies secrete deceit."[26] Even more problematic is that people are not skilled at detecting deception.[27] This inability to identify lying is more pronounced when the communication takes place online.[28] The cartoon, "On the Internet, nobody knows you're a dog," published in 1993, expresses a fear that remains today.

Lack of Trust and Confidence

In the physical world, there are a number of indicators we use to evaluate whether we trust a person and have confidence in that person. When we visit a doctor's office, we can see objects associated with medical care. In a store, we can see and touch the merchandise. Although these cues suggest trustworthiness, they are only a guide. We learn to trust certain people through our regular associations with them. In cyberspace, these indicators are absent. So we do not know whether the neutral we selected is qualified, educated, or otherwise appropriate. We do not know whether the participants can be trusted.

At the present time, there is no way that consumers can identify quality online neutrals because there are no clear regulations or standards.[29] Although some states have minimum requirements to be included on their court rosters of mediators, inclusion on a roster still does not ensure that a mediator has the ability to resolve disputes online. Although one practitioner suggests that online mediators "use generally the same skill set, with the added twist of doing so via the medium of technology,"[30] the Distance Mediation Project reached a different conclusion. "Distance mediation [online mediation] employs different skills, and involves a different mediation style rather than simply new tools in the mediation tool box."[31] The majority of the mediators who participated in the project thought more skills and training were "needed to do this work, including additional training in: appropriate web or other technology platforms; proper cyber "netiquette;" reading the nuances of non-visual or verbal cues and written communication; and the implications of timing and other impacts of distance mediation approaches, as they affect both the process and outcomes of mediation."[32] As a result of the Distance Mediation Project, the Mediate BC [British Columbia] Society published an 81-page guide focused exclusively on distance mediation.[33]

ODR providers acknowledge the importance of ensuring quality services and have created ethical standards that their mediators must follow. Many use the Model Standards of Conduct for Mediators created by the American Arbitration Association, the American Bar Association's Section of Dispute Resolution, and the Society of Professionals in Dispute Resolution (now the Association for Conflict Resolution).[34]

Enforcement of Agreement

Disputants who settle a dispute rely on good faith compliance with the terms of the settlement. If a party does not abide by the agreement, that party may be in breach of the contract. The other party may then need to seek enforcement in court. If this happens, the time, effort, and funds expended in ODR will have been wasted, and the party will find herself in her original position. In such cases, even if the parties request court intervention, there is no certainty that the court will or has the authority to force compliance with the online agreement.

Access to and Proficiency in Technology

Some people are more comfortable and proficient with online technology, giving them an advantage over the other party. For example, although instant messaging is available to most computer users, some may not know how to use it or feel at ease with the technology. Additionally, one party may not have certain technological capabilities such as videoconferencing, scanning, and faxing.

WHAT'S NEXT? HOLOGRAPHY AND ARTIFICIAL INTELLIGENCE

Holography, the next generation of technology, may finally be the magic potion for those critics who argue that mediation works best when the disputants are physically present with each other and the mediator. Holography uses a laser light to transport or beam a 3D image of a person to another location without the use of screens (think *Star Trek: The Next Generation* and the "holodeck").[35] Two companies at the forefront of holography are Cisco Systems and Corning Glassware. Google each company and you will find a number of YouTube videos demonstrating this fascinating new technology. Holotexting is also being developed. Researchers at the University of Tokyo have created "touchable holograms" that will let users send 3D hologram text messages.[36]

Artificial intelligence could also have an impact on ODR. According to David Allen Larson, "artificial intelligence devices will replace the humans who perform complex, interactive, interpersonal tasks such as dispute resolution."[37] Larson points out that "[s]tudies have concluded that persuasive dialogues with computer agents can change attitudes [and] results based on interactions in situations other than ADR, suggest that avatars[38] and robots acting as relational agents,[39] also are capable of behaviors that will facilitate dispute resolution and problem solving."[40] While Larson does not portend the demise of the human mediator, he does believe that artificial intelligence devices and programs will have an impact on dispute resolution:

> There is a generation quickly moving to adulthood that spends significant time interacting with avatars in cyberspace. They rely on technology assisted communication for their most intimate conversations and look to the Internet to find answers to their most pressing questions. They will search for, and will not hesitate to use, artificial intelligence devices to assist them in dispute resolution and problem solving. They are able to interact with avatars, robots, and other forms of relational agents easily and will expect and demand dispute resolvers and problem solvers to be similarly prepared.[41]

Conclusion

ODR is still in its infancy, but its roots are firmly in place. Two of the pioneers in this field, Ethan Katsh and Colin Rule, both predict that as our use and dependence on computers grow, so will disputes. As technology improves, more dispute resolutions will occur online. And, the use of ODR for offline disputes will also expand.

> We are in the midst of a period of dramatic change in terms of what ODR processes can offer disputants as well as what disputants feel comfortable with when communicating online. What we can say is that the trend is towards increasingly richer technologies (at lower costs) and a higher degree of comfort among young users with the online medium. It is our contention, that over time we can expect increasingly complex disputes to be addressed online with higher degrees of comfort and satisfaction among users.[42]

In 2002, Colin Rule wrote:

> Yet the promise of online dispute resolution (ODR) remains as strong as ever. The momentum behind the expansion of ODR, much like the momentum behind the spread of global computer networks, has a tidal inevitability to it. Scholars, governments, non-profits, international organizations, and corporations have all concluded that ODR is an essential part of solutions to the problems raised by the Internet. Eventually, ODR will become an indistinguishable part of the way people around the world resolve their disputes. Whether or not the technology of today is sophisticated enough to fulfill the promise of ODR is not the key issue, because technology will continue to evolve. It may take longer than we previously assumed at the height of the Internet revolution, but the emergence of ODR is all but certain.[43]

Key Terms and Concepts

Artificial intelligence

Assisted eNegotiation

Asynchronous communication

Blind-bidding systems

eArbitration

eMediation

eNegotiation

Holography

Synchronous
communication

Practice Test Questions

True/False

____ 1. Asynchronous communication is when parties are not communicating at the same time.

____ 2. Holography uses a laser light to transport or beam a 3D image of a person to another location without the use of screens.

____ 3. One advantage of ADR is confidentiality.

____ 4. Enforcing an agreement reached online is no more difficult than enforcing an agreement reached in a court-approved ADR process.

____ 5. In assisted negotiation, computer software is used to set up the communication between the parties.

Multiple Choice

____ 1. A disadvantage of ODR is it _____
   a. is slow.
   b. is not convenient.
   c. does not save time and money.
   d. does not guarantee confidentiality.

____ 2. _____ uses computer software to set up the communication between the parties, facilitate with developing agendas, identify possible solutions, and help with writing agreements.
   a. Assisted eNegotiation
   b. Assisted mini-trial
   c. eArbitration
   d. Automated blind bid

____ 3. The use of asynchronous communication in ODR is advantageous in which of the following situations?
   a. When the parties have a history of antagonism or the dispute is extremely emotional
   b. When there is a lack of trust between the parties
   c. When the parties want a speedy resolution
   d. When the parties want to avoid jurisdictional issues

____ 4. Blind-bidding systems are primarily designed to resolve ____
   a. liability disputes.
   b. single-issue disputes.

    c. monetary disputes.

    d. cross-cultural disputes.

___ 5. _____ may be the answer for critics who argue that mediation works best when the mediator and disputants are physically present with each other.

    a. Faster computers

    b. Holography

    c. Skype

    d. Visual platforms

Review Questions

1. Describe the process of ODR.
2. What is "assisted eNegotiation"?
3. Name and explain each step in the AAA's process for online arbitration dispute resolution.
4. There are a number of advantages to using ODR. List and explain those discussed in the chapter.
5. ODR has some disadvantages. List and explain those discussed in the chapter.
6. What is asynchronous communication? Provide at least one example.
7. What is artificial intelligence? What impact will artificial intelligence have on ODR?
8. Name and describe the three types of online mediation.
9. What is the difference between synchronous and asynchronous mediation?
10. What is holography? How can holography be applied to ODR?

Application Questions

1. Some advocates of online asynchronous communication believe it avoids hostility between the parties. Others disagree and believe that asynchronous communication can lead to flaming. Which side do you think is correct? Why? Do you think that parties are less inhibited when not in a face-to-face situation and thus likely to be more outspoken? Rude? Civil? Follow social order?
2. Some critics argue that in automated negotiation, parties could seek a higher or lower amount than their true valuations. This not only discourages bargaining, it also lessens the effectiveness of automated negotiation. Do you agree? Why or why not?
3. David A. Larson suggested three possibilities for the future of ODR:
   i. The dynamic potential that online dispute resolution offers is almost unimaginable, and some day it will become the pre-eminent ADR process;
   ii. Online exchanges capture neither the essence nor nuance of human communication and, consequently, initial excitement will evaporate

quickly and online dispute resolution soon will be relegated to the same lonely space now occupied by monochromatic monitors;

iii. Online dispute resolution increasingly will become a valuable, and perhaps ultimately invaluable, complement to ADR processes; but it always will be, shall we say, a side dish and never the main course.[44]

Which one of Larson's viewpoints do you agree with? Why?

4. Haitham A. Haloush and Bashar H. Malkawi argue that

> [a]lthough many traditional ADR systems draw their strength from face-to-face interactions, online ADR should not seek to replicate those conditions. Instead, it should use the advantages of online technology to forge a new path. This new path should focus on using the networks to maximize the power of technology, a power which may be missing in face to face encounters, instead of duplicating the richness of face-to-face environment."[45]

Do you agree? What do you think is the "power of technology" that Haloush and Malkawi are referring to? Can you think of any other advantages of using technology instead of F2F dispute resolution?

Practice Exercises

1. iCourthouse
   a. Go to http://www.i-courthouse.com and register at http://www.i-courthouse.com/main.taf. (N.B.: This website takes about one minute to load.)
   b. Take the "iCourthouse tour." Click on and review each of the eleven topics on the left-hand side of the page (Plaintiff's Opening Statement through Verdicts).
   c. Find three cases in which the parties have submitted trial notebooks and review each. Submit your verdict for all three cases. Note: select cases that appear to be genuine disputes.
   d. Prepare a written paper in which you evaluate your experience with iCourthouse. Be sure to discuss the strengths and weaknesses of using iCourthouse to resolve disputes. Finally, explain in what ways iCourthouse could be improved.
2. eJury
   a. Go to http://www.eJury.com and review the site.
   b. Explain how eJury operates.
   c. Read "Case No. 0031 – Day Care Crash" and answer questions 1-10. To find this case, go to opening page and click on box "Jurors." Then click on "Learn about." Scroll to bottom of page and click on "Case No. 0031."
   d. Prepare a written paper in which you evaluate your experience with eJury. Compare and contrast eJury with iCourthouse. Which program would you recommend to your supervising attorney and why?

3. Virtual Mediation Lab

Go to http://www.virtualmediationlab.com/videos-2 and watch any dispute on this site that is at least 20 minutes in length. After you finish, address each of the following:

a. Briefly explain the facts of the dispute and each disputant's position.

b. What type of mediation took place: evaluative or facilitative? (Refer to Chapter 4 for an explanation of each type.)

c. Was the dispute resolved? Explain the resolution.

d. Evaluate the effectiveness of the mediator, addressing how the mediator (i) developed and maintained communication; (ii) managed emotions; (iii) maintained interest; and (iv) helped generate solutions.

e. Discuss the strengths and weaknesses of using a mobile device platform for mediating the dispute that you watched. Explain in what ways, if any, the mediation could be improved.

Endnotes

1. Colin Rule, *Technology and the Future of Dispute Resolution*, 21 Disp. Resol. Mag. 4 (2015).

2. Smartsettle Infinity can handle multi-issue, multi-party disputes. Smartsettle One is designed for a single-issue dispute.

3. Jacqueline Nolan-Haley, *Mediation: The New Arbitration*, 17 Harv. Negot. L. Rev. 61, 70 (2012).

4. Lucille M. Ponte & Thomas D. Cavenagh, *Cyberjustice, Online Dispute Resolution (ODR) for E-Commerce* 63 (Pearson Education 2005).

5. Three parties, the two disputants and the third-party neutral, are traditionally involved in ADR. The "fourth party . . . is the technology that works with the mediator or arbitrator." Ethan Katsh & Janet Rifkin, *Online Dispute Resolution: Resolving Conflicts in Cyberspace* 93 (Jossey-Bass 2001).

6. Noam Ebner, *e-Mediation, in Online Dispute Resolution: Theory and Practice, A Treatise on Technology and Dispute Resolution* 369 (Mohamed S. Abdel Wahab, Ethan Katsh & Daniel Rainey eds., Eleven Int'l 2011).

7. Virtual Mediation Lab, http://www.virtualmediationlab.com (last visited Mar. 30, 2017).

8. Llewellyn Joseph Gibbons, Robin M. Kennedy & Jon Michael Gibbs, *Cyber-Mediation: Computer-Mediated Communications Medium Massaging the Message*, 32 N.M. L. Rev. 27, 62-63 (2002).

9. *Id.* at 28. "There is almost universal agreement that mediation is most effective if the parties to the dispute are physically present before the mediator." William T. D'Zurilla, *Alternative Dispute Resolution*, 45 L.A. B.J. 352 (1997).

10. Virtual Courthouse, http://www.virtualcourthouse.com (last visited Mar. 30, 2017).

11. David Allen Larson & Paula Gajewski Mickelson, *Technology Mediated Dispute Resolution Can Improve the Registry of Interpreters for the Deaf Ethical Practices System: The Deaf Community Is Well Prepared and Can Lead by Example*, 10 Cardozo J. Conflict Resol. 131, 140-141 (2008).

12. *Id.*

13. Joel B. Eisen, *Are We Ready for Mediation in Cyberspace?*, 1998 BYU L. Rev. 1305, 1358.

14. *See* David B. Lipsky & Ariel C. Avgar, *Online Dispute Resolution Through the Lens of Bargaining and Negotiation Theory: Toward an Integrated Model*, 38 U. Tol. L. Rev. 47, 56-57 (2006).

15. Gibbons et al., *supra* note 8, at 34.

16. Howard S. Lichtman, *Telepresence and Visual Collaboration @InfoComm 2010—The Telepresence Options Review & "Best of Show" Awards* (June 24, 2010), http://www.telepresenceoptions.com/2010/06/telepresence_and_visual_collab_1.

17. Howard S. Lichtman, *Telepresence, Effective Visual Collaboration and the Future of Global Business at the Speed of Light* 4 (2006), https://pdfs.semanticscholar.org/049e/27f57deda8243d4d3c0043b10fb990ee8ada.pdf.

18. *Id.* at 3.

19. R.J. Lewicki, *Trust, Trust Development and Trust Repair, in The Handbook of Conflict Resolution* 110 (M. Deutsch, E.C. Coleman & E.C. Marcus eds., Jossey-Bass 2006).

20. Noam Ebner, *ODR and Interpersonal Trust, in Online Dispute Resolution, supra* note 6, at 223.

21. Ederyn Williams, *Experimental Comparisons of Face-to-Face and Mediated Communication: A Review,* 84 Psychol. Bull. 963, 971 (1977).

22. Eisen, *supra* note 13, at 1323.

23. *Id.* at 1325.

24. Some researchers disagree, arguing that encryption technology can ensure confidentiality. *See* Philipe Gilliéron, *From Face-to-Face to Screen-to-Screen: Real Hope or True Fallacy?,* 23 Ohio St. J. on Disp. Resol. 301, 320 (2008); M. Ethan Katsh, *Dispute Resolution in Cyberspace,* 28 Conn. L. Rev. 953, 973 (1996); Richard Michael Victoria, *Internet Dispute Resolution (iDR): Bringing ADR into the 21st Century,* 1 Pepp. Disp. Resol. L.J. 279, 296 (2001).

25. Avnita Lakhani, *The Truth About Lying as a Negotiation Tactic: Where Business, Ethics, and Law Collide . . . or Do They?,* 9 ADR Bull. 6 (2007).

26. David Livingstone Smith, *Why We Lie: The Evolutionary Roots of Deception and the Unconscious Mind* 15 (St. Martin's Press 2004).

27. Saul M. Kassin, *Human Judges of Truth, Deception, and Credibility: Confident but Erroneous,* 23 Cardozo L. Rev. 809, 809 (2002); George Giordano et al., *The Influences of Deception and Computer-Mediation on Dyadic Negotiations,* 12 J. Computer-Mediated Comm. (2007), http://jcmc.indiana.edu/vol12/issue2/giordano.html.

28. Brian Farkas, *Old Problem, New Medium, Deception in Computer-Facilitated Negotiation and Dispute Resolution,* 14 Cardozo J. Conflict Resol. 161, 161-162 (2012); Giordano et al., *supra* note 27.

29. The ABA Task Force on Electronic Commerce and Alternative Dispute Resolution acknowledged this concern and suggested a set of guidelines to ensure the quality of online dispute services. *Recommended Best Practices for Online Dispute Resolution Service Providers,* http://www.americanbar.org/content/dam/aba/migrated/dispute/documents/BestPracticesFinal102802.authcheckdam.pdf (last visited Mar. 30, 2017).

30. Susan S. Raines, *Mediating in Your Pajamas: The Benefits and Challenges for ODR Practitioners,* 23 Conflict Resol. Q. 3, 360 (2006).

31. 1 Colleen Getz, *Evaluation of the Distance Mediation Project: Report on Phase II of the Technology-Assisted Family Mediation Project* iii (May 2010), http://www.mediatebc.com/PDFs/1-2-Mediation-Services/Distance-Mediation-Project—Evaluation-Report.aspx.

32. *Id.*

33. Susanna Jani, *Mediating from a Distance: Suggested Practice Guidelines for Family Mediators* (2d ed. Oct. 2012), http://www.mediatebc.com/PDFs/1-14-Family-Mediation—FAQs/Guidelines_Mediating-from-a-Distance-%28Second-editi.aspx.

34. https://adr.org/aaa/ShowPDF?doc=ADRSTG_010409.

35. Susan Nauss Exon, *The Next Generation of Online Dispute Resolution: The Significance of Holography to Enhance and Transform Dispute Resolution,* 12 Cardozo J. Conflict Resol. 19, 38-41 (2010).

36. Luke Yoo, http://luke77.com/holotext-messaging (last visited Mar. 31, 2017).

37. David Allen Larson, *Artificial Intelligence: Robots, Avatars, and the Demise of the Human Mediator,* 25 Ohio St. J. on Disp. Resol. 105, 105 (2010).

38. An avatar is "an electronic image that represents and is manipulated by a computer user (as in a computer game)." *Merriam-Webster Dictionary,* http://www.merriam-webster.com/dictionary/avatar.

39. "Relational agents . . . can have a physical presence such as a robot, be embodied in an avatar, or have no detectable form whatsoever and exist only as software." Larson, *supra* note 36, at 107.

40. *Id.* at 108.

41. *Id.* at 163.

42. Orna Rabinovich-Einy & Ethan Katsh, *Technology and the Future of Dispute Systems Design,* 17 Harv. Negot. L. Rev. 151, 178 (2012).

43. Colin Rule, *Online Dispute Resolution for Business* vii (Jossey-Bass 2002).

44. David A. Larson, *Online Dispute Resolution: Do You Know Where Your Children Are?,* 19 Negot. J. 199, 200 (2003).

45. Haitham A. Haloush & Bashar H. Malkawi, *Internet Characteristics and Online Alternative Dispute Resolution,* 13 Harv. Negot. L. Rev. 327, 333 (2008).

CHAPTER NINE

Restorative Methods

Chapter Outline

Introduction

What Is Restorative Justice?

The Advantages and Disadvantages of
Restorative Justice

    Advantages

    Disadvantages

Restorative Methods

    Victim-Offender Dialogue
    (VOD)

Conferencing

Circles

Conclusion

Key Terms and Concepts

Practice Test Questions

Review Questions

Application Questions

Practice Exercises

Ho'oponopono ("To make right")[1]

INTRODUCTION

We begin our study with a story well known in the restorative justice field, about two teenagers who went on a drunken vandalism spree in Elmira, Ontario, and how it led to the creation of restorative justice in Canada. It is referred to as the "Kitchener Experiment" and is told in the words of one of the participants, Russ Kelly (see Exhibit 9-1).

Exhibit 9-1. **THE KITCHENER EXPERIMENT**

MY FORMATIVE YEARS

My seven siblings and I were raised in Mount Forest, Ontario. When I was six years old, my father died, leaving my mother to look after her eight children. At the young age of fifteen my mother also died and my eldest brother became my official guardian. At the time, he had just gotten married and was putting his life back on track because he had made a few bad choices and poor decisions. Dad was not there to guide him and keep him out of trouble. This was a scary time for me and a challenging time for him. While I

Continued >

lived under his roof I lived under his law because he did not want me to make the same mistakes and I respect him for that. He did his best!

Feeling unjustly victimized, and deeply hurt at the loss of my mother I was a confused teenager. In 1971, there weren't programs in place to properly deal with grief and the trauma that I felt when I lost my mother. At the age of fifteen, I still hadn't understood (or should I say — accepted) the loss of my father. Sure, I went to the school guidance counselor, only to have appointments set up to see a psychiatrist who in turn only told me that I was not crazy. He did not help me deal with my emotions and anger. Talking to my siblings about my problems was not an option and our aunts and uncles didn't have what you would call close ties with our family. Looking for ways to deal with my emotional pain I turned to drugs and alcohol.

BAD HABIT TURNS TO VICE

By 1974, I had developed a strong reliance on drugs and alcohol as well as the people that could feed my established habit. Since the grief and pain wasn't dealt with in a positive way and vented properly, I would get very hostile when I got drunk and often it felt as though my head was going to explode. It was difficult to think clearly and rationalize sensibly. There were times that I would end up in fights and very often have vague memories of what happened the night before. Blackouts were a common occurrence. I was not the person that I wanted to be, nor the person that my parents wanted me to be. They sure wouldn't have been proud of me. I was on a path to nowhere and life went on.

One night in May of 1974, I went to Elmira, Ontario, to visit some of my so-called friends. Of course that visit was to drink and get drunk. My friend and I went for a drive with a case or two of beer. We drove around the back roads for hours drinking beer and getting drunker by the minute. It was after mid-night when we got pulled over by the police. Things were different back then, the officer took what was left of our beer, gave us a stern warning and told us to go home.

A CRAZY SENSELESS NIGHT

We made our way back into town and went to my friend's apartment building. Upon arriving at the apartment building, my friend suggested we go raise some hell. Not being of sound mind, I shrugged my shoulders and said something like, "What the hell, why not?" I asked my friend what he had in mind and he suggested that we proceed to wreak havoc and destroy whatever was in our path. I am not proud of what we did that night in Elmira, but I'll tell you anyway. I had a switchblade and my accomplice had a sharp kitchen knife that we used to slash 24 car tires. We slashed car seats and destroyed a car radiator. Rocks were thrown through large plate glass windows in homes and the front window at the local beer store. A boat was pulled into the street, punctured and overturned. A gazebo was damaged, a flashing light at an intersection was damaged and a cross was broken from a display case at a local church. Side windows and car windshields were smashed with beer bottles. A garden table was thrown into a fishpond and a fence destroyed. In all, 22 properties received damage. All this happened in about a two hour span from about 3:00 a.m. to 5:00 a.m. When we had enough of this craziness we headed back to the apartment and passed-out.

Continued >

BUSTED

The police were pounding at the door at about 7:00 a.m. Someone had seen us running through the back-yards and gave a description to the police. It didn't take long to figure out the two young men that were pulled over the previous night were the likely suspects. My accomplice and I were detained in separate rooms for questioning. The police did not use the good cop-bad cop routine with us. They just asked us if we were the ones that committed all the damage the previous night. I knew we messed up big time and I felt terrible about it, so I admitted my part in the crime spree. However, my accomplice was not as forthcoming with his guilt. Indeed, he did confess to his part of the crime after learning of my confession. We both knew that we messed up severely and it was only right to own up to our mistakes and face the consequences.

JUDICIAL SYSTEM TAKES A TURN

At the time of "The Elmira Case," Mark Yantzi was a probation officer and a volunteer with the Mennonite Central Committee in Kitchener. Mark was handed our case and in a meeting with other volunteer members he suggested, "Wouldn't it be neat for these offenders to meet with their victims?" The offenders could be accountable for their actions and repair the harm done. Mark felt there could be some therapeutic value in this approach. Yet, having this novel idea, he didn't think the idea was any more than just that. Another volunteer, Dave Worth, told Mark that his idea was a great one and it should not only be further investigated, but to suggest it to the judge. Mark attached an addendum to the back of the pre-sentence report for the judge. Judge Gordon McConnell saw no precedence in law to allow this idea. However, Judge McConnell was tired of the revolving door of justice and was looking for a new approach for justice. There was no basis in law to order my accomplice and I to do this, so Mark asked us and advised it would be best for all concerned. My accomplice and I decided it was the right thing to do. If we did not go along with this novel suggestion — we were sure to see the inside of jail for a long time. Having agreed to meet our victims opened the door for the judge to include this as part of our probation order.

MEETING OUR VICTIMS

Meeting our victims was one of the hardest things I had ever done in my entire life. Accompanied by Mark Yantzi (our probation officer) and Dave Worth (a volunteer), we walked up to the victims' front door to apologize, hear what the victims had to say, determine the amount of restitution, ask for forgiveness and assure the victims that they were not targeted. It was a random act of vandalism.

Some victims offered forgiveness while others wanted to give us a good whipping. Nonetheless, we survived meeting the victims of our crime spree and returned a couple of months later with certified cheques to restore the amount of out-of-pocket expenses not covered by insurance. The total damage was around $2,200; my accomplice and myself each had to pay $550 restitution and each paid a $200 fine. As well, we were placed on 18 months' probation. I thought that was the end of that shameful part of my life. Little did I know what would become of this judicial experiment. Unknowingly to me the Victim Offender Reconciliation Program was born.[2]

The Kitchener Experiment was about accepting responsibility and repairing harm, the underpinnings of restorative justice. The term "restorative justice" describes a philosophy or a "social movement to institutionalize peaceful approaches to harms, problem-solving and violations of legal and human rights."[3] The next section discusses the philosophy of restorative justice.

WHAT IS RESTORATIVE JUSTICE?

The term "restorative justice," generally attributed to Albert Eglash, is found in an article he wrote in 1977; however, the roots of restorative justice are not so apparent. Some scholars have argued that restorative justice has been around since the beginning of civilization. Others disagree and posit that it grew from the social justice movements in the United States in the mid-twentieth century. What is clear is that today, restorative justice methods are well established in Western society and are another alternative method for resolving conflicts.

Restorative justice, often associated with criminal justice, focuses on the harm to the victim rather than the actions of the offender. Howard Zehr, considered by many to be "the leading visionary and architect of the restorative justice movement,"[4] defines restorative justice as "a process to involve, to the extent possible, those who have a stake in a specific offense and to collectively identify and address harms, needs, and obligations, in order to heal and put things as right as possible."[5] **Restorative methods** are the mechanisms used for identifying the victim's harm, holding the offender accountable for the harm, and, to the extent possible, restoring the interpersonal relationship. The objectives are to make amends, extend forgiveness, and reintegrate the offender back into the community. To illustrate, let's look at how the traditional system of criminal justice approaches wrongdoing as compared to the restorative view.

Principles of Restorative Justice

- Focus on the harms and consequent needs of the victims, as well as those of the communities and the offenders.
- Address the obligations that result from those harms (the obligations of offenders as well as of communities and society).
- Use inclusive, collaborative processes to the extent possible.
- Involve those with a legitimate stake in the situation, including victims, offenders, community members, and society.
- Seek to put right the wrongs.

Source: Howard Zehr, *Commentary: Restorative Justice: Beyond Victim-Offender Mediation*, 22 Conflict Resol. Q. 305, 307 (Fall-Winter 2004).

Conventional criminal justice focuses on law violations. It centers around the offender—investigation, arrest, arraignment, prosecution, conviction, sentence, and incarceration. Because crime is seen as victimizing the state, the state gets to determine what happens. The individual who actually suffered the harm is viewed only as a witness for the state who provides evidence to help convict the offender. Victims and members of the community have little or no involvement in the process. The criminal justice system focuses on three questions: "(1) What laws have been broken? (2) Who did it? (3) What do they deserve?"[6]

From the restorative justice perspective, the victim is the individual person hurt by the crime. Restorative justice is victim-focused. It acknowledges the victim's needs and requires offender accountability. Restorative justice asks: "(1) Who has been hurt? (2) What do they need? (3) Whose obligations and responsibilities are these? (4) Who has a stake in this situation? (5) What is the process that can involve the stakeholders in finding a solution?"[7] The restorative concept "sees crime as an injury rather than as lawbreaking with the purpose of justice being healing rather than just punishment."[8]

Now that we have described restorative justice as a philosophy for resolving conflict, we will discuss its advantages and disadvantages in the next section.

THE ADVANTAGES AND DISADVANTAGES OF RESTORATIVE JUSTICE

Advantages

Helps Victims

Restorative justice gives victims a chance to meet offenders and tell them how they were affected physically, emotionally, and financially, and to get answers to their questions about the wrongdoing and the offender. Victims feel like the offense has taken away control of their lives. Restorative justice can validate victims' experiences and provide recognition that they are not responsible for the wrongdoing. By participating in a restorative process, they can regain a sense of empowerment. Many victims report that after meeting with the offenders, they felt "a significant reduction in fear and a significant increase in their sense of security."[9] The process helps them move forward.

Sometimes victims want the harmful behavior to stop but do not want to be dragged into the court process. The restorative approach can address the offender's conduct in a way that stops the behavior and repairs the relationship without going to court.

Helps Offenders

The offender learns firsthand from the victim about the impact his actions had on her and allows the offender to apologize and make amends. The objective is to have the offender feel compassion for the victim and thus make it more difficult for the offender to repeat his wrongdoings. "It is hoped that this face-to-face interaction will instill in the offender a sense of compassion for the victim, hence making it more difficult for the offender to replicate his wrongdoings in the future."[10] By accepting responsibility, the offender may also increase his chances for a more favorable sanction.

Another benefit is that the offender plays an active role in the resolution of the wrong rather than just passively accepting punishment or reprimand. "[P]eople will be happier and make positive change when people do things with them (restorative, participatory, engaging) rather than to them (punitive and authoritarian) or for them (permissive and paternalistic)."[11] In restorative processes, victims and offenders communicate and work together to create a mutually agreed-upon resolution (that can include things other than money), answer questions, and talk about the effect of the wrongdoer's behavior.

Offenders also benefit by gaining self-respect and personal integrity and restoring interpersonal trust. As a result, the relationships between the offender and others involved will become stronger. "These outcomes . . . will strengthen relationships among the offender, victim, and others . . . [in the community, school, or] workplace."[12]

Reinforces Social Norms

Wrongdoing conveys a message of disrespect for the victim, community, workplace, or school. While everyone follows the rules, the offender acts as though the rules do not apply to her and she can do whatever she wants. Through restorative processes, the community can collectively censure the offender's behavior and explain how the wrong damaged the trust and equality of the community. By acknowledging the harm, accepting responsibility, and making amends, the offender can be reintegrated back into the community.

Victim and Offender Satisfaction

The restorative justice research shows an increase in victim and offender satisfaction with the processes and outcomes.[13] "This literature has produced remarkably consistent outcomes, and results suggest that offenders and their victims have better justice experiences compared with offenders and victims in traditional justice."[14]

Recidivism

Although research into reoffending is still inconclusive, some studies demonstrate that restorative justice methods have reduced or have the potential to reduce reoffending. The evidence suggests that offenders who meet with their victims are less likely to commit new crimes when compared with offenders who did not participate in restorative justice. "Newly emerging evidence, still tentative in scope, suggests that offenders who mediate with their victims are dramatically less likely to return to crime than comparable offenders who have been dealt with in the usual ways."[15]

Less Costly Than Litigation

Restorative processes, like other alternative dispute resolution methods, can be less expensive than litigation. Because there are no or minimal court hearings and no need to comply with the rules of evidence, there are reduced costs. Also, when lawyers are not involved, there are additional savings in legal fees. In criminal matters, there are the added savings associated with the costs of incarceration.

A Holistic Approach

Instead of focusing solely on punishing the offender, restorative methods address the needs of the victims and offenders and promote healing. The processes are designed to hold wrongdoers accountable, meet victims' needs, and promote social cohesion.

Disadvantages

Repairs Harms but Ignores Wrongs

Critics of restorative processes posit that some harm, especially material harm, can be repaired through restitution, "[b]ut the message of insult or contempt the offender communicated through his conduct—the wrong he did . . . —remains." By extension, the community to which the victim is a member is also wronged. While restorative remedies can repair the harm, they cannot repair the wrong.[16]

No Punishment

Restorative justice advocates think that punishment is unnecessary, however, Stephen Garvey argues that without punishment, the victim cannot be restored.[17] Punishment is necessary

> to convey censure or condemnation of the offender's wrongful action. . . . [This] proclaims to the world—to the victim, to the offender, and to the community as a whole—that the message of superiority implicit or explicit in the offender's crime is a false message. The expressive dimension of punishment broadcasts a true moral message to counteract and annul the false moral message broadcast through the offender's wrongful conduct. Punishment therefore humbles the wrongdoer and vindicates the victim. Without punishment the wrong the victim suffered would go unrepaired, and the victim would remain less than fully restored. Consequently, the victim's full restoration, far from being incompatible with punishment and retribution, actually ends up requiring it.[18]

The absence of punishment is thus viewed by some as a distinct disadvantage of restorative justice.

Victims Can Be Revictimized

The informality of restorative methods could make victims vulnerable to more harm.[19] An offender can use words, tone of voice, or gestures to intimidate and control the victim. This is exacerbated in situations of power imbalances between the victim and offender.

Labor and Time Intensive

Preparing for and participating in restorative processes can be very time consuming. In one workplace harassment case, approximately 25 hours were expended.[20] This included 19 hours for the preconference interviews and 6 hours for the conference. Not included were the inestimable time devoted to follow-up.

No Procedural Safeguards

Critics of restorative methods express concerns about the legal rights of offenders and victims. In the criminal context, offenders have certain due process[21] rights: the right to be presumed innocent,[22] the right against self-incrimination,[23] the right to a fair trial,[24] and the right to the assistance of counsel.[25] Critics question whether offenders who admit their guilt during the restorative process were properly informed of and voluntarily waived these constitutional rights. In noncriminal matters, the accused also has rights and remedies. For example, an employee wrongfully accused of sexual harassment in the workplace can bring an action in civil court and be represented by counsel. There are also the rules of civil procedure and the rules of evidence designed to make the process fair. Finally, there is the concern about confidentiality. If the restorative process fails to result in an agreement, there is worry that the offender's admission of responsibility and other statements made against interests can be used against him.

Discrimination and Power Imbalances

Critics caution that discrimination may affect the restorative process, so that characteristics such as race, culture, gender, and social standing may result in different results for similar wrongs. In addition, power imbalances may exist that could disadvantage the less powerful party. He might accept a less favorable outcome than one that could have been achieved if there was no power imbalance.

Now that we have explored the advantages and disadvantages, we will discuss three prevalent types of restorative methods.

RESTORATIVE METHODS

Restorative methods are the processes wherein victims and offenders, and in some cases other interested parties, meet with a facilitator to discuss the wrongdoing and develop a plan for resolving the conflict. The three common forms are victim-offender dialogue, group conferencing, and circles. All of these involve the victim and offender in face-to-face dialogue with the addition of at least one other person.[26] (As we will see, some forms include supporters of the victim and offender and members of the community.). This "other" person acts as the mediator, facilitator, or circle keeper. The meetings look at what happened, how it affected the parties, and how the harm can be repaired. These forms have been used in a number of different settings, including workplaces, schools, criminal justice settings, and families.

PARALEGAL POINTERS

Is Restorative Justice Appropriate for Your Client?

The following are factors to consider when determining whether a restorative method is suitable for a client:

- A client who admits guilt, or at least, seems to be moving in the direction of accepting responsibility for the offense. A question of guilt is usually not mediable.
- An offender who is at least open to talking about meeting with the victim and negotiating restitution or other issues. A good mediator can often convince a reticent offender of the benefits available to him from mediation.
- An offender who has the capacity to speak for himself in mediation.
- An identified or identifiable victim with whom to mediate. The defense attorney may or may not have any information about the victim's willingness or ability to mediate. If you have not already made contact with the victim, I recommend that defense attorneys leave the victim outreach to the mediator.
- Some loss, damage or harm (monetary or non-monetary), for which restitution or restoration could be mediated. [And, does the offender have the ability/resources to provide restitution?]
- Give extra consideration to mediation for a client who has, or had an ongoing relationship with the victim of the crime.
- Particularly ripe for mediation are situations in which there is a dispute over what losses were suffered, what losses were caused by the offender, or in which there is a dispute over the value of the victim's losses.[27]

Used with permission. © Victim-Offender Reconciliation Program Information and Resource Center.

Victim-Offender Dialogue (VOD)

Victim-offender dialogue (VOD) is a meeting between the victim, offender, and a trained facilitator to talk about the wrong and develop an agreement to make things right. Of all the restorative methods, VOD is the oldest and most widely used and developed restorative method. Some states have passed legislation that support victim-offender mediation in the criminal justice system. Many scholars credit the "Elmira Case" (recounted in the beginning of this chapter) with giving birth to this form.[28] VOD focuses "on victim healing, offender accountability, and restoration of losses."[29] The facilitator's role is to help the parties by

> facilitating dialogue and mutual aid; scheduling separate pre[dialogue] sessions with each party; connecting with the parties through building rapport and trust while not taking sides; identifying the strengths of each party; using a nondirective style of [discussion] that creates a safe space for dialogue and accessing the strengths of participants; and recognizing and using the power of silence.[30]

The process uses four steps: (1) determining whether the matter is suitable for VOD, (2) preparing for the dialogue, (3) conducting the dialogue or meeting itself, and (4) following up.[31]

Stage One — Assessing the Case

The process begins with a referral to a facilitator who reviews the case to determine whether it is appropriate for VOD. The facilitator gathers background information and contacts the victim and offender. If both are willing to participate and there is no appearance of hostility between the parties, the facilitator accepts the referral.

Stage Two — Preparing for the Dialogue

In this phase, the facilitator meets with each party separately; explains the program, purpose, and how it works; and answers questions. Additionally, the facilitator will ensure that each party's participation is voluntary, that they are mentally prepared, and that each has a realistic expectation of what will happen. If the facilitator concludes that the wrongdoing is appropriate for VOD and if both parties agree to participate, a time and place is selected for a face-to-face meeting. If either party does not want to be involved, the process ends.

Stage Three — Meeting

The meeting is intended to generate understanding between victim and offender. The dialogue begins with introductions, followed by the facilitator's explanation of her role. Next, the victim is given uninterrupted time to tell what happened, the impact of the offense, and the losses he suffered. The victim also can ask the offender questions. The offender then has the opportunity to admit to the wrongdoing, explain her participation, and offer an apology.

After the parties have shared their experiences and emotions, the meeting focuses on developing an acceptable agreement between the victim and offender, obligating the offender to do something to make amends. This could be paying money to the victim, performing work for the victim or a nonprofit organization of the victim's choosing, or some other form of obligation. The agreement is reduced to a writing and signed by the parties. If the parties fail to reach an accord, the case is sent back to the person or organization that made the referral.

Stage Four — Following Up

The final phase of VOD is follow-up. After an accord is reached, a designated person will monitor the offender's performance to ensure she is complying with the agreement.

Conferencing

Conferencing, originally called "family group conferencing," began in New Zealand in 1989 as a response to the disproportionate number of minorities involved in the juvenile justice system. Alternative names include community conferencing, restorative conferencing, and workplace conferencing. A major difference from VOD is the participation of family members and supporters of the victim and offender at the meeting. In these conferences, "[e]ach participant has the opportunity to discuss the impact of the incident. Hearing people speak at the conference allows the offender to see the impact of his or her behavior on the victim and those close to the victim as well as on the offender's own family and friends."[32] Leena Kurki suggests that conferencing is "more effective [than victim-offender mediation] in creating positive community involvement, rebuilding relationships, and preventing future offending . . . [because it involves] a broader range of people and family members, and supporters tend to take collective responsibility over the offender and fulfillment of his or her agreement."[33]

One of the key focal points of conferencing is **reintegrative shaming**. This means expressing disapproval of the behavior while also conveying respect for the offender.

Reintegrative shaming communicates to the offender and community "what values/norms/laws have been violated and affirm[s] mutual obligations and accountability."[34] Unlike **stigmatizing shame**, which centers on the person and can make the offender feel humiliated and estranged, reintegrative shame focuses on the act. "By acknowledging the harm, accepting responsibility for the act, and making amends, the shame can be discharged, allowing the individual to be reintegrated into the community. Processing of shame in this manner helps restore social bonds"[35] and acceptance by the community.

Just like VOD, reintegrative shaming involves four steps: assessment, preparation, meeting, and follow-up. Many conferencing methods use a script similar to the one in Exhibit 9-2.

Exhibit 9-2. CONFERENCE FACILITATOR'S SCRIPT

1. PREAMBLE

"Welcome. As you know, my name is (your name) **and I will be facilitating this conference."**

Now introduce each conference participant and state his/her relationship to the offender/s or victim/s.

"Thank you all for attending. I know that this is difficult for all of you, but your presence will help us deal with the matter that has brought us together. This is an opportunity for all of you to be involved in repairing the harm that has been done."

"This conference will focus on an incident which happened (state the date, place and nature of offense without elaborating). **It is important to understand that we will focus on what** (offender name/s) **did and how that unacceptable behavior has affected others. We are not here to decide whether** (offender name/s) **is/are good or bad. We want to explore in what way people have been affected and hopefully work toward repairing the harm that has resulted. Does everyone understand this?"**

"(Offender name/s) has/have admitted his/her/their part in the incident."

Say to offender/s: **"I must tell you that you do not have to participate in this conference and are free to leave at any time, as is anyone else. If you do leave, the matter may be referred to court/handled by the school disciplinary policy/handled in another way."**

"This matter, however, may be finalized if you participate in a positive manner and comply with the conference agreement."

Say to offender/s: **"Do you understand?"**

2. OFFENDER/S

"We'll start with (one of offenders' names)**."**

If there is more than one offender, have each respond to all of the following questions.

- **"What happened?"**
- **"What were you thinking about at the time?"**
- **"What have you thought about since the incident?"**
- **"Who do you think has been affected by your actions?"**
- **"How have they been affected?"**

3. VICTIM/S

If there is more than one victim, have each respond to all of the following questions.

- **"What was your reaction at the time of the incident?"**
- **"How do you feel about what happened?"**
- **"What has been the hardest thing for you?"**

Continued >

• "How did your family and friends react when they heard about the incident?"

4. VICTIM SUPPORTERS

Have each respond to all of the following questions.

• "What did you think when you heard about the incident?"
• "How do you feel about what happened?"
• "What has been the hardest thing for you?"
• "What do you think are the main issues?"

5. OFFENDER SUPPORTERS

To parent/caregiver ask: **"This has been difficult for you, hasn't it? Would you like to tell us about it?"**

Have each respond to all of the following questions.

• "What did you think when you heard about the incident?"
• "How do you feel about what happened?"
• "What has been the hardest thing for you?"
• "What do you think are the main issues?"

6. OFFENDER/S

Ask the offender/s: **"Is there anything you want to say at this time?"**

7. REACHING AN AGREEMENT

Ask the victim/s: **"What would you like from today's conference?"**

Ask the offender/s to respond.

At this point, the participants discuss what should be in the final agreement. Solicit comments from participants.

It is important that you ask the offender/s to respond to each suggestion before the group moves to the next suggestion, asking **"What do you think about that?"** Then determine that the offender/s agree/s before moving on. Allow for negotiation.

As the agreement develops, clarify each item and make the written document as specific as possible, including details, deadlines and follow-up arrangements.

As you sense that the agreement discussion is drawing to a close, say to the participants:

"Before I prepare the written agreement, I'd like to make sure that I have accurately recorded what has been decided."

Read the items in the agreement aloud and look to the participants for acknowledgment. Make any necessary corrections.

Continued >

---

8. CLOSING THE CONFERENCE

"Before I formally close this conference, I would like to provide everyone with a final opportunity to speak. Is there anything anyone wants to say?"

Allow for participants to respond and when they are done, say:

"Thank you for your contributions in dealing with this difficult matter.

Congratulations on the way you have worked through the issues. Please help yourselves to some refreshments while I prepare the agreement."

Allow participants ample time to have refreshments and interact. The informal period after the formal conference is very important.

Used with permission. © International Institute for Restorative Practices.

The third method we will explore is restorative circles. The major difference between VOD, conferencing, and circles is that in addition to the victim, offender, and their supporters, members of the wider community may participate.

Circles

The **circle** method in the United States comes from the Native Canadian peacemaking practice. First used in the Yukon in the early 1980s, the goal of the circle is to resolve "conflict in a manner that advances the well-being of individuals, families, and the community."[36] Three common principles underlie the circle process. First, an offense signifies a violation of the relationship between the offender and victim and offender and community. Second, the community is responsible for healing the violation to preserve stability. And third, the community is best situated to address the causes of the breach of the relationship.

A circular seating arrangement and the use of a "talking piece" are the notable features of circles. The talking piece is an object that has specific meaning or symbolism to the circle keeper (facilitator). Examples might be feathers, stones, sticks, and seashells (see Exhibit 9-3). It is passed to each person in the circle and is used to control the conversation. Sitting in a circle symbolizes the equality of all participants and highlights the interconnectedness and interdependence of everyone in the community.

> In a circle, there is no right or left, nor is there a beginning or an end; every point (or person) on the line of a circle looks to the same center as the focus. The circle . . . is perfect, unbroken, and a simile of unity and oneness. It conveys the image of people gathering together for discussion.[37]

Exhibit 9-3. TALKING PIECES

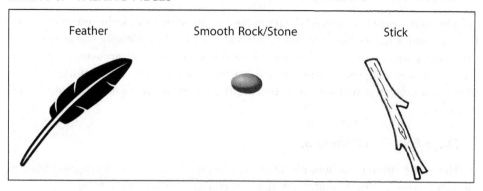

| Feather | Smooth Rock/Stone | Stick |

The talking piece ensures that all participants have an opportunity to be heard because only the person holding the talking piece is allowed to speak.

> When you receive the talking piece, you may speak without interruption, hold the talking piece in silence, or simply pass it in silence to the next person. The use of a talking piece, in essence, slows the pace of dialogue, encourages quieter people to have an equal voice, assists participants in modulating and shaping the expression of strong emotions, and allows for deeper conversation, more careful listening and thoughtful expression.[38]

The circle process uses four distinct stages, similar to those used in VOD and conferencing: assessing, preparing, gathering, and following up.[39]

Stage One — Assessing the Case

In the United States, peacemaking circles are usually organized and facilitated by a community-based organization. The process begins when an offender is referred to the program or submits an application to participate. Members of the organization then determine whether the case is appropriate for a restorative circle. If the case is accepted, the process moves to the preparation stage.

Stage Two — Preparing

During this stage, the circle facilitator, commonly called the "Circle Keeper,"[40] meets separately with each participant and explains the purpose and process of the circle, the role of the Keeper, and what is expected from participants. Sometimes, separate circles are held with victim's supporters and offender's supporters. These circles can be used to prepare participants for the larger circle gathering, discuss concerns, and share ideas. The Keeper also selects the date, time, and location of the gathering; the room arrangement; and the talking piece.

Stage Three — Gathering

The third stage is where all the participants gather in one circle and share their feelings about the victim, offender, and the harm. They identify the issues and develop a plan of resolution that addresses the interests of all circle members. All participants must agree on the solution. Once consensus is reached, the members develop a plan that will lead to repairing the harm to the victim, offender, and community.

Stage Four — Following Up

Here, the circle members monitor the offender's and victim's progress and, if circumstances warrant, make any needed changes to the agreement.

Conclusion

Restorative justice is another approach for resolving conflict. It focuses on the harm to the victim rather than the actions of the offender. Restorative methods are the mechanisms used for identifying the harm, holding the offender accountable for the harm, and, to the extent possible, restoring the interpersonal relationship. The objectives of restorative justice are to make amends, extend forgiveness, and reintegrate the offender back into the community.

Key Terms and Concepts

Circle
Conferencing
Reintegrative shaming
Restorative justice

Restorative methods
Stigmatizing shame
Victim-offender dialogue

Practice Test Questions

True/False
____ 1. Restorative justice focuses on the harm to the victim rather than the actions of the offender.
____ 2. A talking piece is used in the circle method to control the conversation.
____ 3. Victim-offender dialogue is a meeting between the victim, offender, and representatives of the community to talk about the wrong and develop an agreement to make things right.
____ 4. Conventional criminal justice focuses on violations of the law with little or no involvement from victims and members of the community.
____ 5. The circle facilitator is commonly called the Circle Keeper.

Multiple Choice

___ 1. The four stages of victim-offender dialogue are ___
   a. assessment of the case, preparation for the dialogue, the meeting, and follow-up.
   b. assessment of the case, preparation for the meeting, the gathering, and follow-up.
   c. assessment of the case, preparation, the gathering, and conclusion.
   d. assessment of the case, preparation for the meeting, shaming, and follow-up.

___ 2. The three common forms of restorative methods are ___
   a. group conferencing, shaming, and circles.
   b. victim-offender dialogue, mediation, and circles.
   c. victim-offender dialogue, gathering, and circles.
   d. victim-offender dialogue, group conferencing, and circles.

___ 3. All of the following *except* ___ are advantages of restorative methods.
   a. Helps victims
   b. Reinforces social norms
   c. Provides procedural safeguards
   d. Helps offenders

___ 4. A key component of the conferencing process is ___
   a. the talking piece.
   b. reintegrative shaming.
   c. the follow-up.
   d. the mediator.

___ 5. The principles of restorative justice include all of the following *except* ___
   a. focuses on the harm and needs of victims.
   b. focuses on the actions of the offender.
   c. seeks to put right the wrong.
   d. uses collaborative processes.

Review Questions

1. What is restorative justice?
2. What are the principles of restorative justice?
3. List and explain the advantages of restorative methods.
4. List and explain the disadvantages of restorative methods.
5. What are the three common restorative methods? Explain each one.
6. What are the steps in victim-offender dialogue? Conferencing? Circles?
7. What are the three common principles of the circle?
8. Explain the concept of reintegrative shaming. How does it differ from stigmatizing shame?
9. What is the major difference between victim-offender dialogue and conferencing?

10. Why does one scholar think that conferencing is a better restorative method than victim-offender dialogue?
11. What are some alternative names for conferencing?

Application Questions

1. Sally has been employed at the Board of Education for 15 years. Her supervisor Jean, a former worker, feels threatened because Sally knows more about the school system than she does. At least once a week, Jean comes over to Sally's work area and begins to criticize her work. She talks in a very loud voice and tries to provoke Sally. She stays in the area criticizing Sally, walking around looking at her work for upwards of 45 minutes at a time. Sally is thinking of quitting.[41]
   a. Would you recommend using a restorative method in the above hypothetical? Why or why not?
   b. If your answer to "a" is yes, which method would you use? Why?
   c. How would you determine whether Jean is an appropriate candidate for a restorative method?
2. Do you agree or disagree with the following statement? Why or why not?
   [W]hile restitution can repair the material harm (if any) caused by a crime, it cannot and does not fix the wrong. If the offender who stole my car returns it, or buys me a new one, the material injury I've suffered is repaired as far as it can be. But the message of insult or contempt the offender communicated through his conduct — the wrong he did to me — remains. So how can that wrong be repaired? The answer, of course, is through punishment, which restorativists steadfastly reject.[42]
3. Victims of an offender's action include not only the person injured but also the community.
   a. What is meant by community?
   b. How is the community injured?
4. The attorney you work for represents Stan Liu, who stole $7500 from a nonprofit community organization for which he was the treasurer. The members of the organization are stunned and angry. Stan has no criminal record and admitted to you that he stole the money to pay off a gambling debt. After reviewing his case, you see no possible defenses. Why might this be a good case for restorative justice?

Practice Exercises

1. Go to the Centre for Justice and Reconciliation website (http://www .restorativejustice.org) and read one of the articles listed below. (Click on "RJ Library" then on "Read More" and then on "Read Full Article.") Prepare a paper in which you discuss the article. Be prepared to present your paper to the class.

Articles

Abuser and Survivor, Face to Face, by Leah Sottile (Oct. 16, 2015)

I Felt Healed: Mum Met Burglar Who Stole Precious Memories of Her Dead Daughter, by Sally Beck (Feb. 13, 2013)

Just Get a Rock and Talk, by Robert C. Koehler (Sept. 18, 2012)

Restorative Practices Seen by the Court (paper presented Aug. 6-8, 1998)

2. Find a restorative justice program in your state or a neighboring state and provide the following information: an overview of the program, its history, the goals, and the process from the filing or assignment of a case to its conclusion. If possible, interview a person involved in the program and have him or her share with you some actual cases handled by the organization.

3. Go to http://www.cehd.umn.edu/ssw/rjp/DVDs/default.asp and click on "Volume 5 Complete Victim Offender Mediation and Conference Training." Watch both cases and then choose one to prepare a paper in which you discuss the process used, the issue, the facilitator, and any resolution. In addition, discuss what you believe are the negative consequences and positive benefits of the program. Be prepared to present your paper to the class.

Endnotes

1. "Ho'oponopono is a traditional Hawaiian dispute resolution system. . . . The word ho'oponopono literally means 'to make right.'" Andrew J. Hosmanek, *Cutting the Cord: Ho'oponopona and Hawaiian Restorative Justice in the Criminal Law Context,* 5 Pepp. Disp. Resol. L.J. 359, 359 (2005).

2. Used with permission of Russ Kelly.

3. *What Is Restorative Justice?,* Suffolk University, http://www.suffolk.edu/college/centers/15970.php (last visited Mar. 31, 2017).

4. Mark Umbreit, Betty Vos, Robert Coates & Elizabeth Lightfoot, *Restorative Justice in the Twenty-First Century: A Social Movement Full of Opportunities and Pitfalls,* 89 Marq. L. Rev. 251, 256 (2005).

5. Howard Zehr, *The Little Book of Restorative Justice* 37 (Good Books 2002).

6. *Id.* at 63.

7. *Id.*

8. Mary Ellen Reimund, *Is Restorative Justice on a Collision Course with the Constitution?,* 3 Appalachian J.L. 1, 4 (2004).

9. Linda G. Mills, *The Justice of Recovery: How the State Can Heal the Violence of Crime,* 57 Hastings L.J. 457, 458 (2006).

10. Alyssa Shenk, *Victim-Offender Mediation: The Road to Repairing Hate Crime Injustice,* 17 Ohio St. J. on Disp. Resol. 185, 196 (2001).

11. Susan Hanley Duncan, *Workplace Bullying and the Role Restorative Practices Can Play in Preventing and Addressing the Problem,* 32 Indus. L.J. 2331, 2357 (Oct. 2011).

12. Jerry Goodstein & Kenneth D. Butterfield, *Extending the Horizon of Business Ethics: Restorative Justice and the Aftermath of Unethical Behavior,* 20 Bus. Ethics Q. 453, 466 (July 2010).

13. *Id.* at 464; William Bradshaw & Mark S. Umbreit, *Crime Victims Meet Juvenile Offenders: Contributing Factors to Victim Satisfaction with Mediated Dialogue,* 49 Juv. & Fam. Ct. J. 17, 17-18 (Summer 1998).

14. Hennessey Hayes, *Reoffending and Restorative Justice, in Handbook of Restorative Justice* 432 (Gerry Johnstone & Daniel W. Van Ness eds., Willan 2007). "75% of victims and 65% of offenders who mediate report satisfaction with the way that their case was handled; 85% of both victims and offenders who mediate report that a fair result was reached in their case. Typically, less that 40% of victims and less than 20% of offenders report a sense of fairness and satisfaction with the result, in non-mediated cases." Marty Price, *Mediated Civil Compromise—A Tool for Restorative Justice,* Victim-Offender Rehabilitation Program Info. & Resource Ctr., http://www.vorp.com/articles/civil.html (last visited Mar. 31, 2017).

15. Price, *supra* note 15.

16. Stephen P. Garvey, *Restorative Justice, Punishment, and Atonement*, 2003 Utah L. Rev. 303, 306-307.

17. *Id.* at 305.

18. *Id.* at 308.

19. For an interesting case study, see Margaret Thorsborne, *Beyond Punishment—Workplace Conferencing: An Effective Organizational Response to Incidents of Workplace Bullying* 7-15, http://www.thorsborne.com.au/restorative-justice/wp-content/uploads/2013/09/BeyondPunishment.pdf.

20. E-mail from Margaret Thorsborne, Managing Dir. of Transformative Justice Austl. (Queensland) and Thorsborne & Associates in London, UK (July 9, 2014 08:21P.M. EDST) (on file with author).

21. The Fifth and Fourteenth Amendments to the U.S. Constitution prohibit the United States and state governments from depriving a person of "life, liberty or property without due process of law." U.S. Const. amends. V and XIV, § 1.

22. U.S. v. Laurent, 861 F. Supp. 2d 71, 95-96 (E.D.N.Y. 2011).

23. Fernandez v. Rodriguez, 761 F.2d 558, 562 (10th Cir. 1985).

24. U.S. v. Girodano, 158 F. Supp. 2d 242, 244-245 (D. Conn. 2001).

25. U.S. v. Schwartz, 925 F. Supp. 2d 663, 685 (E.D. Pa. 2013).

26. "While programs are often designed around one of these approaches, increasingly these models are being blended, blurring the lines between them." Zehr, *supra* note 5, at 306; *see also* Umbreit et al., *supra* note 4, at 270;. Barbara E. Raye & Ann Warner Roberts, *Restorative Processes, in Handbook of Restorative Justice, supra* note 14, at 211-216.

27. Price, *supra* note 14.

28. Mark Umbreit, Robert B. Coats & Betty Vos, *Victim-Offender Mediation: Three Decades of Practice and Research*, 22 Conflict Resol. Q. 279, 280 (2004).

29. *Id.*

30. *Id.*

31. Shenk, *supra* note 10, at 194-196.

32. Reimund, *supra* note 8, at 10.

33. Leena Kurki, *Restorative and Community Justice in the United States*, 27 Crime & Just. 235, 273 (2000).

34. Goodstein & Butterfield, *supra* note 12, at 463.

35. Susan Hanley Duncan, *Restorative Justice and Bullying: A Missing Solution in the Anti-Bullying Laws*, 37 New Eng. J. on Crim. & Civ. Confinement 267, 286-287 (2012).

36. Barry Stuart, *Building Community Justice Partnerships: Community Peacemaking Circles,* Dep't of Just. Can., Aboriginal Just. Sec. 5 (1997), http://publications.gc.ca/collections/collection_2009/justice/J22-12-1997E.pdf.

37. Robert Yazzie, *Life Comes from It: Navajo Justice Concepts*, 24 N.M. L. Rev. 175, 180 (1994).

38. Jean Greenwood, *The Circle Process: A Path for Restorative Dialogue* (Oct. 2005), http://www.cehd.umn.edu/ssw/RJP/Projects/Victim-Offender-Dialogue/Peacemaking_Healing_Circles/The_Circle_Process.pdf.

39. Jamelle Smith, *Peacemaking Circles: The Original Dispute Resolution of Aboriginal People Emerges as the NewEAlternative Dispute Resolution*, 24 Hamline J. Pub. L. & Pol'y 329, 346, 356 (2003).

40. *Id.*

41. *Workplace Bullies*, United Electrical, Radio & Machine Workers of Am., http://www.ueunion.org/stwd_bullies.html (last visited Mar. 31, 2017).

42. Garvey, *supra* note 16, at 308.

CHAPTER TEN

Court-Annexed Alternatives

Chapter Outline

Introduction: Brief History of ADR in
  the Courts
The Court-Annexed Alternatives
Mediation
Settlement Conference
Early Neutral Evaluation
Nonbinding Arbitration
  Referral
  Prehearing

Hearing and Award
Demand for Trial De Novo
Summary Jury Trial
Mini-Trial
Conclusion
Key Terms and Concepts
Review Questions
Application Questions
Practice Exercises

Justice delayed is justice denied.

—Author Unknown

INTRODUCTION: BRIEF HISTORY OF ADR IN THE COURTS

U.S. courts' adoption of dispute resolution alternatives is fairly recent. Prior to World War II, judges' roles were to decide issues presented by lawyers, not to manage the court. After World War II, this changed. Public funding for courts began to decrease while case filings increased, putting pressure on courts to more efficiently use public resources. One solution was the creation of court administrators to help judges control their calendars. Another was the use of mandatory nonbinding arbitration, mediation, and judicial settlement conferences, with the goal of decreasing the time needed to resolve civil cases.

In 1976, lawyers, judges, law professors, and court administrators came together to study problems in the legal field. At the conference, Harvard Law School Professor Frank Sander gave a speech in which he suggested that courts offer alternative processes for resolving disputes. The procedure would begin with an evaluation of the case, after which it could be channeled to mediation, arbitration, fact finding, a screening panel, or an ombudsperson for resolution. This talk was the impetus for creating a multidoor courthouse that offers disputants a choice of different forms of dispute resolution.[1]

Following Sander's speech, the arbitration, mediation, and judicial settlement conferences, which were already being used by some courts, became known as alternative dispute resolution (ADR) processes. By 1983, Sander's idea of alternative procedures was established in amendments to Rule 16 of the Federal Rules of Civil Procedure. The original rule, as written in the 1930s, permitted judges to hold pretrial conferences at their discretion. The amended rule made this a requirement and encouraged judges to discuss settlement and the use of extra-judicial procedures to settle the dispute.

Rule 16 was again amended in 1993 and provided more information about the judge's role in controlling pretrial matters and discovery, organizing trials, and assisting parties to reach settlement agreements. These changes gave judges the power to require the attendance of the parties or their representatives at conferences or be available by telephone for the purpose of settlement discussions. The amendment led to ADR becoming part of the judicial process.

In December 1990, Congress passed the Civil Justice Reform Act of 1990, which required that federal district courts find ways to reduce costs and delays, including by using ADR. In 1998, Congress passed the Alternative Dispute Resolution Act, which mandated that ADR methods be available to parties involved in civil litigation. In part, the act provided that

> litigants in all civil cases consider the use of an alternative dispute resolution process at an appropriate stage in the litigation. Each district court shall provide litigants in civil cases with at least one alternative dispute resolution process, including but not limited to mediation, early neutral evaluation, minitrial, and arbitration authorized in sections 654 through 658.[2]

THE COURT-ANNEXED ALTERNATIVES

The types of ADR methods frequently used by courts include mediation, settlement conference, Early Neutral Evaluation (ENE), nonbinding arbitration, minitrial, and summary jury trial. There are two ways in which one of the methods becomes annexed to a pending civil suit. First, a court can issue a formal order requiring the parties to participate in one of the alternatives, or second, the court can informally acknowledge that the parties, by agreement, will be using an alternative method prior to any trial.

To help determine which court-annexed method might be appropriate for any given dispute, we need to know how they operate and how they differ. One way to differentiate the processes is by comparing the degree of formality of each. The chart in Exhibit 10-1 positions each court-annexed method on a spectrum that focuses on the formality of the process, with the least formal on the left and the most formal on the right.

Exhibit 10-1. SPECTRUM OF COURT-ANNEXED ALTERNATIVES

Informal					Formal
Mediation	Settlement Conference	Early Neutral Evaluation (ENE)	Non-binding Arbitration	Mini-Trial	Summary Jury Trial

Mediation, as you learned in Chapter 4, is the least structured process in which the parties meet with a third-party neutral and discuss the dispute. Similarly, a settlement conference is an informal conversation with the judge. As we move to the right, each method becomes more formal, the parties' participation changes, and the format is altered. For example, the mini-trial uses a trial format, but the presentation is made to a neutral expert who makes a nonbinding decision. The summary jury trial is more like a jury trial with actual jurors who listen to the presentations of both sides and render a verdict that is also nonbinding.

The court-annexed alternatives can also be differentiated by the extent of the third party's involvement in the process. Generally, mediators facilitate discussions in an effort to help the parties reach agreement. Likewise, in a settlement conference the judge tries to assist the parties to resolve the dispute. ENE, non-binding arbitration, mini-trial, and summary jury trial are more adjudicative in nature. In ENE, the neutral evaluates each side's case and then gives her objective assessment. In the mini-trial and summary jury trial, the neutral is more akin to a judge in that he decides the outcome based on the merits of the dispute. We can also think of ENE, mini-trials, and summary jury trials as advisory processes.

Now that we know the commonly used court-annexed alternatives and some differences between them, we will discuss each process in more detail.

MEDIATION

Parties to civil litigation are often encouraged or required by statute or court rules to participate in **mediation**. Because this type of ADR method is extensively covered in Chapter 4, we are only going to discuss issues that relate to court-ordered mediation. To begin, you need to know that courts can require the parties to attend mediation and other court-annexed alternatives. Courts, however, cannot "force the disputants to peaceably resolve their differences. . . ."[3] The issue that is sometimes raised concerns the meaning of "participation," and what can happen when a court determines that a party did not "participate." For mediation to be meaningful, parties have to participate in good faith:

> If good faith is not present, all we will be left with is a *pro forma* mediation, one more procedural task to be checked off of the long list of items to be covered in order to get to the trial . . . to allow parties to show up without authority, without preparation, and without a desire or an ability to even discuss options and alternatives makes a mockery of mediation.[4]

What does "good faith" mean? Although the definition of good faith in mediation is controversial, "courts have interpreted the concept narrowly to require compliance with orders to attend mediation, provide pre-mediation memoranda, and, in some cases, produce organizational representatives with sufficient settlement authority."[5] For example, in a sexual harassment lawsuit filed in a federal court in Missouri, the court ordered

> that at least seven days before the first ADR conference, each party shall supply the mediator with a memorandum presenting a summary of the disputed facts and its position on liability and damages; that all parties, counsel, corporate representative and claims professionals with settlement authority shall attend all mediation conferences and participate in good faith. . . .[6]

The defendant failed to file a premediation memorandum. At the mediation, the plaintiff and her attorney appeared in person. The defendant was represented by

> outside counsel . . . and a corporate representative who had no independent knowledge of the facts of the case and had permission to settle only up to $500. Any settlement offer over $500 had to be relayed by telephone to [the corporation's in-house counsel] who chose not to attend the ADR conference on the advice of outside counsel. . . . During the [mediation], the plaintiff twice made offers of settlement that were rejected without a counteroffer by [defendant]. The ADR conference ended shortly thereafter without a settlement having been reached.[7]

The plaintiff then filed a motion requesting that the defendant be ordered to pay her attorneys' fees and costs for failing to participate in good faith in the mediation. The court granted her motion, finding that the defendant did not participate in mediation in good faith when it failed to file the premediation memorandum and did not have a corporate representative with settlement authority at the mediation.[8]

Opponents of a good faith requirement argue that inquiry into whether the parties mediated in good faith invades the confidential nature of mediation and has a chilling effect on the process. "The mere prospect of adjudicating bad-faith claims by using mediator testimony can destroy the mediation process by damaging participants' faith in the confidentiality of mediation communications and the mediators' impartiality."[9]

Another concern of critics is with the threat of sanctions. Aware that a court could investigate the parties' behavior during mediation, coupled with the risk of sanctions, the parties may feel pressure to settle.[10]

SETTLEMENT CONFERENCE

Early in the twentieth century, the workload of the federal courts expanded in dramatic fashion. William Howard Taft, Chief Justice of the U.S. Supreme Court, attributed the increase of work to more federal legislative regulations; the stimulating effect of World War I on federal business, which resulted in contract disputes and other claims against the government; and an increase in federal crimes being committed, including bootlegging, in violation of the Volstead Act (Prohibition).[11]

Recognizing the growing problem of expanding dockets, the American Bar Association, along with judges and legal scholars, began working on reforming the federal courts. One result was the creation of the Federal Rules of Civil Procedure in 1938 and, in particular, Rule 16, which was based on a practice by state judges in Detroit in the 1920s who "were the first to require an official meeting between lawyers and judges right before jury trials started."[12] (See Exhibit 10-2.)

Although Rule 16 gave judges and lawyers the chance to meet before trial, they were not required to, and if they did meet, the rule provided no guidance on what to discuss. Some judges, however, saw an opportunity to manage the preparation for trial and to work with the parties toward settlement. Many other judges were hesitant to become involved in this way, and it was not until the 1960s that this changed. During this decade and following, newly appointed judges attended seminars on docket management that included information on judicial

Exhibit 10-2. **RULES OF CIVIL PROCEDURE FOR THE DISTRICT COURTS OF THE UNITED STATES 1938**

Rule 16. Pre-Trial Procedure; Formulating Issues. In any action, the court may in its discretion direct the attorneys for the parties to appear before it for a conference to consider

(1) The simplification of the issues;
(2) The necessity or desirability of amendments to the pleadings;
(3) The possibility of obtaining admission of fact and of documents which will avoid unnecessary proof;
(4) The limitation of the number of expert witnesses;
(5) The advisability of a preliminary reference of issues to a master for findings to be sued as evidence when the trial is to be by jury;
(6) Such other matters as may aid in the disposition of the action.

The Report of the Advisory Committee on Rules for Civil Procedure point out that "[s]imilar rules of pre-trial procedure are now in force in Boston, Detroit and Cleveland, and a rule substantially like this one has been proposed for the urban centers of New York State." Fed. R. Civ. P. 16 (1938).

---

involvement in settling cases. They learned the meaning of "good judging" and how a negotiated settlement is often better than a trial. In one seminar, a sitting judge told new judges that:

> In most cases, a freely negotiated settlement is a higher quality of justice, which is obtainable earlier and at less cost. We know that approximately 90% of all suits filed in the federal courts, civil and criminal, will be disposed of without a trial. And we know that the civil cases, in large part, will be disposed of by a settlement. . . .
>
> I suggest to you that it's the rare case in which the all-or-nothing, black or white result of a trial is really the highest quality of justice. It's just the best we can do to resolve a controversy when it can't be resolved any other way. Trial is the ultimate and last resort resolution of a controversy. But it's the rare case in which there isn't justice in some degree on both sides, and most cases, therefore, are better disposed of, in terms of highest quality of justice, by a negotiated-freely negotiated-settlement, than by the most beautiful trial that you can preside over.[13]

Eventually, the idea of using **pre-trial conferences** as an opportunity to search for settlement and permitting judges to make attendance mandatory at these conferences by representatives with settlement authority, was incorporated in Rule 16 as amended in 1983 and 1993.[14] The rule also gives judges the power to sanction offending parties, a power used in the following case.

Dvorak v. Shibata
123 F.R.D. 608 (D. Neb. 1988)

A settlement conference was held at which plaintiff and plaintiff's counsel were present. At the commencement of the conference, in light of the fact that no representative of the defendant other than counsel was present [the judge] conferred separately with counsel for the defendant and learned that the defendants' insurance carrier had authorized defense counsel to offer no more than $2,500 as a proposed settlement of this case, and that offer had been conveyed to plaintiff's counsel . . . and had not been accepted. Defense counsel had no further authority. . . .

The order scheduling the conference included the following:

> The conference shall be attended by the parties, or, in the case of corporate or organizational parties, those persons who have the authority to negotiate and consummate a negotiated settlement in the action. . . .

There are several reasons for requiring the presence of authorized representatives at a settlement conference. During the conference, counsel for both sides are given an opportunity to argue their clients' respective positions to the court, including pointing out strengths and weaknesses of each party's case. In this discussion, it is often true that client representatives and insurers learn, for the first time, the difficulties they may have in prevailing at a trial. They must, during the conference, weigh their own positions in light of the statements and arguments made by counsel for the opposing parties. It is often true that as a result of such presentations, the clients' positions soften to the extent that meaningful negotiation, previously not seriously entertained, becomes possible. This dynamic is not possible if the only person with authority to negotiate is located away from the courthouse and can be reached only by telephone, if at all. The absent decision-maker learns only what his or her attorney conveys by phone, which can be expected to be largely a recitation of what has been conveyed in previous discussions. At best, even if the attorney attempts to convey the weaknesses of that client's position as they have been presented by opposing counsel at the settlement conference, the message, not unlike those in the children's game of "telephone," loses its impact through repetition, and it is simply too easy for that person to reject, out of hand, even a sincere desire on the part of counsel to negotiate further. At worst, a refusal to have an authorized representative in attendance may become a weapon by which parties with comparatively greater financial flexibility may feign a good faith settlement posture by those in attendance at the conference, relying on the absent decision-maker to refuse to agree, thereby unfairly raising the stakes in the case, to the unfair disadvantage of a less wealthy opponent. In either case, the whole purpose of the settlement conference is lost, and the result is an even greater expenditure of the parties' resources, both time and money, for naught. . . .

I do not find actions of defense counsel in these respects to be contumacious, nor do I find them to have been taken in bad faith, nor vexatiously as that term is used in 28 U.S.C. § 1927. I do find, however, that counsel were "substantially unprepared to participate in the conference," as that term is used in Rule 16(f), and for that reason I impose the sanction of the expenses incurred by the plaintiff for his, and his attorneys' attendance at the conference.

Questions:
1. Who was ordered to appear at the settlement conference?
2. Who appeared at the conference for the plaintiff?
3. Who appeared at the conference for the defendant?
4. According to the court, who should have been at the conference with defense counsel? Why?
5. What was the court's finding?

PARALEGAL POINTERS

Preparing for a Settlement Conference

Many courts require a settlement conference before a case can go to trial. Cases are often resolved at these discussions. Because settlement conferences are an important event, preparation is vital. Addressing the following questions will help you prepare the attorney and client for the meeting.

- What does the client want?
- What issues have been resolved, and what issues remain?
- What are the strengths and weaknesses of the client's case?
- What is the opposing side's position?
- What is wrong with the opposing side's position? What is right with their position?
- What facts do both sides agree with? What facts do they disagree with?
- What legal issues do both sides agree with? What legal issues do they disagree with?
- What are the obstacles to reaching a settlement?
- What are the possible legal remedies?
- Are there any innovative solutions that can resolve the dispute?

EARLY NEUTRAL EVALUATION

Early Neutral Evaluation (ENE) is a nonbinding process intended to help litigants with case preparation and settlement opportunities by providing them with an objective evaluation of the probable outcome of the lawsuit. In ENE, a neutral evaluator, usually a lawyer with expertise in the subject matter of the dispute, meets in a confidential session with the parties and their lawyers early in the litigation process. At this session, both parties make brief presentations of their positions. The neutral then evaluates the strengths and weaknesses of each party's case and gives them her candid assessment. The evaluator can also assist the parties with case planning and, if requested, help with settling the dispute. ENE was developed in the federal courts in California as a response to the expense of litigation on the parties.[15]

Early Neutral Evaluaton: Key Purposes and the Process

ENE provides litigants with a free, nonbinding, confidential opportunity to reduce cost and delay, to improve the quality of justice, and to explore settlement. A confidential ENE session is held before expensive discovery and

Continued >

motion practice are completed. Lead counsel and their clients must attend the session; key witnesses, including experts may attend. Clients may participate actively.

Face to face, in the presence of an evaluator with subject matter expertise, the parties present evidence and set forth their positions. The evaluator clarifies and probes with questions, identifies the key issues, then retires to a separate room to prepare a written evaluation. After the evaluation is presented to the parties, they may choose to engage in settlement negotiations with the assistance of the evaluator. If no settlement is reached, the evaluator helps the parties develop a focused case development plan.

The ENE process expands the parties' information base for decisions about case development and about settlement, improves the quality of parties' analyses, and sharpens the joinder of issues. It also provides litigants with valuable, impartial feedback from an expert about the merits of their positions, and with suggestions about how to acquire efficiently any additional evidence the parties need to engage in more productive settlement discussions.

Source: Wayne D. Brazil, *Early Neutral Evaluation or Mediation? When Might ENE Deliver More Value?*, 14 Disp. Resol. Mag. 10, 11 (2007).

In 1982, Robert E. Peckham, the chief judge of the federal district court for the Northern District of California (San Francisco), was concerned that the high cost of litigation "impair[s] access to justice and might be compromising the quality of the product that emerges from the adjudicatory process."[16] In the fall of 1982, he appointed a task force of lawyers and judges and asked them to create new ways to make litigation less financially burdensome on the parties. One committee examined the court's arbitration and settlement conference processes while a second committee looked specifically for ways to cut litigation costs. After completing its study, the second committee "became convinced that the place where the most [money] could be saved is in the formative stages of litigation. It is in those stages that patterns and expectations are set and thus it is in those stages where an infusion of intellectual discipline, common sense, and more direct communication might have the most beneficial effects."[17] The committee identified some issues that impaired early settlement and contributed to the cost of litigation. The first was that complaints and answers were drafted in ways that made it difficult to determine the parties' positions and the evidence on which they relied. As a result, the parties were forced to undertake extensive discovery that can be very costly. Another barrier was the failure of some lawyers and parties to understand their own positions and theories of the case and to present them in clear and logical ways. With this knowledge, the committee recognized the need to create a process that could happen early in the litigation and that would

- encourage each party, at the outset, to confront and analyze its own situation in the suit;

- provide each litigant and lawyer with an opportunity to hear the other side present its case;
- help the parties isolate the center of their dispute and identify the factual and legal matters which will not be seriously contested;
- help parties develop an approach to discovery that focuses immediately on the key issues and that would disclose promptly the key evidence;
- offer all counsel and litigants a confidential, frank, thoughtful assessment of the relative strengths of the parties' positions and of the overall value of the case;
- after receiving the neutral assessment, provide the parties with an early opportunity to try to negotiate settlement.[18]

The result of this committee's study focused on the development of the ENE process.

ENE requires the attendance of each party and their attorneys at the session. Prior to the meeting, the litigants must present to the evaluator a written statement that identifies the participants, the main issues of dispute, and any discovery that could be helpful to settlement discussions.

A typical ENE session looks something like this (see also Exhibit 10-3):

1. The evaluator explains the purposes of the program and outlines the procedures.
2. Each side in turn presents a 15-minute opening statement, either by counsel, client, or both, without interruption from the evaluator or the other party. The statement presents the side's case and legal theories and describes the supporting evidence.
3. The evaluator may then ask questions of both sides to clarify issues, arguments, and evidence, to fill in evidentiary gaps, and to probe for strengths and weaknesses.
4. The evaluator identifies the issues on which the parties agree (and encourages them to enter stipulations where appropriate) and also identifies the important issues in dispute.
5. The evaluator adjourns to another room to prepare a written case evaluation. The evaluation assesses the strengths and weaknesses of each side's case, determines which side is likely to prevail, and establishes the probable range of damages in the event the plaintiff wins.
6. The evaluator returns to the ENE conference room, announces that she has prepared an informal evaluation of the case, and asks the parties if they would like to explore settlement possibilities before she discloses the evaluation to them. If either party declines the offer to begin settlement discussions, the evaluator promptly discloses her written assessment. If, on the other hand, both sides are interested in working on settlement, the evaluator facilitates these discussions.
7. If the parties do not hold settlement discussions or if discussions do not produce a settlement, the evaluator helps the parties develop a plan for efficient case management. This aid may include scheduling motions or discovery that would put the case in a position for rapid settlement or disposition.
8. After the ENE session, the parties may agree to a follow-up session or other activity. With the consent of the court, the parties may engage the evaluator for additional sessions on a compensated basis.[19]

Exhibit 10-3. UNITED STATES DISTRICT COURT NORTHERN DISTRICT OF CALIFORNIA ADR LOCAL RULES

15-11. Procedure at ENE Session

(a) Components of ENE Session. The evaluator shall:

(1) Permit each party (through counsel or otherwise), orally and through documents or other media, to present its claims or defenses and to describe the principal evidence on which they are based;

(2) Help the parties identify areas of agreement and, where feasible, enter stipulations;

(3) Assess the relative strengths and weaknesses of the parties' contentions and evidence, and explain carefully the reasoning that supports these assessments;

(4) Estimate, where feasible, the likelihood of liability and the dollar range of damages;

(5) Help the parties devise a plan for sharing the important information and/or conducting the key discovery that will equip them as expeditiously as possible to enter meaningful settlement discussions or to position the case for disposition by other means;

(6) Help the parties assess litigation costs realistically; and (7) If the parties are interested, help them, through private caucusing or otherwise, explore the possibility of settling the case;

(8) Determine whether some form of follow up to the session would contribute to the case development process or to settlement.

(b) Process Rules. The session shall be informal. Rules of evidence shall not apply. There shall be no formal examination or cross-examination of witnesses and no recording of the presentations or discussion shall be made.

(c) Evaluation and Settlement Discussions. If all parties agree, they may proceed to discuss settlement after the evaluation has been written but before it is presented. The evaluation must be presented orally on demand by any party. Copies of the written evaluation may be provided to the parties at the discretion of the evaluator. The parties also may agree to discuss settlement after the evaluation has been presented.

NONBINDING ARBITRATION

In 1952, Pennsylvania was the first jurisdiction to institute court-annexed arbitration. With courts facing a three-year backlog of civil cases waiting for trial, the legislature passed a statute that allowed courts to mandate nonbinding arbitration for certain classes of cases determined by the dollar amount of money damages sought and subject matter of the lawsuit.

The experiment was based on the premise that parties were more likely to settle if they were given an opportunity to present their cases in an abbreviated form to three neutral attorneys who would render a non-binding judgment. This would provide an opportunity to "reality test" by comparing the presentation of their case with that of their opponent and to see how neutrals who were familiar with the law would assess the cases.[20]

Other states, facing the same court congestion, soon followed, using Pennsylvania's program as a model.

Court-annexed arbitration (also called court-ordered arbitration, judicial arbitration, or court-administered arbitration) differs from traditional arbitration in the following ways: it is mandatory not voluntary; it is forced on the parties by statute or court rule; a third party, usually a judge, selects the arbitrators; and the

Exhibit 10-4. COURT ORDER TO ARBITRATION

STATE OF NEW MEXICO
COUNTY OF BERNALILLO
SECOND JUDICIAL DISTRICT COURT

D-202-CV-xxxx

XXXX
    Plaintiff(s),

vs.

XXXX

    Defendant(s)

ORDER OF REFERRAL TO COURT-ANNEXED ARBITRATION (7020)

This matter having come before the Court upon a review of the court file by the Arbitration Legal Assistant, which review included any arbitration certifications filed, the Legal Assistant having advised the Court that based on this review no party seeks relief other than a money judgment or seeks an amount in excess of $25,000 exclusive of punitive damages, interest, costs and attorney fees, the Court finds that Court-Annexed Arbitration is mandated and therefore orders that this case be referred to Court-Annexed Arbitration.

                                           —————————————
                                           THE HONORABLE xxx
                                         District Judge, Div. —

Submitted by Court Alternatives Paralegal Endorsed copy mailed by the Court on the date of filing to parties and other persons listed below:

ATTORNEY FOR PLAINTIFFS: XXX
ATTORNEYS FOR DEFENDANTS: XXX

Source: N.M. 2d Jud. Dist. Ct. Local R. 2-603, app. C forms.

---

award is nonbinding. Additionally, whereas traditional arbitration takes place before a lawsuit is filed, court-annexed arbitration occurs after court proceedings have begun.

Mandatory court arbitration programs typically have four stages: (1) referral; (2) prehearing; (3) hearing and award; and (4) demand for trial de novo, or a new trial on the case.

Referral

This stage begins with the filing of a lawsuit in a court and a referral to arbitration (see Exhibit 10-4), if it meets the state's statutory requirements. These usually limit court-annexed arbitration to cases seeking money damages in a set dollar amount that varies by jurisdiction. If the case is referred to arbitration, the court appoints a single arbitrator or panel of arbitrators. Usually, arbitrators are volunteer lawyers with experience in the subject matter of the case or retired judges. After referral takes place, the parties may engage in discovery; discovery is limited, however, by time constraints.

Prehearing

Here the parties get ready for the hearing. They conduct limited discovery, prepare documents for use at the hearing, meet with witnesses, and review issues and claims. Witness lists and copies of documents or exhibits expected to be offered into evidence are exchanged in addition to brief written statements outlining positions and any agreed-to stipulations. The parties also learn the name of the arbitrator. During the prehearing stage, the arbitrator will review the pleadings in the court's file and any documents, exhibits, and statements provided by the parties. The arbitrator can also request additional information.

Hearing and Award

The arbitration hearing, although adversarial, is usually more informal than a court trial. Rules of evidence are not strictly adhered to, but are used to guide the arbitrator in deciding which evidence to hear or exclude. Each side has an opportunity to present witnesses, submit evidence, and make an argument. Hearings are brief, usually lasting no more than two hours, and no record is made of the proceeding.

After the hearing, the arbitrator announces his decision. If a panel of arbitrators is used, its members meet in private to discuss the case, after which they return and announce their decision. In some states, arbitrators are given a certain amount of time to issue their decision. If the plaintiff prevails, the arbitrator will state the amount of money awarded (see Exhibit 10-5). Arbitrators usually do not provide any reason for their finding.

Exhibit 10-5. ARBITRATION AWARD

SECOND JUDICIAL DISTRICT COURT
COUNTY OF BERNALILLO
STATE OF NEW MEXICO

CV-[CASE NUMBER]

[PLAINTIFF'S NAME] Plaintiff(s),

vs.

[DEFENDANT'S NAME], Defendant(s).

ARBITRATION AWARD (8312)

THIS MATTER having been referred by the Court to the undersigned Arbitrator pursuant to local rule, the Arbitrator having heard the evidence, the Arbitrator makes the following award:

In favor of _____

and against _____

in the amount of _____,

plus pre-judgment interest of _____,

plus costs of _____,

plus attorney fees of _____,

for a total award of _____.

_____

_____

_____

[Arbitrator's signature & address block]

I hereby certify an endorsed copy was mailed or delivered to all parties of record on day of _____, 20_____.

_____

Dist. Ct. Local R. 2-603, app. C forms.

Demand for Trial De Novo

A party dissatisfied with the arbitrator's decision can request that the case be tried before a judge (called a bench trial) or jury. This **demand for trial de novo** must be made within a certain number of days. The time limit varies by jurisdiction. At the trial, no one is permitted to reveal that the case was arbitrated.

In some states, the party rejecting the award may be required to pay some or all of the arbitrator's fees and a financial penalty if the outcome of the trial is not better than the arbitrator's award. The reason for this is to deter appeals. "For court-ordered programs to achieve the goals of reduced cost and delay, the number of cases actually tried de novo must be fewer than the number of cases that would be formally tried in the absence of the arbitration program."[21]

SUMMARY JURY TRIAL

The **summary jury trial** was the creation of federal district court judge Thomas Lambros of Ohio. In 1980, Judge Lambros was presiding over two personal injury jury trials. Although the cases should have been settled, the attorneys and their respective clients believed they could obtain a better result from the jury than from their earlier settlement negotiations. Reflecting on these two cases, Judge Lambros thought "that if only the parties could gaze into a crystal ball and be able to predict, with a reasonable amount of certainty, what a jury *would* do in their respective cases, the parties and counsel would be more willing to reach a settlement rather than going through the expense and aggravation of a full jury trial."[22] This was the genesis of what Judge Lambros called "a summarized trial to a jury, and what is now known as the Summary Jury Trial [SJT]."[23]

The SJT should not be confused with the "mini-trial." The SJT is a court-connected alternative using jurors to hear and decide the dispute while the mini-trial is a private, voluntary process "conducted before top management representatives (with settling authority) of each party. It is presided over by a jointly selected neutral advisor or moderator who may have specialized subject expertise."[24]

Usually lasting no more than a day, the SJT is heard by jurors selected from the same pool of jurors as would be used for a "real" trial. The number of jurors selected to hear the case varies by jurisdiction, but six is common.[25] The jurors are informed that the case will be a summary jury trial, but they are not told until after the trial that their decision is not binding on the parties. During the trial, there are no live witnesses, only summaries of their testimony presented by the attorneys. Counsel for each side is also permitted to introduce exhibits to the jury. After closing arguments, the judge instructs the jury, after which they deliberate until they reach a verdict. The jury's decision is presented to the parties to help facilitate settlement negotiations. "An SJT provides the parties with a reality check by indicating how an actual jury may view their cases and opposing arguments."[26] The hope is that "[u]nreasonable demands and offers are reevaluated, and mutually agreeable compromises are worked out in light of the jury's findings."[27]

> The summary jury trial reduces the gap between the parties' perceived probabilities of the outcome at trial by giving them information (in the form of the summary jury's reactions to the case) that should cause them to adjust their perceptions. Because the information is available to both parties, it should help

each to get closer to the true odds, which will usually be somewhere in between the parties' estimates.[28]

The SJT gives the parties "their day in court." They get to tell their story to a jury of their peers and hear their verdict. The decision can then be used a starting point for settlement discussions.

What if a party does not want to participate in a summary jury trial? Can courts make participation mandatory? This was the question addressed in the following case.

Ohio ex rel. Montgomery v. Louis Trauth Dairy, Inc.
164 F.R.D. 469 (S.D. Ohio 1996)

The Defendants' motions raise two issues. First, whether the Court has the authority to order the parties to participate in a summary jury trial. [The second motion requests a continuance of the summary jury trial and is not included below.]

The Defendants rely on a recent decision of the Sixth Circuit which held that "the provisions of Rule 16, as amplified by the Commentary Committee, do not permit compulsory participation in settlement proceedings such as summary jury trials." *In re NLO, Inc.*, 5 F.3d 154, 157 (6th Cir. 1993). For the following reasons, we conclude that *NLO* has been effectively overruled by Rule 16 as amended December 1, 1993. . . .

Rule 16, as amended, states in pertinent part,

> (c) Subjects for Consideration at Pretrial Conferences. At any conference under this rule consideration may be given, *and the court may take appropriate action with respect to* . . .
>
> (9) settlement and the use of special procedures to assist in resolving the dispute *when authorized by statute or local rule*[.]

Fed.R.Civ.P. 16(c)(9) (as amended December 1, 1993). The old Rule 16 did not contain the reference to local rule authorization, nor did it contain the reference to "appropriate" actions.

Furthermore, the Advisory Committee notes state in unambiguous terms that

> [t]he primary purpose of the changes in subdivision (c) are to . . . eliminate questions that have occasionally been raised regarding the authority of the court to make *appropriate orders* designed either to facilitate settlement or to provide for an efficient and economical trial. The prefatory language of this subdivision is revised to clarify the court's power to enter *appropriate orders* at a conference *not withstanding the objection of a party.*
>
> . . .
>
> The Rule acknowledges the presence of statutes and local rules or plans that may authorize use of some of these procedures [mini-trials, summary jury trials, mediation, etc.] *even when not agreed to by the parties.* . . .

... [U]nder the plain meaning of Rule 16 as amended, this Court has the authority to "take appropriate action" with respect to "special procedures [i.e. summary juries trials] to assist in resolving [a] dispute[,]" Fed. R. Civ. P. 16(c), (c)(9), "notwithstanding the objection of a party[.]" *Id.* at Advisory Committee notes. . . .

Southern District of Ohio Local Rule 53.1 states in full,

ALTERNATIVE DISPUTE RESOLUTION

The Court may, *in its discretion*, assign any civil case for a *summary jury trial*, mandatory, non-binding arbitration hearing, settlement week conference, or other alternative method of dispute resolution.

It is readily apparent, therefore, that under Rule 16 as amended, considered in conjunction with Local Rule 53.1, it is within this Court's authority to *order* the parties in a civil action to participate in a summary jury trial, notwithstanding the objection of a party. . . .

[Conclusion.] [T]he Court has power to order the parties to participate in a summary jury trial. . . .

Questions:

1. The defendant cited as precedent *In re NLO, Inc.*, in which the Sixth Circuit Court of Appeals held that Rule 16 does not allow a court to mandate participation in a summary jury trial. How did the court in *Ohio* ex rel. *Montgomery v. Louis Trauth Dairy* address this?
2. What is the language in the amended rule that gives courts the authority to order a party to participate in a summary jury trial?

MINI-TRIAL

According to Thomas D. Lambros,

Telecredit Inc. v. TRW, Inc. was the first widely publicized application of the mini-trial concept. It involved a legally and technically complex patent infringement between Telecredit, Inc., the owner of a number of patents relating to computerized check verification and charge authorization systems, and TRW Inc., the manufacturer of a number of such systems for banks and retail outlets. In nearly three years of litigation, the case had consumed several hundred thousand dollars in legal fees on both sides and still no trial date had been set. Using former United States Court of Claims Judge James Davis as a privately hired neutral advisor, the parties reached a settlement after only two days of presentation time of what had been a long and bitterly fought lawsuit.[29]

The **mini-trial** is a private proceeding, agreed to by the parties and the court, used mainly in business disputes. The length of the trial can range "from half a day to three or four days (two days is average)."[30] At the trial, the parties' lawyers present brief summary presentations of their cases. Parties can use their allotted time in whatever manner they choose. Sometimes the lawyers make the presentation while in other cases, the lawyers present witnesses, introduce documents, and use experts to explain technical matters.

The format varies widely, but "the common goal is to employ a procedure that effectively draws out the strengths and weaknesses of each side . . . in a short time."[31] Senior executives of each party attend the trial, and the hope is that they will be encouraged to reach a settlement and avoid the high cost of litigation.

Conclusion

Court-annexed ADR developed in the second half of the twentieth century as a way to address the increase in court case filings and decrease in court funding. The processes include mediation, judicial settlement conference, ENE, nonbinding arbitration, mini-trial, and summary jury trial. Some of these, such as mediation and judicial settlement conference, are party directed. Others, early neutral evaluation, nonbinding arbitration, mini-trial, and summary jury trial, are similar to traditional litigation. The use of these processes "can contribute significantly to the quality of justice by providing better focused, more productive, and more efficient pretrial case development."[32]

Key Terms and Concepts

Court-annexed nonbinding arbitration
Early Neutral Evaluation (ENE)
Good faith
Mediation
Mini-trial

Pretrial conference
Settlement conference
Summary jury trial
Trial de novo

Practice Test Questions

True/False

____ 1. ENE provides litigants with an objective evaluation of the probable outcome of the lawsuit.

____ 2. Court-annexed arbitration and traditional arbitration are voluntary procedures.

____ 3. Rule 16 of the Federal Rules of Civil Procedure permit judges to make attendance at a settlement conference mandatory.

____ 4. Court-annexed ADR developed in the second half of the twentieth century in response to an increase in the number of court cases and a decrease in court funding.

____ 5. The mini-trial and summary jury trial are both private proceedings.

Multiple Choice

____ 1. ____ is where a neutral evaluates the strengths and weaknesses of each party's case and provides a candid assessment.
   a. Summary jury trial
   b. Early Neutral Evaluation
   c. Nonbinding arbitration
   d. Mini-trial

____ 2. Which of the following court-annexed alternatives is more adjudicative in nature?
   a. Summary jury trial
   b. Settlement conference
   c. Mediation
   d. Negotiation

____ 3. In court-annexed arbitration, the dissatisfied party ____
   a. cannot request a bench trial.
   b. cannot request a jury trial
   c. can file a demand for trial de novo.
   d. has no recourse.

____ 4. The ____ required that federal district courts find ways to reduce costs and delays, including by using ADR methods.
   a. Court Reform Act of 1990
   b. Rule 16 of the Federal Rules of Civil Procedure
   c. Uniform Court Reform Act
   d. Civil Justice Reform Act of 1990

____ 5. The summary jury trial was the creation of ____
   a. William Howard Taft.
   b. Congress.
   c. the Federal Rules of Civil Procedure.
   d. Judge Thomas Lambros.

Review Questions

1. What was the impetus for the creation of court-annexed ADR processes?
2. What are the two ways in which one of the ADR methods becomes annexed to a pending civil suit?
3. How does ENE help the litigants? Briefly describe how it operates.
4. Explain how court-annexed arbitration differs from traditional arbitration.
5. Name and briefly explain each stage of the mandatory arbitration process.
6. Explain the differences between a summary jury trial and a mini-trial.

Application Questions

1. Your client's mother recently passed away. Her husband died two years earlier. Your client's mother was a very well-known and respected pediatrician and generous philanthropist in the community, your client expected a large

number of people to attend the wake and so decided to hold calling hours over a two-day period. When your client arrived at the funeral home on the first night of the wake, about 250 people were in attendance. Your client, his spouse, and their children walked up to the casket and when they peered in, the body was not his mother's. Your client was stunned, and so too were the guests. Your client talked with the funeral home director and was told that he did not know what happened or where to find the body. It took three months before the body was located in a medical school laboratory, partially dissected by medical students.

Your client is despondent and furious at the funeral home. He tells you that he does not care about any money damages but just wants to drive the funeral home out of business.

You file suit and then receive notification from the court that you must participate in one of the following court-annexed dispute resolution programs: nonbinding arbitration, ENE, or mediation. Which program would you advise your client to choose? Why?

2. Your firm represents Leah Baxter in an age discrimination suit against Style Inc., a clothing store. A scheduling conference was held at which the parties were asked whether they wished to participate in mediation pursuant to local court rules. The parties agreed, and the court prepared an Order of Referral that included the following requirements: (1) All named parties and their counsel must attend the mediation, participate in good faith, and possess settlement authority. (2) Not later than seven days before the mediation, the parties shall submit a memorandum to the neutral. The memorandum should include a summary of the facts, including those in dispute; the legal and factual issues; all settlement offers that have been made; and any "roadblocks" to settlement.

Prior to the mediation, the defendant's attorney expressed to Baxter's attorney his concern that mediation would be a waste of time. This opinion was not shared with the court.

On the mediation date, Baxter (who had full settlement authority) and her attorney, the neutral, Style Inc.'s attorney, and the manager of the local Style Inc. store were present. Baxter submitted her memorandum as ordered by the court. Style Inc. did not submit a memorandum. Style Inc.'s representative had settlement authority up to only $500, contrary to the court's order that the representative have full settlement authority.

Baxter made an offer of settlement that Style Inc. rejected, and no counteroffer was made. After this, the mediation was terminated.

Baxter's attorney has filed a motion seeking attorney's fees and costs because Style Inc. did not participate in good faith. Will she be successful? Why or why not?

3. Read the following hypotheticals and choose which court-annexed alternative dispute method (mediation, settlement conference, ENE, nonbinding arbitration, mini-trial, or summary jury trial) you think is most appropriate. Then

explain how the neutral and the interaction of the participants in that particular method can help overcome settlement obstacles.

a. A divorcing couple with three children, a boy age 11 and two girls ages 7 and 4, cannot agree on which parent should have primary custody or on a visitation schedule for the noncustodial parent.

b. A tenant fractured his ankle after falling on the stairs in the common area of the apartment building where he resided. The tenant claims that the stairs needed to be repaired. The landlord disputes this, claiming that the tenant fell because he was carrying a heavy box.

c. A consumer purchased a washing machine that broke one month after the manufacturer's warranty ran out. The consumer claims that because of poor design, the bolts securing the cement ballast broke, causing the ballast to fall and making the machine inoperable. The cost to repair the damage exceeds the cost of purchasing a new washing machine.

   The consumer has knowledge that as a result of similar complaints, the manufacturer stopped making that particular washing machine two years prior. The manufacturer claims that the washing machine broke from misuse, but in any event, the warranty had run out. The jurisdiction in which the consumer lives has an "implied warranty of merchantability" statute, which may negate the manufacturer's claim that the warranty had expired.

4. Plaintiffs have filed suit against defendant Fly Right Air Lines, alleging breach of contract, negligence, battery, assault, slander, and infliction of emotion distress. They were passengers on a flight from Boston to Dallas. They claim that they were wrongfully ejected from the flight during a stopover in North Carolina after two events on board during which each displayed or possessed a knife. Pursuant to court rules, the judge referred the case to mandatory arbitration. The case was heard by the arbitrator. Plaintiffs and their attorneys attended the hearing, but only the defendant's lawyer was present.

   The arbitrator found in favor of each plaintiff, finding that the defendant's attorney did not participate in the arbitration in a meaningful way. He specifically found that:

   • Defendant's attorney did not produce any witnesses because they were all on assignment.

   • She provided only position summaries and fact summaries about what the defendant's employees may have said in their depositions.

   • When the arbitrator asked whether she wanted the damage award divided into compensatory damages and punitive damages, if he awarded such damages, she responded, "Do what you want, we won't pay it anyway."

   Defendants filed a motion for a trial de novo within the mandatory 30-day time period. Plaintiffs objected, arguing that the defendant did not participate in the arbitration in a meaningful way, as required. The court rules allow a judge to impose appropriate sanctions, including denying a demand for a trial de novo, if a party does not participate in arbitration in a meaningful way.

You are the judge. What sanction would you impose and why? The court rules allow for whatever sanction the court deems is appropriate. The sanction can range from awarding attorneys' fees and costs to the attorneys for preparing for and attending the arbitration hearing to denying a trial de novo. (Remember that there is a constitutional right to a jury trial and denying the demand for a trial de novo, although permitted, is a very harsh sanction.)

Practice Exercises

1. Is there a court-annexed or court-referenced ADR program in your state or a neighboring state? Write a paper in which you describe the program, including the following: What ADR methods does the program include? Is participation by the parties mandatory? What sanctions can be imposed on a party who refuses to participate? Who serves as third-party neutrals? How are neutrals chosen for a case? What are the qualifications for becoming a third-party neutral? Who pays for the neutrals? Are any types of cases excluded from the program? Why? Can decisions be appealed, and if yes, how? Be sure to provide references for applicable statutes, rules, and cases.

2. Find a case in your jurisdiction or neighboring jurisdiction that involved a court-annexed ADR. Brief the case, and then write a statement either agreeing or disagreeing with the court's decision. Include your reasons for agreeing or disagreeing. Be prepared to present your paper to the class.

3. Read and brief *Darcy v. Lolohea*, 886 P.2d 759 (Hawai'i App. 1994), which discusses Hawai'i's Court Annexed Arbitration Program. Be prepared to discuss the case in class.

Endnotes

1. 70 F.R.D. 111, 131 (1976).
2. 28 U.S.C. § 652 (2012).
3. Decker v. Lindsay, 824 S.W.2d 247, 250 (Tex. App. 1992).
4. Kimberlee K. Kovach, *Good Faith in Mediation—Requested, Recommended, or Required? A New Ethic*, 38 S. Tex. L. Rev. 575, 595-596 (1997).
5. John Lande, *Using Dispute System Design Methods to Promote Good-Faith Participation in Court-Connected Mediation Programs*, 50 UCLA L. Rev. 69, 84-85 (2002). "Attendance at mediation along with an exchange of information are treated as critical elements of good faith." Kovach, *supra* note 4, at 583.
6. Nick v. Morgan's Foods, Inc., 270 F.3d 590, 593 (8th Cir. 2001).
7. *Id.*
8. *Id.* at 594.
9. Lande, *supra* note 5, at 102.
10. In re A.T. Reynolds & Sons, Inc., 452 B.R. 374, 381 (S.D.N.Y. 2011).
11. William Howard Taft, *Possible and Needed Reforms in Administration of Justice in Federal Courts*, 8 A.B.A. J. 601, 601 (1922).
12. Judith Resnik, *Trial as Error, Jurisdiction and Injury, Transforming the Meaning of Article III*, 113 Harv. L. Rev. 924, 935 (2000).

13. Hubert L. Will, *Judicial Responsibility for the Disposition of Litigation, in Proceedings of Seminar for Newly Appointed United States District Judges*, 75 F.R.D. 117, 123 (1976).

14. Fed. R. Civ. P. 16 (as amended 1983, 1993).

15. Around the same time, a similar scheme was developed in Michigan courts. Carrie Menkel-Meadow, Lela Porter Love, Andrea Kupfer Schneider & Jean R. Sternlight, *Dispute Resolution: Beyond the Adversarial Model* 568 (Aspen 2011).

16. Wayne D. Brazil, Jeffrey P. Newman & Judith Z. Gold, *Early Neutral Evaluation: An Experimental Effort to Expedite Dispute Resolution*, 69 Judicature 279, 279 (1986).

17. *Id.*

18. *Id.* at 280.

19. Joshua D. Rosenberg & H. Jay Solberg, *Alternative Dispute Resolution: An Empirical Analysis*, 46 Stan. L. Rev. 1487, 1490-1491 (1994).

20. Alan Scott, Edward F. Sherman & Scott R. Peppet, *Mediation and Other Non-Binding ADR Processes* 225 (2d ed. Foundation 2002).

21. Kinsland Edwards, *No Frills Justice: North Carolina Experiments with Court-Ordered Arbitration*, 66 N.C. L. Rev. 396, 400 (1988).

22. Thomas D. Lambros, *The Summary Jury Trial and Other Alternative Methods of Dispute Resolution*, 103 F.R.D. 461, 463 (1984) (emphasis in original).

23. *Id.*

24. *Id.* at 467.

25. Lambros, *supra* note 22, at 469; Richard C. Reuben, *Constitutional Gravity: A Unitary Theory of Alternative Dispute Resolution and Public Civil Justice*, 47 UCLA L. Rev. 949, 970 (2000);

26. Reuben, *supra* note 25.

27. Lambros, *supra* note 22, at 469.

28. Richard A. Posner, *The Summary Jury Trial and Other Methods of Alternative Dispute Resolution: Some Cautionary Observations*, 53 U. Chi. L. Rev. 366, 371 (1986).

29. Lambros, *supra* note 22, at 467.

30. Thomas J. Klitgaardt & William E. Mussman III, *High Technology Disputes: The Minitrial as the Emerging Solution*, 8 Santa Clara Computer & High Tech. L.J. 1, 3 (1992).

31. Eric D. Green, *Corporate Alternative Dispute Resolution*, 1 Ohio St. J. on Disp. Resol. 203, 240 (1982).

32. Dorothy Wright Nelson, *ADR in the Federal Courts—One Judge's Perspective: Issues and Challenges Facing Judges, Lawyers, Court Administrators, and the Public*, 17 Ohio St. J. on Disp. Resol. 1, 4 (2001).

CHAPTER ELEVEN

The Paralegal and ADR

Chapter Outline

Introduction

Paralegal Mistakes Become Attorney
  Mistakes

Paralegal Tasks
  Motions
  Explain the Designated ADR
    Process to Client
  Write Legal Memoranda of the Facts
  Research the Neutral
  Prepare Subpoenas
  Prepare Memoranda Summarizing
    Each Witnesses' Expected
    Testimony

Preparation of Exhibit List

Attend the Proceeding and Take
  Notes

Prepare Agreements and Other
  Documents

Conclusion

Key Terms and Concepts

Practice Test Questions

Application Exercise

Practice Exercises

> It should be apparent that the modern litigator must manage and
> organize an effort resembling a military campaign. The foot
> soldiers in this organization will increasingly be paralegals,
> persons without law degrees who have training and/or experience
> in assisting lawyers with the pretrial preparation of lawsuits.[1]

INTRODUCTION

Some years ago, the Philadelphia Paralegal Association made a movie that began
with people on the street being asked for their definition of a paralegal. The
replies included:

> A paralegal, ah, isn't that like half a legal?
> Paralegal, isn't that when there is a very difficult case so they need two attorneys?
> You know, a pair of legals![2]

There is a lot of uncertainty about the work of a paralegal or legal assistant. (These
terms are interchangeable). This may be because the profession is unregulated,
and a license to practice is not needed.

The American Bar Association (ABA), a national voluntary organization of lawyers, and the National Association of Legal Assistants (NALA), a national voluntary organization of paralegals, define a **paralegal** as

> a person, qualified by education training or work experience who is employed or retained by a lawyer, law office, corporation, governmental agency or other entity who performs specifically delegated substantive legal work for which a lawyer is responsible.[3]

In this chapter, we examine what paralegals do to assist attorneys in preparing cases for dispute resolution. Although you learned in Chapter 2 that litigation may be the appropriate dispute resolution process because there are numerous textbooks on litigation for paralegals, this discussion focuses on the alternatives. Let's begin by listing what paralegals do and then discuss each. This list is not meant to be exhaustive. There are other tasks specific to particular areas of law that paralegals perform, such as drafting petitions, schedules, disclosures, and other required forms for bankruptcy cases; articles of incorporation, shareholder agreements, and financial documents for corporate cases; and purchase and sale agreements, mortgages, deeds, and record documents in the registry of deeds for real estate cases.

PARALEGAL MISTAKES BECOME ATTORNEY MISTAKES

As the quote in the beginning of this chapter points out, paralegals are the "foot soldiers" in litigation, and attorneys rely on them to assist in the battle. However, paralegal mistakes become attorney mistakes, as the case below illustrates. Errors not only affect the client, but also may subject the attorney to a malpractice lawsuit and cost the paralegal his job. In the following case, the paralegal failed to file an opposition to defendant's motion for summary judgment. As a result, plaintiff's lawsuit was dismissed.

Henderson v. Pacific Gas & Electric Co., **187 Cal. App. 4th 215 (2010):** Susan Henderson retained attorney Rod McClelland to represent her in an employment discrimination lawsuit against Pacific Gas & Electric Co. When he failed to timely file an opposition to defendant's motion for summary judgment, the court dismissed the suit. McClelland blamed his paralegal, who "assured him the preparation was going well and the opposition would be filed timely."[4] Because the paralegal was leaving on a cruise, she promised him she would have the document ready for his review before she left, three days before the filing deadline. When the paralegal's computer crashed, she took the entire file with her on the cruise and promised to have it filed by the due date. When McClelland checked with the court on the date the opposition was due, he learned it had not been filed. As a result, defendant's motion for summary judgment was granted, and the lawsuit was dismissed.

On appeal, McClelland argued that his paralegal's mistake was excusable and the court should vacate the trial court's granting of defendant's summary judgment motion. The appellate court found that McClelland's neglect was inexcusable. He "gave his employee, the paralegal, the task of preparing the opposition to the summary judgment motion. The responsibility for preparing the opposition, however, ultimately was his. . . . Thus, McClelland was responsible for supervising his paralegal's work and is responsible for her work product, including the failure to have the opposition filed on time."[5]

The court reasoned that "[w]hile counsel might not have expected the paralegal's computer to crash, that she would take the client file with her on vacation, or that she would not have the documents filed while on her trip, ordinary prudence certainly could have guarded against these events. . . . A reasonably prudent [attorney] would not have expected a paralegal, even a trusted one, to prepare an opposition to a summary judgment on her own and then, upon learning that the opposition would not be available for review before filing, simply wait to see if in fact the opposition is filed. . . . McClelland's conduct was inexcusable. . . . [6]

Questions:
1. What reason did the paralegal give for failing to timely file the opposition?
2. Why did the court reject the attorney's "excusable neglect" argument?

PARALEGAL TASKS

Paralegals perform a variety of tasks to support lawyers including preparing motions, drafting documents, and legal research. Courts have recognized that the work performed by paralegals can reduce litigation costs and contribute to the efficiency of lawyers. In the following case, the court listed some of the substantive legal work performed by paralegals and acknowledged the value of this work.

McMackin v. McMackin
651 A.2d 778 (Del. Fam. Ct. 1993)

. . . The United States Supreme Court has found that the term "attorney's fee" refers not only to the work performed by members of the Bar but also to reasonable fees for the work product of an attorney, which includes the work of paralegals, law clerks and recent law graduates at market rates for their services. . . .

Paralegal fees are not a part of the overall overhead of a law firm. Paralegal services are billed separately by attorneys, and these legal assistants have the potential for greatly decreasing litigation expenses and, for that matter, greatly increasing the efficiency of many attorneys. By permitting paralegal fees, the danger of charging these fees off as the attorney's work is hopefully extinguished. By the same token, the danger of charging off a secretary's services as those of a paralegal is very real and present, thereby mandating that certain information be provided by the supervising attorney before paralegal fees can be awarded by this Court in the future. Those criteria are as follows:

1. The time spent by the person in question on the task;
2. The hourly rate as charged to clients (will vary based on expertise and years of experience);
3. The education, training or work experience of the person which enabled him or her to acquire sufficient knowledge of legal concepts. . . .
4. The type of work involved in detail. The work must *not* be purely clerical or secretarial in nature. Such work would fall under costs and may not be charged as paralegal fees at the market rate. The task must contain substantive legal work under the direction or supervision of an attorney such that if the assistant were not present, the work would be performed by the attorney and not a secretary. However, the assistant may not do work that only an attorney is allowed to do under the rules of practice and ethics. Substantive legal work which may be performed by legal assistants and billed at the market rate includes, but is not limited to, such activities as:
   a. Factual investigation, including locating and interviewing witnesses;
   b. Assistance with depositions, [interrogatories] and document production;
   c. Compilation of statistical and financial data;
   d. Checking legal citations;
   e. Correspondence with clients/opposing counsel/courts; and
   f. Preparing/reviewing/answering petitions and other pleadings. . . .

Questions:

1. What was the criteria the court looked at to determine whether the work performed could be billed as paralegal fees?
2. What was the substantive legal work the court recognized that paralegals could perform?

Now we will explore some of the common duties paralegals are responsible for on a day-to-day basis. These include the following.

- Preparing motions
- Explaining the process of the designated dispute resolution method to the client
- Writing memorandum of the facts underlying a dispute
- Performing legal research pertinent to the case
- Researching the mediator or arbitrator
- Preparing subpoenas
- For arbitration, summary jury trial, and minitrial:
  - preparing memoranda summarizing each witness's expected testimony and
  - preparing a list of possible exhibits to be introduced

- Attending the proceeding and taking notes
- Preparing settlement agreements and other documents such as lien releases and personal property transfers

Motions

A **motion** is "[a] written or oral application requesting a court to make a specified ruling or order."[7] The various motions that can be made are found in the Federal Rules of Civil Procedure and civil rules of procedure for each state. For example, a motion to compel discovery (Fed. R. Civ. P. 37) is a request for a court order to require the opposing party to answer the party's discovery request; a motion for summary judgment (Fed. R. Civ. P. 56) is "[a] request that the court enter judgment without a trial because there is no genuine issue of material fact to be decided by a fact-finder."[8]

For illustrative purposes, we will look at a motion to vacate, or nullify, an arbitration award. Remember, in arbitration there are certain grounds for vacating an award (see: Chapter 7). Let's assume the following facts.

A law firm's client, Peterson and Sons Painting, Inc., located in Florida, was hired to paint the exterior of 15 multiunit apartment buildings in Florida owned by Zest Realty Properties, Inc., a Georgia corporation. The total amount of the contract was for $135,000, with $13,500 due at signing and $9000 payable at the completion of each building. Peterson and Sons Painting finished painting three building and received a total of $27,000. Peterson and Sons completed two more buildings, but Zest Realty failed to pay despite repeated demands. Peterson and Sons then stopped work and on March 22, 2016, filed suit in the U.S. District Court for the Middle District of Florida, for the full amount of the contract. The contract contained the following provision for arbitration:

> Article 9: If any question of fact arises under this contract about any unpaid balances, either party may demand arbitration with a Board of Arbitration. Zest Realty will select one arbitrator, Peterson and Sons will select one arbitrator, and these two shall select a third. The written decision of two of the three arbitrators shall be final and binding upon both parties.

When arbitration was held, the Board declined to award Peterson and Sons the full contract amount and instead awarded Peterson and Sons $18,000, the amount for the two buildings not previously paid, minus the $13,500 paid at the signing of the contract for an award of $4,500.

Since the arbitration, the attorneys for Peterson and Sons have learned that the third arbitrator and chairman of the Board of Arbitration had a prior association with Zest Realty that had not been disclosed. Had Peterson and Sons known this, it would not have agreed to his appointment as an impartial arbitrator.

The paralegal's supervising attorney has asked her to draft a motion to vacate the award on the grounds of fraud and/or evident partiality of an arbitrator.

Section 10 of the Federal Arbitration Act (FAA) provides that courts can vacate arbitration awards for "corruption, fraud, or undue means" (§ 10(a)(1)) or "evident partiality or corruption in the arbitrators" (§ 10(a)(2)).

The paralegal drafted the motion shown in Exhibit 11-1.

Exhibit 11-1. MOTION

UNITED STATES DISTRICT COURT FOR THE MIDDLE DISTRICT OF FLORIDA

Peterson and Sons, Inc.

        Plaintiff

                              Motion to Set Aside Arbitration Award

v.   Civil No. 15-3347

Zest Realty Properties, Inc.

        Defendant

NOW COMES the Plaintiff, Peterson and Sons, Inc., by and through its attorney, and respectfully states and moves as follows:

1. On March 22, 2015, Plaintiff filed suit against Defendant for breach of contract and unjust enrichment.
2. Pursuant to the parties' contract, an arbitration hearing was held at which the arbitrators awarded Plaintiff $4500.
3. Since the arbitration award, Plaintiff discovered that one arbitrator, who served as chairman of the board, had a prior association with the Defendant.
4. Had plaintiff known about this prior association, it would not have agreed to the appointment of this arbitrator.
5. Pursuant to the Federal Arbitration Act § 10(a)(1) and § 10(a)(2), the award should be vacated because of fraud and/or evident partiality of the arbitrator.

WHEREFORE, Plaintiff respectfully prays that this Honorable Court vacate the award, order another arbitration hearing, order Defendant to pay Plaintiff's attorney's fees and costs, and grant whatever additional relief it deems proper and fitting under the circumstances.

Dated: _____, 20_____   _____

                                            William J. Barry, Esq.

                                          Attorney for Plaintiff

                                          Peterson and Sons, Inc.

Through the course of a legal dispute, numerous motions may be filed. A paralegal who understands and masters the skill of motion writing will be highly valued by an attorney. In addition to writing motions, paralegals need to understand each dispute resolution method and be able to explain it clearly and succinctly to the client. This is the topic of the next section.

Explain the Designated ADR Process to Client

Paralegals are frequently responsible for educating the client about the process of the chosen dispute resolution. This can be done in a letter, in a face-to-face meeting, or both. Let's say that a paralegal's supervising attorney represents the wife in a divorce matter. The couple reached agreement on all issues except child custody and visitation. They have two boys, ages 10 and 7. The court requires mandatory mediation when there are children under the age of 18. The supervising attorney has asked her paralegal to write a letter to the client explaining the mediation process. An example is shown in Exhibit 11-2.

Exhibit 11-2. LETTER EXPLAINING THE MEDIATION PROCESS

Barry, Coulombe, Hernandez & Associates
1178 Congress Street
Portland, Maine 04101

Telephone (207) 555-5555
Fax (207) 555-5556
e-mail: BCK@innet.com

May 16, 20_____

Ms. Amanda Pearson
34 Oceanside Avenue
Cape Elizabeth, ME 04107

Re: Mediation

Dear Ms. Pearson:

A mediation between you and Charles is scheduled for June 1, 20_____, at 1:00 p.m. at the Superior Court, 175 Middle Road in Portland. Attorney Barry asked me to write and explain mediation so that you will know what to expect. The issues will be child custody and visitation. Attorney Barry will be there, however, his role will be limited because the mediation is designed for the parties to discuss and resolve the issues with the help of the mediator. Of course, at any time during the mediation, you can consult with Attorney Barry.

Mediation is a process where you and Charles will discuss child custody and visitation with the help of a third-party neutral called the mediator. Selected by the court, the mediator will try to help both of you define the issues, communicate effectively,

---

Continued >

and search for a way to resolve any disagreement. Ultimately, you and Charles decide the outcome.

Here is what will happen at the mediation:

The session will begin with the mediator explaining that the process is informal and consensual, that she is impartial, and that the parties are responsible for identifying the issues and setting the agenda. Next, she will tell you and Charles the ground rules: no interrupting the other party when he or she is speaking; no using abusive language; the need to attend all sessions on time; bathroom breaks, and coffee and lunch breaks. The mediator will explain that anything said or learned during the mediation is confidential and is not admissible at a trial if a settlement is not reached. The confidentiality rule applies to you, Charles, and the mediator.

After the mediator's opening remarks, you and Charles will have an opportunity to make uninterrupted statements. This is an opportunity to explain your feelings about the disagreement, identify what you believe to be the issues, and give your view on how they should be resolved. After Charles's statement, with the help of the mediator, you and Charles will discuss the conflict, clarify the needs and interests of both of you, and create an agenda on the topics for discussion.

After the issues have been identified, you and Charles will make and discuss suggestions for ways to resolve them. The mediator will help you both discuss and analyze each proposal and determine whether you agree. From time to time, the mediator may meet privately with each of you. This is called caucusing and gives each party an opportunity to tell the mediator his or her feelings about a particular issue. These discussions are private and will not be shared with the other party without permission.

When an agreement is reached, it will be put in writing. If the discussions are unsuccessful, the mediator will summarize for you and Charles any areas of agreement and give an opinion about the prospect for settlement.

I hope that this has given you a better understanding of what will happen at mediation. If you have any questions, please do not hesitate to call me or Attorney Barry.

Very truly yours,

Kayla Barry
Paralegal

As just illustrated, paralegals must have the ability to write effectively. While subject matter knowledge is important, paralegals must know how to write letters, motions, and memoranda. The next section discusses another type of writing, the limited legal memoranda.

Write Legal Memoranda of the Facts

A **legal memorandum** is a written document that provides information about a case, issue, or other legal matter. Frequently referred to as "memos," these documents are written for use within a law firm. The more formal memos, called a memorandum of law, follow a particular format that can include the following sections: introduction, question presented, brief answer, statement of facts, analysis, and conclusion. These memos are usually covered in a legal research and writing course. Our discussion addresses the limited memo, such as one summarizing a client interview, witness statement, or facts of the case. To demonstrate, assume the following facts.

Attorney Campbell and her paralegal met with Eloise, a 10-year-old girl, and her parents, Rachel and David Thompson. Rachel explained that they have lived near the Green Basket Supermarket for the past 5 years. The market has been in business in the same location for more than 20 years. The owners are very involved in the community and well liked. Customers frequently take the shopping carts home to unload their groceries. The owners are aware that carts sometimes would be returned to the lot at night or on Sundays when the market was closed.

Rachel said that on Sunday, July 28, 20__, Eloise and three of her friends walked to the Green Basket Supermarket parking lot. Eloise said there were a lot of shopping carts in the area. She didn't know the exact number, but said there were more than three because she and her friends each pushed one around the lot and they could see other carts. Eloise explained that she climbed into one of the carts and one of her friends, Amy, began to push her around. She said that something happened and the cart fell over and she remembers hurting and crying. Another friend, Alexis, ran home and told her mother, who called the police and Rachel, who rushed to the parking lot and saw Eloise on the ground crying and screaming that her arm hurt a lot. A police officer and ambulance arrived shortly after. Eloise was transported to the hospital, where she had surgery for a fractured left arm. The paralegal learned from the police report that one of the cart's wheels hit a small pothole that caused it to tip over.

Assume that the paralegal's supervising attorney has asked him to write a memorandum of the facts. The document might look Exhibit 11-3.

Memo writing is a task paralegals may be asked to perform; therefore, paralegals must learn how to write clearly and concisely. Finding and researching a neutral is another paralegal job and is discussed in the next section.

Research the Neutral

Selecting a neutral is as important, and sometimes more so, than learning about the judge who might hear the case, especially for arbitration. In mediation, early neutral evaluation, and summary jury trial, the outcome is binding only if agreed to by the parties. An arbitrator, however, unlike a judge, is not constrained by rules of procedure and court decisions, and her verdict is subject to limited

Exhibit 11-3. MEMORANDUM OF FACTS

MEMORANDUM OF FACTS

Date: September _____, 20_____

To: Mary Campbell, Esq.

From: Jorge Rivera, Paralegal

Re: Eloise Thompson: Negligence (Attractive Nuisance) – File No. 00-5677

STATEMENT OF THE FACTS

Ten-year-old Eloise lives near the Green Basket Supermarket. On Sunday, July 28, 20_____, she and her three friends walked onto the parking lot of the supermarket. There were at least four shopping baskets in various places on the lot. Eloise climbed into one, and her friend pushed the cart around the parking area. At one point, a wheel struck a small pothole. The cart fell over, throwing Eloise to the ground. Eloise's left arm suffered a fracture that required hospitalization and surgery. The store's owners were aware that customers would sometimes bring the carts home after shopping and return them when the store was closed at nights or Sundays.

---

review. So selecting the appropriate neutral can sometimes be vital to a fair hearing and a favorable outcome for a client. Paralegals can be assigned the task of finding the appropriate neutral. Locating biographical information is usually the easy part because neutrals have resumes available. The more difficult undertaking is learning about the neutral's reputation within the field of the dispute, finding written works authored by the neutral, and discovering whether the neutral typically favors one side of the dispute over the other side.

Let's use the following hypothetical to demonstrate how to select an arbitrator for a construction case. A paralegal's firm represents Rashid and Nancy Karim, who have sued DCB Builders, Inc., for breach of contract. On January 20_____, DCB Builders gave Rashid and Nancy a floor plan, with specific dimensions, for a home with five rooms, a garage, and unfinished basement. DCB Builders agreed to build the residence in a workmanlike manner on a lot owned by it and then sell the property to the Karims for $265,850. The Karims secured a loan through the U.S. Department of Agriculture, paid DCB Builders $265,850, and in the same year on August 20, 20_____, DCB Builders conveyed the property to the Karims by warranty deed. The Karims moved into the home the next day, August 21, 20_____.

In April of the following year, the tile floors in the kitchen and living room began to buckle or lift from the subfloor surface. Additionally, the kitchen cabinets pulled loose from the ceiling approximately ¼ inch, the hardwood floors in the bedrooms and hall squeaked, nail heads were sticking up from the floor, and the door leading to the backyard would not open or close properly. Rashid Karim contacted the builder, who looked at the "defects" and said he would make the necessary repairs; however, he never appeared to do the work.

Pursuant to the contract, if a dispute arose, the parties agreed to arbitration. The case would be heard before a panel of three arbitrators. Each party would select one arbitrator and those arbitrators would select the third.

Your supervising attorney wants you to research arbitrators and recommend one for an interview. The first step in the selection process is to review resumes. While doing this, consider the following:

- What did the person do prior to becoming an arbitrator?
- What training does he or she have in arbitration?
- What experience does he or she have as an arbitrator?
- Does the person have any experience in arbitrating construction cases?
- What is his or her hourly rate?

Once the list is narrowed down to two or perhaps three candidates, the next step is to learn about their reputations. To do this, talk to lawyers in the area and ask the following questions:

- Are they impartial?
- Do they have good case management skills?
- Do they implement cost-effective and efficient arbitration procedures?
- Do they know the area of law involved?
- Are they generally available? What is their approach to pre-hearing discovery — liberal or restricted?
- Are they diligent in making pre-hearing rulings?
- Are they known for intelligence, common sense, open-mindedness, patience and a sense of humor?
- What is their judicial temperament?
- Do they take firm control of the proceedings?
- How do they apply the rules of evidence at arbitration hearings?
- Do they take a more legalistic or more equitable approach in rendering awards?
- Do they comply with ethical rules?
- Do they write thorough, comprehensive and well-reasoned awards?
- Are their fees reasonable?[9]

Be sure that you avoid any ex parte communication with potential arbitrators,

except you can discuss the general nature of the case, the identities of the parties, counsel and witnesses and ask questions regarding the suitability and availability of candidates. You cannot, though, get into specifics about the dispute or discuss the merits of the case. If you have any improper communications with arbitrator candidates, you may be faced with a successful motion to vacate an arbitration award in your client's favor.[10]

Selecting a party-appointed arbitrator in the US
David McLean

When appointing a neutral, party-appointed arbitrator, parties often attempt to maximize their chance of winning while remaining cognizant of the arbitrator's neutrality. As one commentator expressed, in selecting a party-appointed arbitrator, the candidate with the "maximum predisposition towards" the client, but "with the minimum appearance of bias" is often favored (M. Hunter, *Ethics of the International Arbitrator*, 53 Arb. 219, [223] (1987)).

Even when an arbitrator must be neutral and impartial, parties nevertheless seek candidates who are predisposed towards their position, whether based on philosophy, prior rulings or predilection. Without a doubt, all else being equal, to select an arbitrator likely to view one's case favourably should increase the chances of a favourable award. For example, depending on the case, one may seek to appoint "pro-business" or "pro-consumer" arbitrators. Similar dichotomies include "pro-employee" and "pro-employer" jurists in an employment dispute or "strict constructionist" and "liberal constructionist" in a contract dispute. Likewise, potential arbitrators, like judges, sometimes can be distinguished by the degree to which they are likely to focus on equitable considerations as opposed to implementing the business deal as written on the four corners of the contract. Parties might find clues into such predispositions in previous academic writings or prior decisions. Even though the modern arbitrator is neutral and not an advocate for the appointing party, the neutral's legal perspective, political views and other such factors could colour his or her decision. Under somewhat analogous circumstances, litigants often speak of being assigned to a judge whom they believe will look favourably on their side, such as when a judge has previously expressed views on relevant legal theories consistent with one's position in litigation. These considerations are often germane as one approaches arbitrator selection.

Source: Produced by Latham & Watkins LLP for LexisPSL Arbitration (Nov. 3, 2014), https://www.lexisnexis.com/uk/lexispsl/arbitration/home.

The paralegal in the *Karim v. DCB Builders, Inc.* hypothetical above has selected five potential arbitrator candidates. Assume you are the paralegal. Read each of the following resumes and choose the one you think would be the best candidate.

Resume Example 1

Kevin Hamilton
222 Court Street
Hillsboro, MO 63050
Phone: (555) 555-5555

A. Educational Background

B.A., University of Maryland (1975)
J.D., Saint Louis University School of Law (1982)

B. Current Employment and Experience

Hearing officer for Missouri Department of Elementary and Secondary Education; Adjunct Faculty at local community college

C. Formal Dispute Resolution Training

Basic and advanced mediation training (100 hours); employment mediation training; mediating civil and commercial disputes

D. Other ADR Panels and ADR Rosters on Which Neutral Serves

Community Mediation Services

E. Experience as a Neutral

Over 500 hours of mediations, including business, employment, and family law

F. Fees

$200.00/hour plus travel time over one hour each way at $85 hour

G. References

Available upon request.

H. Professional Organizations

American Bar Association, Dispute Resolution Section; Missouri Bar

Resume Example 2

Julia Mendoza, Esq.
178 Western Avenue
Hillsboro, MO 63050
Phone: (555) 555-5555

A. Educational Background

B.A., DePauw University (1982)
J.D., Tulane University Law School (1985)

B. Current Employment and Experience

Law Office of Julia Mendoza, specializing in construction law

C. Formal Dispute Resolution Training

American Arbitration Association (Construction Industry Arbitrator Training)
Mediation (40 hours training)

D. Other ADR Panels and ADR Rosters on Which Neutral Serves

E. Experience as a Neutral

Arbitrations – 12 construction disputes, including three as chair of a three-person
panel

F. Fees

$250/hour

G. References

David Burns, Esq., Burns, Rappold, and Pelletier; (555) 555-5555

Michael Silva, Esq. (555) 555-5555

H. Professional Organizations

American Bar Association, Dispute Resolution Section; Missouri Bar

Resume Example 3

Sarah Goodwin
88 Monroe Street
Hillsboro, MO 63050
Phone: (555) 555-5555

A. Educational Background

B.A., Boston College (1978)
J.D., Boston College Law School (1981)

B. Current Employment and Experience

Shareholder, Palmer, Goodwin, and Larson, LLC, specializing in construction, insurance, and professional negligence litigation, as well as alternative dispute resolution

C. Formal Dispute Resolution Training

Over 500 hours of training, including over 150 hours in advanced conflict resolution

D. Other ADR Panels and ADR Rosters on Which Neutral Serves

Chair, State Board of Arbitration (2001-present); Federal Mediation & Conciliation Service (labor arbitrator, 2000-present); Social Security Administration panel of arbitrators (2006-present); Home Improvement Construction Arbitration Panel (2003-2012)

E. Experience as a Neutral

Mediated over 325 cases; arbitrated over 230 cases

F. Fees

$275/hour plus travel time at $75/hour

G. References

Available upon request

H. Professional Organizations

Missouri Association of Dispute Professional (past president); American Arbitration Association; Missouri Bar

Resume Example 4

Hon. Juan Lopez
Fuller, Buckman, & Lopez, LLC
224 W. Washington Street, Suite 122
Hillsboro, MO 63050
Phone: (555) 555-5555

A. Educational Background

B.A., Northwestern University (1970)
J.D., Baylor Law School (1973)

B. Current Employment and Experience

Of Counsel, Peters, Bryant, and Flynn, LLC; formerly, Circuit Court Judge (1990-2010)

C. Formal Dispute Resolution Training

National Judicial College — Advanced Mediation, Settlement
American Bar Association — Dispute Resolution

D. Other ADR Panels and ADR Rosters on Which Neutral Serves

American Arbitration Association Commercial Arbitration Panel

E. Experience as a Neutral

Twenty years' experience adjudicating, managing, or settling cases in Missouri Circuit Courts

F. Fees

Mediation Per Day

Two-party cases — $1000 per party
Three or more party cases — $750 per party

Arbitration Per Day

$2000

G. References

Brent Jackson, Esq., Jackson & Abbott (555) 555-5555

Linda Phillips, Esq., Phillips & Associates (555) 555-5555

H. Professional Organizations

American Bar Association; Missouri Bar

Resume Example 5

Douglas Hammond
68 Woodward Avenue
Hillsboro, MO 63050
Phone: (555) 555-5555

A. Educational Background

B.A., University of Michigan, Ann Arbor 1990
J.D., University of Michigan Law School 1993

B. Current Employment and Experience

Partner Blackwell and Fisher, LLP

C. Formal Dispute Resolution Training

Mediation certificate; American Arbitration Association (Construction Industry Arbitration Training)

D. Other ADR Panels and ADR Rosters on Which Neutral Serves

Volunteer mediator small claims court

E. Experience as a Neutral

Mediations – 50 small claims, 2 residential real estate, 1 construction

F. Fees

$150/hour

G. References

Gary Thompson, Esq., (555) 555-5555

Jay Townsend, Esq. (555) 555-5555

H. Professional Organizations

American Bar Association; Missouri Bar

Now that you've made your selection, let's review them together. Keep in mind that there is no "correct" candidate, and the one recommended at the end of this discussion may not be your choice. The first candidate eliminated is Douglas Hammond because he has never arbitrated a dispute. Similarly, Kevin Hamilton's background is in mediation, and he has no training or experience as an arbitrator and therefore is not a good choice. The next person we will eliminate is Sarah Goodwin. Although her resume is impressive with legal experience in construction law, chair of the State Board of Arbitration, and a member of the Home Improvement Construction Arbitration Panel, we do not know whether any of the 230 cases she has arbitrated involved construction. We may want to do some additional research to find out. The next candidate, the Hon. Juan Lopez appears to be highly qualified, having served as a circuit court judge for 20 years, but because of his judicial experience, he may focus more on the law than equity.[11] This may not be favorable to the Karims, who are looking for fairness rather than a strict legal interpretation. The candidate that may be the best choice for the Karims is Julia Mendoza for the following reasons: her law practice appears to be limited to construction law; she has training as a construction arbitrator; and she has arbitrated 12 construction cases, including three as chair of a three-person panel.

Prepare Subpoenas

A **subpoena** is a written court order compelling a person to appear in court, at a deposition, or at another legal proceeding to testify. It may also compel her to bring documents, books, photographs, e-mails, or other types of evidence under her control. A subpoena duces tecum only requires an individual to produce a document or documents at a particular proceeding. Preparing subpoenas is usually the responsibility of paralegals. See Exhibit 11-4 for a sample subpoena.

Prepare Memoranda Summarizing Each Witness's Expected Testimony

Witnesses can be divided into two categories: lay witnesses and expert witnesses. A lay witness is any person who gives testimony in a case and is not an expert. Lay witnesses can testify only to matters of which they have personal knowledge. An expert witness is a person who has "scientific, technical, or other specialized knowledge [that] will help the trier of fact to understand the evidence or to determine a fact in issue."[12]

In our *Karim v. DCB Builders, Inc.*, hypothetical, the Karims will offer two witnesses, Rashid Karim and expert witness Martin Wagner. Exhibit 11-5 is an example of a memorandum summarizing the expected testimony of these witnesses.

Exhibit 11-4. SUBPOENA

AO 88 (Rev. 02/14) Subpoena to Appear and Testify at a Hearing or Trial in a Civil Action

UNITED STATES DISTRICT COURT
for the

_____ District of _____

_____)	
Plaintiff)	
v.)	Civil Action No.
_____)	
Defendant)	

SUBPOENA TO APPEAR AND TESTIFY
AT A HEARING OR TRIAL IN A CIVIL ACTION

To:
_____
(Name of person to whom this subpoena is directed)

YOU ARE COMMANDED to appear in the United States district court at the time, date, and place set forth below to testify at a hearing or trial in this civil action. When you arrive, you must remain at the court until the judge or a court officer allows you to leave.

Place:	Courtroom No.:
	Date and Time:

You must also bring with you the following documents, electronically stored information, or objects *(leave blank if not applicable)*:

The following provisions of Fed. R. Civ. P. 45 are attached – Rule 45(c), relating to the place of compliance; Rule 45(d), relating to your protection as a person subject to a subpoena; and Rule 45(e) and (g), relating to your duty to respond to this subpoena and the potential consequences of not doing so.

Date: _____

CLERK OF COURT

OR

_____   _____
Signature of Clerk or Deputy Clerk   *Attorney's signature*

The name, address, e-mail address, and telephone number of the attorney representing *(name of party)* _____
_____ , who issues or requests this subpoena, are:

Notice to the person who issues or requests this subpoena
If this subpoena commands the production of documents, electronically stored information, or tangible things before trial, a notice and a copy of the subpoena must be served on each party in this case before it is served on the person to whom it is directed. Fed. R. Civ. P. 45(a)(4).

Continued >

AO 88 (Rev. 02/14) Subpoena to Appear and Testify at a Hearing or Trial in a Civil Action (page 2)

Civil Action No.

PROOF OF SERVICE
(This section should not be filed with the court unless required by Fed. R. Civ. P. 45.)

I received this subpoena for *(name of individual and title, if any)* _____

on *(date)* _____ .

☐ I served the subpoena by delivering a copy to the named person as follows: _____

_____ on *(date)* _____ ; or

☐ I returned the subpoena unexecuted because: _____

_____ .

Unless the subpoena was issued on behalf of the United States, or one of its officers or agents, I have also tendered to the witness the fees for one day's attendance, and the mileage allowed by law, in the amount of

$ _____ .

My fees are $ _____ for travel and $ _____ for services, for a total of $ ___0.00___ .

I declare under penalty of perjury that this information is true.

Date: _____   _____
                                                    Server's signature

                                          _____
                                                    Printed name and title

                                          _____
                                                    Server's address

Additional information regarding attempted service, etc.:

Exhibit 11-5. MEMORANDUM SUMMARIZING EXPECTED WITNESS TESTIMONY

MEMORANDUM

Date: September _____, 20_____

To: Mary Campbell, Esq.

From: Deanna Barry, Paralegal

Re: Karim v. DCB Builders, Inc. – File No. 14-9398

SUMMARY OF PLAINTIFFS' WITNESSES

There are two witnesses we will present at trial.

Rashid Karim – Plaintiff/Client

Mr. Karim will testify that he entered into a contract with DCB Builders, Inc., to construct a house on a certain parcel of property. Approximately eight months after moving into the house, the tile floors in the kitchen and living room began to buckle. Also, the kitchen cabinets separated about ¼ inch from the ceiling, the floors in the bedrooms and hall squeaked when walked on, nail heads were sticking up from the floor, and the back door would not open or close properly.

Martin Wagner – Expert Witness

Mr. Wagner has extensive experience in the construction field. He is certified by the National Floor Safety Institute as a Walkway Auditor Safety Specialist and holds a Building Code Certification issued by the International Code Council. Additionally, he is licensed as a Commercial and Residential Construction Supervisor. Mr. Wagner has testified as an expert in numerous construction cases and has performed many on-site inspections of various residential and commercial buildings. He will testify as follows:

Tile buckling: attributable to defective plywood used for the subflooring.

Cabinets separating: the fasteners used to attach the cabinets were not designed for the purpose they were used.

Squeaking floors: the subflooring was not properly secured.

Exposed nail heads: an improperly installed steel beam is the likely cause of the nail heads being exposed.

Mr. Wagner will also testify to the cost of repairing all of the defects.

Preparation of Exhibit List

Many cases take months or years of work gathering evidence. In large cases, there are frequently hundreds of exhibits containing thousands of documents that will be presented at trial, arbitration, summary jury trial, or mini-trial. The attorney must be able to access these quickly and efficiently. An attorney who has difficulty locating evidence may appear incompetent. Preparation of trial exhibits is key to ensuring that the presentation will go smoothly. Additionally, parties are required to file with the court or arbitrator and opposing party "evidence it may present at trial. . . ."[13]

Exhibits are physical or documentary evidence presented during a hearing. These include written documents, physical objects, animations, e-mails, text messages, and audio- and videotapes. The judge or arbitrator determines whether a particular exhibit is admissible. The paralegal is responsible for organizing all exhibits so they can be quickly retrieved. There are many software programs and forms readily available for organizing and presenting exhibits at trial. Every exhibit must have a numbered "Exhibit" sticker so that it can be readily identified. Each jurisdiction may have its own requirements for exhibits, including numbering, color, placement, and content of the labels; be sure to check your local court rules. After each exhibit is marked, you should create a master index with the date the exhibit was created, the author, type, and brief description. Prepare at least three copies of each exhibit: the original, a copy for your attorney, and a copy for opposing counsel. The copies should be attached to the original so they can be quickly provided to opposing counsel at the time the original is offered into evidence.

Deadlines for exchanging and filing trial exhibits differ by jurisdiction. In federal court, exhibit lists must be filed 30 days before trial.[14] Be sure you allow sufficient time to prepare. Exhibit 11-6 shows an example of an exhibit list.

Exhibit 11-6. **PLAINTIFFS' LIST OF EXHIBITS**

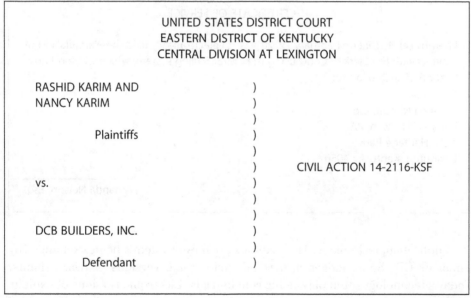

UNITED STATES DISTRICT COURT
EASTERN DISTRICT OF KENTUCKY
CENTRAL DIVISION AT LEXINGTON

RASHID KARIM AND
NANCY KARIM

　　　　Plaintiffs

vs.

DCB BUILDERS, INC.

　　　　Defendant

)
)
)
)
)
)
)
)
)
)
)
)

CIVIL ACTION 14-2116-KSF

Continued >

PLAINTIFFS' LIST OF EXHIBITS

Pursuant to the Court's Scheduling Order and Fed. R. Civ. P. 26 (a)(3), Plaintiffs Rashid Karim and Nancy Karim, by and through undersigned counsel, respectfully submit the following list of exhibits they may present at trial:

1. Report from Martin Wagner.
2. Deposition of Martin Wagner.
3. Deposition of Steve Woodhill, DCB Builders, Inc.
4. Contract to purchase property at 22 Meadow Lane.
5. Photo of tile floor in kitchen.
6. Photo of tile floor in living room.
7. Photo of bedroom floor.
8. Photo of hallway floor.
9. Photo of exposed nail heads.
10. Photo of kitchen cabinets.
11. Photo of door.

Respectfully submitted,

Amanda Nelson, Esq.
Attorney for Plaintiffs
7388 New Meadows Road
Lexington, Kentucky 40507
(555) 555-5555

CERTIFICATE OF SERVICE

I hereby certify that on February 12, 20_____, I electronically filed the Plaintiffs' List of Exhibits with the Clerk of Court using the CM/ECF filing system, which will send notification of such filing to:

Amanda Nelson, Esq.
Barry and Nelson, PA
1212 Heritage Park
Lexington, Kentucky 40507

_____
Amanda Nelson, Esq.

A note about technology. Trial exhibits are now frequently being exchanged by e-mail or CD. Some judges also require electronic versions of trial exhibits. Today's technology often plays a big role in trials. Electronic versions of exhibits can be easily projected during trial, making them more compelling. The use of technology depends on each attorney.

Attend the Proceeding and Take Notes

Experienced paralegals attend various proceedings, including formal trials, arbitration hearings, summary jury trials, and mini-trials. At these events, the attorney is intently focused on the proceeding—questioning witnesses, formulating cross-examination questions, and making objections. The paralegal's role is to assist the attorney by listening to testimony and taking notes. These notes can then be compared with a witness's deposition or answers to interrogatories. If any inconsistent statements are found, the paralegal can then inform the attorney. Because people speak words faster than they can write them, paralegals need to learn some form of shorthand note taking. One method to help take notes quickly is using a short form of a word or an abbreviation of the word. This can be accomplished by

- leaving out articles and conjunctions (the, a, and, but);
- leaving out vowels or other letters;
- using abbreviations and symbols for commonly used words.

Exhibit 11-7 gives some common examples of abbreviations and symbols. There are many, many more, which can easily be found on the Internet. You can also invent your own. Remember to make and keep a list of the meanings of your abbreviations and symbols so you can refer to them if needed.

Prepare Agreements and Other Documents

Settlement Agreements

A **settlement** ends a lawsuit by mutual agreement. Most cases are settled before trial. Sometimes a settlement happens after an ADR process. Paralegals must know how to draft settlement agreements. A **settlement agreement** is a written document, sometimes lengthy, detailing what the parties agreed to. It is a form of contract, and like all contracts must meet certain requirements, including acceptance by the offeree, consideration, and mutual intent to be bound to the terms. Paralegals should be aware that local laws may apply. Most law offices keep on file standard settlement agreements for various legal matters. Because agreements affect the present and future rights, obligations, and duties of the parties, precision is important. All settlement agreements must be reviewed by the supervising attorney. Exhibit 11-8 is an example of a basic settlement agreement. Of course, settlement agreements can be very lengthy, depending on the subject matter, and an attorney might deem additional information necessary.

Exhibit 11-7. ABBREVIATIONS AND SYMBOLS

LEGAL SHORTHAND AND SYMBOLS

aka	also known as	ex	exhibit
amt	amount	f	fact
ans	answer	H	husband
atty	attorney	hrg	hearing
c/a	cause of action	inj	injury
cc	child custody	LL	landlord
cf	compare	oc	opposing counsel
K	contract	prop	property
ct	court	v or vs	versus, against
d/e	direct examination	W	wife
depo	deposition	xe	cross examination
dkt	docket	π	plaintiff
dmg	damage	Δ	defendant
ev	evidence	§	section

GENERAL SHORTHAND AND SYMBOLS

a/b	about	w/	with
b/c	because	w/i	within
btwn	between	w/o	without
b/4	before	=	equals
cf	compare	$\neq$	does not equal
diff	different/difference	$\approx$	similar to
dob	date of birth	<	less than
ea	each	>	greater than
ee	employee	~	approximately
eg	for example	↑	increase
er	employer	↑↑	rapid increase
est	estimate	↓	decrease
excl	excluding	↓↓	rapid decrease
4	for	∴	therefore/
fr	from		consequently
ie	that is	→	leads to or causes
p/pp	page/pages	←	comes from
pt	point	x	not correct
NB	important, note well	?	unproven
no.	number	√	correct
re	about	+	and
sim	similar	!	not
viz	namely		

Exhibit 11-8. SETTLEMENT AGREEMENT AND RELEASE

This Settlement Agreement and Release ("Agreement") is entered into as of November 10, 20_____, by and between Rashid Karim and Nancy Karim and DCB Builders, Inc. Collectively, Rashid Karim, Nancy Karim, and DCB Builders, Inc., shall be referred to as the "Parties." The purpose of this Agreement is to fully and finally settle and resolve all claims between the Parties.

WHEREAS, disputes have arisen between the Parties, which disputes have resulted in litigation; and

WHEREAS, the Parties desire to settle their disputes by entering into this Agreement. For good and valuable consideration, the receipt and sufficiency of which is hereby acknowledged, the Parties agree as follows:

1. DCB Builders, Inc., will pay Rashid Karim and Nancy Karim the total sum of Twelve Thousand dollars ($12,000.00). The Parties acknowledge and agree that they are solely responsible for paying attorneys' fees and costs.
2. The Parties acknowledge that the Twelve Thousand dollars ($12,000.00) is in full settlement of all claims or losses of whatsoever kind that they have, or may ever have had, against the other Party and by signing this Agreement they are forever giving up any right to seek further monetary or other relief from the other Party.
3. Each party shall take whatever actions necessary to ensure that the lawsuit is dismissed in its entirety with prejudice.
4. The Parties intend that this Agreement be legally binding upon and shall inure to the benefit of each of them and their respective successors, assigns, executors, administrators, heirs, and estates.
5. This Agreement represents the entire agreement and understanding of the Parties and supersedes all prior negotiations or agreements concerning the subject matter hereof. And, no modification of this Agreement shall be binding unless in writing and signed by each of the Parties.

The Parties acknowledge that they have read and understood the contents of this Agreement and sign the same of their own free will.

Dated: November 20, 20_____

_____
Rashid Karim

Dated: November 20, 20_____

_____
Nancy Karim

Dated: November 20, 20_____

_____
President, DCB Builders, Inc.

Liens

A **lien** is "a claim or charge on, or right against, personal property, or an encumbrance on real property, for the payment of a debt. A lien may be created by statute (Examples: a tax lien; an attachment lien) or by agreement between the parties (Examples: a mortgage on real estate; a security agreement covering personal property)."[15] A fairly common lien that a paralegal may be assigned to draft is a **mechanic's lien**, which is created by statute "to secure a priority of payment for the performance of labor or the supply of material to buildings or other improvement to be enforced against the particular property in which they have become incorporated."[16]

To illustrate the drafting of a mechanic's lien, we will use the following hypothetical: On October 20, 20____, our client, KRB Builders, Inc., and Thomas Richardson entered into a contract for repairs to Richardson's house. The contract provided that KRB Builders would remove all shingles, and repair damaged wood on the roof and around the chimney. Additionally, the contract provided that KRB Builders would install porch steps and level a corner of the foundation. The total contract price was $13,183.73. Richardson made a down payment in the amount of $2,500.00, leaving a balance of $10,683.73 due upon completion of the work.

Our client completed the repairs on October 30, 20____, and sent an invoice to Richardson. After 45 days, payment had not been received, so our client called Richardson and requested payment. Richardson said that there were a couple of problems that needed to be corrected before he would pay; the roof was leaking and the steps were not installed correctly. On November 2, 20____, our client made repairs; however, Richardson still refused to pay. KRB Builders now wants to file a mechanic's lien in the amount of $10,683.73.[17] Exhibit 11-9 represents the mechanic's lien prepared by the paralegal.

When the prerequisites of the mechanic's lien statute are met, the completed Statement of Claim must be filed or registered in the Office of Registrar of Deeds. If it is not, then it is not perfected,[18] and the collateral is not encumbered and could be sold without any claim for funds by the lien holder.

Now let's assume that KRB Builders, Inc., and Thomas Richardson resolved their dispute through mediation. Richardson agreed to pay KRB Builders, Inc., $9000; KRB Builders, Inc., agreed to accept $9,000 in full settlement of its claim; and KRB Builders, Inc., agreed to discharge the mechanic's lien. Exhibit 11-10 is an example of a release of the mechanic's lien.

Exhibit 11-9. MECHANIC'S LIEN STATEMENT OF CLAIM

STATE OF OKLAHOMA   )
)
COUNTY OF OKLAHOMA   )

Know all men by these presents: That I, KRB Builders, Inc., have a claim against Thomas Richardson for the sum of Ten Thousand Six Hundred Eighty-Three Dollars and Seventy-Three Cents ($10,683.73) due to me, and that the claim is made for and on account of repairs and that such work was performed and materials supplied by me on or between October 20, 20_____, and October 30, 20_____, according to an itemized statement thereof, hereto attached marked "Exhibit A" and made part of this statement; that such work, labor, and materials were done in pursuance of a contract with Thomas Richardson and was performed upon the building and premises owned by Thomas Richardson and described as follows to wit: removing roof shingles, repairing damaged wood on the roof and around the chimney, installing porch steps, and leveling a corner of the foundation in said County and State; that the sum is just due and unpaid, and I have claimed a lien upon said building and upon the said premises on which the same is situated, to the amount of $10.683.73 as above set forth, according to the laws of the State of Oklahoma.

      Dated this _____ day of _____, 20_____.

                                                      _____
                                                      James Webber, President
                                                      KRB Builders, Inc.

     STATE OF OKLAHOMA   )
)
     COUNTY OF OKLAHOMA   )

James Webber, of lawful age, being first duly sworn, upon oath, says: That he is the claimant mentioned in the foregoing Statement of Mechanic's Lien; that he had read said statement and knows the contents thereof; that the name of the owner, name of the contractor, the name of the claimant, the description of the property upon which the lien is claimed, and the items of the account as therein set forth, are just, true, and correct.

Subscribed and sworn to before me this _____ day of _____, 20_____

                                                        _____
                                                          Notary Public

My commission expires: _____

Source: http://countyclerk.oklahomacounty.org/files/rod_ucc/mechanics_materialmans_lien.pdf.

Exhibit 11-10. RELEASE OF MECHANIC'S LIEN

NO. _____

THIS IS TO CERTIFY that the indebtedness secured by the Mechanic's Lien filed on the _____ day of _____, 20_____ in Book _____ Page _____ against Thomas Richardson covering the following described property to wit: a single family residence located at 222 Old Jackson Road, Edmond, Oklahoma in the County of Oklahoma, State of Oklahoma, has been paid and said lien is hereby released and discharged of record and the county clerk is hereby authorized and directed to enter the satisfaction of said Lien on the Lien Journal.

                                        _____
                                        James   Webber,
                                        President
                                        KRB Builders, Inc.

State of Oklahoma

County of Oklahoma

Before me, a Notary Public, in and for said County and State.

On this _____ day of _____, 20_____ personally appeared James Webber to me known to be the identical person who executed the within and foregoing instrument and acknowledged to me that he executed as his free and voluntary act and deed for the use and purposes therein set forth. Given under my hand and seal the day and year last above written.

My commission expires: _____

Commission Number: _____   _____
                                            Notary Public

Source: http://countyclerk.oklahomacounty.org/files/rod_ucc/release_of_mechanics_lien.pdf.

Conclusion

This chapter discusses some of the tasks assigned to paralegals in dispute resolution. One cannot overstate the importance of precision when researching, writing letters, and drafting documents. One careless error can not only hurt the firm's client but may also end a paralegal's employment.

Key Terms and Concepts

Exhibit

Legal memorandum

Lien

Mechanic's lien

Motion

Paralegal

Release

Settlement

Settlement agreement

Subpoena

Practice Test Questions

True/False

_____ 1. A legal memorandum and a memorandum of law are two terms with the same meaning.

_____ 2. Selecting a third-party neutral is important because in some ADR processes the outcome is binding, even if not agreed to by the parties.

_____ 3. A subpoena is a written court document requesting that a person appear in court.

_____ 4. A lien is an encumbrance on a person's property to secure the payment of a debt.

_____ 5. Paralegals frequently educate the client about the procedure of the selected dispute resolution method.

Multiple Choice

_____ 1. A memorandum of law is
   a. sometimes called a legal memorandum.
   b. a written document that explains the facts of a case, statutes, and/or case law.
   c. a written document that explains to a client the likelihood of success of his or her dispute.
   d. filed with the court.

_____ 2. The more difficult task when researching a third-party neutral is
   a. locating his or her resume.
   b. determining his or her field of expertise.
   c. finding out his or her fee.
   d. discovering whether the neutral tends to favor one side of a dispute.

_____ 3. Lay witnesses can testify to all of the following *except*
   a. specialized knowledge.
   b. what they saw.
   c. what they heard.
   d. what they smelled.

_____ 4. Because a settlement agreement is a contract, it must include the following:
   a. offer, acceptance, and intent to be bound.
   b. offer, acceptance, and consideration.
   c. offer, acceptance, consideration, and intent to be bound.

        d. offer, consideration, and intent to be bound.

____ 5. All of the following are examples of liens *except* a

        a. tax lien.

        b. promise lien.

        c. mortgage lien.

        d. mechanic's lien.

Short Answer

Prepare a list of paralegal tasks and indicate those that can be billed as paralegal fees.

Application Exercise

In this exercise, you will perform a number of paralegal tasks. To begin, read the facts below.

FACTS

Mark and Lisa Merrill live in a rural residential area with their two children, Jack (eight years old) and Ben (five years old) and their one-year-old pot-bellied pig Mabel. Jeff and Emma Quinn live in the house next door. The Merrills' home is situated on a four-acre lot.

Mabel, like a lot of pot-bellied pigs, is very intelligent. She can open doors and learn tricks like sit, circle, wave, and bow. Mabel lives in the house but spends time outside in an enclosed gated pen, which includes a structure similar to a dog house where she can go. Occasionally, one of the children forgets to close the gate, and Mabel escapes. Mark and Lisa have also seen Mabel open the gate and walk out.

There have been three incidents when one of the Merrill children left the gate open, allowing Mabel to escape and wander over to the Quinns', where she damaged their property. On April 20, 20____, Emma saw Mabel dig ruts in their lawn. On June 14, 20____, Emma watched Mabel dig up her vegetable garden. And on August 12, 20____, Mabel escaped and destroyed the prize tomatoes Emma planned to enter in the fall county fair. Jeff called Mark and complained. He also expressed his concern for their prize-winning rose bushes growing in a corner of his yard.

On August 20, 20____, Emma was working in her garden when Mabel again got loose and began to uproot the rose bushes. Emma got very upset and chased her with a broom. This startled Mabel, and she bit Emma on the hand. Mark heard the commotion and retrieved Mabel. Jeff drove Emma to the hospital, where she had four stitches to close the wound. The cost for this was $1025. On August 24, 20____, Emma's hand got badly infected, and she had to spend seven days in the hospital for treatment of blood poisoning. The bill for the hospital stay was $11,575. Because Emma had catastrophic health insurance with a $5000 deductible, she had to pay $6575 out of pocket. The total amount of the medical bills was $12,600. Emma also missed two weeks of work.

Jeff took pictures of Emma's hand before and after the stitches and on the fourth and fifth day after the bite. He also photographed the rose bushes before and after they were dug up, Mabel's outdoor pen, and Mabel.

Emma wanted the Merrills to pay her medical bills, her lost wages, and $500, the value of the two rose bushes. The Merrills refused. Emma then hired an attorney who filed a lawsuit in district court. The court rules require litigants to participate in an ADR method before certifying the case for trial. Both parties have agreed to binding arbitration. Each party agreed to select one arbitrator. The two arbitrators would then select one arbitrator who will hear the case.

Your supervising attorney represents Emma and has assigned you the following tasks:

1. Prepare a memorandum of facts.
2. Draft a letter to Emma explaining binding arbitration and what will happen at the hearing.
3. Research arbitrators using those listed on the JAMS website (http://www.jamsadr.com). Write a memo to your supervising attorney, Matthew Gilman, with three recommendations. Include your reasoning for each selection and attach each arbitrator's resume.
4. Determine the exhibits to introduce at the hearing and prepare an exhibit list.

Additional information needed for the assignment:

Supervising attorney:
Matthew Gilman, Esq.
Gilman, Cook & Moore, LLC
375 North Main Street
Ann Arbor, MI 48104
(555) 555-5555

Address for the Merrills:
248 Northwood Road
Ypsilanti, MI 48197
(555) 555-5555

Practice Exercises

1. Research your jurisdiction and determine whether it has any form requirements for the items listed below. Provide an explanation for each, and if examples are provided, download and print them.
   a. Motions
   b. Subpoenas
   c. Mechanic's liens
   d. Memorandum of law (a brief)
   e. Exhibits
2. Find out which ADR processes are available through the courts in your state.
3. Do the courts in your jurisdiction provide a list of neutrals? For which ADR methods?
4. Prepare a list of paralegal tasks and indicate which can be billed as paralegal fees.

Endnotes

1. Richard L. Marcus & Edward F. Sherman, *Complex Litigation: Cases and Materials on Advanced Civil Procedure* 545 (2d ed., West 1992).

2. Katherine A. Currier & Thomas E. Eimermann, *Introduction to Paralegal Studies: A Critical Thinking Approach* 14 (4th ed., Aspen 2010).

3. Adopted by the ABA House of Delegates, August 1997. In July 2001, the National Association of Legal Assistants (NALA) membership approved a resolution to adopt the ABA definition. http://www.nala.org/terms.aspx (last viewed Apr. 6, 2017).

4. 187 Cal. App. 4th 215, 222 (2010).

5. *Id.* at 231.

6. *Id.* at 232.

7. *Black's Law Dictionary* 1168 (Bryan A. Garner ed., 10th ed. 2014).

8. *Id.* at 1171.

9. Stewart Edelstein, *The Best Strategies for Choosing Arbitrators*, Conn. L. Trib., Dec. 16, 2004, http://www.ctlawtribune.com/id=1202681186513/The-Best-Strategies-for-Choosing-Arbitrators.

10. *Id.*

11. Equity denotes "a system for insuring justice in circumstances where the remedies customarily available under conventional law are inadequate; a system of jurisprudence less formal and more flexible than the common law, available in particular types of cases to better ensure a fair result." *Ballentine's Legal Dictionary and Thesaurus* 218 (1995).

12. Fed. R. Evid 702.

13. Fed. R. Civ. P. 26(a)(3).

14. Fed. R. Civ. P. 26(a)(3)(B).

15. *Ballentine's Legal Dictionary and Thesaurus* 379 (1995).

16. Lake Ozark Const. Indus., Inc. v. Osage Land Co., L.L.C., 168 S.W.3d 471 (Mo. App. 2005).

17. Mechanic's liens are a creature of statute and may vary from state to state. Failure to follow the requirements may render the lien invalid to the detriment of your client. Therefore, it behooves paralegals to pay close attention and be sure to comply with each condition.

18. "Perfect" means "to take all legal steps needed to complete, secure, or records (a claim, right, or interest); to provide necessary public notice in final conformity with the law." *Black's Law Dictionary* 1318 (Bryan A. Garner ed., 10th ed. 2014). "Perfection" means "validation of a security interest as against other creditors, usually by filing a statement with some public office or by taking possession of the collateral." *Id.*

Uniform Mediation Act
[Last Revised or Amended in 2003.]

SECTION 1. TITLE.   This [Act] may be cited as the Uniform Mediation Act.

SECTION 2. DEFINITIONS.   In this [Act]:

(1) "Mediation" means a process in which a mediator facilitates communication and negotiation between parties to assist them in reaching a voluntary agreement regarding their dispute.

(2) "Mediation communication" means a statement, whether oral or in a record or verbal or nonverbal, that occurs during a mediation or is made for purposes of considering, conducting, participating in, initiating, continuing, or reconvening a mediation or retaining a mediator.

(3) "Mediator" means an individual who conducts a mediation.

(4) "Nonparty participant" means a person, other than a party or mediator, that participates in a mediation.

(5) "Mediation party" means a person that participates in a mediation and whose agreement is necessary to resolve the dispute.

(6) "Person" means an individual, corporation, business trust, estate, trust, partnership, limited liability company, association, joint venture, government; governmental subdivision, agency, or instrumentality; public corporation, or any other legal or commercial entity.

(7) "Proceeding" means:

   (A) a judicial, administrative, arbitral, or other adjudicative process, including related pre-hearing and post-hearing motions, conferences, and discovery; or

   (B) a legislative hearing or similar process.

(8) "Record" means information that is inscribed on a tangible medium or that is stored in an electronic or other medium and is retrievable in perceivable form.

(9) "Sign" means:

   (A) to execute or adopt a tangible symbol with the present intent to authenticate a record; or

   (B) to attach or logically associate an electronic symbol, sound, or process to or with a record with the present intent to authenticate a record.

SECTION 3. SCOPE.

(a) Except as otherwise provided in subsection (b) or (c), this [Act] applies to a mediation in which:

    (1) the mediation parties are required to mediate by statute or court or administrative agency rule or referred to mediation by a court, administrative agency, or arbitrator;

    (2) the mediation parties and the mediator agree to mediate in a record that demonstrates an expectation that mediation communications will be privileged against disclosure; or

    (3) the mediation parties use as a mediator an individual who holds himself or herself out as a mediator or the mediation is provided by a person that holds itself out as providing mediation.

(b) The [Act] does not apply to a mediation:

    (1) relating to the establishment, negotiation, administration, or termination of a collective bargaining relationship;

    (2) relating to a dispute that is pending under or is part of the processes established by a collective bargaining agreement, except that the [Act] applies to a mediation arising out of a dispute that has been filed with an administrative agency or court;

    (3) conducted by a judge who might make a ruling on the case; or

    (4) conducted under the auspices of:

        (A) a primary or secondary school if all the parties are students or

        (B) a correctional institution for youths if all the parties are residents of that institution.

        (C) If the parties agree in advance in a signed record, or a record of proceeding reflects agreement by the parties, that all or part of a mediation is not privileged, the privileges under Sections 4 through 6 do not apply to the mediation or part agreed upon. However, Sections 4 through 6 apply to a mediation communication made by a person that has not received actual notice of the agreement before the communication is made.

SECTION 4. PRIVILEGE AGAINST DISCLOSURE; ADMISSIBILITY; DISCOVERY.

(a) Except as otherwise provided in Section 6, a mediation communication is privileged as provided in subsection (b) and is not subject to discovery or admissible in evidence in a proceeding unless waived or precluded as provided by Section 5.

(b) In a proceeding, the following privileges apply:

    (1) A mediation party may refuse to disclose, and may prevent any other person from disclosing, a mediation communication.

    (2) A mediator may refuse to disclose a mediation communication, and may prevent any other person from disclosing a mediation communication of the mediator.

(3) A nonparty participant may refuse to disclose, and may prevent any other person from disclosing, a mediation communication of the nonparty participant.

(c) Evidence or information that is otherwise admissible or subject to discovery does not become inadmissible or protected from discovery solely by reason of its disclosure or use in a mediation.

SECTION 5. WAIVER AND PRECLUSION OF PRIVILEGE.

(a) A privilege under Section 4 may be waived in a record or orally during a proceeding if it is expressly waived by all parties to the mediation and:

(1) in the case of the privilege of a mediator, it is expressly waived by the mediator; and

(2) in the case of the privilege of a nonparty participant, it is expressly waived by the nonparty participant.

(b) A person that discloses or makes a representation about a mediation communication which prejudices another person in a proceeding is precluded from asserting a privilege under Section 4, but only to the extent necessary for the person prejudiced to respond to the representation or disclosure.

(c) A person that intentionally uses a mediation to plan, attempt to commit or commit a crime, or to conceal an ongoing crime or ongoing criminal activity is precluded from asserting a privilege under Section 4.

SECTION 6. EXCEPTIONS TO PRIVILEGE.

(a) There is no privilege under Section 4 for a mediation communication that is:

(1) in an agreement evidenced by a record signed by all parties to the agreement;

(2) available to the public under [insert statutory reference to open records act] or made during a session of a mediation which is open, or is required by law to be open, to the public;

(3) a threat or statement of a plan to inflict bodily injury or commit a crime of violence;

(4) intentionally used to plan a crime, attempt to commit or commit a crime, or to conceal an ongoing crime or ongoing criminal activity;

(5) sought or offered to prove or disprove a claim or complaint of professional misconduct or malpractice filed against a mediator;

(6) except as otherwise provided in subsection (c), sought or offered to prove or disprove a claim or complaint of professional misconduct or malpractice filed against a mediation party, nonparty participant, or representative of a party based on conduct occurring during a mediation; or

(7) sought or offered to prove or disprove abuse, neglect, abandonment, or exploitation in a proceeding in which a child or adult protective services agency is a party, unless the
[Alternative A: [State to insert, for example, child or adult protection] case is referred by a court to mediation and a public agency participates].

[Alternative B: public agency participates in the [State to insert, for example, child or adult protection] mediation].

(b) There is no privilege under Section 4 if a court, administrative agency, or arbitrator finds, after a hearing in camera, that the party seeking discovery or the proponent of the evidence has shown that the evidence is not otherwise available, that there is a need for the evidence that substantially outweighs the interest in protecting confidentiality, and that the mediation communication is sought or offered in:

(1) a court proceeding involving a felony [or misdemeanor]; or

(2) except as otherwise provided in subsection (c), a proceeding to prove a claim to rescind or reform or a defense to avoid liability on a contract arising out of the mediation.

(c) A mediator may not be compelled to provide evidence of a mediation communication referred to in subsection (a)(6) or (b)(2).

(d) If a mediation communication is not privileged under subsection (a) or (b), only the portion of the communication necessary for the application of the exception from nondisclosure may be admitted. Admission of evidence under subsection (a) or (b) does not render the evidence, or any other mediation communication, discoverable or admissible for any other purpose.

SECTION 7. PROHIBITED MEDIATOR REPORTS.

(a) Except as required in subsection (b), a mediator may not make a report, assessment, evaluation, recommendation, finding, or other communication regarding a mediation to a court, administrative agency, or other authority that may make a ruling on the dispute that is the subject of the mediation.

(b) A mediator may disclose:

(1) whether the mediation occurred or has terminated, whether a settlement was reached, and attendance;

(2) a mediation communication as permitted under Section 6; or

(3) a mediation communication evidencing abuse, neglect, abandonment, or exploitation of an individual to a public agency responsible for protecting individuals against such mistreatment.

(c) A communication made in violation of subsection (a) may not be considered by a court, administrative agency, or arbitrator.

SECTION 8. CONFIDENTIALITY.   Unless subject to the [insert statutory references to open meetings act and open records act], mediation communications are confidential to the extent agreed by the parties or provided by other law or rule of this State.

SECTION 9. MEDIATOR'S DISCLOSURE OF CONFLICTS OF INTEREST; BACKGROUND.

(a) Before accepting a mediation, an individual who is requested to serve as a mediator shall:

(1) make an inquiry that is reasonable under the circumstances to determine whether there are any known facts that a reasonable individual would consider likely to affect the impartiality of the mediator, including a financial or personal interest in the outcome of the mediation and an existing or past relationship with a mediation party or foreseeable participant in the mediation; and

(2) disclose any such known fact to the mediation parties as soon as is practical before accepting a mediation.

(b) If a mediator learns any fact described in subsection (a)(1) after accepting a mediation, the mediator shall disclose it as soon as is practicable.

(c) At the request of a mediation party, an individual who is requested to serve as a mediator shall disclose the mediator's qualifications to mediate a dispute.

(d) A person that violates subsection [(a) or (b)] [(a), (b), or (g)] is precluded by the violation from asserting a privilege under Section 4.

(e) Subsections (a), (b), [and] (c), [and] [(g)] do not apply to an individual acting as a judge.

(f) This [Act] does not require that a mediator have a special qualification by background or profession.

[(g) A mediator must be impartial, unless after disclosure of the facts required in subsections (a) and (b) to be disclosed, the parties agree otherwise.]

SECTION 10. PARTICIPATION IN MEDIATION. An attorney or other individual designated by a party may accompany the party to and participate in a mediation. A waiver of participation given before the mediation may be rescinded.

SECTION 11. INTERNATIONAL COMMERCIAL MEDIATION.

(a) In this section, "Model Law" means the Model Law on International Commercial Conciliation adopted by the United Nations Commission on International Trade Law on 28 June 2002 and recommended by the United Nations General Assembly in a resolution (A/RES/57/18) dated 19 November 2002, and "international commercial mediation" means an international commercial conciliation as defined in Article 1 of the Model Law.

(b) Except as otherwise provided in subsections (c) and (d), if a mediation is an international commercial mediation, the mediation is governed by the Model Law.

(c) Unless the parties agree in accordance with Section 3(c) of this [Act] that all or part of an international commercial mediation is not privileged, Sections 4, 5, and 6 and any applicable definitions in Section 2 of this [Act] also apply to the mediation and nothing in Article 10 of the Model Law derogates from Sections 4, 5, and 6.

(d) If the parties to an international commercial mediation agree under Article 1, subsection (7), of the Model Law that the Model Law does not apply, this [Act] applies.

SECTION 13. UNIFORMITY OF APPLICATION AND CONSTRUCTION.   In applying and construing this [Act], consideration should be given to the need to promote uniformity of the law with respect to its subject matter among States that enact it.

SECTION 14. SEVERABILITY CLAUSE.   If any provision of this [Act] or its application to any person or circumstance is held invalid, the invalidity does not affect other provisions or applications of this [Act] which can be given effect without the invalid provision or application, and to this end the provisions of this [Act] are severable.

SECTION 15. EFFECTIVE DATE.   This [Act] takes effect................

SECTION 16. REPEALS.   The following acts and parts of acts are hereby repealed:

(1)

(2)

(3)

SECTION 17. APPLICATION TO EXISTING AGREEMENTS OR REFERRALS.

(a) This [Act] governs a mediation pursuant to a referral or an agreement to mediate made on or after [the effective date of this [Act]].

(b) On or after [a delayed date], this [Act] governs an agreement to mediate whenever made.

Sample Mediation Agreement

AGREEMENT TO MEDIATE

_____ and _____ agree to participate in
      Party   Party

mediation for the purpose of resolving issues relating to: _____

_____

_____ .

The mediation will be conducted by _____ .
                                   Mediator

1. The parties agree to make a good faith attempt to settle their dispute through mediation.
2. The parties agree to compensate the mediator at the rate of _____ per hour. Each party is responsible for paying one-half of the mediator's fee.
3. The parties understand that the mediator is an impartial third party and does not represent either of the parties. The parties also understand that the mediator must work on behalf of each party equally and cannot give legal advice to either party.
4. The mediator may meet separately with a party for private discussions. Unless that party gives consent, the mediator will not disclose any information learned in the private session.
5. To assist the mediator, each party shall provide an information statement to the mediator one week before the first mediation session.
6. The parties and the mediator understand that the mediation is confidential. All mediation discussions and written and oral communications will not be disclosed to any third party either by the mediator or the parties.
7. Any party, including the mediator, may withdraw from or terminate the mediation at any time for any reason.

The undersigned acknowledge that they have read and understand this agreement.

Dated this ____ day of _____ , 20 ____ .

Signature: _____

Signature: _____

Mediator: _____

Proposed Arbitration Fairness Act of 2013

SEC. 2. FINDINGS.   The Congress finds the following:

(1) The Federal Arbitration Act (now enacted as chapter 1 of title 9 of the United States Code) was intended to apply to disputes between commercial entities of generally similar sophistication and bargaining power.

(2) A series of decisions by the Supreme Court of the United States have interpreted the Act so that it now extends to consumer disputes and employment disputes, contrary to the intent of Congress.

(3) Most consumers and employees have little or no meaningful choice whether to submit their claims to arbitration. Often, consumers and employees are not even aware that they have given up their rights.

(4) Mandatory arbitration undermines the development of public law because there is inadequate transparency and inadequate judicial review of arbitrators' decisions.

(5) Arbitration can be an acceptable alternative when consent to the arbitration is truly voluntary, and occurs after the dispute arises.

Source: S. 878, 113th Cong. (2013), and H.R. 1844, 113th Cong. (2013). These are identical bills.

Answers to Practice Test Questions

CHAPTER ONE

True/False
1. True
2. True
3. True
4. True
5. False

Multiple Choice
1. b
2. d
3. a
4. d
5. c

CHAPTER TWO

True/False
1. True
2. True
3. True
4. False
5. True

Multiple Choice
1. b
2. d
3. c
4. a
5. b

CHAPTER THREE

True/False
1. True
2. True
3. True
4. False
5. True

Multiple Choice
1. b
2. c
3. b
4. d
5. a

CHAPTER FOUR

True/False
1. True
2. True
3. True
4. True
5. False

Multiple Choice
1. d
2. b
3. b
4. a
5. d

CHAPTER FIVE

True/False
1. True
2. True
3. False
4. False
5. True

Multiple Choice
1. d
2. c
3. a
4. d
5. b

CHAPTER SIX

True/False
1. True
2. False
3. True
4. True
5. True

Multiple Choice
1. d
2. d
3. a
4. b
5. c

CHAPTER SEVEN

True/False
1. True
2. True
3. True
4. True
5. True

Multiple Choice
1. d
2. b
3. b
4. a
5. c

CHAPTER EIGHT

True/False
1. True
2. True
3. True
4. False
5. True

Multiple Choice
1. d
2. a
3. a
4. c
5. b

CHAPTER NINE

True/False
1. True
2. True
3. False
4. True
5. True

Multiple Choice
1. a
2. d
3. c
4. b
5. b

CHAPTER TEN

True/False
1. True
2. False
3. True
4. True
5. False

Multiple Choice
1. b
2. a
3. c
4. d
5. d

CHAPTER ELEVEN

True/False
1. False
2. True
3. False
4. True
5. True

Multiple Choice
1. b
2. d
3. a
4. c
5. b

GLOSSARY

Alienation Can cause a person to be unfriendly, mistrustful, and even hateful (Ch. 1)

Adhesive arbitration agreements Agreement, usually forced on one of the parties, requiring mandatory arbitration for any dispute that arises between the parties (Ch. 6)

Answer Document where the defendant admits or denies the allegations in a complaint and asserts any defenses (Ch. 2)

Alternative dispute resolution (ADR) Any means of settling legal disputes that do not involve litigation; traditionally refers to negotiation, mediation, and arbitration (Intro.)

Appeal The process by which a party requests a higher court to review a lower court's decision (Ch. 5)

Arbitrability The determination of whether there was an agreement to arbitrate (Ch. 6)

Arbitral clause Clause in contract that binds the parties to arbitrate future disputes (Ch. 6)

Arbitration A dispute resolution process in which the parties present evidence and argument, to one or more third-party neutrals, who then issue a judgment, or award (Ch. 5)

Arbitrator Neutral party in an arbitration who decides the dispute (Ch. 5)

Artificial intelligence Devices that replace humans who perform complex tasks (Ch. 8)

Assisted eNegotiation Computer software is used to set up the communication between the parties, facilitate with developing agendas, identify possible solutions, and help with writing agreements (Ch. 8)

Asynchronous communication Communication when parties are not communicating (email, text messaging) at the same time (Ch. 8)

Automated eNegotiation See Blind-bidding systems (Ch. 8)

Award The remedy or relief issued after the arbitrator's decision (Ch. 5, Ch. 6)

Blind-bidding systems Primarily designed to resolve monetary disputes; use an automated algorithm to evaluate bids, or dollar settlement offers submitted by the disputants (Ch. 8)

Caucuses Private meetings with one party and the mediator that take place during mediation (Ch. 4)

Coercive power Ability to force agreement, but can lead to alienation (Ch. 1)

Commercial arbitration Involves a dispute between two businesses (Ch. 6)

Compensatory damages Intended to compensate the plaintiff for the loss suffered by the wrongdoing of the defendant (Ch. 2)

Competitive negotiators Negotiators who employ various tactics and ploys to pressure or mislead the other party into accepting their demands (Ch. 3)

Complaint Initiates a lawsuit; summary of the plaintiff's claims and facts supporting the lawsuit and the relief plaintiff is seeking (Ch. 2)

Conferencing A meeting between the victim, offender, and a trained facilitator with participation of family members and supporters of the victim and offender (Ch. 9)

Conflict Competition between people or groups who have incompatible interests (values, goals and needs) (Ch. 1)

Constructive conflict Can lead to invention, creativity, and positive change (Ch.1)

Consumer arbitration Arbitration between a consumer and a business (Ch. 6)

Contextual bias Refers to the relationship between the arbitrator and one of the parties that may disqualify the arbitrator from hearing the case (Ch. 5)

Contract of adhesion A standardized contract, which, imposed and drafted by the party of superior bargaining strength, gives the other party only the opportunity to agree or reject the contract (Ch. 6)

Cooperative negotiators Negotiators who approach the dispute as an opportunity to solve a problem or problems (Ch. 3)

Court-annexed nonbinding arbitration Arbitration 1) that is mandatory not voluntary; 2) that is forced upon the parties by statute or court rule; 3) where a third party, usually a judge, selects the arbitrators; and 4) where the award is non-binding. Occurs after court proceedings have begun (Ch. 10)

Cultural norms Behavioral standards of a society as a whole, followed when interacting with one another (Ch. 1)

Defendant The party alleged to have caused a harm in a civil lawsuit (Ch. 2)

Discovery Process used before trial to provide the parties with facts and information known only to the opponent; it helps each party to better prepare for trial (Ch. 2, Ch. 5)

Distributive negotiation Focuses on what the negotiator wants for her client (Note: Negotiation may not be over resources) (Ch. 3)

Due process As described in the Fifth and Fourteenth Amendments to the United States Constitution, the principle that an individual cannot be deprived of life, liberty, or property without appropriate legal procedures and safeguards (Ch. 2, Ch. 5)

eArbitration Arbitration involving the use of online tools (Ch. 8)

Early neutral evaluation (ENE) Nonbinding process intended to help litigants with case preparation and settlement opportunities by providing them with an objective evaluation of the probable outcome of the lawsuit (Ch. 10)

Ecological power Ability to manipulate or alter the environment to make another person behave or not behave in a certain way (Ch. 1)

eMediation Mediation where parties negotiate with the support of the mediator via email or on specially created Internet sites that provide virtual "rooms" in which the parties congregate electronically (Ch. 8)

Employment arbitration Involves job related disputes between non-union employees and employers (Ch. 6)

Empowerment Sufficient power to attain an objective, free from interference from other people or other things (Ch. 1)

eNegotiation Negotiation with the use of computers or other electronic communications; eNegotiation can be either assisted or automated (Ch. 8)

Equitable relief Awarded in situations where a plaintiff wants the defendant to do or to refrain from doing, a specified act (Ch. 2)

Evaluative mediation Mediation that centers on the legal rights of the disputants, such as the contract, the accounting principles involved, industry practice, or the applicable law; the mediator evaluates the dispute and suggests an appropriate resolution (Ch. 4)

Exchange power See Reward power (Ch. 1)

Executory arbitration agreement Agreement where the parties have agreed to arbitrate any dispute that may arise in the future (Ch. 5)

Exhibit Physical or documentary evidence presented during a hearing (Ch. 11)

Expert power Power based on the superior knowledge or skill one has over another (Ch. 1)

Facilitative mediation Mediation that centers on the needs of the parties; the focus is on communication and understanding between the parties (Ch. 4)

Fact finder In litigation, the judge or jury (Ch. 2)

Federal Arbitration Act (FAA) Provides a legal framework for managing arbitrations and applies to all maritime transactions and interstate or foreign commerce; does not apply to employment disputes (Ch. 6)

Finality The concept in arbitration that when the arbitrator issues an award, the dispute is over (Ch. 5)

Flamewars Individual conflicts occurring in text-based listservs and virtual worlds on the Internet in the early 1990s (Ch. 7)

Holography Uses a laser light to transport or beam a three-dimensional person to another location without the use of screens (Ch. 8)

Human needs Structured hierarchy beginning with physiological (air, food, water, shelter, sleep, sex), followed by safety, love, esteem, and self-actualization (Ch. 1)

Information exchange Takes place during discovery; the rules of civil procedure provide specific methods and procedures for this phase of a lawsuit (Ch. 2)

Interest-based mediation See Facilitative mediation (Ch. 4)

Interim relief When a court makes a ruling on a temporary basis until a decision on the case is made (Ch. 2)

Internet service providers (ISPs) Private companies that provide Internet access for a fee to anyone with a computer (Ch. 7)

Labor arbitration Involves job related disputes between unions and employers (Ch. 6)

Legal memorandum A written document that provides information about a case, issue, or other legal matter (Ch. 11)

Lien A claim on personal property, or an encumbrance on real property, for the payment of a debt (Ch. 11)

Listserv In the 1990s, this text-based forum was where most discussions took place (Ch. 7)

Maslow's Hierarchy of Needs Seeks to explain human development by positing that people seek to satisfy certain needs which are structured hierarchically (Ch. 1)

Mechanic's lien Created by statute, it permits a claim to be attached to a particular property to secure payment for labor or material used to improve the property (Ch. 11)

Med-arb Combination of mediation and arbitration that begins with mediation; if mediation fails, the neutral acts as the arbitrator and issues a binding decision (Ch. 4)

Mediation Negotiation that involves the help of a neutral third party; the parties decide the outcome but have the benefit of guidance by a person knowledgeable about the mediation process and often the subject matter of the dispute (Intro., Ch. 4, Ch. 10)

Mini-trial A private proceeding used to highlight the strengths and weaknesses of each party's position. Attorneys are allotted a finite time within which to present their case. The attorneys can do this by offering a brief summary or by using witnesses, documents, and experts (Ch. 10)

Motion A written or oral request of a court seeking a specified ruling or order (Ch. 11)

Negotiation A process in which two or more parties seek to move forward in their relationship (Intro., Ch. 3)

Normative power Ability to convince others that a proposal is the correct thing to do and that they should act accordingly (Ch. 1)

Online dispute resolution (ODR) An expansion of alternative dispute resolution which adds the use of technology to facilitate the resolution of disputes between parties (Ch. 7)

Ouster of jurisdiction English law concept where courts found arbitration against public policy because it ousted the courts of jurisdiction over a dispute (Ch. 5)

Personal bias The arbitrator's class-based prejudices; includes race and ethnicity (Ch. 5)

Plaintiff The party who initiates the lawsuit by asserting that the defendant caused a harm (Ch. 2)

Power over Refers to the power of a person over another person or a group of people over another group of people (Ch. 1)

Power with Power developed jointly by combining the knowledge and experience of each individual (Ch. 1)

Powerlessness The inability of a person to affect the outcome of a situation (Ch. 1)

Precedent Requires judges to follow past decisions in similar cases (Ch. 2, Ch. 5)

Predispute agreement See Arbitral clause (Ch. 6)

Pretrial conference See Settlement conference (Ch. 10)

Private adjudication Private process not open to the public (Ch. 5)

Problem-solving or interest-based negotiation Negotiation where the goal is to reach a mutually satisfactory agreement. The negotiators work together to identify the interests and needs of each side in an effort to reach a fair settlement. Also referred to integrative, collaborative or principled negotiation (Ch. 3)

Procedural unconscionability When a party has no meaningful choice at the time of entering the contract because the terms of the contract are presented on a "take-it-or-leave-it" basis (Ch. 6)

Punitive damages Awarded to punish the defendant for conduct considered malicious, grossly reckless, or fraudulent (Ch. 2)

Referent power Power to influence others' desire to be like some person or group (Ch. 1)

Reintegrative shaming In restorative conferencing this means expressing disapproval of the offender's behavior while also conveying respect for the offender and helping him or her reintegrate back into the community (Ch. 9)

Release Terminate any legal liability between the releasor and the releasee(s) (Ch. 11)

Remedies In civil litigation, there are two types of remedies: money damages or equitable relief (Ch. 2)

Restorative justice A system of justice that focuses on the harm to the victim rather than the actions of the offender (Ch. 9)

Restorative methods Processes wherein victims and offenders, and in some cases other interested parties, meet with a facilitator to discuss the wrongdoing and develop a plan for resolving the conflict (Ch. 9)

Revised Uniform Arbitration Act (RUAA) Functions much like the FAA. Governs enforcement of arbitration awards, the appointment of arbitrators, the procedure for arbitration hearings, methods for compelling testimony and evidence at the hearing, and the reviewability of awards. It has been adopted, in whole or part, by well over half the states (Ch. 6)

Reward power Offer of something of value such as money, property, recognition, etc. as a reward or exchange for what is wanted (Ch. 1)

Rights-based mediation See Evaluative mediation (Ch. 4)

Securities arbitration Involves investor/broker disputes (Ch. 6)

Settlement Ends a lawsuit by mutual agreement (Ch. 11)

Settlement agreement A written document, sometimes lengthy, detailing what the parties agreed to (Ch. 11)

Settlement conference Meeting between the lawyers and judges to search for settlement; judges are permitted to make attendance mandatory by representatives with settlement authority (Ch. 10)

Specific performance When a court orders a person to do a specified act (Ch. 2)

Stigmatizing shame Centers on the person and can make the offender feel humiliated and disaffected (Ch. 9)

Subject matter Determines which court hears a particular dispute (Ch. 2)

Subpoena A written court order compelling a person to appear in court, at a deposition, or other legal proceeding to testify (Ch. 11)

Submission agreement An agreement to arbitrate a present dispute (Ch. 6)

Substantive unconscionability Substantive unconscionability is found when an agreement is unfair or so one-sided that no reasonable person would think otherwise (Ch. 6)

Summary jury trial Court-connected alternative using jurors to hear and decide the dispute (Ch. 10)

Summons A document delivered to the defendant informing him or her that he or she is being sued and in what court (Ch. 2)

Synchronous communication "Real-time" communication, meaning that after one party finishes talking, the other party responds (Ch. 8)

Transformative mediation Mediation that focuses on empowering each party to make decisions and to gain the ability to recognize each other's perspectives (Ch. 4)

Trial de novo A new trial on the case (Ch. 10)

Unconscionability The contract defense courts rely on when an agreement is so one-sided that it violates the contractual obligation of good faith (Ch. 6)

Victim-offender dialogue (VOD) Meeting between the victim, offender, and a trained facilitator to talk about the wrong and develop an agreement to make things right (Ch. 9)

Virtual world A computer-simulated environment inhabited by users who interact through their on-screen avatars (Ch. 7)

INDEX

A

AAA (American Arbitration Association), 98, 118, 169, 185–186
ABA (American Bar Association), 98, 112, 246
Accommodation, 10
Adhesive agreements, 136–143
  sample language, 137
  supporters, 143
  unconscionability, 140–141
Age Discrimination in Employment Act (ADEA), 145
Aggressive avoidance, 12
Agreement (negotiation), 62
Agreement to mediate, sample, 285
Alienation, 13, 18–19
Alternative Dispute Resolution Act, 222
American Arbitration Association (AAA), 98, 118, 169, 185–186
American Bar Association (ABA), 98, 112, 246
Answers (litigation), 31
Appeals, 36–37, 115
Arbitrability, 136
Arbitral clauses, 135–136
Arbitration, 107–154
  adhesive agreements, 136–143. *See also* Adhesive agreements
  arbitral clauses, 135–136
  Arbitration Fairness Act of 2013 (proposed), 143, 287
  arbitrator selection, 150
  bias, 121–123
  commercial arbitration, 148–149
  consumer arbitration, 144, 146
  cost, 114, 121
  court-annexed, 232
  decision maker, 117
  demand, 150
  discovery, 120, 150–151
  due process, 119
  electronic, 185–188
  exchange of information, 150–151
  Federal Arbitration Act, 132–134
  finality, 115–116, 119–120
  flexibility, 117
  hearing, 151
  history, 108–112
  informality, 116
  judicial enforcement, 152–154
  labor and employment arbitration, 144–146
  litigation compared, 112–122
  nonbinding, 222, 231–235. *See also* Nonbinding arbitration
  overview, 107–108
  paralegal role, 114, 151
  precedential effect, 115
  prehearing conference, 150
  preliminary meeting, 150
  privacy, 115
  process, 149–152
  relationship preservation, 117–118
  Revised Uniform Arbitration Act, 134–135
  securities arbitration, 146–148
  similarity to litigation, 121
  speed, 114, 121
  types of, 143–149
  written record, 120–121
Arbitration Act of 1888, 81
Arbitration Fairness Act of 2013 (proposed), 143, 287
Arbitrators. *See also* Arbitration
  AAA online resolution, 186
  bias, 121–123
  defined, 107
  party choice of, 117, 150, 186
  researching, 253–263
Aristotle, 107
Artificial intelligence, 194–195
Assisted eNegotiation, 183
Association for Conflict Resolution, 98
Asynchronous communication, 182
Attorney preparation for negotiation, 58–59
Avoidance of conflict, 10, 12
Awards (arbitration), 107, 151
  AAA online resolution process, 186
  judicial enforcement, 152–154
  nonbinding arbitration, 233–234

B

Baruch-Bush, Robert, 92
Beliefs, 9
Better Business Bureau, 162
Bias of arbitrators, 121–123
Biblical arbitration, 108–109
Binding arbitration, 108. *See also*
Arbitration
Blind bidding systems, 183

C

Caucuses, mediation, 92
Center for Public Resources, 2
Child custody negotiation, 52
"Circle Keeper," 215
Circle method, 214–216
Civil Justice Reform Act of 1990, 222
Civil Rights Act of 1964, 81
Claims (litigation), 32
Client preparation (negotiation), 58
Coercive power, 13, 17, 18
Collaborative processes. *See* Restorative
justice
Collapse of negotiation, 63
Collective bargaining, 67
Commerce Department, 175
Commercial arbitration, 144, 148–149
Communication as source of conflict, 9
Community conferencing, 211–214
Community Court of Modria.com, 176
Community Relations Service, 81
Compensatory damages, 33
Competitive approach, 10
Competitive negotiators, 54–56
Complaints (litigation), 30
Compromise, 10
Conferences
prehearing, 150
pre-trial, 226
settlement, 225–227
Conferencing, group, 211–214
Conflict, 5–23
approaches, 10–11
avoidance, 10, 12
constructive conflict, 23
culture and, 19–21
definition, 7
factors affecting, 9–10
human needs, 7–9
overview, 5–7
paralegal role, 21–22
power, 12–19. *See also* Power
sources of, 9
Consideration, 63

Constructive conflict, 23
Consumer arbitration, 144, 146
Contextual bias, 122
Contracts of adhesion. *See* Adhesive
agreements
Convention on the Recognition and
Enforcement of Foreign Arbitral Awards
(New York Convention), 144, 149
Cooperative/collaborative approach, 10
Cooperative negotiators, 56–57
Cost of litigation, 38–39
arbitration compared, 114, 121
online dispute resolution, 188
restorative methods compared, 207
Coulson, Robert, 121
Court Alternative Dispute Resolution
Service (CADRES), 95
Court-annexed alternatives, 221–238
early neutral evaluation, 222, 228–231
history, 221–222
mediation, 223–224
mini-trials, 222, 237–238
nonbinding arbitration, 222, 231–235.
See also Nonbinding arbitration
overview, 222–223
paralegal role, 228
settlement conferences, 225–227
summary jury trials, 222, 235–237
Court-annexed arbitration, 232
Cox, Trey, 121
CPR Commission on the Future of
Arbitration, 117
Criminal cases
negotiation, 51–52
restorative justice, 201–208. *See also*
Restorative justice
Cultural norms, 19–21
Cybersettle, 173

D

Dabdoub, Alan, 121
Defendants, 30
Demand for trial de novo, 234–235
Denial, avoidance through, 12
Deutsch, Morton, 7
Discovery, 32–33, 35
AAA online resolution, 186
arbitration, 120, 150–151
Discrimination, 208
Distance zones, 21
Distributive/competitive stage of negotiation,
61–62
Divorce agreements, 68
Divorce negotiation, 52
Domestic relations negotiation, 52

Due process, 35–36, 119
Duty to disclose, 65

E

Early neutral evaluation, 222, 228–231
EBay, 169, 171–172
Ebner, Noam, 184–185
Ecological power, 17
Eglash, Albert, 204
Elmira Case, 201–203, 210
EMediation, 184–185
Employment arbitration, 143–146
Empowerment, 15–16
ENegotiation, 183
Equitable relief, 33
Erdman Act of 1898, 81
Erving, Julius, 122–123
Ethics
    mediators, 98–99, 289–290
    negotiation and, 68–70
Evaluative mediation, 80, 92–93
Exchange power, 17
Executory arbitration agreements, 111
Exhibits, 266–268
Expert power, 18

F

Facial expression, 20–21
Facilitative mediation, 80, 93–94
Fact finders, 33
FairOutcomes.com, 176
Family group conferencing, 211–214
Federal Arbitration Act, 112, 132–134.
    See also Arbitration
Federal Mediation and Conciliation
    Service, 81
Federal Trade Commission, 175
Finality, 115
Financial Industry Regulation Authority
    (FINRA), 144, 148
Flamewars, 165
Folding, avoidance through, 12
Folger, Joseph P., 92
Formalities (negotiation), 63
Fraud and misrepresentation, 64

G

Garvey, Stephen, 207
Gestures, 20–21
Gilmer v. Interstate/Johnson Lane Corp.,
    145
Government adjudication, 112
Greek arbitration, 109

Griswold, Erwin N., 41
Group conferencing, 211–214

H

Hall, Edward T., 21
Hand, Learned, 117
Hearing, arbitration, 151
    AAA online resolution, 186
Heraclitus, 5
Hierarchy of needs, 7–8
High-context cultures, 19–20
Holography, 194
Hopelessness, 12
Human needs, 7–9

I

Information/positioning stage of negotiation,
    60–61
Integrative/collaborative stage of
    negotiation, 62
Interest-based mediation, 80
Interest needs, 8
Interim relief, 37
International arbitration, 144, 149
International negotiation, 52
Internet bubble, 171
Internet Service Providers (ISPs), 163
Interpersonal space, 20–21

J

Juripax.com, 176
Juveniles and conferencing, 211–214

K

Karon, David R., 122
Katsh, Ethan, 161, 165, 169, 171, 195
Kelly, Russ, 201
Kent, Fred I., 148
King, Martin Luther, 29
Kitchener Experiment, 201–204

L

Labor arbitration, 143–146
Labor-management negotiation, 50–51
Labor Management Relations Act, 144
LambdaMOO (virtual online community),
    167–168
Lambros, Thomas, 235, 237
Larson, David Allen, 194–195
Leone, Giuseppe, 184
Liens, 272–274

Lincoln, Abraham, 29, 79
Listservs, 165
Litigation, 29–42
   advantages, 33–38
   appeals, 36–37
   arbitration compared, 112–122. *See also*
     Arbitration
   attorneys, need for, 41
   claims, 32
   costs of, 38–39
   disadvantages, 38–41
   discovery, 35
   due process, 35–36
   enforcement of, 34
   fact finder, 33, 41
   finality of, 33–34
   flexibility and, 40
   indirect communication and, 37
   information exchange, 32–33
   interim relief, 37
   justice and, 38
   location, 31
   openness of, 36
   outcomes, 33
   overview, 29–30
   pace of, 40
   paralegal role, 31
   participants, 30
   precedent and, 34–35
   predictability of, 34
   privacy and, 40
   relationships and, 40
   remedies, 33
   stages of, 30–31
Low-context cultures, 19–20

M

Maryland Family Mediation Project
   (Mediate-net), 170–171
Maslow's Hierarchy of Needs, 7–8
Mayer, Bernard, 12
Mechanic's liens, 272–274
Med-arb, 99–100
Mediate-net (Maryland Family Mediation
   Project), 170–171
Mediation, 79–100. *See also* Mediators
   abuse of process, 87
   advantages, 83–87
   agreements, 90, 285
   bargaining power, 87
   caucuses, 92
   communication and trust, 86–87
   cost, 83
   court-annexed, 223–224
   defined, 80–81

   disadvantages, 87–88
   electronic, 184–185
   empowerment of parties, 86
   ethics, 98–99
   evaluative, 92–93
   exploration of party relationship, 86
   facilitative, 93–94
   form for sample agreement, 285
   forms of, 92–95
   history, 81–83
   med-arb, 99–100
   non-precedential, 87
   opening statements, 89
   overview, 79–80
   paralegal role, 88
   precedent, 87
   privacy, 83–86
   procedural ease, 83
   process, 88–90
   remedies, 86
   settlement, 87–88
   speed, 83
   stages, 88–90
   transformative, 94–95
   Uniform Mediation Act, 279–284
Mediators. *See also* Mediation
   communication and, 91
   educating parties, 90
   ethics, 98–99
   generating agreement, 91
   issue identification, 89
   maintaining interest, 91
   managing emotions, 91
   organizing sessions, 91
   qualifications, 95
   researching, 253–263
   role, 90–91
   selection, 89
   skills, 95–98
Middle Ages arbitration, 109–110
Miller, Geoffrey P., 36
Mini-trials, 222, 237–238
Misrepresentation and fraud, 64
Modria.com, Community Court of, 176
Moore, Christopher W., 8
Moses, 108–109
Multidoor courthouse approach, 2, 82

N

National Association of Legal Assistants, 246
National Center for Automated Information
   Research, 168
National Conference of Commissioners on
   State Laws, 112, 134
National Labor Relations Act, 67, 81, 144

National Mediation Board, 81
National Science Foundation Acceptable
    Use Policy, 167–168
Negotiation, 47–70
    agreement stage, 62
    attorney preparation stage, 58–59
    child custody, 52
    civil disputes, 50
    client preparation stage, 58
    collapse of, 63
    competitive negotiators, 54–56
    consideration, 63
    cooperative negotiators, 56–57
    criminal cases, 51–52
    defined, 48–49
    distributive, 53
    distributive/competitive stage, 61–62
    divorce, 52
    domestic relations, 52
    duty to disclose in, 65
    electronic, 183
    ethics and, 68–70
    formalizing agreement, 63
    information/positioning stage, 60–61
    integrative/collaborative stage, 62
    international, 52
    labor-management, 50–51
    laws affecting, 63–68
    lawyer-client relationship, 52–53
    methods of, 53
    misrepresentation and fraud in, 64
    offer and acceptance, 63
    overview, 48
    paralegal role, 60
    policy favoring settlement, 63–64
    preliminary stage, 60
    preparation stage, 57–59
    problem solving, 53
    process, 57–63
    styles, 53–57
    subject-matter specific regulations, 67–68
    transactions, 50
    types of, 49–52
    writings, 63
Neighborhood Justice Centers, 2, 81
Newlands Act of 1913, 81
New York Arbitration Act, 112
New York Convention (Convention on the
    Recognition and Enforcement of
    Foreign Arbitral Awards), 149
Nonbinding arbitration, 222, 231–235
    award, 233–234
    demand for trial de novo, 234–235
    hearing, 233
    prehearing, 233
    referral, 233
Nonverbal communication, 20–21

Normative power, 18
Norms
    influence in creating conflict, 19–21
    reinforcement of, 206
Nuisances, 9

O

Offer and acceptance, 63
Online dispute resolution (ODR), 161–195
    advantages, 188–190
    artificial intelligence, 194–195
    blind bidding systems, 183
    communication, 189
    confidentiality, 192
    convenience, 188
    cost, 188
    Cybersettle, 173
    data storage, 189–190
    deception, 192–193
    defined, 163–164
    disadvantages, 190–194
    eArbitration, 185–188
    eBay, 169, 171–172
    eMediation, 184–185
    eNegotiation, 183
    enforcement, 194
    equalizing effect, 189
    evolution, 164–175
    first period, 165–168
    government role, 174–175
    holography, 194
    hostility level, 189
    jurisdictional issues, 189–190
    location, 189
    Maryland Family Mediation Project,
        170–171
    Online Ombuds Office, 169–170
    overview, 161–163
    paralegal role, 174, 185
    Smartsettle, 173–174, 183
    speed, 188
    SquareTrade, 172
    technology access and proficiency, 194
    trust, 193–194
    Virtual Magistrate Project, 168–169
Online Ombuds Office, 169–170
Ouster of jurisdiction, 111

P

Paralegals, 21–22, 245–274
    arbitration, 114, 151
    definition, 246
    explaining processes to client, 251–252
    liens, 272–274
    litigation, 31

mediation, 88
memorandum, 253
mistakes by, 246–247
motions, 249–251
negotiation, 60
notetaking, 269
online dispute resolution, 174, 185
overview, 245–246
preparing exhibits list, 266–268
preparing subpoenas, 263
researching neutrals, 253–263
restorative justice, 209
settlement agreements, 269–271
settlement conferences, 228
summarizing expected testimony, 263–266
tasks, 247–274
Parker Follett, Mary, 6
Passive aggressive avoidance, 12
Passive avoidance, 12
Peacemaking circles, 214–216
Peckham, Robert E., 229
Personal bias, 122
Plaintiff, 30
Pound, Roscoe, 81
Pound Conference, 1–2, 81–82
Power, 12–19
    alienation and, 18–19
    application of, 17–18
    co-active, 14
    coercive, 17, 18
    context-based, 16–17
    defined, 13
    ecological, 17
    empowerment, 15–16
    exchange, 17
    expert, 18
    lack of, 15
    normative, 18
    over people, 13
    overview, 12–13
    with people, 13–14
    powerlessness, 15
    referent, 18
    reward, 17
    situation-based, 16–17
    sources of, 16
    types of, 17–18
Precedent, 34, 115
Predispute agreements, 135–136
Preferences, 9
Prehearing conferences, 150
Preliminary meeting (arbitration), 150
    AAA online resolution, 186
Presumption of innocence, 208
Pre-trial conferences, 226
Private adjudication, 112

Problem solving, 53
Procedural interests, 8
Procedural unconscionability, 141
Psychological interests, 8
Punitive damages, 33

R

Racketeer Influenced and Corruption
    Organization Act (RICO), 147–148
Railway Labor Act, 81
Real estate transactions, 68
Recidivism, 206–207
Referent power, 18
Reintegrative shaming, 211
Remedies
    litigation, 33
    mediation, 86
Resource disputes, 9
Restitution, 209
Restorative methods, 201–216
    advantages, 205–207
    circles, 214–216
    conferencing, 211–214
    cost-effectiveness of, 207
    definition, 204
    disadvantages, 207–208
    discrimination, 208
    holistic approach, 207
    ignoring wrongs, 207
    Kitchener Experiment, 201–204
    labor-intensive, 208
    methods, 204, 209–216. *See also*
        Restorative methods
    offenders, effect on, 205–206
    overview, 201–204
    paralegal role, 209
    power imbalances, 208
    principles, 204–205
    procedural safeguards not part of, 208
    punishment and, 207–208
    recidivism, 206–207
    revictimization, 208
    social norms and, 206
    time-intensiveness, 208
    victims, effect on, 205, 206
Revised Uniform Arbitration Act, 134–135
Reward power, 17
RICO (Racketeer Influenced and Corruption
    Organization Act), 147–148
Rifkin, Janet, 165, 169
Rights-based mediation, 80
*Rodriguez de Quijas v. Shearson/American
    Express, Inc.*, 148
Roman arbitration, 109
Rule, Colin, 163, 181, 195

S

Sander, Frank E.A., 2, 82, 221–222
Schellenberg, James, 5–6
Securities Act of 1933, 146–147, 148
Securities arbitration, 144, 146–148
Securities Exchange Act of 1934, 146–148
Self-incrimination, 208
Settlement agreements, 269–271
Settlement conferences, 225–227
    paralegal role, 228
Seul, Jeffrey R., 30
Shaming, 211
Shearson/American Express, Inc. v.
    McMahon, 147–148
Smartsettle, 173–174, 183
Specific performance, 33
SquareTrade, 172
Stages of litigation, 30–31
Stare decisis, 120
Steelworkers Trilogy, 144
Stigmatizing shame, 211
Stipanowich, Thomas, 121
Subject matter (litigation), 32
Submission agreements, 135–136
Substantive interests, 8
Substantive unconscionability, 141
Summary jury trials, 222, 235–237
Summons, 31
Surrogates, avoidance through, 12
Synchronous communication, 182

T

Taft, William Howard, 225
Taft-Hartley Act. *See* National Labor
    Relations Act

Talking piece, 214–215
Thiessen, Ernest M., 173–174
Transaction negotiation, 50
Trial de novo, demand for, 234–235
Trials
    mini-trials, 222, 237–238
    summary jury trials, 222, 235–237

U

Unconscionability, 140–141
UN Convention on the Recognition and
    Enforcement of Foreign Arbitral Awards
    (New York Convention), 144, 149
Uniform Arbitration Act, 112, 134
Uniform Mediation Act, 82
    text, 279–284

V

Values, 9
Victim-offender dialogue (VOD),
    210–211
Virtual Lab Mediation Project, 184
Virtual Magistrate Project, 168–169
Virtual worlds, 165
Voice volume, 20–21
Volstead Act, 225

W

Wilko v. Swan, 147, 148
Workplace conferencing, 211–214

Z

Zehr, Howard, 204